The Aesthetics of Television

Media & Cultural Studies

Interactive Television
TV of the Future or the Future of TV?
Edited by Jens F. Jensen & Cathy Toscan
Media & Cultural Studies 1
1999

The Aesthetics of Television
Edited by Gunhild Agger & Jens F. Jensen
Media & Cultural Studies 2
2001

The Aesthetics of Television

Media & Cultural Studies 2

Edited by Gunhild Agger & Jens F. Jensen

Aalborg University Press
Aalborg, Denmark

The Aesthetics of Television
Media & Cultural Studies 2

Edited by
Gunhild Agger & Jens F. Jensen

© 2001 This collection of essays: Aalborg University Press
© 2001 Individual essays: Individual authors
© 2001 Cover illustration: Itshimtoo Inc.

Printed and bound in Denmark by Narayana Press, Gylling
Publisher: Aalborg University Press
ISBN 87-7307-623-6
ISSN 1399-1752

Distribution:
Aalborg University Press
Langagervej 6, 302
9220 Aalborg East
Denmark
Phone: (+45) 96 35 71 40, Fax: (+45) 96 35 00 76
E-mail: aauf@forlag.auc.dk
Homepage: <http://www.forlag.auc.dk>

All rights reserved. No part of this book may by reprinted or reproduced or utilized in any form or by any electronic, mechanical, or other means, now known or hereafter invented, including photocopying and recording, or in any information storage or retrieval system, without permission in writing from the publishers, except for reviews and short excerpts in scholary publications.

Media & Cultural Studies:
Professor Jens F. Jensen, Series editor
VR Media Lab & Department of Communication
Aalborg University, Denmark

Media & Cultural Studies 1:
Interactive Television. TV of the Future or the Future of TV?, 1999
(Edited by Jens F. Jensen & Cathy Toscan)

Media & Cultural Studies 2:
The Aesthetics of Television, 2001
(Edited by Gunhild Agger & Jens F. Jensen)

Contents

About the Authors 7

Gunhild Agger & Jens F. Jensen
Foreword: The Aesthetics of Television 11

Jørgen Stigel
Department of Communication, Aalborg University
Aesthetics of the Moment in Television
Actualisations in Time and Space 25

Gunhild Agger
Department of Communication, Aalborg University
**National Cinema and TV Fiction
in a Transnational Age** 53

Poul Erik Nielsen
The Danish School of Journalism
Comedy Series in Danish Television
– for Better or Worse 89

Gunhild Agger
Department of Communication, Aalborg University
Crime and Gender in the Provinces
– an Analysis of *Island Cop* 121

Rasmus Dahl
Department of Information and Mediascience
University of Aarhus
Distinctions in Documentary Television 173

Preben Raunsbjerg
Department of Communication, Aalborg University
TV Sport and Aesthetics.
The Mediated Event   193

Hanne Bruun
Department of Information and Mediascience
University of Aarhus
The Aesthetics of the Television Talk Show   229

Stig Hjarvard
Department of Film & Media Studies
University of Copenhagen
Journalism as Company   257

Tove A. Rasmussen
Department of Communication, Aalborg University
So – That's Your Life?
Authentic Forms of Television Talk   287

Jørgen Stigel
Department of Communication, Aalborg University
TV Advertising Virtually Speaking
The Invisible Voice Elaborating
on the Space between Screen and Viewer   321

Jens F. Jensen
VR Media Lab & Department of Communication,
Aalborg University
"So, what do *you* think, Linda?"
Media Typologies for Interactive Television   349

About the Authors

Gunhild Agger is Associate Professor in Communication at the Department of Communication, Aalborg University, Denmark. Her current research interests include television drama, theory of genre and style, history of the media, and cultural theory. She has contributed to a history of the Danish Media 1996-97 1-3 (co-editor of part 2) and to a history of Danish literature 1-9 (first ed. 1983-85, third ed. 2000). She has published a number of articles on television drama, advertisements in a historical context, cultural theory and practice, and Russian and Danish literature. Agger participated in the national research programme on "The Aesthetics of Television" 1993-99. She has participated in the European research network on television drama "Eurofiction" since 1998. She was appointed to The Danish Research Council for the Humanities in 1997, to The Research Committee of the Ministery of Culture 1999, and to The Board of the Danish Institute for Advanced Studies in the Humanities in 1999.

Hanne Bruun, MA and Ph.D., is Assistant Professor in Media Studies at the Department of Information and Mediascience, University of Aarhus, Denmark. Hanne Bruun has published several articles and a book on the talk show genre and the use of the genre in Danish television. She recently edited and contributed to a book on the Danish public service television channel TV 2: *TV 2 på skærmen – analyser af TV 2's programvirksomhed* (co-editors K. Frandsen and H. Søndergaard), Samfundslitteratur, 2000. Hanne Bruun participated in the national research program "The Aesthetics of Television" 1993-1999. Currently she is taking part in the national research program "Global Media Cultures" (1999-2001) funded by the Danish Research Councils (http://www.global.media.ku.dk). Her subproject is a comparative textual analysis as well as a qualitative audience analysis of young Danish women watching American and Danish daytime talk shows.

Rasmus Dahl, Master Degree in Filmscience (1994), Department of Film & Media Studies, University of Copenhagen, Denmark. Doctoral student (1995-98) at Department of Information and Mediascience, University of Aarhus. Part of "The Aesthetics of Television"-research project. Currently finishing a dissertation on "The Viewer, Television and Reality". Now teaching courses on media sociology, media aesthetics and media language at University of Copenhagen. Research interests include: the audiovisual representation of reality, documentary theory, television theory and analysis, the aesthetics of television reception and the psychology of media use.

Stig Hjarvard, Ph.D., Associate Professor at Department of Film & Media Studies, University of Copenhagen, Denmark. Among his research interest are journalism, international communication, political communication, media history and the relationships between mediated and face-to-face communication. Recent books are *Internationale tv-nyheder* [International TV news], Akademisk Forlag, 1995, *Audiovisual Media in Transition* (co-edited with Thomas Tufte, 1998), *Tv-nyheder i konkurrence* [TV news in competition], Samfundslitteratur, 1999, and *News in a Globalized Society* (editor, Nordicom, 2000). He is head of the research programme "Global Media Cultures" (http://www.global.media.ku.dk), financed by The Danish Research Council for the Humanities, 1999-2001.

Jens F. Jensen is Professor in Interactive Multimedia at VR Media Lab and the Department of Communication, Aalborg University, Denmark. His current research interests include networked multimedia, interactive television, Internet and WWW, interaction and interactivity, the aesthetics of multimedia, and inhabited 3D Virtual Worlds. Jensen is on the editorial board of the Danish scientific journal *K&K,* and is the general editor of the series *Media & Cultural Studies* as well as the *FISK-series* from Aalborg University Press. He is the editor of several anthologies, such as *The Computer as Medium* (co-edited with P.B. Andersen and B. Holmqvist), Cambridge University Press, 1993; and *Interactive Television. TV of the Future or the Future of TV?* (co-edited with C. Toscan), Aalborg University Press, 1999. He has published several articles and papers on new media and the social and cultural implications of information and computing technology. Recently, Jensen participated in the national research program on "The Aesthetics of Television" in a subproject on "Media and interactivity" (1993-1999), and currently, he participates in a national research program on "The Staging of Virtual, Inhabited 3D Spaces" (1998-2001) funded by the Danish Research Councils as well as in a research project on "Multimedia in the Home" (1998-2001). Further information on http://www.hum.auc.dk/ansatte/jfj/.

Poul Erik Nielsen, Ph.D., is Associate Professor in Media Studies at the Danish School of Journalism, Denmark. His research interests include the relation between the organisation of television production and the aesthetics of television. Recent publications include "Dansk tv-fiktion i det nationale bakspejl – TV 2's bidrag" in *TV 2 på skærmen – analyser af TV 2's programvirksomhed,* Samfundslitteratur, 2000, and "Scandinavian television fiction in transition", in *Television Fiction and Identities*, Napoli, 2000.

Tove Arendt Rasmussen is Associate Professor in Communication at the Department of Communication, Aalborg University, Denmark. With a background in television research, media ethnography and qualitative methodology she is currently co-managing a project on "Multimedia in the Home" (1998-2001) where she focusses on use and reception of interactive television. Rasmussen is on the editorial board of the Danish journal of media research, *MedieKultur*, where she is co-editing an issue on reality television and docu-soap. Recent publications include: "Hverdagens samtaler i TV: Interaktion", "Hverdagens samtaler i TV: Programanalyse", working papers 22 & 23 from the research project "The Aesthetics of Television", Aarhus, 1998; and "Construction of Authenticity" in *Live is Life – Constructing Mediated Authenticity*, DFG-Sonderforschungsbereich "Bildschirmmedien", Siegen, 2000.

Preben Raunsbjerg is a Ph.D.-student at the Department of Communication at Aalborg University, Denmark. He is part of "The Aesthetics of Television"-project and currently writing a Ph.D.-dissertation on the subject of the aesthetics of televised sport. Preben Raunsbjerg holds a Cand. Phil. degree in Danish from Aalborg University and currently lives in London, England.

Jørgen Stigel is Associate Professor in Communication Theory and Mass Communication at the Department of Communication, Aalborg University, Denmark. His current research interests include TV-genres, (TV-)advertising and the aesthetics of audiovisual media. He has been director and designer of the research project "Advertising – the Cultural Dimension" (1991-94) sponsored by The Central Research Committee, Aalborg University, and co-designer of the research project "The Aesthetics of Television" sponsored by The Danish Research Council for the Humanities (1993-99). He has been co-editor of major works on Danish literary history and Danish media history and advertising. During the past ten years he has published several articles on TV-genres and the quality of TV, TV-advertising, advertising and aesthetics, and the aesthetics of 3-D interactive media. He is currently participating in the national research program on "The Staging of Virtual, Inhabited 3D Spaces". Further information on http://www.hum.auc.dk/ansatte/js/.

Foreword: The Aesthetics of Television

Gunhild Agger
& Jens F. Jensen
Department of Communication
Aalborg University

Writing a foreword to an anthology is to provide an offer of a framework of understanding and a pattern of connections which, when put together, form a picture. The framework and the connecting lines in this case are not difficult to draw, as the anthology originates in a joint research project, "The Aesthetics of Television" which has taken place in the period from 1993-99 with the support of The Danish Research Council for the Humanities. For this reason, the articles in this anthology have a number of common features, because of their identical theoretical background, common theories, and approach. On the theoretical level we shall emphasise three essential areas of attention, viz.: 1) the medium, 2) the genres, and 3) the aesthetics. The significance of these three areas will be elaborated on below. In addition to this, the common elements are, to a great extent, determined by the situation of the medium upon which the articles are written, and to which they relate. The medium is marked by a period of transition common to a great many countries, which, under pressure of technological as well as political development in the 1980s, moved away from a predominantly public service system towards a competitive system in which one or more channels became wholly or partially financed commercially. As well as this, there are a number of national peculiarities. Both these conditions will be characterised briefly. The articles are placed in the collective framework according to their particular focus. The order in which they appear and their relation to one another will be commented on at the end.

The attention given to *the medium* and the various forms of expression to which it avails itself, is a recurring factor of the anthology. The television medium is, in a quite unexceptional way, part of the everyday lives of most people, first and foremost in their leisure time, and as a source of information and entertainment. It is a *fleeting* medium: quickly seen and quickly forgotten. However, it is also a *powerful* medium in the sense of its customary ability to set the agenda, and it can have a very great influence on the fate of politicians and talk show victims alike. It is also powerful in the sense that it can convey both simultaneity and togetherness, as can be seen, for example, in the broadcasting of sporting events of national importance. Viewers, quite rightly, demand that television should be good at everything, but the history of the medium shows that its strengths and weaknesses have primarily been developed the hard way, i.e. by producing fiascos, the repetition of which is later avoided, and successes, the emulation of which is attempted – and with no guarantee whatsoever for either. Media research is unable to help in these circumstances, but hopefully it can contribute to a wider understanding by offering viewers, producers and critics concepts with which the fiascos, the successes, and what lies in between, can be discussed and analysed. In recent years the body of researchers has focused a great deal on the medium, and what is finally emerging is a more precise understanding of it, its interaction with the audience, and its opportunities relative to available technology at any given time. Ironically, this is happening at a time when radical changes are taking place in the medium, or at any rate, when sweeping changes in the function of the medium are beginning to emerge with increasing clarity. With the latest technological development, varying degrees of interactivity between the computer and television have already become a reality. The key factors in the process of change are media convergence, the possibility of integration, digitisation and interactivity.

In a direct extension of the perspective of the medium, attention is given to *the genres*. Genre and medium are connected on so many levels, that the genres can be considered as an actualisation of the opportunities of the medium when it functions well, and vice versa when it functions badly. In such cases it is often a question of the genre and the medium opposing each other or failing to relate to each other. This relationship is registered colloquially, both in conversations about television and in TV reviews, when one often refers to 'good TV' or 'bad TV' as opposed to e.g. 'a good documentary' or 'a bad series'. In addition to this, our daily lives provide convincing examples of the degree to which we think in terms of genres and the prominence of the role of genre level. In any TV guide in any newspaper or magazine, the classification and the references which are used, are governed by a consciousness of genre. In connection with a general discussion of genre, it might be enlightening to distinguish between a *vertical* (historical) and a *horizontal* (simultaneous, geo-sociological) level of analysis. The existence of the genre level, though a certainty, is marked by instability in the sense that genres are in a constant state of change. This applies to any medium, but in television it applies, seemingly, with an even greater force, and an explanation of this can be found both on the horizontal, and on the vertical level.

The genres of television have *historical* origins in existing genres of other media, and these genres have been converted and adapted for the television medium. In particular, the genres of radio were originally of great importance, not only because many television pioneers were recruited from radio, but also because radio and television originally shared the element of simultaneity as a condition of broadcasting. Simultaneity was a force in the elevated moments when an event was actually captured on air. The Danish Social Democrat and culture historian Hartvig Frisch characterised this quality precisely in the expression, "the fluttering pulse of the present", in connection with a radio broadcast in 1940. In other situations the condition of simultaneity was clearly a drawback, i.e. when one was not in the right place at the right time – or when the camera accidentally caught a stage manager in TV Theatre. The possibility of using tapes in radio existed from the mid-1930s and in television from the end of the 1950s. This changed the dependence of the media on the here and now. In addition to this, literary formats (serialisations) and those genres which were known from films (especially Hollywood) and theatre, played a significant role in the fictive genres in television, just as newspaper reports, weekly reviews in cinemas, and documentary films were important precursors for television news broadcasts and documentary programmes. A development in the direction of independent television genres, sensitive to the medium, began to accelerate in the course of the 1970s and 80s. The historical consciousness of genre is a central factor in an analysis of genre because the medium is, in a sense, so historically orientated. Assuming that they are recorded on tape, old television programmes can be re-broadcast at any time. The same applies to films since the film industry has given up its opposition to television and has begun to co-operate with it.

Another central factor in the analysis of genre stems from the horizontal consideration: an awareness of the opportunities of the individual genres, and the ability to define these and their levels at a given time. The horizontal level is important for both large and small TV-producing nations, but for different reasons. The large nations are characterised by a low level of programme exchange with other countries. The USA and India, for example, broadcast only a very small percentage of foreign programmes. In this way they set a standard that is their own and have no external yardstick. On the other hand there is tough competition between the different networks – particularly in the USA – and this competition is based on viewer ratings. This means that achieving favourable ratings is bound up with the development of popular genres. In contrast, international orientation has always been important for middle-sized and smaller TV-producing nations, e.g. Australia, Canada, and most European countries, because domestic production has simply not been sufficient to cover air time. In the television service of these countries both domestic, nationally-developed genres and genres primarily created and based in other countries, circulate constantly. Although these productions are primarily from the USA, other countries contribute too. In south-European countries, Spain in particular, Latin-American fiction, for example, is an influential force.

These circumstances lead to an extremely extensive consciousness of genre in connection with television. Whether consciously or unconsciously, viewers are constantly being invited to draw parallels and carry out comparisons; vertically these comparisons are to previous editions of popular programmes, and horizontally they consider how one's national favourite talk show compares to the American *Ricki Lake,* or whether they have finally succeeded in creating a national sitcom of the calibre of *Roseanne* or *Yes, Minister.*

In television, scenographers take great pains with studio scenography, no matter whether the genre is a talk show, a book programme, a quiz, a sporting magazine, or a drama. Outdoor events are not neglected either. Obviously, the scenography of a football pitch is a constant, but camera angles, and thereby the way the event appears on television, are by no means constant. It has almost become standard procedure to position twenty cameras and their operators in connection with a football match in the European Championship or the World Cup in order to secure the important moments from perfect angles. The use of the term *aesthetic* in connection with fiction genres, is a matter of course, but the use of the term *dramaturgy* in connection with news broadcasts and documentary programmes, has gradually become accepted in media research. Aesthetic elements, which were originally connected with the theory of fiction, have been used increasingly in fact-orientated genres by producers, programme personnel, internal instructors in TV stations, and media researchers alike. Nevertheless, aesthetics is often considered as notably unremarkable in fact-orientated genres and entertainment genres, and it can, on occasion, completely escape attention. The background for this, of course, is the impression that television provides a direct representation of reality in these genres.

The knowledge that this is not the case is child's play for the vast majority of viewers and media researchers alike. But *why* it is not the case is a question that still requires more detailed explanation. It is in this connection that the aesthetic level comes into play relative to both medium and genre. In order to characterise the relationship between the medium and the genre more specifically than with the expressions, 'good TV' or 'bad TV', its aesthetics must be characterised. What are the special, and common elements that exist between programmes and genres? Why are so many cameras vitally important in transmissions of football games? What is the significance of the hand-held camera in the documentary and in police fiction respectively? What role does dramaturgy play in the sequencing of the talk show? What is the function of the TV audience that is indispensable in certain TV genres? It is only on the aesthetic level that it is possible to specify how the apparently obvious representation of reality in television, actually works, whether representation of reality is an existing factor at all, and whether it is a question of interpretation, what the framework for representation is, and which ground rules apply. In this context the analysis of new television genres also raises the question of *method*: are the methods we use sufficiently sensitive to capture the special nature of the new genres?

As regards time, the articles refer to topical television from the 1990s, take their examples from, and analyse genres and tendencies from this period. The examples which apply specifically in a Danish context can result in displacement in terms of time, relative to other countries, but they are otherwise representative of the main tendency, the extremities of which are the local and the global. In Denmark, 1988 was the year which marked the definite break with the hitherto monopolistic system: de-regulation and competition between the two leading national channels, DR (Danmarks Radio) and TV2 on the one hand, and on the other, between these and the satellite channels, leading to numerous changes in consequence.

On the institutional level, the situation gave rise to an increased focus on ratings, satisfied and dissatisfied users, increased openness about 'viewers' television', but also greater pressure to achieve quantitative success at the expense of 'narrow' programmes. Discussions on the notion of quality, the rearrangement of management structures in DR, rearrangement of programme policy, and the introduction of strategic slotting, in both DR and TV2, became part of the daily lives of both institutions. At viewer level the situation gave rise to greater choice – but in a number of cases, this was undeniably a choice between more of the same.

These conditions and debates are widespread. Although the examples in the anthology might be Danish, they can, with comparative ease, be related to similar phenomena in other places, e.g. the development towards entertainment journalism in breakfast television (Stig Hjarvard), the opportunities offered by the talk show for the democratisation of access to television (Hanne Bruun), or the striking fiascos that came in the wake of translating the American sitcom to national television (Poul Erik Nielsen). Even the fact that a national audience prefers to watch nationally produced television – news from a domestic perspective, and nationally produced fiction – is a widespread phenomenon at international level (Gunhild Agger).

Having pointed out the common elements in television, it should also be made clear that there are differences too. There are, of course, in Denmark as in all other countries, particular national traditions in television. Anyone who has watched television in a foreign country, or merely zapped through channels at home, knows how similar, yet different, national television can be. Even American series appear different in Denmark than in e.g. the USA, because in public service channels in Denmark, interrupting programmes is not allowed. This means that the dramaturgy, whose aim it is to keep hold of viewers through commercial blocks, can fall flat with a single cut. The channel voice with its 'intros' and 'outros', its references and explanations, is probably one of the most nationally-anchored institutions we have. There are also differences which are bound up with the vertical genre level in the form of particular, historically-based genre versions, particular accentuation and references, etc. Additional differences are determined by the horizontal genre level which can breed similarity, as well as small differences, appreciable differences, and even direct opposition. Even in the case of identical concepts, such as many popular quiz shows and entertainment programmes, they generally function best when they are adapted to form a national version.

The anthology is built up in such a way that the most general contributions introduce the issues that have been mentioned. In "Aesthetics of the Moment in Television", Jørgen Stigel focuses on the particular communicative and aesthetic logic, by emphasising that even though most television is edited before it is broadcast, the illusion of *simultaneity,* and the possibility of actual simultaneity, are nevertheless of vital importance. Television can create a sensation of shared time and space, of *proximity* in spite of distance. *The channel voice* constantly carries out a process of temporal placement by using expressions like, 'now', 'tomorrow', 'this evening' and so on. In the same way, we are continually kept informed about *where* we are: 'in the studio', 'on the spot', 'back to the studio' etc. The channel voice constantly guides us around time and place, thereby creating a sensation of togetherness. Consequently, Jørgen Stigel has good reason to suppose that the aesthetics of television is based on proximity, participation and simultaneity. What he refers to as the "aesthetics of the moment" embodies, in a sense, the aesthetics of television as such. Time and place, here and now or there and then become, therefore, central elements in an analysis of the genres of television and their inter-relationship, in the model advocated by Jørgen Stigel. In this way, the genres become a point of convergence for the medium and aesthetics.

The features described by Jørgen Stigel exist at a level of generality where they apply to television as such, no matter what its national affiliations might be. But what happens if we include the national level in a discussion of genre? Globalisation and localisation are often considered to be widespread tendencies today: on the one hand there is a great media community of transnational character, on the other, a propensity for absorption and acknowledgement in the media community of local societies. According to Gunhild Agger's analysis in "National Cinema and TV Fiction in a Transnational Age", national factors do play a vital role in the television of every country. The picture, however, is by no means clear cut. Inspired by modern film theory of national film, Gunhild Agger sees the genres of national television as a place where there is ongoing *dialogue* about, and *negotiation* with the genres of other countries. It is a place where the national and the international constantly mirror themselves in each other, and is, therefore, a place where aesthetics is constantly being tested. The way in which this is done is illustrated by way of a description of developmental tendencies in Danish TV fiction.

Following the two introductory articles, there are a number of genre analyses covering various fiction and non-fiction genres, entertaining interactive genres, such as talk shows, breakfast television, video-realism, and television advertisements. In his article, "Comedy Series in Danish Television", Poul Erik Nielsen raises the question of the national versus the international – in particular the American – in connection with the sitcom genre. Through a concrete analysis of genre, Poul Erik Nielsen shows that the American sitcom clearly functions as a *pattern* and a *yardstick* for Danish series. He also shows that attempts to create a successful national product have so far been fruitless. The reason for this is to be found in the lack of respect for the level of craftsmanship.

Similarly, the relationship between national and international genre traditions is the subject of Gunhild Agger's, "Crime and Gender in the Provinces". The Danish police series *Island Cop* is related, in terms of genre and aesthetics, to dominating developmental tendencies in the history of Danish crime fiction, seen in the light of the dominance that British and American series have always exerted in this area in Denmark. The orientation towards *everyday life* and consequently also the orientation towards everyday realism in television fiction, which has had a dominant position in Danish TV drama in the 1970s and 80s are both pitfalls for comedy series and crime series. However, Danish crime series have, from time to time, succeeded in utilising the orientation constructively, especially in searches of particular milieus both in the provinces and in the city. The international tendency towards giving the police officer a personal life, thereby making him or her more interesting and vulnerable as a character, towards complicating relationships between the sexes, and towards making the general series plot as interesting as the plot of the individual episode, can also be traced in the Danish version.

However, the genre mix is unusual in that *Island Cop* adopts elements from soap opera, popular comedy, and the Danish tradition for provincial series, at the same time as it operates with a certain melodramatic touch.

In the police series genre, morality tales are played, in the sense that the relationship between crime/criminals, and society/law-enforcers/justice system, has a central place in the genre. In this way, the fiction also functions as a forum of discussion relative to changes in the perception of crime and punishment, society's responsibility versus the responsibility of the individual, in which the questions are the same but the answers different. In the 1990s we have seen a significant increase in a police-related genre which has a more utilitarian aim, namely reconstruction and police station programmes which, with varying degrees of emphasis, endeavour to unite the basic excitement connected with criminal investigation with gaining help from citizens to solve crimes. This also happens with the use of aesthetic combinations which have gradually become common to fiction and non-fiction; handheld cameras, angular shots and grainy pictures. In the USA the Rodney King video was an obvious source of inspiration, and the phenomenon which can be termed video-realism also belongs in this context.

The raw, versus the adapted presentation of reality, is taken up as a problem and a challenge in Rasmus Dahl's "Distinctions in Documentary Television". In connection with the documentary, Rasmus Dahl believes that it is more meaningful to refer to several prototypes or sub-genres instead of one large genre. For this reason Dahl suggests a division according to, first of all, the degree of *intervention* relative to the raw material, dependent on whether there is a very direct influence on, or a more indirect presentation to viewers. Secondly, he suggests a division according to the degree of *restriction*, i.e. according to whether there is a high or a low degree of restriction. In a discussion, primarily with Bill Nichols and Carl Platinga, Rasmus Dahl argues for three basic types. 1) A type in which intervention is minimal, and the intention is to show. 2) An intermediate type in which there is more influence/control, in a delicate balance between openness and restriction. 3) An authoritative type, the intention of which is to control the viewers' reception. Rasmus Dahl's contribution, then, is an element in the ongoing debate about the impression of deception given by the TV medium in the presentation of live reality when analysed in relation to the genre which is often considered to be the mainstay of public service broadcasting. That the documentary is, in Jørgen Stigel's terminology, a 'there and then' genre, might contribute to the explanation of why, in spite of its close-to-reality affinity, it is so amenable to various forms of aesthetics and rhetoric.

The debate on the representation of reality continues in Preben Raunsbjerg's "TV Sport and Aesthetics. The Mediated Event", which following the same terminology, is a 'now and there' genre. Preben Raunsbjerg points out that sport, and sport on television are many things. The basic forms are the magazine programme and the live sporting transmission, and Preben Raunsbjerg takes his point of departure in the latter, on the grounds that it provides material for the former. The event which is taking place in reality, while it is simultaneously being observed on screen, embodies at one time both the "aesthetics of the moment" (Stigel) which is the hallmark of the medium, and the national feeling of togetherness, which can be detected in the voice of the commentator. Traditionally, content-bearing considerations have been dominant vis à vis sport. As regards this, Preben Raunsbjerg emphasises the significance of aesthetics on the four levels of analysis, and he distinguishes between: 1) The photographic, in which camera angles can be decisive for the instants which almost always, when shown in slow motion, become the privileged moments of highlight. 2) Graphics, in which development is at full gallop owing to the increased use of computers. 3) The actual sound which contributes to the feeling of spacial togetherness, and 4) the roles of principal and secondary commentators in which the rules governing who may say what, and when, accurately correspond to the rule-bound world of sport itself.

In transmitting sporting events, television functions, at one and the same time, as a transmitting medium and a reporting medium, which assisted by various aesthetic and rhetorical devices, tell of a reality that exists outwith television. What is in focus in the talk show, is another type of simultaneity which is especially suitable in relation to the television medium's ability to present non-fictive pictures in the space of leisure time: 'here and now' in the studio, in the company of the *studio host*. In "The Aesthetics of the Television Talk Show", Hanne Bruun illustrates how the talk show, whether it is live or on tape, to a very great extent also avails itself of "the aesthetics of the moment", and in this connection, it is particularly *the uncertainty factor* that is so vitally important for the vigour of the talk show. On the other hand, this uncertainty factor is balanced with the element of *sociability* and with it the etiquette, politeness, and congenial social conventions which are also part and parcel of the talk show. The two common, incompatible elements are stage-managed in various dramaturgic juxtapositions for which Hanne Bruun, amplifying on Sonia Livingstone and Peter Lunt, has drawn up a typology. The fundamental models she works with are: Debate, Research, Therapy, and Consultation. The reason for the success of the talk show genre, according to Hanne Bruun, is that it is particularly suitable for the television medium, and that the genre, via the indispensable TV audience, interacts with its wider audience.

A common topic of discussion is what happens to journalism when it is used in the talk show genre. This discussion is taken up by Stig Hjarvard in "Journalism as Company", in an analysis of Danish breakfast television on TV2. Breakfast television consists of a mixture of genres, from news to cartoons, games, interviews with famous and unknown people, cookery, and discussions of topical issues. Breakfast television shares a sphere with talk shows in the sense that here too, it is *togetherness* that is the central element, presented by studio hosts. The mirroring function relative to the viewing public is obvious, and as Stig Hjarvard points out, the two worlds exist parallel to each other. Because of this, the journalist can only allow himself a limited degree of aggression, because the host function and the journalistic function are juxtaposed, just as the uncertainty factor and the element of sociability are juxtaposed in the talk show. Stig Hjarvard concludes that both the journalistic and the host function are *modified* in breakfast television's presentation of political, personal, and everyday issues.

A similar tendency can be observed in other reality-based genres, e.g. in 'video-realism' which is the subject of Tove Arendt Rasmussen's "So – That's Your Life?". It appears that these genres are cultivated to just as high a degree in public service stations as in commercial stations, as there is a growing tendency for public service stations to adopt the foci of the commercial stations. In this way, as with breakfast television, the focus is shifted from politics to the politician, from subjects to people, from a political discussion based on an authoritatively-set agenda to an observed interaction between various people, in a gathering which combines the personal with the political, and in which strangers treat each other as though they were close friends (or bitter enemies). But unlike the talk show, in which the uncertainty factor is balanced with the sociability factor, and unlike breakfast television, in which the studio host clearly harmonises the role of host with the role of journalist, the unexpected and the spontaneous elements of video-realism, according to Tove Arendt Rasmussen's analysis, have a greater potential to convey what is authentic.

An interesting point of view about television sport is that it embodies all the genres: games, competition, documentary, fiction etc. Similar views could be expressed about television advertising which, even more obviously, uses and processes other genres. In "TV Advertising Virtually Speaking", however, Jørgen Stigel considers, not so much the much-publicised fiction genre in television advertising, but rather, the more overlooked, unspectacular, but much more commonplace genres which use the device of voice-over. Through close analysis of an example Jørgen Stigel offers a number of explanations for this choice. Just as the channel voice has an anchoring function which is often unnoticed, but which is nevertheless central to the notion of affiliation, the voice-over function too, possesses the ability to create intimacy, familiarity, and communication, which functions effectively between the screen and the audience in an interaction between proximity and distance.

Audience has always been centrally positioned in television as the object of attention for the channel voice, who guides them around, and as those to whom both fiction and factual programmes address themselves, but this central positioning is even more important for genres which operate with a degree of interactivity, for example, via the telephone or computer. We are indeed moving towards a media situation in which the interactive element, to a much greater extent, is becoming an integral part of technology, and therefore the public is being compelled to relate to it. This aspect, which is at once a contemporary and a futuristic aspect, is developed by Jens F. Jensen in "So, what do *you* think, Linda?". The dream of changing the one-way communication of mass communication, which was to be found among radical critics in the 1930s and 1960s, the dream that simulated interaction opposes in a limited way, can now be fulfilled. The technological conditions exist. But how much interactivity do we really want, and in what way? Jens F. Jensen, amplifying primarily on Bordewijk and Kaam, provides a commentatorial overview and an illustrative discussion of the new typologies, which are necessary elements in defining these opportunities. The prospect is that television can be transformed from being, primarily, a transmitting medium, to also become, in varying degrees, a medium for consultation, registration, and conversation. The potential to give users greater influence now exists.

If the television medium changes fundamentally, such that interactivity becomes a dominant feature, then all the analyses which are presented here can be called into question, with the exception of the final one. However, it is a general condition in media history that the media and their functions are in a constant state of change, and so analyses have a limited durability. In spite of the changes which are emerging it will probably take a considerable time before television's function as a transmitting medium has had its day.

CHAPTER ONE

Aesthetics of the Moment in Television
Actualisations in Time and Space

Jørgen Stigel
Department of Communication
Aalborg University

Television is a medium which, in principle, is able to absorb many different genres and aesthetic expressions, and to transmit them. On the basis of this it could be claimed that the aesthetics of television[1] might consist of a multiplicity of aesthetic forms which these genres embody, and, therefore, that television could, in principle, be used to communicate almost anything.

The following is an attempt to deploy a different approach; that is, to take a point of departure in television as a special medium with special strengths, but which also has special limitations. In keeping with this, television carries out a relatively clear prioritising within genres and promotes particular forms of expression and formats of programme. This does not necessarily occur at the cost of others, but it occurs to an increasing extent, based on what might be termed a special communicative and aesthetic logic of television.

The following will, therefore, take a point of departure in which television in some sense appears as visible actor.

Involvement

One of the special characteristics of television is the very banality, as with radio, that it broadcasts in real-time and seemingly disseminates concrete sensory impressions of the places from which broadcasting takes place. The actual broadcast and the reception of it are synchronous. Also, the individual programme element of broadcasting, such as news broadcasts, other studio-based programmes, and outside broadcasts, can be shown as they happen. The greater part of programmes and their individual items are not live, but consist of pre-edited and pre-produced material. However, a great many of these programmes attempt to give the impression of being live, and very often it can be fairly difficult, on the face of it, to ascertain whether a programme is live or not. This is because, among other things, the programme, or its host presenter, adopts a direct form of address to the viewing public, and also because the programme takes place in a studio.[2] In any case the transmission itself makes sure, in principle, that everything that takes place is placed *within a framework* of happening here and now. The notion of things happening here and now is almost always emphasised by a speaker.

The creation of this framework on an overall level, i.e. on the station's range of programmes, is handled by the *channel-voice*. This is the station's ultimate communicative authority. It appears continuously between programmes and its function is, among other things, to create continuity between the range of programmes. Most Danish television stations simply have one voice (DRTV, TV2, TV3, Kanal Danmark) used as a voice-over which, though it has a particular presence, is kept discreetly behind a screen of illustration. On other stations a person on screen addresses the viewer directly as the station's host or presenter. However, no matter which form this speaker takes, he or she represents an authority whose function it is to emphasise a temporal feeling of togetherness with the viewers. He or she familiarises the viewers with parts of the content of the programme range (right now, in a while, later, tomorrow) and attempts to be the confidant of the viewer. Viewers are encouraged to join the programmes and to come into their world. The speaker attempts constantly to create closeness between the channel and its viewers. This is attempted by emphasising a commonly-felt experience of 'we' with the viewers, and by uniting the elements in the programme range.

The live and simultaneous communication from screen to viewer is constantly expressed on the *programme level* several times a day in the form of news broadcasts. Discounting special or thematic channels, news broadcasts are the *principal element* of television stations. They are indispensable programmes for television stations and are to a great extent the face which the station presents to the outside world. They also have an effect of forming a framework around the station's range of programmes, as they typically frame the station's prime-time broadcasts, and form the entrance and exit points of prime-time viewing.

The presenter, or studio host, of news programmes manages and presents the individual items or mini programme elements in the programme. In principle, this is the same method as at station level. The programme host creates continuity between programme items with 'lead-ins' and 'leadouts', and addresses the viewers directly with emphasis on a collective 'we' which is often ambiguous, because it can be interpreted at one and the same time as meaning, "we on the programme or station", "you and I", or even, "all of us in the country". The form of address is of simulated interaction[3] and it is *always* simultaneous.

The presenter form or host form is used in a variety of versions in a series of other (studio) programmes. It may not always be live, but will simulate being live. It is precisely the interactional feature of this form of address which conveys the impression of simultaneity. In these programmes the studio host has significantly more free scope. This applies both to the definition of his role and in terms of what is presented to the audience. Also of significant importance is the way in which the host, and his or her mode of address to the viewers, along with the 'guests' in the studio contribute to supporting an impression of immediacy – of something that is taking place *now* and *here*. In cases of simultaneity (or simulated simultaneity) there is always an accompanying voice which carries out an anchor role, and which establishes contact with the viewers. The person behind the voice need not, however, be visible to the viewers. Nowhere is this more obvious than in the live transmission or the on-the-spot report, when it can sometimes occur that not a great deal is happening or where it is not always obvious what is happening or why. This can, for instance, occur in cases when so much of an event is taking place out of shot, and is seen at events such as live sports transmissions, transmissions of major events in parliament or ceremonial events involving heads of state (royal weddings, funerals, etc.).[4]

In this way it can be seen that the basic ability of television is that it can present an impression of having a fusion in time and place, and at the same time it can convey a very concrete and emotional experience of place, events and players, through sight and visual impressions. It can thus create for the viewer an experience of proximity in time, in spite of distance in space, in such a way that something happening far away is experienced at close quarters. It is experienced as *now and here* even though it might be happening *now and there*, and although it might even have been recorded several days previously. In this sense television is the modern equivalent of antiquity and classicism in which the requirement was for unity of time, place and action.[5]

Unlike radio, television can, to a certain extent, deliver *versions* of the *complete picture* of something which is happening with some people, and among some people. It can show physical action in a specific context. However it does this notably *only* to a certain extent, and *only* in versions of the complete picture. Television is always subject to the parameters of a picture framework and a limited vision which involuntarily create meanings through the process of selection, just as it is subject to the basic condition that visual images are often unable to convey a definite meaning on their own. For this reason they tend to be anchored or accompanied by verbal comment.

Unlike so many other aesthetics, the aesthetics of television are founded, not on distance, but on proximity, participation and immediacy. Neither does the communication of television appear as an aesthetic structure. Despite the fact that the very picture framework and the limited vision are in themselves basically artificial and aesthetic, television appears, for the most part, as a direct representation which defies aesthetic artificiality. Television operates within the part of the aesthetic field which is concerned with the creation of illusions of reality, intensity, and a likeness of proximity for an audience. This happens in the special way that the audience, from their ordinary daily lives, can tune into other worlds and be directly connected to them. Television is the controlling presentation form and it is a window to the world through which the viewer can 'go out' into the world and 'become a part' of it.

Taken literally, it is this adoption of the possibility to go out and become a part of something which is emphasised by the channel-voice.[6] The voice speaks in straight-forward terms about places and spaces which viewers can *visit* and *go to* along with the channel and which they can move *in and out of*. The station and its hosts invite viewers inside where they can *take part*, meet various people and *do* things along with them. The programmes, too, accommodate the metaphorical speech by presenting themselves as places where the viewers are present and from where people address the screen as though it were merely a window between themselves and the viewers.

The intensity which is inherent in simultaneity in time and place is further reinforced by the personal eye contact with viewers via the person who is communicating through the screen. As well as this, intensity is, of course, closely connected to *the expectation* to the event, and the quality of the tele-visual presentation of incidents as and when they occur. It is a condition of reporting live from the scene of an event, that something will, in fact, take place, and that in the course of the transmission, one or more *decisive incidents* will develop. Yet another vital condition is the nature of the event itself and the expectation of cultural togetherness which it embodies.

The problem for television is that providing decisive incidents is fraught with unpredictability while programme planning, on the other hand, is dependent on a certain amount of predictability. On television, time also becomes programmed time and measured units of time within television's own schedule, and as such, its limits are seldom breached. The rule is that the programme must keep within the boundaries of a time-slot. So virtually all programmes are subject to pressure of time in the form of a framework of time. As a structural organisation, television is a steady, fixed programme machine with a circular sequence of regularity, and a constant programme format from day to day and from week to week. In that respect television resembles a number of other media phenomena which appear continually and recurringly, such as the printed press. Unlike these however, television is in a completely different kind of potential conflict with itself: on one side there is the need for scheduled programming, and on the other, the opportunity, in principle, of being able to broadcast real events as they happen.

Given this background it might also seem logical that television should create its own events – or more accurately, the places where events take place, and to a great extent turn itself and its programmes not only into events, but also into rituals. This happens firmly and continuously by the way in which the channel-voice creates contact with, and proximity to, the viewers, and by attempting to involve viewers in the programme as a place one can be. But it also happens in a symbolically concrete sense in completely different ways – prototypically, for example, when the news programme claims, both visually and in person, to be close to the centre of events. It broadcasts its reporters in real time and in full figure on, or rather, in front of, the place that has a connection with the story in question. This on-the-spot reporting can also involve interviewees, and in the same way the studio host can simultaneously question the reporter 'in the field'. It is seldom, however, that this on-the-spot reporting is connected with pictures of a concurrent event – breaking news – taking place here and now, discounting, of course, the report itself, and possible interviews connected with it. The action is the action of relating, and it takes place in an exchange between visible participants, each in his own space: the television studio and some version of the place where the news is being made. Typically a background picture like a recognisable emblem of state will attempt to create the atmosphere of this place (the White House, or, in Denmark, Christiansborg etc.).

The form is a visual effect or a transference of attention, and one of the effects of this, apart from 'illustrating topicality' is to provide visual proof of the programme's ability to achieve a form of omnipresence.

Apart from the live transmission, television's constant and repetitive place where events take place is, to a very great extent, either the television studio itself, or a form of transferred or extended television studio in the 'real world' via a reporter/interviewer. From here television creates its own events and does it within a fairly predictable framework which takes account of the time limitations imposed by programme planning, while at the same time giving or maintaining a perception or simultaneity and immediacy which go beyond the limitations of space.

The places[7] or spaces from which television works consist, in all, of:

- the home of the range of programmes and the station, typically represented by the regular channel voices.
- the space of the programme – typically represented by the visible and easily recognisable studio setting and the regular programme host or hosts.
- the place where the action happens or an external location which is typically represented by way of an on-the-spot reporter whose live report takes place against the background of a (well-known) locality.
- the place where the action happens in the form of the programme's space. This consists typically of the presenter's conversation, interview or other means of testing and challenging guests or outside representatives in the studio itself
- and finally, the actual real location or place where action takes place; a limited arena or route as shown in the transmission of sporting events, live speeches and live ceremonial events.

In cases of the latter, television can only to a very limited extent define the limits of the place and enclose it within a framework. It is first and foremost the place, the participants themselves and their actions within the setting which dictate the conditions independently of television. Television can, however, as we shall consider in more depth later, establish certain set-ups which frame participants in situations without their realising it or being prepared. If television is to spend time and energy transmitting live or recording events, then it also expects that the main sequence of the events is predictable, but also has the potential to develop spontaneous and surprising elements. The point here is that the main sequence of events can contain these elements (ritualised events) or can be engineered to have them (television's own framing and set-ups within a piece of reality).

Live transmission in which television simply transmits the event and is merely the tele-visual channel is the exception. The rule, is the planned schematised programme and the edited (post-fabricated) programme which is guaranteed to fit into the time frame and the programme pattern. So what television provides, first and foremost, are *intermediate forms* in which the course of events and the passage of time are controlled by television itself, and in which television as its own authority and communicating organ, takes over the function of presenting to the receiver its own version of here and now. Television's various reformed versions of here and now become in this respect a substitute, a replacement, or a metaphor for the there and now of events.

Television's Self-limiting Space I: the Studio

Due to the fact that they share the studio as the place where the event takes place, and due to the role of the studio host, there are, strangely enough, certain common elements between, for example, news broadcasts and game shows, quiz shows and talk shows (GQT shows). Both the television news, and GQT shows are anchored in television's own constructed world and created space. In concrete terms their anchor point is the studio, the studio host and the set up – the rules and boundaries for the conduct of participants which are represented by him (the concept). In common they have an artificial space, or an artificial delimitation of space, as their point of departure. On a completely abstract level they also have in common an understanding that identity in time is of vital importance, albeit in varying versions. In addition, they share the trait that for each their reference to reality is vital. The people must be who they claim to be, and the actions, course of events, and places which are shown must be in accordance with something that really exists. This is not fiction. Another common element is the situational unpredictability and the requirement of being able to handle a situation and be *in* the situation. The course of events as a whole, is, therefore, either framed in an extremely tight set up or else is in itself defined by limitations or a set of rules. The programme host is the controlling, anchoring factor and is the vital link with the audience as well as other links in the programme itself (moderator role). And it is at this point that the similarities cease, for the perspectives and intentions of the two programme types are vastly different.

The perspective of television news is principally directed towards the constantly problem-filled space and time of social reality. The orientation and point of reference is directed towards something (i.e. places, events, cases) outside the programme. As regards time, there is an emphasis on giving viewers an experience of being synchronised and on a level with what is currently happening/has happened and (perhaps) what is about to happen (the weather) within the given common universe, its 24-hour time horizon and in relation to its main themes and relevance criteria. For this reason it is also important that the programme shows its intention, albeit if only in the form of the more symbolic figure expressed by, for example, the live (stand-up) reporter. And when the news broadcast creates events in the studio by involving outside participants the main intention is that these participants should shed light on, or provide greater detail to a story or item and not upon themselves as individuals.

The energies of GQT shows are, on the other hand, to a far greater extent directed inwards towards the programme's own enclosed space and special set ups. Among the ways in which this is shown is by the fact that they are generally enframed by a studio audience and in this way take place on stage. They are, in some respects, governed by a time factor which is connected with tests or achievement/luck involving speed or quick-wittedness, and at the same time they also challenge, or are connected with the abilities of the viewers (quizzes and games and to a lesser extent, talk shows). But the energies are also directed towards the (mutual) relationships of the participants and the participants' personal revelations about themselves or others, their personal stories, fate and dreams within the framework and set up of the show (talk shows and, to a lesser degree, games). Finally, the energies can be directed towards an issue and become a question of competing opinions and arguments within a specific issue or a topical problem (talk show as debate). Without actually appearing to do so, GQT shows stage participants by providing varying degrees of a narrow framework for their appearance and by creating constellations and staged situations between them. The participants are the variables. The framework (i.e. the scenography and programme concept of the studio) and the style of the programme host are invariables, and the programme host is the central leading figure – often to the extent that the talk show very often bears the name of the programme host. The family resemblance to the game show category in all its variants is great. The role of the programme host as a moderator in relation to guests, the studio audience and viewers is often that of a referee, or at least someone attempting to achieve fair play.

In studio programmes it is the studio host who makes the topicality link to the viewers. The studio host speaks in the present tense at all times as if the programme were taking place here and now (which it often, in fact, does).

Games and quiz shows are apparently the most regulated studio programmes. Their time is partly a time in which the object is to manage a task within a given time limit, and partly a co-ordinated time with the viewer, such that the viewer can also take part in the guess work, answer and consider, and in which the viewer by way of parallel activity, and in a sense via the pressure of time itself, also shares the same space as the programme and its clear limited intention: to refer to itself and its own institutionalised set of rules.

Debate and talk shows would appear to be less regulated and governed by fewer rules. In terms of content (i.e. concerning what is talked about) their reference is usually found outwith the studio in the form of a definite issue as a specific subject. But concrete and manifestly visual is the immediate reference person in the discussion/debate situation's here and now. Seen from a cynical and phenomenological viewpoint, what would seem to be of vital importance are the conduct, reactions and mannerisms of the participants in the situation, and in the situations that can arise. It is, at any rate, these things which carry the programme. These basic conditions are utilised radically and consistently by the more extreme talk shows. This happens by presenting the participants with some kind of challenge. They are exposed to something for which they are perhaps quite unprepared, and which catches them off guard forcing them into some kind of spontaneous or even very intimate or sensitive reaction in front of the camera.

Every studio programme exposes its participants to some form of calculated set-up and a distribution of roles. But in the very hard-hitting talk shows the expectation of spontaneous reactions becomes the vital element, so much so that the programme and its producers have no scruples about creating intrigues, confrontations and situations designed to catch participants on the wrong foot.[8] This can cause them, for example, to reveal more than they had intended because they are directly confronted with something, or suddenly become pawns in a game which they had not anticipated. The time co-ordinate to the viewers is, in this way, the very development and revelation in the situation which is seen spontaneously, and they are players from real life it is happening *to* – or rather *in,* being typically articulated in facial expressions and posture. There is no script, because what is played upon is the audience's reaction as it learns more, the spectacle of the victim and, not least, the intense emotion at the moment of the victim's exposure. The ingredients of this exposure consist of varying degrees of psycho-somatic stress, authentic agony and mortification. In this way the proximity in question is the kind of proximity which is arranged by way of intrusion into people's lives, artlessness and basic values. What is created is insecurity and disquiet over the conception of everyday life and its basic relationships of trust. It is this which can evoke the feelings of immediate identification and emotion in the viewers. Apart from the desire to watch and experience sensations, the feelings of viewers can presumably vary from sympathy, through indignation, to contempt and condemnation. Perhaps, too, viewers are made to examine the emotional defences in their own lives.

Although these studio-based programmes are extreme, they only become so because they radicalise a certain dimension of the aesthetic-constructive potential inside the television studio and the enclosed space of the studio audience. However, television can also move out of the studio to broadcast sensational revelations.

Television's Self-Limiting Space II: Set Ups With Cameras On-the-Spot

Breaking into the daily lives of people in a more concrete way, surprising them with a camera in the middle of their daily affairs, and thereby watching and documenting their conduct (with a wide variety of purposes in mind) have now become common elements in, or concepts for, television programmes.[9]

Establishing set ups in which people (usually people in power or authority) are confronted in actual situations with agonising facts and become hesitant or dumbstruck and appear to be on shaky ground, or suddenly become involuntary embarrassed participants in the programme, is also commonly used in hard-hitting exposé documentaries. The situation recorded, sometimes with, sometimes without, a hidden camera and its revelations are used by way of argument; – "Dear viewers, you can see for yourselves...". However, it is television that creates the situation and does so with the intention of capturing the definite, vital, dramatic, hesitating, or silent moment.

The same devices are also used in more 'innocent' ways and in 'pure fun' in the form of practical joke programmes in which different kinds of hidden camera and various set ups bring people into situations which they believe to be perfectly plausible, commonplace, everyday situations and in which they behave accordingly, while the audience is aware that the events are shenanigans designed to make a spectacle of the person in question.[10]

The Experience of Time – Simultaneity

The *experienced* time factor in connection with television is not merely something which in simple terms is connected with an actual *now,* 'an hour ago', 'today', 'yesterday' or 'the day before yesterday' (as it applies fundamentally for news broadcasts). It is also something constructed by television by way of the interaction between the programme's own simulated *now* (as on-going actions) and the viewers, as those experiencing the *now*, and participants through the television screen. The programme host's presentation (via the form of address and speech tempo) of this common *now* is of vital importance. The viewers' opportunity to experience being subject to the same psychological and situational pressure (of time) as the participants in the programmes is of vital importance. And the viewers' opportunity to feel they are witnessing something *immediate* which is taking place in the world of reality, is also of vital importance. In this way a programme might very well be recorded several months prior to broadcasting but be experienced by viewers as being bound together with their *now*.

This presentation form is closely connected with the situational representation of reality, the showing of (everyday) people and their immediate actions, reactions, and statements, expressed by words and gestures in a specific context, and most often in a well-arranged enclosed space. This is connected with having the experience of being close to something authentic, an experience which nevertheless is ambiguous, because while one is, in a sense, close, one is, at the same time, at a distance. In this context time is not chronological time, but comes about as a condensation of the expressive and vital situation which is attended. What we have is a compressed, synthetic time which greatly resembles the one which television fiction and drama attempt to create, build up, and let culminate in climactic situations. But it is also substantially different, partly because the participants are not fictive: they exist, and their actions (including those on television) have, or can have, consequences in the real world for themselves and other individuals. They are not merely enclosed in an artificial, limited world. There is something at stake partly because there often exists a relatively lengthy and extensive series of events which have taken place prior to the condensed situation.

Scales of Time and Place

As regards both time and place, television works on scales or axes which are not pure time/place axes, but axes which are greatly influenced by television itself as participant in a time/place.

One of the extremities of the place axis is the place where the event takes place in the real world. Its other extremity is the event which takes place in television's created and regulated world, but with reality's people as participants. These regulated conditions can be formalised in varying degrees. Those which are formalised most definitively, and where the limitations are greatest, are to be found in the game show and the quiz show. At the same time, the quiz is a form that puts the viewer in the same scale of time as the participants. In connection with the live transmission, it is another time element that is the prevalent one, i.e. the sensation of being present while the event is under way. But as a rule this place is an extremely delimited place with a clearly regimented course of action. In other words, both ends of the scale are characterised by delimitation and clear limitations also as regards the participating role of television itself.

Television's own role as a participant grows when we move from the extremities of the axis towards the mid-point. This applies with regard to the internal world of the studio, by taking representatives from the real world in, and with regard to the outer world to which television moves out to seek contact with people from real life with on-the-spot reports, (hidden) cameras, and transmissions from the space of reality.

In terms of time, television moves on a similar axis, where the mid-point of the axis is television itself, as a channel which broadcasts here and now and does it day after day. Both the television channel itself and the television news lie on this axis, and it is also here that the time axis intersects the space axis. As regards time, television can move in two directions from this intersection. In one direction the correlation between programme time and actual real time is crucial, just as what is offered directly to viewers, and how it is offered, is also crucial. That is to say, the simulated, mutually-understood, direct interaction with the home audience is crucial in varying degrees, including the interaction which is predetermined by, for example, games having to be completed within a fixed time limit. For that reason the spontaneous, the provisional, the incomplete and the fragmentary, are generally also acceptable. In the other direction the interaction between actual real time and programme time abates, just as what if offered to the viewers and the interaction with them also abates. This means that, to an increasing extent, it is programme time along this axis which controls the time relationship. Time is the function of things accumulated, and accumulated narratives, which are to be woven together, and of anecdotes to be bound together. Here, at the other end of the scale the attempt to create simultaneity between what takes place and the viewers no longer applies. Television alone decides the way in which events are to be cut and shaped, and how long they will last. In principle, everything is placed in 'one time' or is told 'once upon a time'. Single events have to be cut, combined with others, formed to meaningful structures and framed by various levels of enunciation.

Television itself is the central participant and expressive form in time and space, and a main actor that establishes itself, with its characteristic expression, in this game, relative to the viewer. As previously mentioned, this appears by emphasis of the programme's here and now in relation to the receiver. The continuously present aspect is the television station itself, represented by the channel-voice or else by the programme hosts. These are the channel's personalities. It is first and foremost television itself as a person-focused medium that is situated precisely at the intersection of the axes, and by *its* domestication of this intersection develops or delivers various versions of time and place in relation to the viewers, including delivery of them in various intermediate forms and symbolic manifestations which claim to co-ordinate and actualise the viewer relative to time and place.

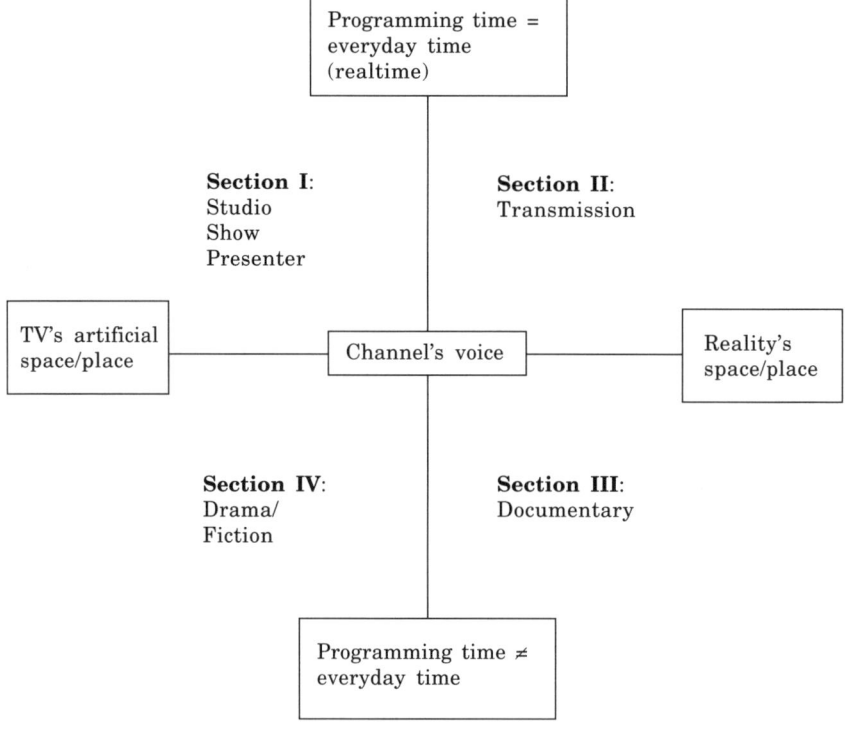

Figure 1

The channel-voice claims explicitly that the viewers, at any given time, are present as active participants on the spot. The channel-voice is also, in a way, merely the directly expressed version of the various forms of contact strategies deployed by the programmes, and whose aim it is to promote a sense of proximity and closeness. The direct form of address to the viewers actualises a now and here and a simulated closeness. The studio or programme host must be able to actualise and crystallise. The studio or programme host's personal qualities and 'natural', 'living', and 'dynamic' charisma in this respect is, therefore, vitally important. His or her adaptability and readiness to improvise is usually supported by a constant (invisible) back-up and feed-back from the production room. The studio host, therefore, represents an indicator of, and a crystallising figure for, not only the place-seeking, (that which takes place, that which is created), but also for the involvement of the viewer. In order to carry out this function the studio host must be, literally, two-faced.

Television's central base is, in other words, television itself as a participant in time and space, and is its own organiser of these conditions and the attempt to synchronise them with the viewers, while taking account of the synchronisation of real time and television time. This can be carried out in a variety of ways.

The Genres in Television's Co-ordination System

By using a system of co-ordinates on an axis it is possible to plot in the genres of television and to see them in terms of their position between centre and periphery.

In the two top sections, then, we find programme types or television genres in which the common elements are the direct form of address to the viewers, the attempts to involve the viewers, and the various attempts to actualise shared time (whether or not, in reality, time is actually shared). Another common element is the reference to the real world, either in the form of the programme bringing people into the studio from the real world, or by the programme moving out into the real world. Yet another common element is the situational unpredictability and the condition that situations must be able to be steered, i.e. the ability to respond and react immediately *in* the situation. Intensity is anchored in the special temporal and situational interaction, and the awareness of the authenticity of the participants and/or the places.

If we move down into the bottom left-hand section (IV) into the world of fiction, it is also characteristic that of the constant television formats, television comedy – or situation comedy – is to be found very close to the boundary area. As the name suggests, situation comedy is built around situations, swift exchanges, like a string of pearls of varying sizes. Situation comedy also has a conscious address to its double audience – a play for two stages – in which the situational, mainly in the form of verbal exchanges, is in focus. Another television genre which is probably even closer to the intersection of the axes, and in which the action to a great extent is based on speech, is the *soap* or the daily-recurring series. The soap is a serialised drama of everyday life with a high, slowly developing profile of interpersonal relationships, taking place within a comparatively closed universe, relatively few localities (like the sitcom), and a fairly primitive light setting and scenography which makes the genre and its studio setting easy to decode no matter which country it is produced in. The special characteristic of the soap is its regular programme time slot and its muted thematising of everyday personal problems. And the term 'everyday' should be understood literally. The action of a single episode is limited to a twenty-four hour period. As with television news which has a time co-ordinate to viewers relative to the events of a twenty-four hour period, and which also, as a daily programme, can become a central part of the viewers' time structure, the soap is similarly geared between television programme and the everyday programme of people's lives. It is also a characteristic of both television comedy and soap that the backdrop of the dramatic development is typically based on family or family-like relationships in a work place, and so constitute the close, everyday problems of ordinary life. It is in this respect, as with television as a whole, that proximity or closeness is the important element: this includes daily proximity and the co-ordinate relative to viewer time.

Television can provide the same experience of proximity in a documentary, non-fictive, but factual form. Here, we are over in the lowest right-hand section (III). This is achieved, for example, by following people at close range as they function in their own environment, their daily lives, in their institution or work place where television is present as a 'fly on the wall'. Television provides 'a slice of life', a series of situations, a piece of an event with very few accompanying remarks. Television can appear both as a participant (for example, by way of an interview or in the role of reporter), or it can play down its role as a participant. Here the focus is on a limited aspect of the lives of the real participants, their actions and their environment. And the intention is to allow these qualities to speak for themselves and illustrate themselves. The documentary element consists of the presentation of the lives of definite people, the ways in which they act and react in a number of situations, – not necessarily with the aim of proving any point. It is a look inside a particular reality and the framework surrounding that reality. Proximity in time is less important here, because proximity is created when television provides the constant, insistent insight which brings the viewers, so to speak, to the place, and close to the participants, following on their heels as they go about their business. What is caught on camera is often caught in such a way that it appears as if the viewers themselves are in the situation. The authenticity and the seemingly matter-of-fact form of registration is what is important, but equally or more important is the dominance of the close, intimate, intrusive focus on the people concerned. This sets the scene for the viewers' simulated proximity. The participants' immediate actions (including statements, facial expressions and gestures) in situations captured on film 'bear witness' to them and their reality rather more than other declarations about themselves. And it is the film montage of these actions in given situations which gives the programme planner the possibility of creating a more constructed narrative and a programme sequence governed by an invisible narrative thread leading to a contrived point. One can, in addition, attempt to fuse this form illustrating life as it is lived, or everyday life, with a clearer television-designed version of the same events by allowing people to 'play themselves' within a television-supervised framework by which a kind of 'docu-soap' is achieved.

44 • *Aesthetics of the Moment in Television*

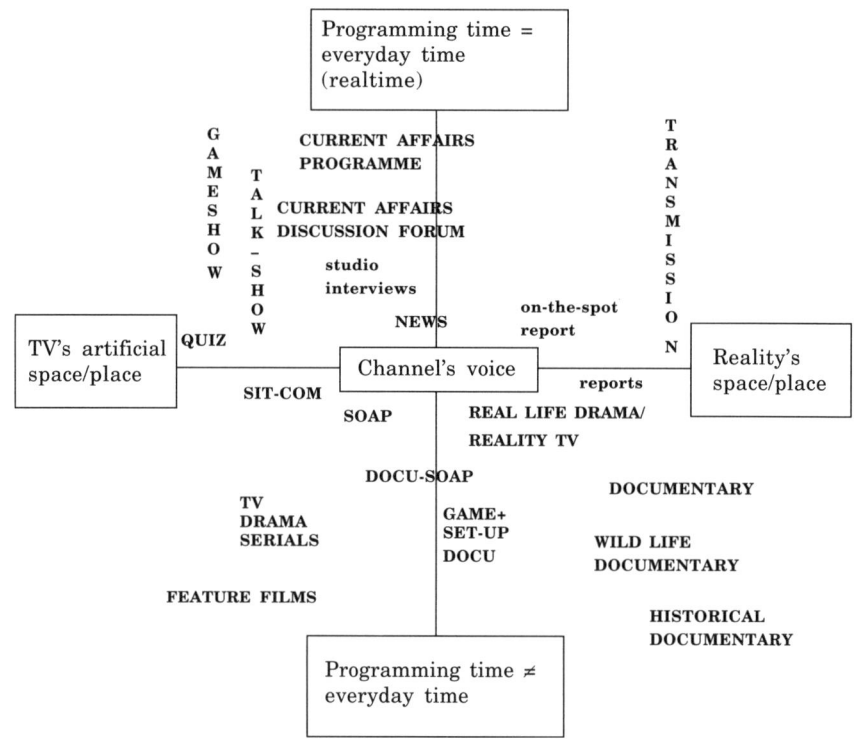

Figure 2

The Entire Genre Universe of Television

Of course television contains more genres than those mentioned here. The claim is that most of them could be placed within the surface of the two-dimensional chart with varying degrees of distance to the intersection and positioned in relation to each of the other genres. This can take place within four main sections, and, what is more, with regard to the gradings already mentioned. The first section might be called the 'home ground' of television. For this reason it is very important for television that the people who come into their home ground (which is an 'away ground' for them) come to feel at home in these unfamiliar surroundings. This is characteristic of programmes that take place in television's self-defined and self-constructed space (usually the studio) and which have some kind of corresponding relationship to the viewers' everyday time or twenty-four hour rhythm, and which tries to make sure that the programme/viewer relationship is experienced as a simultaneous relationship. As far as time is concerned, precisely the same conditions apply to the programmes in the second section. However, with regard to place, the same conditions do *not* apply. In this case actual places, i.e. places which television has not been able to define in advance, and the events in these places, play the vital role. Television can place its regular characters in these settings, but the occurrence at a particular place has its own level of autonomy and is governed by rules which are independent of television. It is precisely this condition, for example, which participants in the actual real world can make use of to attract the attention of television in connection with actions, demonstrations, hostage-taking and the like. For this reason we might call this section television's 'away ground'.

In the third section authenticity of time and the conduct of participants is also crucially important. Just as it is important to show, it is also crucially important to prove or illustrate. The relationship to viewers' time and experience of simultaneity is of less importance. What is important are actions and situations which can be documented, as well as recurring patterns among participants in these real situations. These can be developed into formulated hypotheses or authenticative allegations about these patterns of action and the intentions that these actions might suggest. Seen in its ultimate form this might be described as television's intervening, argumentative and documental ground, or television on the field of reality. This demands a stringent, comprehensive rhetorical and narrative arrangement, or else some relatively narrow, well-defined limits as regards participants and course of events. The same applies in the fourth section, but here the obligation to authenticity, relative to time and place, is removed, and replaced by the regularity of fiction and drama and the demands, for example, of verisimilitude, plot etc.

We shall not fill out the various sections in detail here,[11] but it might be appropriate to mention that a third, and as yet undiscussed dimension makes itself felt in television's total system. This is the system that has to do with television's own communicative dimension and predominant cultural code. This in itself can become the object of an examination in television involving television's handling of the outside world, such that television's ways of *being* television becomes a conspicuous working part in the presentation of this outside world. If this dimension is included then the model become three dimensional and extremely complex. It might, however, be necessary to do so, because by doing so it also becomes clear that: (1) television in itself is a convention-bound, symbol-producing institution which first and foremost has a propensity towards realistic (i.e. mimetic) reproductions of reality, but which does not touch upon the codes according to which these reproductions are perceived or created on television, and (2) that television also possesses a certain free scope with which to render these codes and conventions visible. In mundane terms, most programme types/series have their own travesties and parodies on television. But aside from this it is characteristic that it is mainly one-off programmes that break the tradition of television aesthetics' dominant and 'naive' joy of seeking, framing and reproducing 'reality', and which attempt to challenge the conventions and illusions of viewers in this area.

Conclusion. Instant Aesthetics

This account has, perhaps rather brutally, chosen to ignore the fact that television is, of course, more than programmes which closely connect with a daily or weekly chronicle, which does this within its own pre-determined framework and which copes with the limitations of recurring places formulae and events. Television is also, for example, feature films and one-off documentaries in which form and content are co-ordinated and in which the programme as a whole has the character of a complete unit of work, and in which television means the transmission of one-off events.

This account has chosen to do this because programmes having this characteristic of 'one-off' do not constitute the basis of the range of programmes. Over the past ten years it has become the rule in Danish television that the single programme has a subordinate position relative to programmes with a serialised quality, and are made to adapt to the design of the programme range (Søndergaard, 1994), and that news broadcasts, in particular, comprise the regular entry point into the range of programmes. The news, the positioning of news and the extent of news in the range of programmes has become a vital parameter in the competition between stations. The same applies to programmes which, in various ways, are slotted beside news programmes and/or which in various ways can be woven together with them i.e. current affairs programmes in the form of in-depth magazine programmes, debate programmes, special reports, documentaries, and, in general, programmes which promote the idea that television can move into real life situations and report on what and how something is happening or has happened. Television's qualities of topicality and realism (Fiske and Hartley, 1978) have been cultivated and developed, but to a great extent this has been done in forms which first of all attempt to create formal, as opposed to aesthetic, finality.

It can be seen then that the central dimension of the aesthetics of television has become the aesthetics of expediency which make a virtue of making and communicating contingence and circular, or cyclical, recurrence. It takes only stop-gap measures and does only what is strictly necessary in terms of aesthetic construction or in its way of *being* television, but it places great emphasis on appearing dynamic, active and challenging in all areas of reality. The aesthetic form need not even contribute to developing the content. The aesthetic forms of television are, to a great extent, pre-determined, firmly-established frameworks, slots and formats within which pre-arranged content (realised through people) are handled according to fairly regular sequence patterns, in definite places and communicated via regular television personalities. This form-determined aesthetic which mainly provides a half-fabricated product is possible, indeed successful, for various reasons. It takes advantage of the elementary fact that it can generate an isolated focus on something or someone by a visual process and make things literally accessible at a glance, so that the viewer is given an immediate experience 'self-seeing' and 'self' from minute to minute. This is the immediate tele-visual involvement which takes advantage of contact-seeking involvement appearing via the central participants' play to the camera, via the informal mode of verbal address and via the asserted direct communication and form of address: "it is as though I were being directly spoken to" and, "things are shown to me as though I were actually present".

The provisional, the fragmentary and the kaleidoscopic are compensated for, to a great extent, by the circumstance that what takes place, does so in various forms of well-defined situations and in various versions of now and here. The fixed framework contains a certain element ensuring that what is unexpected and spontaneous can, in fact, happen. Dependent on the way in which the interaction between the framework and the participant(s) is pre-calculated, various forms of pressure are exerted on the participants. Expressed on a scale from the spontaneous to the calculated, the participants' (1) immediate, momentary actions and reactions (2) their mastery of the situation and (3) their constructive ability to improvise are of fundamental importance. These are the same basic elements we find expressed both in terms of actions and figuratively in, for example, a football match with its limited framework and space: the stadium. On the same parallel: in the football match actual finality or concentrated highlights (for example, goals) are phenomena which occur only seldom. The formal finality only appears, in actual fact, when the game is over i.e. when the framework of time has been filled.

It is these conditions which, first and foremost, comprise the main ingredients of television's instant aesthetics. And it must in dialectical terms be considered against the background of its converse: the formal and recurring framework, and also of lengthy periods within its framework. This mix of lengthiness and momentary intensity exists in a form of symbiosis with the everyday lives of the viewers. Thus there is the third vitally important condition which the aesthetics of television take advantage of, that is, that a great many of television's programmes and content are calculated and co-ordinated in series in keeping with the relevant interests of large viewer groups, their problem horizons, and their daily and weekly routines. When the channel-voice speaks of programmes as places one can go into, or out of, or visit, these metaphors are anchored in actual experience. Programmes are, in themselves, moments in a daily rhythm. The lengthiness can, therefore, in certain circumstances, be stretched comparatively long – in principle to infinity, as is the case, for example, with soaps.

The positive aspect in this elucidation of some of television's special aesthetic qualities lies in: (1) The opportunity that the medium has to take a position, flexibly and in effect, instantly, on what is topical, and on current agenda. (2) The opportunity that the medium has to show processes, including courses of events among people in different versions of professional, intimate, and everyday reality, and so-called ordinary/ extraordinary people as participants in various forms of a television-arranged reality. (3) The fact that aesthetic and communicatively functional aspects can, to a high degree, be found in a comparatively raw and unpolished interaction with an audience, and not merely with its immediate problem horizon and relevance horizon, but also with its need to express itself, and its need to see relationships made specific and emotionally crystallised in close-up.

On the other hand, the negative aspect is television's very abbreviated perspective, and what one might call an apparent 'innocence' with regard to the role of communicator and messenger. They say, of course, that one mustn't shoot the pianoplayer or the messenger, but as has been emphasised above, it is television itself that is the central participant with regard to the construction of its 'places' and what has, or can have, immediate impact. It is important, therefore, that television maintains and develops the presentation methods which, to a considerable extent, utilise its instant aesthetic and concrete sensory potential, with an aim to constructing and reconstructing more complete perspectives. Perspectives in this sense are understood as methods and places from which things are seen, illustrated and considered. Reconstruction and construction of perspectives can be understood as methods by which the perspective of the viewing public is also considered, and considered as a dynamic quality that can be emotionally affected and adapted, such that television does not merely provide insight, but touches on methods of achieving varying viewpoints and *shifting* insight.

According to a communicative and formal aesthetic criteria the minimal programme units of television advertising operate within this latter sphere. They are forced to, if they are to have any effect. That television advertising is able to occupy this sphere to a higher degree than actual programmes, and thereby achieve a special aesthetic weigh in the range of programmes, has happened without anyone's conscious planning. Or has it?

Notes

1. In this context the term TV stands for the programming activities which are incorporated in public service stations such as Danish DR and TV2, and commercial stations such as TV-Danmark and TV3, i.e. stations with an all-round or broad range of programming material in terms of thematic issues and genres.
2. The above, and the following characteristics of TV are summaries of what is normally agreed upon by media researchers. The qualities as regards live broadcast (Eco 1977) and the live character of the medium in general are necessary platitudes. The latter, Ellis (1982) labels as the "immediacy effect", which is generated by the directness of the TV image primarily in, e.g. a presenter's direct address and its "co-present intimacy". Focusing on this aspect of direct address, the predominance of talk and discourse, Morse (1985) has made specifications of the talkative nature of TV, but not made clear that although TV presents itself as "discourse" it is "history" (cf. Larsen 1989). Respecting this, and including the station or schedule level, Kozloff (1992) has presented applications of narrative theory in order to show how TV as a whole, works as a text with a hierarchy of narrators. Morse (1990) has further elaborated on the aspects of directness and intimacy in order to establish a graduated or hierarchical system of the spatial relationships between TV and its audience, including the schedule level. As for co-ordinates of time, place and space between programming content/programme schedule and audience, primarily Scannell (1988, 1993, 1995) has delivered substantial definitions.
3. The term indicates the same as Horton and Wohl's (1956) parasocial interaction.

4. On media event cf. Dayan & Katz (1992).
5. Although differences exist between Aristotle's *On Poetry* and French classicism – Boileau-Despreaux's L'Art Poetique – these differences are not significant in the present context.
6. The channel-voice emerges/expresses itself in lead-ins (and lead-outs) 1) in between programmes, 2) during credits, as well as 3) in contexts of separate sequences of the station's promos (time-tables and trailers etc.) of programmes of the day. The definitions of how the channel voice acts are an outcome of a comparative study of Danish TV stations' (TV1, TV2, TV3) programming between 1993 and 1996. The sample represents one week each year and the schedule in total. The study, which is both quantitative and qualitative is to be published in Danish.
7. On the general social implications of "place" on TV, see also Meyrowitz (1985).
8. The extreme edition of the talk-show genre has been developed on US channels over the past 5-6 years. In Denmark we do not find anything like *The Jerry Springer Show* or *The Ricky Lake Show*, but shows which exploit the same elements of setting up the main character(s) in order to provoke immediate and (un)-expected reactions have had some success (e.g. *Udfordringen (The Challenge)* on Danish TV2, 1996).
9. Cf. Tove A. Rasmussen's article in the present volume.
10. A situativity of parallel nature is captured and dominant in programmes based on home videos and on TV's own, or filmmakers cuts, of missed or abortive takes.
11. Stigel (1997) has used a variation of the same system of co-ordinates with slightly different definitions of the time axis, due to the fact the hypothetical viewer formed the central point-of-view, or agent, in that context or model. The article presents a more elaborated exemplification of the implications of the third axis (culture/code: presumed intimacy, or familiarity with primarily referential dimension, on the one hand, vs. intimacy or familiarity with symbolic frame or form, on the other) in order to construct a three-dimensional model of TV's principal and total potentials as regards genre and aesthetic development. As such, a model in itself raises conceptual problems on flat paper, and as the more steady aesthetic developments on TV are, in fact, of a more 'flat' character i.e. are possible to conceptualise as mixtures or hybrids of already given genres, I shall refrain from expounding the complications here.

Bibliography

Dayan, Daniel, & E. Katz (1992). *Media Events: The Live Broadcasting of History*. Cambridge, Mass.: Harvard University Press.

Eco, Umberto (1977). *Das offene Kunstwerk*. Frankfurt a.M.: Suhrkamp [*The Open Work*. Cambridge, Mass.: Harvard Univeristy Press].

Ellis, John (1982). *Visible Fictions. Cinema, Television, Video*. London: Routledge & Kegan Paul.

Fiske, John, & J. Hartley (1978). *Reading Television*. London: Methuen & Co.

Horton, Donald, & R.R. Wohl (1956). "Mass Communication and Para-Social Interaction. Observations on Intimacy at a Distance". In: *Psychiatry*, no 19.

Kozloff, Sarah (1992). "Narrative Theory and Television". In Robert C. Allan (ed.): *Channels of Discourse. Re-assembled*. London: Routledge.

Larsen, Peter (1989). "TV: Historie og/eller diskurs?". In: *EDDA*, hefte 1, Oslo [TV: Histoire and/or Discourse?].

Meyrowitz, Joshau (1985). *No Sense of Place. The Impact of Electronic Media on Social Behaviour*. Oxford: Oxford University Press.

Morse, Margaret (1985). "Talk, Talk, Talk. The Space of Discourse in Television News, Sportscasts, Talk Shows and Advertising". In: *Screen*, Vol. 26 no 2.

Morse, Margaret (1990). "An Ontology of Everyday Distraction: The Freeway, The Mall, The Television". In P. Mellemcamp (ed.): *The Logics of Television*. London: British Film Institute.

Scannell, Paddy (1988). "Radio Times: The Temporal Arrangements of Broadcasting in the Modern World". In P. Drummond & P. Paterson (eds.): *Television and its audience*. London: British Film Institute.

Scannell, Paddy (1993). "Time, Place and Space in Broadcasting". In K. Skretting (ed.): *Kringskasting og kino. Levene bilder*, nr. 2/93. Trondheim: Universitetet i Trondheim.

Scannell, Paddy (1995). "For a Phenomenology of Radio and Television". In: *The Journal of Communication*, Vol. 45, no. 3.

Stigel, Jørgen (1997). "The Aesthetics of Television, The Quality of Television. On Distinctions and Relations of Programme Form and Quality of Address". In M. Eide, B. Gentikow & K. Helland (eds.): *Quality Television*. Bergen: University of Bergen.

Søndergaard, Henrik (1994). *DR i tv-konkurrencens tidsalder*. Copenhagen: Samfundslitteratur [*Denmark's Radio in the Era of TV Competition*].

CHAPTER TWO

National Cinema and TV Fiction in a Transnational Age

Gunhild Agger
Department of Communication
Aalborg University

Purpose

During the 80s and 90s the concept of the national – as opposed to the international and the transnational on the one hand and the local or regional on the other – has been examined from an increasing number of different angles, reflecting different processes going on in different societies during these years. A common point of departure for much thinking about these matters has been Benedict Anderson's concept of the idea of nationhood as an 'imagined political community' (Anderson, 1996: 6), basically a patchwork compounded of different ways of imagining national belonging. A vital part is made up of the process of imagining, and in this process the systems of language, education, and mass communication play an important role (cf. Higson, 1997: 6). In the process of developing the concept of nationhood historically, Anderson makes some hints about the ways in which the system of mass communication works. For instance he has an interesting note on radio:

"Invented only in 1895, radio made it possible to bypass print and summon into being an aural representation of the imagined community where the printed page scarcely penetrated." (Anderson, 1996: 54)

Concentrating on developing an explanation of the origins of nationhood Anderson does not elaborate much on the role of modern media though it is obvious from the general unfolding of the arguments that they assume a vital role in sustaining the imagining of nationhood. It is useful therefore to elaborate the hints made by Anderson on the significance of the media. This has been done by Anthony D. Smith, among others. In his book on *National Identity*, he lists 'a common, mass public culture' as one of the fundamental features of national identity, defining a nation as

"a named human population sharing an historic territory, common myths and historical memories, a mass, public culture, a common economy and common legal rights and duties for all members." (Smith, 1991: 14)

On a more general level the significance of the media has been elaborated by Jürgen Habermas, of course, but what is interesting in this connection is the ways in which the questions of national identity and the questions of mass media are intermingled. In other words: How do the media contribute to and support the imagining of national identity? And can they still be said to do that in an age when transnational trends in many ways have started to prevail, when you are met by the same advertisements in Tokyo as in New York, when you can watch the same movies when flying by Thai Air as when flying by SAS, and when you can watch *The Simpsons* at almost any hotel in any city where you happen to have landed?

All these questions cannot be illuminated here. What I propose to do is to concentrate on two areas within mass media: cinema and television, by discussing which concepts of national identity are worth using and why. The area of cinema has been chosen because, especially within the field of national cinema, some interesting ways of seeing this connection have emerged recently. The field of national television has not been the object of similar scrutiny. Nevertheless, the question of the relationship between international and transnational developments versus national ambitions in national television begins to pose itself.

My assumption is that in spite of many obvious differences between the two media and their fictional products, it is possible to use key concepts from the same theoretical framework when trying to define what it means to imagine national belonging. And that it is illuminating to do so because certain differences become discernible, which characterise the two media.

I shall start by discussing three supplementary levels on which nationhood in cinema can be defined: the basic national level, the representational level, and the institutional level. In one way or another, all these concepts are based on an opposition between national and international. In varying degrees, however, it seems to be useful to see them from a relational aspect. From the area of cinema, I proceed to the area of television and discuss what the application of the same concepts implies. I trace recent transnational developments in genre and style, and I finish by relating these tendencies to recent developments in Danish TV fiction in order to show that though international/transnational formats, formulas, and genres prevail, the question of national belonging is still negotiated in several ways. The series *Taxa* can be seen as an 'answer' to and a negotiation with international formats in technique, style, etc., and the serial *The Kingdom* can be seen as a further elaboration of the Danish tradition of TV fiction dealing with the state of the nation and combining national and transnational genre traditions.

The Basic National Level

A limited but illuminative angle on the national would be to define it by way of the cultural products which are not exportable to other countries and therefore exclusively target a national audience. Soila, Iversen and Widding state that Nordic cinema consists of films that not or only to a very limited degree have been exported.

"This means that it is national in a basic sort of way: a culture that stays within itself, something which exists only for that country." (Soila, Iversen & Widding, 1998: 2)

In small countries most cultural products are national in this basic sense. Whether the cultural products are just unknown to or ignored by leading international critics, or whether they are – or are considered – obsolete or provincial, they never become the focus of international attention. Directors from small nations have to make up their minds what to do in these circumstances. A distinction advanced by Mette Hjort might be useful to outline possible strategies. She distinguishes between 'opaque' and 'translatable' cinematic elements and gives the following definitions of the two:

"Cinematic elements are opaque when they are so firmly rooted within a given national imagery that international audiences cannot be expected to understand their meaning without the help of native informants ..." (Hjort, 1996: 530)

... whereas the cultural specificity of 'translatable' elements is close enough to foreign audiences to enable them to grasp the meaning. Especially within the domain of humour, national tradition and history, opaque elements tend to have a stronghold. On the other hand, what is sometimes believed to be a specially national kind of humour can be found to possess a broader and more universal appeal, e.g. the humour of John Cleese. Cultural products of small nations can have a universal appeal, too, of course, but the possibility of making an appeal which transcends the basic national level lies primarily in what Mette Hjort calls 'cross-filming', which can be defined as a conscious 'dual orientation' toward different audiences (Hjort, 1996: 529). Hence both an opaque and a dual orientation can often be found in the cinema of small nations.

This points to the close connection between the basic national level and the national audience and its expectations in domains such as language, favourite genres, topics, treatments, actors and actresses. All national audiences have their expectations, and it is up to the film industry, if necessary supported by national institutions, to fulfil them, since foreign films, by definition, can only fulfil certain expectations of certain groups. But just as directors might have cross-filming ambitions, national audiences often go for both national and transnational trends.

The Representational Level

A broader angle is provided by the concept of representation. At a certain level of abstraction, national cinema represents a national identity which might be quite unnoticed by a national audience, but easily discernible to an international audience. From a foreign point of view, the domestic element risks being given a greater degree of national representation than is intended. According to Thomas Elsaesser, an obvious example is the new German cinema. It was often received in a way which implicitly turned the directors into ambassadors of a new, legitimate German culture, and he comments:

> "If for the domestic spectator it is more a matter of identifying with this or that character or stance and recognising certain experiences, in the international context, a national cinema will be perceived as presenting or projecting an identity, a narrative image of an entire country." (Elsaesser, 1989: 6)

Due to historical circumstances, this representational angle with its demand for legitimisation might have been especially awkward to the Germans. Discussing the representational angle and comparing certain aspects of similarity between German and Australian cinema, Tom O'Regan makes the following reassuring statement:

> "The national cinema, the national culture, the national identity are always impure and hybrid assemblages of the good, the bad and the dull." (O'Regan, 1996: 135)

Confronted with the challenge of being assessed by an international audience, every single nation will always aspire to deliver the best representations of its own national identity. This can be done in numerous ways, explicitly or tacitly, in an official manner or in a subdued fashion. And there is never any guarantee that it is represented in a convincing manner. According to O'Regan, the rule of thumb is that the more ostentatiously national identity is represented, the more 'dull' (or even 'bad') is the film. National identity is best represented in a tacit or subdued fashion. In any case, the representational angle can be applied to any cinema linked to the idea of a nation, especially when seen from the point of view of another nation or just more generally from an international point of view, e.g. at international film festivals.

At the core of the representational point of view lies a common aspiration to a national geographical and cultural orientation. 'Where is it from?' is often a first question about a new film when a viewer tries to establish a framework before watching it, and the answer to that question suggests a whole range of associative expectations. National stereotypes are often negotiated in this connection. A common Scandinavian comment on films from Hollywood is 'They are so American', meaning that they are well narrated with set-up and pay-off in the right places, setting and characters are convincingly represented, they have at least one scene where lovers or parents and children confirm 'I love you – I love you, too', often they operate within the concepts of winning and losing, and they have a happy ending. This frame of stereotyping is based on experiences with mainstream Hollywood cinema, but it does not consider the exceptions. By contrast, in a North American or French context, Scandinavian cinema is often comprehended in quite a narrow way as a tradition based on the films of Carl Dreyer and Ingmar Bergman. This way of thinking concentrates on the obvious exceptions, the great renowned auteurs, but it does not consider main stream cinema (cf. Soila, Iversen & Widding, 1998: 3).

Only on a second thought comes the question 'Is it good?' The prominence of the representational angle is closely linked to this widespread national geographical and cultural framework of orientation. Whether this framework means less to the young generation brought up on international images than to the older generations is often discussed. But even if the national cinema is often something which the young generation wishes to ignore, or treat with contempt or irony it is still conceived, and perhaps rejected, fundamentally within the same conceptual framework.

The question whether it is good, on the other hand, is crucial to the destiny of national cinema. Tom O'Regan discusses the paradox that it is both an advantage and a disadvantage for a national cinema that its directors' first and second films are really good (O'Regan, 1996: 51-55). An advantage because if they are successful this can be credited to a favourable production milieu, lots of talent and creativity inherent in the national cinema, and that is good for the prestige and fame of the national cinema, of course. A disadvantage because within a relatively short time, successful national directors will go international and perhaps vanish altogether from the national film scene. The same is the case with actors, actresses, and photographers all of whom help to boost a national cinema. And then the national reputation runs the risk of dissolving into talent drain, and the next time the national audience is confronted with talents, they might easily appear in a Hollywood setting.

Opposing national obligations and limitations, some directors without further fuss aim directly at being internationally recognised, either using the above-mentioned dual orientation or by refusing to appeal to a limited national audience. An example of the first strategy is followed by Bille August, the Danish director. When he achieved his international breakthrough with *Pelle Erobreren* (*Pelle the Conqueror*, 1987), it was the result of years of hard work for primarily national, and secondarily Scandinavian, and then international recognition.[1] An obvious example of the second strategy is Lars von Trier, another internationally well-known Danish director, whose strategy was to avoid any national element, with the same purpose: starting with *The Element of Crime* (1984) he made most of his films in English and in a 'German' expressionist setting, financed through various kinds of co-production, directly targeting an international, primarily European avant-garde (festival) audience. An effort, which on the other hand, made a great contribution – as did Bille August's – to the development of Danish national cinema. It was not until the television serial and film *The Kingdom*, 1994, that Lars von Trier started explicitly relating to themes connected with the national tradition of handling problems in Danish society in a satirical way. This was done by drawing on famous international genre traditions as well, and thus it is illustrative of the strategy of dual approach.[2] This approach raises the question: what does it take to be internationally recognised, and which standards are on the whole international? Before discussing that, however, it is necessary to illuminate a third supplementary level.

The Institutional Level

As suggested by Richard Paterson, when we deal with the concept of nationhood, we should supplement any analysis with the 'top down' and the 'bottom up' approach (Paterson, 1993: 4). The institutional level can be regarded as an appropriate representation of the 'top down' approach. The institutional level is closely connected to the representational level. In fact, they can be regarded as interrelated in the sense that one presupposes the other. The representational level obviously could not manifest itself with any strength if it was not supported by national institutions, and the institutional level has to be represented in both a national and an international context to justify itself.

Without a strong interest on the part of government, most European – or Australian – productions for cinema and also some for TV would look different or perhaps would not exist. Governments have undertaken the stimulation and promotion of national film industries as a national obligation. But although a concern for the expression of nationhood, of keeping up national culture, is part of the way in which the whole enterprise is legitimised, there are interesting traits indicating a development towards an international trend on this level as well.

If we examine the latest Danish film legislation from 1997 for instance and take it to represent the latest tendencies in the matter of the balance of national and international elements, the definition of a Danish film is interesting:

"According to this law a Danish film should be defined as a film which has a Danish producer. The film should be in Danish or contain a special artistic or technical effort which will contribute to advancing the art and culture of film in Denmark."

This is quite a liberal interpretation of the national: neither the director, nor the actors, nor the language is required to be Danish. Of course the definition is designed to fit the conditions of production, which increasingly demand international co-production, and as such it is a very clear expression of the terms of negotiation a national cinema has to cope with. For a small nation with a minor film production the conditions risk placing the very issue – the national – at stake. One can abstract from the requirements of the national language to get something else which is defined in rather vague terms to meet the implicit demand of international standards and quality, and which in its turn is hoped to improve the national film art and film culture. Which it sometimes does, and sometimes does not.

As far as films are concerned, there might be a connection between the liberal definition and the fact that there is a strong tendency to reinforce Americanisation in this decade. The definition allows any form of international co-operation, but various kinds of Nordic and European co-operation are the most frequent. The explanation can be found at the supply level.

During the period 1991-95, American first-performance films in Denmark have risen from 1/2 to about 2/3 of all first-performance films. European films have dropped from 1/2 to 1/4, while Danish films have kept a share of about 6-7% of all new films (Mortensen, 1997: 310). This can be accounted for in various ways: the massive come-back of the American film industry starting in the 70s, the aggressive marketing, the huge budgets for both production and marketing, the professionalism of narration, directing etc. – and not least the persistence of genre films as the prevailing form.

One explanation of some significance might be that the production of genre films by the state-supported film industry has declined. If we take Danish development as an example again, we get an interesting picture when comparing the situation in the 50s to the present situation concerning genre films. In Denmark, a film subsidy law was approved in 1949, but it did not favour 'author'-films. On the contrary, during the 50s, genre films prevailed:

> "Of the 138 films [released during the period 1950-60, GA] forty-eight were counted as belonging to the genre of folk comedies and thirty-eight as being light comedies. To this we can add twelve farces, six crime films, thirty-three 'serious' films and one travel film." (Soila, Iversen & Widding, 1998: 19)

Based on the figures supplied by Vicki Synnott in Bondebjerg et al. (1997: 423-430) I made a similar survey for the period 1985-95 for the purpose of comparison. It should be noted that the film law of 1989 was favourable to producers, giving 50% government support to a film which could attract the other 50% from private production companies or other sources. The figures show that out of 130 films released during this period, only 21 could be counted as genre films (covering light comedies, farces, crimis/thrillers, but excluding genre films for children and youth films). There were 10 documentaries, and 40 of the films could be categorised as films for children and youth films. Of course, some of the 'serious' director's films belong to different genre traditions as well, just as it would increase the number if genre films from the children and youth film category were added. Nevertheless, the figures show that the adult audience's demand for genre films (which seems to be a fact) has had to be satisfied in other ways, for instance by Hollywood movies, by reruns on TV, where old Danish genre films are a success according to ratings, and by the TV genres that have elaborated the genre system to fit the new medium.

Within the restrictions always crucial to the concept of supply: what is available? – these numbers give a hint of the 'bottom up' level as far as it indicates that there is an audience for approximately the same number of Danish films now as during the 50s, a period when the market for Danish films culminated. The following table of the most popular films from the period 1972-1996 demonstrates the constant contest in the Danish mind between American and Danish during the last two decades. Popularity is here measured by number of sold tickets. I only list the first 10 films, but the general idea is confirmed by the following 40, the first non-American and non-Danish film on the list being a British 007 film which is number 19.

Number	Title	Country of origin	First performance in DK	Number of sold tickets
1	*The Olsen Gang Sees Red*[3]	DK	1976	1,199,751
2	*One Flew Over the Cuckoo's Nest*	USA	1976	1,119,769
3	*The Olsen Gang on the Run*	DK	1977	1,044,505
4	*E.T.*	USA	1982	1,018,707
5	*Grease*	USA	1978	1,006,102
6	*The Olsen Gang at War*	DK	1978	1,005,498
7	*Out of Africa*	USA	1986	998,856
8	*Walter and Carlo – on Father's Hat*	DK	1985	953,743
9	*The Lion King*	USA	1994	944,749
10	*The House of the Spirits*	DK	1993	940,605

Table 1: Most popular films 1972-96
(Vicki Synnott in Bondebjerg et al., 1997: 403)

It is interesting to note that two films of mixed origins figure on the list: *Out of Africa* and *The House of the Spirits*. Sydney Pollack's film *Out of Africa* was extremely popular in Denmark. One of the reasons could be that many Danes found it intriguing to watch such a spell-binding authoress as Karen

Blixen (Isak Dinesen) played by Meryl Streep – supported by an international setting. Small nations are often flattered by the attentions of the big, and in this case it did not matter that the credibility of the cinematic biography could be discussed.[4] With *The House of the Spirits*, it is the other way round. The director is Danish, but the film is as international as it could be, based on Isabel Allende's Chilean bestseller, with British and American actors and a German producer. This cocktail did not prevent the interest of the Danish fans from being interested in Bille August, the director.

Inherent in the three levels of defining the concept of national cinema, so far, are the binary concepts of either domestic and international or local/regional and transnational. The basic national level concentrates on opaque cinematic elements directly targeting the expectations of a national audience and thus excluding the participation of an international audience. The representational level is orientated towards representing national identity to an international audience, so the contrast between domestic and international is at the core of its construction. Similarly, the institutional level has the dual obligation of providing the national audience with national films and ensuring that they are on an international level. The binary concept functions in various ways, so apparently it is necessary to try to develop it a little further, by trying to explore the nature of the relationship between the contrasting elements.

Essence or Relations?

Thomas Elsaesser argues that Hollywood constitutes the norm and sets the standards of the international because Hollywood films are universally widespread and an integral part of every country's film culture. He applies a little irony quoting Dusan Makavejev's statement "If you can't stand the heat, get out of the kitchen; living in the twentieth century means learning to be American" (Elsaesser, 1994: 24), but he very directly points to an important problem. Can national cinema be understood in terms of essence or can it better be understood in terms of relations? Is there something specific, not necessarily non-exportable, but something essentially specific in the use of genres, traditions, style, themes, music that could be said to constitute national cinema, or should we rather imagine national cinema in terms of "re-assignment of meaning, this fluctuation of critical, cultural and economic currency between one country and another" (Elsaesser, 1994: 25)?

Higson poses the same dilemma:

"If Hollywood standards constitutes the international standard, then in a sense a distinctive national film production is by definition non-standard and marginal ... for a cinema to be nationally popular, it must paradoxically also be international in scope; that is to say, it must work with Hollywood's international standards ... But there is also the possibility of working with different standards, whether economic, or cultural, or both." (Higson, 1997: 8-9)

He concludes his investigation by saying that the British films he has been examining are "the products of a series of dialogues" (1997: 276) with both international (Hollywood) and domestic traditions of different orientation and values (popular and elite). Resulting from these dialogues Higson can discern certain distinctive stylistic characteristics as an essential part of British cinema, the key aspects being "modes of narration, types of looking, and uses of space" (1997: 276). Applied to the terms mentioned above Higson suggests that the dialogue or the relational aspect can be used to define the essential one.

A similar approach is adopted by O'Regan. He makes the relational aspect his point of departure in his search for different angles on Australian national cinema – and finds in this very aspect one of the most Australian characteristics, an observation which might apply to other nations of a comparable size as well:

"I find Australian cinema's specificity to lie, not in any particular set of attributes, so much as in its relational character. This specificity emerges, on the one hand, from its diversifying, unifying, importing and indigenizing, blending and Othering dynamics, and, on the other hand, from its negotiation of its political and cultural weakness and the related importance to it of projecting Australian ugliness and ordinariness." (O'Regan, 1996: 7)

What O'Regan calls "Negotiating cultural transfers" (1996: 213) is a vital issue in this dialogue. It is not a dialogue on equal terms because the partners in it do not operate that way. The dialogue between small, medium-sized and large countries, their ways of seeing, their different productions, take place on an unequal basis where flows and transfers to Australia are more compact than the other way round. Which is indeed the case for most countries except the USA and India, and which is more obvious the smaller the nation is.

The phenomenon of mutual influence, inspiration, loaning and borrowing, is known from any domain of culture, of course, but it seems to present itself with extraordinary force in the domain of film and TV fiction because of the impact of the visual, the international traditions of trade in this field, and all the empty slots on TV that have to be filled. O'Regan suggests that a 'hybrid forms of analysis' should be developed to make sense of the dispersed elements and all the continued dialogues on the screens. Following Lotman's model of cultural transfers[5] O'Regan stresses that the conditions of negotiation, the relative strengths of the participants, the asymmetry between small and large nations, should be taken into account when trying to map the relations. A 'politics of recognition' (Hjort, 1996: 520) is inherent in the creation of every national cinema as it will aspire not only to a local audience, but also to be recognised on equal terms by an international audience. If not, it would deem itself inferior right from the beginning, and that is not acceptable for any national culture, since the idea of equality and thus of equal worth is so deeply rooted in the idea of national identity. According to Benedict Anderson, a bilingual dictionary is the most evident demonstration of this idea as it is structured by the concept that for every word in one language there is an equivalent in another, and this is not dependant on the size of the nation (Anderson,

1996: 71). Anderson gives a convincing description of the processes during the last two centuries that advanced the spread of the concept of equality to other vital cultural domains as well.

In conclusion, we can state that the ambition to define what is specifically national is realisable on the basic national level. The question of essence is still a meaningful question in this connection, and it can help to explain the opaque elements. On the level of representation and on the institutional level, the question of relations seems to force itself on any attempts at thinking in terms of essence. This hinders a clean-cut division between the characteristics which various nations believe to be unique to themselves, and makes it increasingly difficult to avoid the relational approach which seems to be at the very core of small and minor nations' cultural ambitions. For large nations, the question of relations is less crucial, but in connection with the renewal of genre traditions and the assumption of a universal appeal, it has a certain impact.

Returning to Benedict Anderson's general concept of the imagined community it is obvious that the angles from which the question of nationhood are discussed in a cinematic context make a contribution to exploring the ways in which the processes of imagining are carried out in contemporary societies. They occupy themselves with attempts to work out concepts which express the ways in which all the connections between the different levels of signification function. Central in this respect is the concept of a relational approach conceived as a dialogue between the local, the regional, and the national levels on the one hand, and the international (concerning different nations) and transnational (concerning common professional standards, commonly set by Hollywood) on the other. Thinking in terms of relations seems to be essential – also as a condition of catching the essence of the national. Another important concept in the relational approach concerns the negotiations of cultural transfer. This is a domain where the common idea of equality which we have inherited from the Enlightenment is being challenged by problems posed by reality.

Genre Concepts

On the whole, the concept of genre seems to be worth considering when trying to find concrete ways of imagining nationhood in a national cinema. Though the concept of genre is roughly international, a genre always assumes a certain national flavour applied by a national cinema. In this way, the concept of genre can be seen as a crossroads where different traditions meet and where a special national coining of a genre is the result. Higson combines genre and style, claiming that

> "the processes of repetition and reiteration which constitute a genre can be highly productive in sustaining a cultural identity." (Higson, 1997: 5)

Talking of popular genres, Thomas Schatz uses the concept of "a structured mental image" as a way of imagining a genre:

> "We steadily accumulate a kind of narrative-cinematic *gestalt* or "mind set" that is a structured mental image of the genre's typical activities and attitudes." (Schatz, 1981: 16)

In both cases the processual aspect of the genre concept is emphasised, as is also the case in Stephen Neale's useful reflections on the concept:

> "The process-like nature of genres manifests itself as an interaction between three levels: the level of expectation, the level of the generic corpus, and the level of the 'rules' or 'norms' that govern both." (Neale, 1997: 463)

The processual aspect of the genre concept in many ways corresponds to the concept of dialogue launched in relation to the concept of nationhood. In this way, the area of genre can be seen as a meeting place of dialogues, of attempts to combine the essential with the relational aspects. These suggestions cannot directly be transferred to any other medium, but on a general level they are productive when we consider television genres.

National Television

If we look at national television, an even more complex image evolves. If the concepts of relations and dialogue are essential to an understanding of what is going on in national cinema, we might need the concept of 'heteroglossia' to signalise the dimensions of intertextuality on national television. In an interesting attempt to apply Bakhtinian concepts in the area of mass media, Robert Stam advances the idea of television as 'an electronic microcosm', a sort of contemporary electronic novel where all kinds of issues are debated from all kinds of angles. Taking his point of departure from the area of cinema, Stam briefly develops the possibilities of the Bakhtinian approach in television in the following way:

> "Within a Bakhtinian approach, there is no unitary text, no unitary producer, and no unitary spectator; rather, there is a conflictual heteroglossia pervading producer, text, context, and reader/viewer. Each category is traversed by the centripetal and the centrifugal, the hegemonic and the oppositional." (Stam, 1992: 221)

True remarks, but how can one make them operational? Some years ago and inspired by the Bakhtinian angle, John Fiske advanced three levels of 'intertextuality' to make the concept more operational in a television context. He distinguishes 1) "horizontal relations" between primary texts, 2) "vertical intertextuality" between primary texts and other texts of a different type referring to the first (e.g. criticism), and 3) "tertiary texts" as letters or talk about primary texts (Fiske, 1992: 108). In this context it is worth noticing that Fiske considers the concept of genre the most influential for horizontal intertextuality.

However, neither Stam nor Fiske focus on the dialogue between the national level and the international or transnational. In order to discuss how this can be done, I shall try to apply some of the insights from national cinema to the bewildering domain of television – the three supplementary ways of defining the national concept and the discussion of essential or relational angles. Although crucial differences are evident, there are enough similarities between the areas of cinema and TV fiction to make a comparison rewarding. This has been convincingly demonstrated by John Ellis in *Visible fictions*. I shall limit myself to considerations mostly of TV fiction because that is a domain which shares some essential conditions with film. A national production of TV fiction involves the production industry of a nation, and it draws on all the national traditions of genre, style etc. However, it also involves relations with foreign and transnational production industries and the traditions of their products, hence the typical hybridity of TV fiction. When considering the national, I shall in what follows primarily draw on the case of Danish nationhood.

My suggestion is that the *basic national* angle is more important in the television medium than in cinema because TV is more important as a domestic medium, targeting the national audience in the first place, international audiences in the second place. Television as a medium invites its producers to make use of the national language more than is the case with the film industry. It is evident that national genre traditions survive on television in different ways, though international formats and genres prevail. On the whole, TV is a more domestic medium. Its products do not require the same degree of attention as the cinematic, they do not have the character of an event, and they are not watched in the same way.

These characteristics have been convincingly demonstrated by researchers such as Joshua Meyrowitz and Roger Silverstone, but perhaps John Ellis has made the most striking remark about it. Comparing film and television, John Ellis draws attention to precisely the domestic aspect of television and in a pertinent analogy relates it to nationhood:

"Broadcast TV is the private life of a nation-state, defining the intimate and inconsequential sense of everyday life, forgotten quickly and incomprehensible for anyone who is outside its scope" (Ellis, 1993: 5).

This may serve as a direct comment on the question of opaque elements. Much television is not directly translatable and neither is it supposed to be. Though satellite television, often with a more transnational character, has attracted a certain percentage of viewers in most countries, the old-fashioned terrestrial national television is still more watched, even in the USA (Cunningham and Jacka, 1996: 18).

For the same reasons, the *representational* angle is less important in television than in cinema because there is less attention to TV festivals; TV criticism is seldom or never considered an issue of importance, and the flow means that there is less attention to specific programmes. This does not mean that what is represented is not important, it just means that this level plays a less significant role in an international context. For a domestic audience on the other hand, this angle may be more important than in cinema. Many people have the chance of being represented on television in one way or another, and again especially TV fiction assumes a very important role by representing and negotiating all the little changes in everyday life, historical issues, fatal and melodramatic moments, or complex art.

When we look at the *institutional* angle, representing the 'top down'-level many countries still have public service institutions with certain obligations towards both the national audience and the national production industry. Denmark is only one example of how much has been done to ensure a national production of TV fiction in terms of money, laws, and public support. TV fiction is considered important as a public service obligation. During the years of monopoly it was the task of Radio Denmark to develop TV genres and formats, a task which in many ways succeeded so that different traditions were developed. After 1988 TV2 has participated to a certain degree, although this might be one of the domains where it has not taken its avowed public service obligations seriously enough.

The *relational* ambition is as important on television as in cinema, if not more so, because programming in most countries consists of a mixture of domestic and foreign, forcing comparisons upon the viewer (although there are exceptions). Looking at the bottom-up perspective and relating that to the national aspect is illuminating, when we consider choice of channels and favourite programmes.

As far as channels are concerned, in Denmark we can register a strong tendency to choose Danish: The public service channels' share of viewers in 1997 was 68.6%.[6] This figure represents a more or less stable situation. The share is falling at a very slow rate, being 75% in 1992 and 70% in 1995 (Nordahl Svendsen, 1996: 7). On the other hand, if we include the share of viewers held by all channels transmitting in Danish in 1997 the 'national' tendency becomes even stronger:

TV2	39.4%
DR1	27.8%
TV3	11.0%
TV DK	6.2%
DR2	1.4%
Local channels	0.7%
DK4	0.4%
3 +	1.3%
Totally	88.2%[7]

Table 2: Share of channels transmitting in Danish (1997)

But of course it should be noticed that in the programme offer, American fiction plays a leading role, the rule of thumb being that on commercial channels (TV3, TV DK) almost all fiction is produced in the USA, whereas the public service channels see it as one of their aims to provide a certain amount of Danish TV fiction – in Danish.[8]

A supplementary way of measuring what Danes prefer is to look at the ratings. A survey of the most watched programmes on a yearly basis is equally clear showing that the 30 most popular programmes screened in 1997 were all produced in Denmark. The top ten list illustrates the general line concerning the connection between main categories and preferences:

Number	Channel	Programme	Rating
1.	DR1	World Championship in handball for women: Denmark – Norway	47%
2.	DR1 & TV2	The Queen's New Year address	40%
3.	TV2	'Island Cop' (TV-fiction: crime) (average of 6 transmissions)	40%
4.	DR1	World Championship in handball for women: Denmark – Hungary	40%
5.	DR1 & TV2	Prime Minister's New Year address	39%
6.	DR1	World Championship in handball for women: Denmark – Russia	39%
7.	DR1	'The Brewer' (historical TV-fiction) (average of 11 transmissions)	39%
8.	TV2	'My Sister's Children Upset the Town' (Danish comedy)	34%
9.	TV2	'Father of Four in Style' (Danish comedy)	33%
10.	TV2	'The Moelleby-affair' (Danish folk-comedy)[9]	33%

Table 3: Top ten programmes in Denmark (1997)

The priorities and the categories are revealing. *Sport* is important whenever Denmark is involved. It is remarkable that the women's league in handball was able to attract so much attention as a national issue, a level of attention usually bestowed only on men's football championships and events such as the Olympic Games, but on the whole this has been the case since the Danish women began to show excellence in handball in 1993. The official *yearly addresses* by the Queen and the Prime Minister are considered important. *Danish TV fiction* is considered important. And *old Danish genre films* attract unusually large audiences – considering the quality. The rest of the list confirms these priorities, containing the same categories – plus two entertainment shows. And the tendency of the list is not a unique 1997 phenomenon. This picture is confirmed by the annual lists made since 1992, when ratings were first introduced on a systematic basis.

The tendency to prefer more American films in the cinema thus seems to be balanced by a tendency to give Danish TV fiction and Danish films priority when watching television. This does not mean that American films and TV productions are not watched, often with relatively high ratings. It just means that usually they do not have quite the same power of attraction as certain national productions. Viewed from this angle, national Danish television still seems to be a primary source of negotiation of what it is to be Danish and a primary source of consensus. This seems to confirm that the status attributed to TV fiction some years ago by John Ellis is still worth considering. I shall discuss this later, but in order to raise this discussion to a higher level, a brief outline of prevalent trends in genre and style is needed.

Transnational Trends in Genre

The top ten list shows that genre is an important issue in TV fiction. Any survey in any newspaper or magazine would show the same. How important the genre system is to European TV fiction is convincingly confirmed in the following table, assembled by five research groups, partaking in the Eurofiction project for 1996, showing domestic production of fiction in five European countries that can be compared in size (see table 4).[10]

The category of 'drama', it should be noticed, covers soap operas as well as other dramatic subgenres which accounts for the fact that – with the exception of France – drama is prevalent. Buonanno ascribes this to the many serials (cf. Buonanno, 1998: 12). Though the table is not very precise in its use of genre concepts, it is clear as a manifestation of the dominance of the genre system in TV fiction. And then it must be remembered that domestic production is only a limited part of what

Genre	Germany hours	%	UK hours	%	France hours	%	Spain hours	%	Italy hours	%
Drama	1010	60	633	60	239	35	242	53	89	40
Action/Crime	548	32	262	25	141	20	–	–	56	25
Comedy	111	7	164	15	297	43	205	45	64	29
Other	21	1	–	–	13	2	11	2	12	6
Total	1690		1059		690		458		221	

Table 4: Genres of domestic fiction in five European countries (1996) (Buonanno, 1998: 14)

	Germany	UK	France	Spain	Italy
Domestic	24 %	50 %	19 %	13 %	5 %
Europe	4 %	–	22 %	9 %	6 %
USA	69 %	30 %	57 %	67 %	70 %
Lat.Am.	–	–	–	10 %	15 %
Other	3 %	20 %	2 %	1 %	4 %

Table 4: Origins of TV fiction in five European countries (1996) (Buonanno, 1998: 19)

is screened. The following table shows the distribution of the origins of TV fiction for the five countries in question (see table 5).[11]

Contemplating these figures one is tempted to quote once again: "living in the twentieth century means learning to be American". The only exception worth noting in this context is the UK which has an extraordinarily high share of domestic production during the sample week, higher than would be expected considering the figures for domestic production in Table 4, where Germany is outstanding. As noted by Schatz, commercial television has been:

> "the primary vehicle for the regeneration and continuation of these popular formulas, having co-opted Hollywood's industrial and technological base as well as its mass audience and narrative formulas" (Schatz, 1981: 265).

So international formats and international genres and formulas prevail. This does not mean that there is no space at all for negotiations of cultural transfers corresponding to what seems to be the case in cinema. But it does mean that the ways in which this can be done are more limited, even if there is so much more time and so much more space to carry it out, considering all the slots that have to be filled. The apparent heteroglossia may have certain limits. Besides, transnational trends may manifest themselves in other ways as well, e.g. very strongly in technique: number of cuts, way of photographing etc. – all the innumerable ways which together make the audience suddenly feel that a certain programme recorded in a certain way is outdated.

I do not have comparable figures for Denmark for 1996, but a sample week in 1998 gives the following results:

Domestic	26%
Europe	11%
USA	52%
Lat. Am.	–
Other (Australia)	11%

Table 5: Origin of TV fiction in Denmark[12]

In the case of a small nation, however, statistics might be a helpful indicator, but perhaps it is not the most appropriate method to get a picture of the situation concerning domestic TV fiction and special ways of coping with the massive international pressure in genre or style.

Transnational Trends in Style

The notion of a 'Golden Age' seems to be inherent in much thinking of media history in general and of each medium in particular. For TV fiction in Britain the 'Golden Age' is often supposed to be the period of development during the 60s, 70s and part of the 80s when classics were being serialised, series developed, and (post)modernists such as Dennis Potter allowed their screen education in single plays and "nurtured"[13] into eminent growth.

For Danish television, Ib Bondebjerg has adopted a similar periodisation, reckoning three phases of development: 1) *the Paternalistic Period* 1951-1964, when an educational ideology prevailed, 2) *the Classic Public Service Period* or *the Golden Age* of Danish television 1964-1980 when a broad range of programmes and genres was developed, and 3) *the Period of Mixed Culture* from 1980 until today when the monopoly of DR was gradually broken first by so called 'neighbouring TV',[14] then by local TV and last by commercialised TV in 1988 and all the possibilities provided by satellites leading to TV3 etc. (Bondebjerg & Bono, 1994: 45-46). On the whole this periodisation seems correct in its main diagnosis of prevailing traits, and Danish public service TV has always depended heavily on the BBC as have, indeed, most other European public service TV channels. The notion of a 'Golden Age' is inherent in other national television histories as well as it is in much media history. But there is one catch in it. The concept of a 'Golden Age' inevitably implies the notion of decline, and I am not sure whether this is true of TV fiction (or for that matter of news or documentaries). Change is taking place, and it is important to characterise in which ways changes occur and what causes them.

Robin Nelson discusses this problem in his book *TV Drama in Transition* (1997). His diagnosis is that there are surely lots of important changes in TV drama – in reception, in prevailing formats, in the TV studios and the ways of producing – but they are not all for the worst! Using a traditional social-realist serial like *Boys from the Blackstuff* (repeat showing in 1993) and *Twin Peaks* (first showing in the UK 1990-91) as prototype examples he contrasts traditional social-realistic fiction with post-modern fiction. The prevalent traits of realist fiction are that it is referential to everyday reality, its characters are credible, and it is structured and narrated in the form of cause and effect. Whereas post-modern fiction refers more to other media – productions, styles and genres – than to reality, it operates with odd, stylised characters in a collage of events. Summing up, Robin Nelson characterises the alternatives:

> "The TV space has begun to depart from a (humanist) depiction of characters and events grounded in a historical world in which actions have consequences to a (post-modern) collage of attractive but dislocated images and sounds." (Nelson, 1997: 17)

Consequently the keyword for Nelson becomes change or transition, and his analysis shows that there is still appeal in the realist tradition and possibilities in different forms of combinations between realist and post-modern approaches. This kind of change seems to be of a kind that transgresses national borders and permeates ways of rendering reality and dreams as well as ways of conceiving them for audiences of different kinds and nationalities.

Another catch is that we do not know when or how the present period will end or when the phase of transition will be over. That is also the trouble with the term 'post-modern'. The end is still to come. But that cannot be helped for the present. In order to discuss mechanisms of dialogue and cultural transfer I shall now turn to the concrete level of programmes in a Danish setting.

Mapping the Landscape of Danish TV Fiction

TV fiction's flagships on the different channels during Spring 1998 can be taken as a symptom for prevalent tendencies concerning genres and cross-cultural relationships. For weeks, DR1 has had two certain hits at the top of the rating list, *Matador* (*Monopoly,* 1979-81) which in a repeat showing for a new generation with 35-37% of the population as its audience is doing it again, and *TAXA*, a new series launched in 1997, which every Sunday has regularly attracted 26-27% of the population for 40 minutes. 24 episodes have been shown, a total of 72 are planned.

Monopoly represents the great tradition from the 'Golden Age'; it is historical fiction in the realist tradition, with a sense of humour and nostalgia in it. It is the outstanding story of the formation of Danish society during the period from the 1920s to 1949, seen through the eyes of three different families in a provincial town. All Danes can recognise some parts of their own history in it, hence its everlasting popularity as the mother of all Danish TV serials – the serial the others measure themselves against, denounce or compete with.

TAXA represents DR's most recent attempt at a contemporary way of making TV fiction. It is a series. The format is transnational. Technically it is avowedly inspired by American series such as *Homicide* and *New York Blue*, shot by two-camera technique, edited in a fast cutting rhythm. Symptomatically enough its scene of action is not the provincial town[15] but the city. Still, the series has the ambition to be more than just entertaining. Adapting some transnational tendencies e.g. in technique, it opposes others, e.g. the usual tendency that a series should strictly match a distinct genre.

The genre of *TAXA* could be defined as a kind of soap, treating everyday life and having a certain melodramatic tone, but it is not pure soap: it mixes elements from crime, satire and comedy into it. A new generation of directors got their opportunity with the series, competing and co-operating, whereas the actors represent both renowned and new faces.

Back in December 1997, TV2 was triumphant, attracting every day for 24 days more than 20% of the viewers for its original and special family Christmas Calendar-fiction and about 10% for its 'Christmas Calendar for grown-ups', a satirical and harsh police serial in the tradition of film noir. This is a tradition of TV2, and it means that it is harder to compete with DR in the domain of fiction for the rest of the year, a certain part of the fiction money having been spent lavishly on December's fiction. Nevertheless TV2 launched an erotic 30 minute serial in 1998, *Karrusel (Merry-go-round)* 1-10, which in spite of its non-family appeal got quite high ratings (about 17% on an average). The idea, borrowed from Arthur Schnitzler's *Reigen*, was to show a number of erotic meetings and departures, thus revealing the role of coincidence in modern city life. In this case young actors as well as a new generation of directors had their opportunity, demonstrating new ways of being and acting.

In a way, these choices are representative of the current policies of the two main channels. DR is making a hard attempt to come back and improve its share which has been declining ever since TV2 was launched. So it has tried to aim at more popular combinations of the requirement of public demand and those of programming, using the supplementary channel DR2 for public service programmes with narrower appeal. And it seems to work. During recent years TV2 has often been accused of not taking its public service obligations seriously enough within the domain of TV fiction. Thus it has been motivated for renewal in an area far removed from Christmas calendars, though still maintaining this traditional stronghold which it wrested out of the hands of DR, the originator and previous dominator of this genre.

Finally it should be noticed that TV3 has launched a new series, *White Lies*. TV3 has little experience with TV-fiction, having formerly only produced one or two comedy series. The new attempt is pure hospital-soap, transmitted every evening for 30 minutes. 3% watched it during the first week. It can be characterised as transnational TV fiction directly transferred to Danish circumstances, in Danish, with Danish scriptwriters, actors and directors, but really an expression of a clean-cut transnational formula in a discount edition. For the last decade and more, Danes, ironically enough have tried hard to make sitcoms like the Americans, but with poor results. TV2's *Hjem til fem* (*Home to Five*) 1997-98 can be mentioned as an example. It seems to be difficult just to import genres when you lack traditions of your own. The Danes are much better at satire where there is a strong tradition. This does not mean that it is impossible to import genres, but it means that they are out of tune when only translated and not converted and made homely.

Summing up prevalent tendencies as they were manifested during the Spring of 1998, we get the following characteristic features:

1) The formats of series and serials dominate the range of programmes, in accordance with international and transnational trends. Single plays or TV-films still exist, but only as a result of the foundation of 'Dansk Novellefilm' 1994, a co-operative arrangement between the film industry and the public service TV channels. Unfortunately they are scarcely visible in the programme planning, mostly not being allowed their own slot.
2) Genre and style negotiations with transnational and national traditions are on-going; it is considered important to raise the issue of what it means to be Danish just now, to ask questions like who we are, what do we want from society, what about the individual, what about sex etc., but genre and style are integral elements of how it can be done.
3) The traditional roles of DR1 and TV2 concerning TV fiction have been reversed – to a certain extent – as far as viewer-appeal and willingness to risk ratings are concerned, and a purely commercial channel, TV3, has chosen to produce a transnational soap in Danish, presumably to help establish itself as 'the' third national channel in a situation of growing competition from TV DK.[16] But it is not enough merely to translate the usual formulas without creating anything new.

Conclusions

Associating the tendencies mentioned above with TV fiction of the last decade can only be done in a general manner and with some reservations concerning accuracy. Nevertheless it seems worth while to make a rough outline in order to relate the process of change to the perspectives outlined by Nelson and to international developments. I consider the traditional realist traditions which have had such a strong position in Danish TV fiction – from *Monopoly* and the single plays of Leif Panduro from the 70s and till today – to be under pressure. Put in another way: The realist tradition seems less convincing now if not expressed in an unusual manner. This is the case in Denmark as elsewhere.

Let us briefly look at some other productions. In 1997 DR1 screened the most expensive serial ever, *Bryggeren (The Brewer)* 1-12, a historical biographical serial depicting the life and times of the great brewer and later patron of the arts, Jacob Christian Jacobsen (1811-87), the founder of Carlsberg, named after his first and only son, Carl Jacobsen (1842-1914) – who also became a brewer and patron of the arts in keen competition with his father. At the core of the narration is the painful, tragically expanding conflict between father and son, a conflict which lasted all their lives.

Despite all the efforts to recreate the atmosphere of the last century in a convincing manner, the extras in the streets and markets, the skilled photographer, the soft light, i.e. all the accuracy that belongs to the realist tradition of conveying atmosphere, the serial failed to make an impact. The usual audience was there, the ratings were extraordinarily high, but nobody in discussions or interviews afterwards seemed really content with the result. Part of the public interest might be understood in terms of expectations, part of it might be due to the popular actors – or the above-mentioned many details of delight from a traditionally aesthetic angle.

Just like *Monopoly, The Brewer* was an attempt to provide us with our history, but this time from the last century, to remind us from where we have come (conflicts of descent), of the conflicts between husbands and wives (conflicts of gender) and especially fathers and sons (conflicts between generations), of the difficult process of maturing (with beer as a metaphor). The good intentions of the producers matched the good intentions of the audience, but the result was, to use O'Regan's term, neither good, nor bad, but dull. From the well-known biography of brewer J.C. Jacobsen we knew the plot to be true on the whole, but the problem was that it was narrated by way of repetition. The conflicts between husband and wife, father and son continued from different angles and in different editings through all 12 parts. Thus plot and way of narration did not fit with all the realist details. And worst of all: the drama's representational ambitions on behalf of nationhood, including the main developments in 19th century Danish history and society, made it impossible to feel really involved.

That fact that the realist tradition is challenged, however, does not mean that it is outdated. On the contrary it can be quite strong as was seen in another historical biographical serial, *Call me Liva*, DR 1992. Here the realist tradition was supported by the way in which the female protagonist constantly mirrored today's problems and issues, and by the scenic performance.

Some outstanding examples of Danish TV drama of the 90s are seen in *The Kingdom* I 1:4, 1994 and II 1:4, 1997, DR1, directed by Lars von Trier – in Danish for once,[17] and on a more popular level TAXA 1:24, 1997-98, DR1. Both of them use transnational formats and aesthetically they can be seen as both results of and contributions to a transnational postmodern technique. They differ, however, on the level of ambition and way of addressing the audience.

The Kingdom can be seen as a kind of drama where everything is questioned and where nothing can be said or understood for sure, not even if you catch all the intertextual and -cultural references conveyed visually and auditively. Ways of seeing and different themes are driven to extremes, the audience is offended more than once (do they discover it?), strange and grotesque characters flourish, and all the genres you can think of are parodied. It is a story with many meanings. One of them being that the kingdom is a symbol not only of the hospital but also of all the institutions which function as a hospital, and in the very end of the state. This represents another way of dealing with the national dreams and traumas.

TAXA is less extreme by far. Using bits and pieces from transnational genres and post-modern techniques it draws basically on the realist tradition in lots of ways, being less intertextual and more straight. And still, like *The Kingdom*, it asks some of the same questions about the state of the nation, perhaps in a more devious manner. KroneTAXA[18] can easily be seen to represent the nation with all its gender and racial conflicts and the multinationals threatening to swallow it up, with its uncertainty about what is the responsibility of the welfare state, and what is the responsibility of the individual?, with its annual Christmas and New Year celebrations, with its stress on careers, divorces, etc.

The Kingdom demonstrates the excesses of post-modernist fiction in a very convincing way. *TAXA* shows that it is worth while for realist fiction to take up the challenge of post-modernist fiction. And perhaps both show that "All good art is national, and all national art is bad". *The Kingdom* has already shown that its appeal is not limited to the nation which it primarily mirrors and ridicules. It has been screened on television and in the cinema worldwide. As a series it might be more difficult to promote *TAXA* internationally, but in many ways it has the potential of being just as 'national' as *Kingdom*.

Notes

1. Cf. Hjort, 1996: 529, and Hjort & MacKenzie, 2000: 75.
2. Cf. Agger, 1997: 144-149.
3. The translations of the Danish titles are mine.
4. Mette Hjort has even pointed out that the film becomes a vehicle for misrecognition, because it ignores what is central to Karen Blixen's self-understanding (Hjort in an unpublished paper, *The Ethics of Cinematic Biography*, 1995).
5. As it is explained in a very condensed manner, against the background of a broad study of European cultural transfers, in Yuri M. Lotman (1990) *Universe of the Mind*, London: Tauris pp. 146-147. Cf. Agger 1999.

6. Covers DR1, DR2 = public service channels, financed by license fee, and TV2 = public service channel, financed partly commercially, partly by license fee.
7. Channels which are occasionally commented in Danish or texted are Eurosport (share in 1997: 1.2%) and Discovery (share in 1997: 0.9%. Source: *Gallup TV-meter*).
8. As is confirmed in Medieudvalget: *Betænkning om de elektroniske medier* (1995: 33).
9. The translations of the titles are mine. 'Island Cop' is the official title of a police serial which has been exported to the Nordic countries, Ireland, and Slovenia.
10. For methodology cf. Buonanno (1998: 3-5). For the purpose of simplifying the survey I have rounded off the figures.
11. On the basis of one common sample week, March 2 – 8, 1996.
12. The table has been provided by Alexander Nielsen, DR. Represented by Alexander Nielsen and Gunhild Agger, Denmark has started cooperating with Eurofiction from 1998.
13. Potter's own expression in his last TV interview with Melvyn Bragg, transmitted by DR 18.6.1994.
14. Television from Sweden, Norway and Germany which could be seen in different regions of the country dependant on geographical location.
15. The provincial setting has enjoyed a certain popularity in Danish TV fiction in different genres, including both police series and historical serials such as *Monopoly*.
16. Local channels were allowed to network in 1996. Before that, networking was prohibited.
17. As in his film *Idioterne (The Idiots)*, 1998.
18. The name of the firm connotes 'kingdom': the number plate of a particular royal Rolls Royce being 'KRONE 1'.

Bibliography

Agger, Gunhild (1997). "The 'Sideplays' Aesthetics'". In Martin Eide, Barbara Gentikow & Knut Helland (eds.): *Quality Television*. Bergen: Department of Media Studies.

Agger, Gunhild (1999). "Intertextuality Revisited: Dialogues and Negotiations in Media Studies". In Ib Bondebjerg & Helle K. Haastrup (eds.): *Intertextuality and Visual Media, Sekvens 99*. Copenhagen: Department of Film and Media Studies.

Agger, Gunhild, & Alexander P. Nielsen (1999). "The Good, The Bad and the Dull. Danish TV Fiction in 1998". In Milly Buonanno (ed.): *Eurofiction. Report 1999*. Strasbourg: Council of Europe.

Agger, Gunhild (2000). "Modernisation, Nostalgia and the Ultimate Zapping Experience. Danish TV Fiction in 1999". In Milly Buonanno (ed.): *Eurofiction. Report 2000*. Strasbourg: Council of Europe.

Andersen, Michael Bruun (1996). "TV og genre". In *K&K*, no. 80.

Andersen, Jesper (1997). "I lommerne på Europa". In Jesper Andersen, Ib Bondebjerg & Peter Schepelern (eds.): *Dansk film 1972-97*. Copenhagen: Munksgaard/Rosinante.

Andersen, Benedict (1996). *Imagined Communities*. London & New York: Verso.

Buonanno, Milly (ed.) (1998). *Imaginary Dreamscapes. Television Fiction in Europe. First Report of the Eurofiction Project*. Luton: John Libbey Media.

Bondebjerg, Ib & Francesco Bono (eds.) (1994). *Nordic Television History, Politics and Aesthetics, Sekvens*. Copenhagen: Department of Film- & Media Studies.

Bondebjerg, Ib (1997). "Dansk film 1972-1997", "Danske virkelighedsbilleder", "Fra Brønshøj til Hollywood". In Jesper Andersen, Ib Bondebjerg, & Peter Schepelern (eds.): *Dansk film 1972-97*. Copenhagen: Munksgaard/Rosinante.

Collins, Jim (1999). "Miramaxing the Literary". In Ib Bondebjerg & Helle K. Haastrup (eds.): *Intertexuality and Visual Media, Sekvens 99*. Copenhagen: Department of Film & Media Studies.

Cunningham, Stuart, & Elizabeth Jacka (1996). *Australian Television and International Mediascapes*. Cambridge: Cambridge University Press.

Ellis, John (1993). *Visible Fictions*. London & New York: Routledge.

Elsaesser, Thomas (1989). *New German Cinema*. New Brunswick: Rutgers University Press.

Elsaesser, Thomas (1994). "Putting on a Show: The European Art Movie". In: *Sight and Sound* vol. 4, 4. London.

Fiske, John (1992). *Television Culture*. London: Routledge.

Gallup (1997). *TV-meter*.

Higson, Andrew (1997). *Waving the Flag. Constructing a National Cinema in Britain*. Oxford: Clarendon Press.

Hjort, Mette (1996). "Danish Cinema and the Politics of Recognition". In Noël Carroll & David Bordwell (eds.): *Post-Theory*. Madison: University of Wisconsin Press.

Hjort, Mette, & Scott Mackenzie (2000). *Cinema & Nation*. London & New York: Routledge.

Jensen, Klaus Bruhn (1999). "Intertextualities and Intermedialities". In Ib Bondebjerg & Helle K. Haastrup (eds.): *Intertexuality and Visual Media, Sekvens 99*. Copenhagen: Department of Film & Media Studies.

Lotman, Yuri M. (1990). *Universe of the Mind*. London: Tauris.
Medieudvalget (1995). *Betænkning om de elektroniske medier*. Copenhagen: Statsministeriet.
Mortensen, Frands (1997). "Film skal ses". In Jesper Andersen, Ib Bondebjerg & Peter Schepelern (eds.): *Dansk Film 1972-97*. Copenhagen: Munksgaard/Rosinante.
Neale, Stephen (1990). "Questions of genre". In: *Screen* 31, no 1.
Neale, Stephen (1980). *Genre*. London: BFI.
Nelson, Robin (1997). *TV Drama in Transition*. Chippenham: Macmillan Press.
Nissen, Dan (1997). "Den populære kunst". In Jesper Andersen, Ib Bondebjerg & Peter Schepelern (eds.): *Dansk film 1972-97*. Copenhagen: Munksgaard/Rosinante.
O'Regan, Tom (1996). *Australian national cinema*. London: Routledge.
Paterson, Richard (ed.) (1993). *National Identity and Europe*. London: BFI.
Scannell, Paddy, & David Cardiff (1997). "The National Culture". In Oliver Boyd-Barrett & Chris Newbold (eds.): *Approaches to Media*. London: Arnold.
Schatz, Thomas (1981). *Hollywood Genres*. New York: McGraw-Hill.
Schepelern, Peter (1997). *Lars von Triers elementer*. Copenhagen: Munksgaard, Rosinante.
Smith, Anthony D. (1991). *National Identity*. London: Penguin Books.
Soila, Tytti, Astrid Widding & Gunnar Iversen (1998). *Nordic National Cinemas*. London & New York: Routledge.
Stam, Robert (1992). *Subversive Pleasures. Bakhtin, Cultural Criticism, and Film*. London: Johns Hopkins University Press.
Svendsen, Erik Nordahl (1996). *TV-medieforskning i Danmarks Radio 1994-95*. Forskningsrapport nr. 1B/96 (1996). DR.
Todorov, Tzvetan (1978). "L'origine des genres". In: *Les genres du discours*. Paris: Éditions du Seuil.
Todorov, Tzvetan (1981). *Mikhaïl Bakhtine: le principe dialogique*. Paris: Éditions du Seuil.
Tybjerg, Casper, & Peter Schepelern (eds.) (1996). *A Century of Cinema, Sekvens 1995/96*. Copenhagen: Department of Film & Media Studies.

CHAPTER THREE

Comedy Series in Danish Television
– for Better or Worse

Poul Erik Nielsen
The Danish School of Journalism

Comedy in a Genre Perspective

The main purpose of this article is to discuss why Danish so-called popular series and especially comedy series, with a very few exceptions, have been a string of mediocre series. The hypothesis is that until recently, the former public service monopoly and the creative community in Denmark have been stuck in a romantic conception of art, which has made them unable to take popular television series seriously.

The problems facing the Danish drama production community are part of a more general problem. The Danish television system is in a revolutionary transition from a system of public service monopoly to a multi-channel system. This transition is causing fundamental changes, because the public service tradition historically has been rooted in the public sphere, while the new television system is more market-oriented. This paper gives a general historical review of Danish television as background information for an understanding of the current development in drama production.

Genre is a key notion in understanding the current development of Danish drama. The paper examines the concept of genre and the basic features of the successful American and British situation comedy genre using mainly the American series *Roseanne* as an example. The hypothesis is that the situation comedy genre establishes a specific mode of address, and that this mode of address and some other textual features are essential for the success of a comedy series.

Many Danish series that strive to be humorous have deliberately ignored these basic generic features and instead tried to stay within a romantic conception of art where experimenting with form is essential. To demonstrate this, the article analyses the serial *Tre ludere og en lommetyv (Three whores and a pickpocket)* and the series *Hjem til fem (Home for five)* in a genre perspective. Finally the article discusses a recent shift of paradigm in Danish popular series to popular genres like soaps and situation comedies.

Danish Television in Transition

As a starting point, I would like to give a historical review of the main tendencies in Danish television in general and drama production in particular. Denmark had a public service television monopoly, *Danmarks Radio (DR),* until the mid-1980s. The main ideology has been, and to a certain extent still is, that television should be used as a public service in the interest of the citizens in a democratic society, and therefore DR has been strictly regulated.

Public service radio and television did in many ways succeed in Denmark in the monopoly era. Along with a thriving national and local press, *DR* has been a significant force in creating the Danish welfare state, but at the same time *DR* managed its monopoly position in a problematic way. Under shelter of the public service obligations to enlighten and give the public access to a unified culture, *DR* presented the values of the middle- and high-brow culture in a paternalistic manner (Bondebjerg, 1993). A contributory cause of this form of paternalism was that the general public was not the primary audience for the TV stations. Instead the primary audience was the politicians, who decided the size of the license fee, and the public opinion makers and the critics, who gave the only public feedback. The general public was rarely heard, and there were no regular ratings. This paternalistic attitude and a bureaucratic organisation have made it difficult for the public service monopoly to adjust to the new, competitive television situation. Part of the problem is that these new competitors are addressing the audience as consumers in a market instead of as citizens in a democratic society (Søndergaard, 1992), and the public service stations are struggling to find a new role as a player in the marketplace but with non-commercial objectives.

By the mid 1980s, the incipient competition came from trans-national satellite stations, and this 'threat' from the sky caused Denmark in 1988 to launch a terrestrial non-profit public station, *TV2*, partly financed by commercials partly by license fees. It is worth mentioning that *TV2* is subject to approximately the same public service obligations as *DR*.

Danish television policy has so far been successful in containing the influence from foreign transnational television stations. Danes prefer to watch national programmes because of the languages and the cultural heritage, even though subtitled foreign programmes (American and British) are a significant and popular part of the programme supply on the national channels. The only significant challenge to *TV2* and *DR* has come from a Swedish-owned private satellite station, *TV3*, which has a special feed to Denmark.

Television Fiction in Denmark

After this general survey, I would like to focus on Danish television drama. First, it is important to stress that the high cost of producing drama is a key factor in Denmark. National fiction is essentially more expensive than other programme types, and national fiction is usually around 20 to 100+ times more expensive than imported fiction, so the total production of national fiction is limited, even though the total output has increased recently.

The heritage of the monopoly era has great importance for the current production of national fiction. In the field of fiction the above-mentioned cultural conflict caused by the old public service stations' paternalistic attitude has crystallised in the conception of romantic art and the distinction between high and popular culture.

As a part of its public service obligations, *DR* has been obliged to participate actively in the creative arts and to promote artistic and cultural innovation. In early television, the general idea was to challenge the viewers with new ideas and to encourage progressive cultural development. The department for drama production, symptomatically called the department for TV Theatre, produced mainly classical and experimental modernist single plays by international authors like William Shakespeare, Eugene Ionesco, Harold Pinter, and Samuel Beckett, and by classical and contemporary national playwrights.

There is a paradoxical problem tied to this tradition. *DR* produced primarily single plays by playwrights and stage directors working within a romantic conception of art, where the key words were originality and uniqueness, but at the same time, the playwrights, the directors, and the executives in the department of TV Theatre detested TV as a medium. Therefore, these single plays were produced to elevate the comprehension of artistic expressions by the mass audience to the level of high culture, but by using television as the medium the distinction of taste was re-established. Besides that, the general public did not even want this hegemony of high culture. The single plays were produced into a vacuum, and this tradition rarely created a poignant cultural significance outside the closed circle of critics, even though there were prominent exceptions. In the 1970s, the playwright Leif Panduro had great impact by castigating the hollowness of the upper-middle-class way of life in several single plays. Besides the modernistic and classical single plays, the department of TV Theatre produced a few, often novel-based, serials.

Popular Drama

The core of the problem in current drama production is the transition from the high culture concept to a new orientation toward popular series. *DR* is still producing a few high culture serials and made-for-TV movies, but the general policy is to produce more intentionally popular series and serials. From the very beginning, these series have been, and still are, the Achilles' heel of *DR*, just as they are for TV2 and TV3.

In the 1970s and the early 1980s a successful popular tradition was built up around the movie director Erik Balling. Among many other series, he produced the first long-running Danish series *Huset på Christianshavn (The House in Christianshavn)* (83 half-hour episodes 1970-77 and a theatrical movie 1971), but Balling's experience and professionalism were never passed on to a new generation of talents.

DR has produced an increased number of intentionally popular series since the mid 1980s, but they have not been so successful, because they have been mediocre in all aspects. A fundamental problem has been that the series were addressed to a broader audience, but the executives and the creative people did not know what the audience liked and expected, because they came from the TV theatre tradition, and they were bearers of the above-mentioned paradoxical problem. This problem was given a further twist in this transition, because the playwrights and directors were not only producing for a medium they detested, but they also had to produce series which they themselves despised.

The single most important problem in all this has been, that the reminiscences of the romantic conception of art sustained a very deep contempt for the popular genres. Even though the creative people had agreed to produce intentionally popular series, they continued to produce innovative series that ostentatiously tried to avoid the popular genres like the situation comedy, the soap, the police series, etc. To demonstrate how this lack of respect for the popular genres has been problematic, I will discuss the genre concept briefly and the situation comedy genre more thoroughly before taking a closer look at some Danish series.

Genre

Genre is a key notion in analysing television drama, even though it is a problematic term to use, because genre is used within two different discourses, a common and a theoretical.

In the common discourse, we all use genres like western, situation comedy, and soap to describe and discuss film and television series. In this discourse, genre is a complex and dynamic concept developed as a common set of expectations, a kind of tacit agreement between producers, programmers, and the audience.

In the theoretical discourse, the concept of genre historically has been used in different ways. One dominant use has been the categorising of all texts by arbitrary criteria to create order out of chaos. But the concept has also been used to understand the function of different types of texts. The current use of the concept reflects continuing confusion. It is not my intention in this paper to undertake a greater examination of the concept. Instead I will present the genre concept that I intend to use in what follows.

The genre concept is used here in an extended meaning, following the ideas of Stephen Neale.

"Any one genre is, simultaneously, a coherent and systematic body of film texts, and a coherent and systematic set of expectations." (Neale, 1980: 54-55)

This comprehension of genre acts as a bridge between the common and the theoretical discourse, the aim is to understand the function of the genre texts within the communication process. Genre is therefore a dynamic concept depending on both the common expectations and some textual features. The focus is to establish a precise and qualified knowledge of the textual features tied to these expectations, and qualify, so to speak, the tacit knowledge within the common discourse.

As a point of origin I would like to state that popular genres are well established successful products that have demonstrated their ability to provoke significant viewer loyalty through a specific way of presenting historical, cultural, and social matters. In the tension between repetition and innovation, generic texts satisfy cultural, social, and aesthetic needs.

Through the reception of innumerable popular film and TV series, the audience has developed a cultural competence that, in a partly unconscious way, controls the expectations with which it meets new products. Genres are an important part of this cultural competence. It is worth mentioning that even if the producers do not consciously relate to genres, the products will always be received in relation to the genre expectations of the audience, and genre expectations change continuously and are specific to different demographic groups.

Genre as text is not a systematic concept but likewise dynamic. A genre emerges where there is a coherent body of texts with common features that are constituent to the reading of those texts. These common features are of different kinds from genre to genre. The Western and the Gangster genres are characterised by distinct geographical spaces and specific milieus, among other things. Musicals and situation comedies are examples of genres that are not bound by setting, but rather by mode of address, acting style, and other features. Film noir makes use of lighting and other such technical features, among other things, to establish its generic identity. Besides these paradigmatic features, each genre is constituted by specific syntagmatic features – narrative forms, set up/pay off, editing styles, etc. Genre as text is system and process.

It is necessary to conduct comprehensive textual analyses of the different genres to expose and understand each genre's constitutive features and pattern of variation, knowing that each genre text will always be a reciprocal action between repetition and innovation – "reality-maintenance and reality-change" (Threadgold, 1989) or "difference *in* repetition" (Neale, 1980).

Situation Comedy

An interesting matter concerning situation comedies is that the genre has different cultural meanings in the US, in Britain, and in Denmark. Situation comedies like *The Honeymooners, I Love Lucy, All In The Family, The Cosby Show, Roseanne,* and *Home Improvement* are an integrated part of American culture, as are *Fawlty Towers, Steptoe and Son,* and *Yes Minister* of British culture.

In Denmark, the situation comedy genre has never been developed domestically, and even though we are familiar with

American and British situation comedies, the genre has never been a significant part of our culture. This is one of the reasons why the TV stations have had great difficulties in producing successful comedy series in Denmark.

In the US the specific genre features of the situation comedy are common basic knowledge among viewers and producers.

> "Roseanne isn't television-ish. We have attempted to give the series the most real texture possible in terms of characters and setting. The conversations are the kind that go on in real life. The sets are designed and dressed to look as though the audience has just walked into someone's home. The washer and dryer are actually running when we shoot in the laundry room. The children in the series grow out of their clothes when money is tight, and everything's not beautiful in the Conner home all the time. We do fall into a bit of a trap because everybody always wants to look good, but we try to stick with realism the best we can". (Producer Gayle Maffeo, in Mayerle, 1994: 101)

Anyone taking one brief look at the hit series *Roseanne* knows very well that this is not the kind of conversation that goes on in real life, but a comic fictional representation of 'real life' in television. *Roseanne* is a situation comedy that follows all the essential features of the genre, and in that sense the series has generic verisimilitude, but the essential features of all sitcom series are that they break with the intended realism and stress instead that this is fictional television. How can the producer of the series, Gayle Maffeo, then say quite the opposite? Maffeo knows by heart all the genre features from the production of other situation comedies, and it is a truism that *Roseanne* has to use these features of the situation comedy. Maffeo is probably talking about the features that distinguish *Roseanne* from other series, or with an often-used term in the industry, the freshness of the show. The texture of the show is indeed an important feature distinguishing *Roseanne* from shows like *The Cosby Show* and *Family Ties*.

In a way, the creator and executive producer of *Roseanne*, Matt Williams, is demonstrating a corresponding lack of consciousness of the essential genre features.

> "Saying that the most important thing he [Matt Williams] learned from writing for The Cosby Show was that the key to a successful television series was audience identification. "I always remembered Bill saying he wanted the people at home to ask, 'How did you get inside my house?'"" (Mayerle, 1994: 103)

The key problem here is audience identification. Williams is probably using the concept of identification in the meaning recognisable, and in that sense of course Williams is right, the audience has to recognise the situations to laugh at them, but this form of recognition is different from the form of identification you find in other dramatic forms. But as we will see in the following, one of the determining features of the situation comedy is that the mode of address in the genre counteracts genuine audience identification, in which the viewer experiences a more thorough psychological identification.

Mode of Address
– Taped Before a Live Audience

The single most important feature of the situation comedy genre is the mode of address, which in many ways creates a distance between the viewer and the text. The mode of address is closely related to the specific mode of production – taped or filmed in sequence in a studio with limited settings in front of a live audience. This mode of production creates certain aesthetic possibilities and limitations, and it is often argued that because of this mode of production, the genre is inexpensive and aesthetically uninteresting, but that is a problematic way of seeing things. First of all, in commercial American television the price per minute is just as high for situation comedies as for hour-long dramatic series, even though the money is spent in a different way. Second it is obvious that situation comedies are subject to aesthetic limitations but so are all other genres, and to discuss what is most interesting is to compare apples to oranges.

The basic element of a situation comedy production is a large sound stage with 3 permanent sets and 1 or 2 replaceable swing sets for each episode (Fig 1). The shooting mode is multiple camera, where the four cameras are filming simultaneously on the 'golden line' just outside the set. Behind the cameras there is a live audience looking at the set from the outside through a proscenium consisting of all the technical gear.

The mode of production revolves around the fact that the live studio audience is important, otherwise the troublesome live audience would have been dropped.

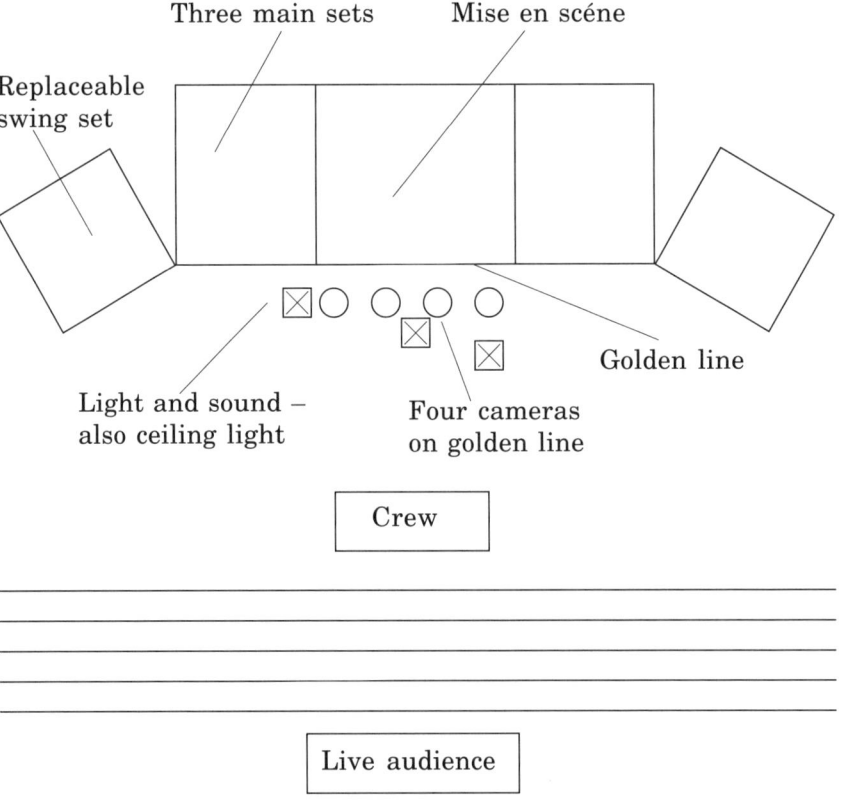

Figure 1: Situation comedy sound stage

Seen from the point of view of the live audience, the audience is watching a kind of theatre play and at the same time witnessing and participating in the production process of a television series. Because the actors are relying on a trustworthy reaction from the audience, it is necessary for the audience to experience the show as a play. Therefore the taping/filming has to be done in sequence and without too many intervals and retakes, so the weekly episode is rehearsed and performed as a play. The live audience does not care about the intervals, because it is also interested in the production process, but this interest threatens to harm their involvement in the play, so in all intervals the live audience is entertained by a stand-up comedian to ensure a comic mood and constantly re-establish focus on the play. The producers use so many resources on the live audience, because they know that the reaction from the live audience is important for the acting.

The reaction from the studio audience or in many cases an edited artificial laugh track is also important for the television audience, because the studio audience through the laugh track represents the television audience watching the show. The laugh track makes it possible for the viewers in a pseudo way to be part of a group, and it is more comforting to laugh within a group than on your own. The laugh track also reassures the viewers that the show is funny and in this way creates a specific mode of reception.

At the same time as the laugh track involves the television audience in a collective group feeling, it also creates a distance from the drama. The television audience and the studio audience (as their representatives) are namely looking at the play from the outside instead of getting involved as in traditional dramatic television, where an important factor is the audience's suspension of disbelief. This specific comic mode of address is further supported by textual features.

If we take a new look at Fig. 1, we can see that the four cameras are situated just outside the proscenium on the 'golden line', just like the first row of seats in a theatre. The cameras are kept in a fixed position and may not cross the 'golden line' partly because of the mode of production, where the situation comedy is taped in sequence. Otherwise, one of the cameras would be seen in the picture. Therefore the cameras and the audience are looking at a 'mise en scéne' from the outside, unfolding in front of the cameras. The 'Golden line' separates the camera space from the performer space (Barker, 1994). In the sitcom genre, it is not possible to use the conventional camera work known from single-camera shooting, such as shot-reverse shots, subjective camera angles and travelling; but neither is it desirable, because the camera work used in this genre sustains a consistent and, for this genre, desirable mode of address.

David Barker has analysed the performer space in the situation comedy *All In The Family*. In the analysed episode, 92% of the performer blocking was on the horizontal x-axis parallel to the 'golden line', while a similar analysis of an episode of *M*A*S*H* showed that 78% of the performer blocking was on the z-axis. The overwhelming use of x-axis blocking in situation comedies means that the set and the 'mise en scéne' are described as flat without any depth. This two-dimensional description is further supported by the lighting, which usually is another way of creating depth in space, but in situation comedies the primary function of lighting is to make sure that everything is visible.

Camera space, performer space, and lighting are a result of the mode of production and they can be seen as strong limitations. But on the other hand, all these features reinforces the decisive feeling of looking at something instead of getting involved in the drama.

> "The basically two-dimensional set design of *All In The Family* – drab and nondescript – and the minimal visual information provided concerning the outside world, encouraged the viewer to focus attention on those things inside the Bunker house that were three-dimensional: the characters and their confrontations." (Barker, 1994: 97)

It is arguable that the characters and their confrontations are three-dimensional in situation comedies. In fact they rarely are, but the main point is that situation comedies in a specific mode of address focus attention on other matters, such as character relations, thematic conflicts, and humour, and to do this the genre needs to employ other aesthetic means, such as acting style, timing, language, and narrative structure.

Acting Style

In one of the opening credit sequences of *The Cosby Show*, the Huxtable family members dance in turn with Cliff Huxtable (Bill Cosby). At the end of the credit sequence, Cliff Huxtable (or is it Bill Cosby) finishes the dance and turns around towards the camera hidden behind his own hands. He removes his hands and looks directly at the television viewers visually saying 'I know that I am dancing for you, and that you are watching'. He is thereby violating the rules of representational drama by stepping out of character, and at the same time he is focusing attention on one of the central features of the difficult art of acting in situation comedies.

Acting in situation comedies is a delicate art of performing on two stages at the same time. The main stage is the acting in character in the 'mise en scéne' on the set. On this stage the acting style establishes believable characters within the series' own logic (generic verisimilitude) and the flow of the narrative is clear. The core element of this acting is the traditional 'realistic' method acting. Co-instantaneously playing to the other characters on the first stage, the character is indirectly addressing the double audience on the second stage. The most subtle way of doing this is a delicate look out at the camera and the audience. Bill Cosby is the master of doing this, and Roseanne Barr (Arnold or whatever her last name is), John Goodman, and many others of the best comic actors are also capable of doing it. There are different ways of establishing this double stage acting. The acting style in situation comedies is usually exaggerated compared with that in traditional film and television drama, this exaggerated style, the timing of the reaction shot, and waiting the extra beat for laughs before continuing the story comprise playing for the second stage. The performer blocking on the x-axis further supports the significance of the second stage, because the 'mise en scéne' is always presented to the cameras.

This performing on two stages is like tightrope walking, because it is the balance between the two stages that makes the difference, and it is possible to fall down on either side. If the acting is too 'realistic' the series easily loses the comic mood, while an exaggeration on the second stage easily loses the comic edge and instead looks foolish and insane.

A different way to look at the acting style in situation comedy is to compare it with stand-up comedy. In his book, *Comic Visions*, David Marc discusses the essential features of stand-up comedy.

> "Without the protection of the formal mask of a narrative drama, without a song, dance, or any other intermediary composition that creates distance between performer and performance, without even, necessarily, some remarkable physical trait or ability to gratuitously display, the stand-up comedian addresses an audience as a naked self, eschewing the luxury of a clear-cut distinction between art and life." (Marc, 1989: 13)

The mode of address in presentational stand-up comedy is obviously different from the mode of address in representational situation comedy. The stand-up comedian is addressing the audience or a single person in the audience directly, while the actors in situation comedies are taking part in a drama as characters. But what is the relation between the acting on the second stage in a situation comedy and the direct mode of address in stand-up comedy?

In the early days of situation comedy, many of the actors had backgrounds in stand-up comedy, e.g., Jackie Gleason in *The Honeymooners*. Since the success of Bill Cosby in *The Cosby Show* and Roseanne Barr in *Roseanne*, we have seen many stand-up comedians become situation comedy stars – Tim Allen in *Home Improvement*, Ellen DeGeneres in *Ellen*, and Jerry Seinfeld in *Seinfeld*. Many of the situation comedies are named after the stars, and thereby we see a blurring of the distinction between representational and presentational forms. In *Seinfeld* this distinction is even more blurred because Jerry Seinfeld plays a stand-up comedian named Jerry Seinfeld in the series.

Even in the case of *Seinfeld*, situation comedies remain representational drama. The actors are covered by the masks of the characters they are playing. Jerry Seinfeld, Bill Cosby or Roseanne Barr are addressing the audience in a representational form. The second stage acting is much more subtle, and it is subordinate to the first stage acting. Situation comedy is representational drama and not something in between a presentational and a representational form. On the other hand, the mode of address in situation comedy is a specific form within representational drama, and stand up comedy is obviously a very good training ground for acting on two stages in situation comedy.

I would now like to conclude on the special mode of address in situation comedy. The two-dimensional description of the set and the characters, the separation of, on the one side, camera and audience space and on the other, performer space, the laugh track, and the acting style are all features creating a distance between the play and the audience, and these features all impede audience identification. Instead the audience is looking at the play from the outside with a comic distance. This is further supported by the fact that the audience usually feels superior to the characters in a comedy (the opposite being true in tragedy).

"As in most sitcoms, the narrative structure of *Yes, Minister* and *Yes, Prime Minister* positions the audience in ironic mode, in possession of a greater knowledge of the situation than any single character – particularly in terms of the knowledge of other characters' motives, actions and feelings ...

In terms of narrative address, this carefully designed comic structure rigorously maintains a position for the audience apart from the characters, allowing only a certain degree of sympathy rather than any sentiment approaching empathy." (Adams, 1993: 70)

The audience sees through the disguise of the character's intention, and the pleasure of watching a situation comedy is not so much the narrative plot resolution or the character development as it is the comic and surprising way in which recognisable conflicts are dealt with.

> "As Mulvey suggests, narrative's potential lies not in the static resolution of conflict with which it invariably ends, but in the upheaval and change before that resolution, where binary oppositions dissolve into process and events are linked in time. Here narrative gives representation to the struggle for change and to collective but unspoken conflicts with the rule of law." (Rowe, 1995: 8)

To discuss more precisely, how situation comedies deal with these problems, would demand extensive analyses of specific features concerning the nature of the humour, the character of the narrative, the relation between the narrative and humour, and the relation between character and thematic conflicts. For instance it is of great importance whether a plot is driven by confusion, primarily fuelled by mistakes and misunderstandings, or by complication, which gives room for more depth in the character's psychological reaction to a substantial dilemma. It is beyond the range of this paper to analyse all these complicated matters, but I would like to stress that a thorough understanding of situation comedy as text requires an investigation of above-mentioned matters.

Situation Comedy
– Thematic Limitations

The last subject I would like to elaborate on concerning the situation comedy genre is its thematic possibilities and limitations.

> "Two types of stand-up comedy emerged: one based on social consciousness and one based on social consensus; ... while the sitcom came to occupy the oceanic middle." (Marc, 1989: 45-46)

In a Danish context, series like *Father Knows Best, Major Dad,* and *The Cosby Show* are far to the right rather than being part of the American 'Oceanic middle' but the concept the 'oceanic middle' raises the question of whether this 'middle' is an intrinsic textual feature of the genre, or whether it is merely a specific attribute of the conventions of American prime-time network television.

Marc further argues:

> "Whereas sitcoms depend on familiarity, identification, and redemption of popular beliefs, stand-up comedy often depends on the shocking violation of normative taboos ...
>
> Compare for example, Don Rickles insulting a member of the audience on *The Tonight Show* to Archie Bunker making a racist remark on *All in the Family:* ...
>
> A moment of danger has passed: Rickles has broken taboo in mass-culture rhetoric ...
>
> In *All in the Family,* racism is embedded as a character flaw of Archie, who is ultimately sympathetic, even loveable." (Marc, 1989: 24-26)

As previously mentioned, the two genres address the audience in different ways, but even so it is arguable that the two genres have different ideological spheres in which to operate. First, it is questionable whether televised stand-up comedy is capable of creating this 'moment of danger' for the television audience, since the viewers are sitting at home without the risk of becoming the butt of the next joke. Secondly, I would argue that situation comedy is capable of offering 'shocking violations of normative taboos' just as stand-up comedy does, even if it does so less often.

Roseanne Barr has been an extremely controversial figure in American culture since she started out as a stand-up comedian in Denver in the early 1980s. Rowe has examined the different public and performative roles of Roseanne Barr in the analysis "Roseanne: The unruly Woman as domestic goddess" (Rowe, 1995: 50). Rowe comments here on the ideological difference between Roseanne Barr as a stand-up comedian on stage and in cable television and as the leading character in the series *Roseanne*.

"This shift in emphasis from narrative to stand-up comedy allows her to sharpen her critique of the family, showing that it is threatened less by external monsters than by those within. In the mode of stand-up comedy, Arnold continues to invite identification with her character, but through moments of *recognition* delivered by each punch line rather than through the emotional engagement and resolution of narrative. Using the direct address of stand-up comedy aimed at a visible studio audience, she delivers a monologue about men, fatness, children, yuppies, male impotence. She establishes a perspective and style that are resolutely working class and uses sarcasm to puncture sentimental illusions about domestic life. She is aggressive and vulgar." (Rowe, 1995: 72)

Roseanne Barr is most powerful and poignant as a stand-up comic. The lengths to which she is capable of going in the presentational mode were demonstrated in an incident several years ago. She was asked to sing the American national anthem before the start of a baseball game. She gave a satirically vulgar, off-key performance, which included mimicking the way baseball players spit chewing tobacco on the field. It caused a sensation in the national press. The situation comedy *Roseanne* has been far less radical.

""A something for everyone" form of television drama, the sitcom often teaches a kind of cheerful resignation to one's lot in life (*Laverne and Shirley 1976-1983)* or adjustment to prevailing institutions (The Norman Lear sitcoms). But it can also subvert or discredit those institutions, and such is the case with *Roseanne*." (Rowe, 1995: 77)

Going from stand-up comedy to situation comedy, Roseanne Barr has had to adjust to prime-time network television, but she has been fighting the powerful Hollywood and network executives to get creative control, and the production of the series has been surrounded by spectacular scandals. However, the series has dealt with essential social conflicts in a serious way.

Over the course of its production run, *Roseanne* has evolved around two fundamental conflict axes, of opposing discourses, that were delineated in the pilot: gender and class. In the pilot, Roseanne has to go to the school because the history teacher, Miss Crane, is complaining about Darlene's behaviour in class – she has been barking like a dog. Roseanne has to get off early from work, and when she arrives 15 minutes late the very fit Miss Crane is just finishing stretching exercises. She tells Roseanne they will have to postpone their meeting because she has an appointment to play squash. After agreeing to go on with the meeting, Miss Crane entrenches herself behind the teacher's desk with the star-spangled banner beside it, while she asks Roseanne to sit in the low, humbling position of a pupil's desk. Roseanne is too fat to squeeze into the chair. She challenges Miss Crane by sitting in an equal position on the pupil's desk.

> "Miss Crane: Darlene has been demonstrating behavioural problems.
> Roseanne: What does that mean?
> Miss Crane: She has been barking in class.
> Barking!
> Miss Crane: Like a dog!
> Roseanne: Well did you tell her to stop it?
> Miss Crane: I did.
> Roseanne: Did she stop it?
> Miss Crane: She stopped.
> Roseanne: What's the problem?
> Miss Crane: I feel this barking is an aggressive manifestation of deeper internal problems.
> Roseanne: Ha!
> Miss Crane: Let me explain. We have found that when behavioural problems arise in the class room it usually indicates a problem at home.
> Roseanne: Aha!
> Miss Crane: How would you describe your relation with your daughter?
> Roseanne: Oh I will say it's typical.

> Miss Crane: Typical, not special?
> Roseanne: Typical!
> Miss Crane: Do you feel you spend enough time with your daughter?
> Roseanne: You mean like quality time!
> Miss Crane: Do you spend any free time with Darlene?
> Roseanne: I have three kids, and I work, so I do not have any free time.
> Miss Crane: Hm, see that may be the problem.
> Roseanne: Hm, well I think that the problem is that there is no problem.
> Miss Crane: Your daughter barks.
> Roseanne: Our whole family barks!"

The scene is a clash between the hegemony of the institutionalised middle class norms and an oppositional set of values represented by the working class Conner family: middle class vs. working class, fitness vs. fatness, looseness, and excess, self-realisation/squash vs. survival, institution/desk vs. self-managing/sitting on the table, dissimulation vs. spontaneity, ideology vs. pragmatics, and abstract vs. concrete. This clash of oppositional discourses, as is the case with gender too, is very critical to the dominating discourse. Roseanne is winning all the sympathy, and she nails Miss Crane by showing that she has seen through her institutionalised teacher psychology, 'You mean like quality time'. *Roseanne* is an ambivalent series that insists on being critical from its own standpoint of never giving in to institutions or the oh-so-right liberal position on gender and social issues.

> "But it also indicates a refusal to flatten contradictions. Much of Roseanne's appeal lies in the delicate balance she maintains between individual and institution and in the impersonal nature of her anger and humor, which are targeted not so much at the people she lives with as at what makes them the way they are." (Rowe, 1995: 210)

The price for reaching a much larger audience on prime-time network television may have been that *Roseanne* is a diluted version of the poignant critique known from Roseanne Barr's other performances, but the series is still a critical show, which raises essential problems seldom dealt with on American television. It seems that even within the boundaries of American network television, there are some series which push the limits in search of an audience. The Fox Network has led the way in this regard. Its raunchy 'white trash' series, *Married ... with Children* has been a successful satirical and grotesque depiction of suburban family life, that does not by any sense relate to the 'oceanic middle'. But how far can the genre go?

In an episode of *Fawlty Towers,* "'The Germans", Basil (John Cleese) while serving some German guests constantly mentions the war, as if by a slip of the tongue.

> "Basil: Certainly, why not, why not indeed? We are all friends now, eh?
> 2nd German: A prawn cocktail.
> Basil: ... All in the Market together, old differences forgotten, and no need to mention the war ... Sorry! ... Sorry, what was that again?
> 2nd German: A prawn cocktail.
> Basil: Oh, prawn, that was it. When you said prawn I thought you said war. Oh, the war! Oh yes, completely slipped my mind, yes, I'd forgotten all about it. Hitler, Himmler, and all that lot, oh yes, completely forgotten it, just like that ...
> 2nd German: Will you stop talking about the war?
> Basil: Me? You started it.
> 2nd German: We did not start it.
> Basil: Yes you did, you invaded Poland." (Cleese & Booth, 1977: 155-56)

In *Fawlty Towers* the comic features usually, as here, evolve around Basil's character flaws, but his character flaws are also violations of normative taboos. In the above-mentioned example, it is a shocking violation which links repressed hate deriving from European history to the on-going economic and cultural integration policy in Europe. The episode creates an uneasy tension, not to say a moment of danger, which is resolved in comic relief.

The point is that it is very difficult to set formal limits for the thematic and ideological content of the situation-comedy genre. The textual features of the genre are indeed more suitable for certain issues. Guiding lectures on normative questions are supported by the overarching narrative of each episode, where the disturbed equilibrium is restored in the end, so that the next episode can begin with a new disturbance of the equilibrium. The narrative resolution and the setting right of the norm-breaking character are in some cases important, but as previously mentioned, it is just as much the narrative process that is important, the continuous set-up and pay-off in each situation. The taboos are broken in *Fawlty Towers*, no matter whether Basil is punished for his character flaws or not.

It is less the limits of the genre that matter, but instead the pragmatic use of the genre, and here it comes down to institutional practices. Within a non-commercial, public-service broadcasting system like the Danish, DR has been obliged to promote artistic and cultural innovation, therefore it would have been possible to explore the limits of the genre, but instead the station until recently has rejected the genre.

Danish Popular Fiction

This analysis of the situation comedy genre might seem unprofitable in relation to Danish popular fiction since Danish series have ostentatiously avoided the genre, but this contempt for the genre is exactly the main problem for Danish fiction intended to be popular, because all other things being equal, it is much more difficult to be genre-innovative in each production and re-invent the wheel again and again. Working within innovative forms and transgressing genre conventions, the creative people will have to be much more aware of every single textual feature used. The mode of production, the lighting, the acting style, etc. are all features that have a function, and the question is, do these features support the intended mode of address and thematic intentions of the series? Or do these features pull in different directions? Second, by transgressing the genre conventions, a series starts out by neglecting the expectations of the audience, and it is necessary to establish a new contract between the series and the audience in order to create viewer interest. By using the textual features of a well-known genre some basic elements are given, and the creative people can focus on features that really matter.

Three whores and a pickpocket is a 6-part serial (each episode lasts between 26 and 37 minutes) produced by DR in 1993, written by Niels Schou and directed by Piv Bernth. The serial revolves around a modern, atypical family running a small cafe. The mother, Mirza Høeg (Helle Hertz) has three teenage children, John (19), Donna (17), and Maria (15) by three different fathers, and she is living happily with a fourth man, Thor, for the seventh year. The last member of the family is the basset hound Henriette Jensen (a very common last name in Denmark). Jensen comments on the plot and on life in general in an inner monologue, and in a few sequences, Jensen is the bearer of the point of view.

First episode introduces the chaotic but amiable family, and Mirza and Thor are discussing whether or not to have a child of their own. At the end of the first episode, Thor accidentally falls off the roof and dies. Mirza cannot acknowledge his death, so she goes into shock and lives in a psychotic state, sometimes acting normally, sometimes interacting with Thor as if he was present. The three teenagers decide to get help from their fathers, who proceed to move into the house. The three fathers are all emotionally immature persons and they turn out to be no help at all; in fact, on the contrary, they create even more problems. In the end, the children have to solve all their problems themselves.

The problems of modern family life are the core of most situation comedies and soaps, and the idea of having a family with a mother, three children, three different fathers, and a lover is in itself fine and could obviously be a good setting for either a situation comedy or a soap. But *Three whores ...* is neither of them.

DR presents the serial as a "modern fairy tale about love and chaos, adults and their children, and a dog called Jensen.

In the middle of everything stands Mirza played by Helle Hertz." This presentation does not precisely say what the audience can expect of the serial. The opening sequence is low key with still photos of the milieu and the characters underscored by instrumental music with a sentimental tone. The first scene takes place in the kitchen. It is written from the point of view of the dog. In an inner monologue Jensen is complaining that the alarm clock portends disturbance of the quiet morning peace. When Maria comes out into the kitchen she talks to Jensen, and we hear Jensen's thoughts. This fantasy-like realism is replaced by ordinary kitchen sink realism, when the three teenagers and their problems are presented. The young inexperienced television actors struggle to establish some credibility in their roles, but whatever credibility is established is squandered immediately after in an amateurishly overacted comical incident in which Maria hits the legs from under John with a broom. The dialogue is primarily realistic and conveys plot, but there are some moments of absurdity in the dialogue which support a comic effect.

From the very beginning, the serial mixes different genres and stylistic features, and this continues throughout. In the beginning the above-mentioned kitchen sink realism familiar from soaps and melodramatic serials dominates, and this realism plays an essential role throughout the serial. Likewise the fantasy-like realism pops up throughout the serial, besides the dog Jensen we follow Mirza's materialisation of her dead lover, Thor.

There are two other recurring styles: a more traditional comic style, where the acting is more exaggerated and the dialogue loaded with absurdity, and a more specific style – a kind of montage of pantomime with rhythmic background music. The latter is often used as an elliptical sequence of action in subplots and milieu presentation. Besides these dominating genres and styles, several other genres and stylistic features pop up: the above-mentioned fairy tale, farce, a mixture of detective and comedy, and psychological drama with expressionistic camera work. The serial also attempts badly supported suspense in cliff-hangers at the end of two episodes. The genre confusion is so pervasive that all aspects appear to be permeated with it: set design, 'mise en scéne', lighting, acting style, timing, narrative structure, editing, etc.

Mixing genres and styles is not a problem in itself, there are several examples of very good and successful films and television series that have mixed genres and styles with great virtuosity, let me just mention Dennis Potter's *The Singing Detective* and Lars von Trier's *Riget (The Kingdom)*. In the successful genre mix you may say that a thesis and an antithesis melt together into a synthesis, but this is not the case in *Three whores...* Different features in the serial point in different directions and instead of supporting a general vision the different features compete against each other.

The main problem is that none of the genres succeeds in its own right. The realistic soap genre dominates, but even though the subplots present important social issues about youth criminality, teenage pregnancy, and traumatic experiences in childhood, the problems are not taken seriously. There is not sufficient dramatic conflict, and therefore the problems are not developed into interesting dilemmas. Instead the plots are resolved by accident; in fact the main plot is resolved by fifth grade psychology, when John gets a revelation that they shall re-enact the accident in which Thor dies. The recurring breach of genre expectations obviously enforces the feeling that the social issues raised should not be taken seriously. It is also a breach of the generic verisimilitude of the serial that Maria's father, the thick-skinned elephant Hannibal, who has been characterised in this pantomime style as an emotionally immature businessman, suddenly changes character and in an expressionistic psychological scene re-experiences a childhood trauma and turns out to be a new and better person.

Three whores... does not work as a comedy either, except for two or three scenes. The process of completing all the various plots governs the realistic narrative form, so space is not created for the narrative forms of the comedy. Furthermore, the lack of dramatic conflicts with their dilemmas and essential complications is just as problematic for the comedy as it is for the soap, and the intendedly funny incidents look like tomfoolery without any dramaturgic significance.

The reason I have spend so much time on a problematic and mediocre serial like *Three whores ...* is that it is a typical Danish serial of many, all of which dismiss the genre conventions. Let me just mention a few, *Fæhår og Harzen, Dr Dip*, and *Station 13*. In *Three whores ...* the genre mix and the over loading of styles are done on purpose, because the relics of the romantic conception of art make a serial more interesting per se, if it experiments with genre and styles. Likewise it is considered to be a better show if the characters develop throughout the serial as in the literary novel and most films. In *Three whores ...* all the main characters go through a development, but this development is not dramatically, psychologically, or thematically motivated.

No doubt *Three whores ...* is unique and has some original features, but these features do not add quality to the serial seen as a popular serial. Within a modernistic tradition, form is interesting in itself, but in popular culture, form is less important in itself. As I have demonstrated in the genre analysis of the situation comedy, form is very important in popular culture, but it is not supposed to point to itself.

Three whores ... is obviously an attempt to reach a large audience, but the idea of loading the serial with a little bit of everything, believing that there would be something for everyone, is wrong, because there is not sufficient nourishment in any of the elements.

Home for five. A Different Institutional Frame

The series *Home for five* is produced for the second Danish terrestrial TV station, TV2, by a small but still one of the largest Danish independent production companies, *Metronome*. This different institutional background has an influence on the series. First, TV2 has, in general, had a different attitude towards the audience than DR, and this has also been evident in the stations' few fiction series. Second, TV2 has been less tied to the romantic conception of art, even though this conception has been a common cultural heritage in the creative milieu. Third, TV2 has less money to spend on programming, so the station has produced a limited amount of Danish fiction and is quite inexperienced in series production.

In 1994, TV2 decided for the first time to bank on a long running series for prime time. The station felt that the creative milieu was not able to deliver right away, either because of reluctance by the established writers to write popular drama, or because the inexperienced writers were not good enough. Therefore TV2 asked *Metronome* to conduct a working seminar for young and inexperienced, as well as more established, writers. An American writer-producer was brought in as teacher and supervisor. After the seminar, seven of the participants and two executives from respectively TV2 and *Metronome* in a collective process developed the family series *Home for five*. 13 episodes of the series were broadcast in 1995-96, and even though it has not been the expected or hoped for qualitative and popular success, TV2 has produced 13 episodes more.

Home for five is a half-hour series about a brought-together family, where the lawyer Elisabeth and her teenage son Victor in the first premise episode are moving in with the unemployed salesman Ulrik and his two teenage girls Silke and Rosa. The series deals with the problems of living together in a new family, jealousy, men's vanity and self deception, teenage love, and women's search for power. The series is primarily episodic with a few minor themes running through several episodes.

It is difficult to decide to what genre the series belongs, because it is neither a soap nor a situation comedy. Instead it is part of a specific Danish genre consisting of series/serials like *Parløb (Partner Race), Mor er major (Mother is a Major), Far på færde (Daddy is on the go)*, and *Altid om søndagen, (Always on Sundays)*. These series are intentionally popular humorous series, which have avoided the situation comedy genre because the above-mentioned contempt for the too American and commercial genre, and because of the opinion that the genre is too difficult to translate into Danish terms. This specifically Danish genre (or maybe more correctly, this non-genre) has convincingly demonstrated that it has never had the potential to satisfy an audience.

In *Three whores* ... I discussed how the relics of the romantic conception of art meant a conscious breach of the genre expectation by overloading the serial with different genre features and styles. In *Home for five* the problems are of a different kind, because the romantic conception of art did not play any significant role, since all involved in the project accepted the conditions governing the production.

The main problem is that TV2 insisted on developing the series within the above mentioned non-genre, because the station did not think the Danish script writers were capable of creating a successful situation comedy and therefore wished to hide behind parallel emotional action. As a result, the series has huge problems with the mode of address, the acting style, and the narrative form.

The mode of address is closely related to the mode of production. *Home for five* has been taped with a cheap two-camera technique known from daytime soap. This mode of production has been developed to produce 25 or 50 minutes a day, but it does not utilise the aesthetic possibilities of lighting, camera movement, etc. known from single-camera taping, and gets nothing substantial in return, as does the mode of production used for situation comedy, as mentioned above.

By using this mode of production, *Home for five* ends up with a style and a mode of address in between a traditional dramatic mode and the situation comedy mode. The visual style is ordinary and dull, much like the daytime soap and thus the series is not capable of establishing the same depth in the emotional action as traditional one-camera drama. The visual style, the set design, which is a typical situation comedy living room, and the 'mise en scéne' supports the situation comedy mode of address, but several features prevent the outsider's feeling of looking in at the drama: the lack of studio audience, z-axis action, the editing style, and the lack of separation between the camera space and the performer space.

One of the main problems caused by this inconsistency in the mode of address is the acting style. The actors have an impossible task, because the realistic and the comic acting styles are in conflict. The realistic style loses its credibility because it alternates with an exaggerated acting style, while the latter never succeeds in itself, because it does not have two stages to play on. In situation comedies, the comic acting style is an integrated part of the mode of address, while in *Home for five* the mode of address changes continuously. Moreover, the series has not been able to create characters that can work within this ambivalent situation. These are the main reasons for the actors in the series looking like 'Bambi on ice'.

The narrative also tries to serve two masters at the same time. In several episodes the series presents interesting plots with complications that open up for depth in the characters' reactions. In the episode "Mor er den bedste i verden" ("Mother is the best in the World") for her birthday, Rosa wants a cat, and Rosa's mother will probably give it to her. Elisabeth does not want to have a cat in the house, so she is in a real dilemma, because she also wants to get Rosa's love – to be the mother in her life. Instead of focusing on the dilemma and further developing the complication, the dramatic substances evaporate into thin air, when Elisabeth decides to give Rosa a cat herself, and the narrative plot changes focus to a giddy confusion of identity; not about the identity of the best mother but of the identity of the two cats given by the two mothers.

All these problems are linked with the concept of the series, and even though it is possible to point out several problems in the scripts, in the directing, and in the acting, it is essential to understand that this non-genre has some inherent problems that are very difficult to solve – it is an uphill struggle.

During the past few years, both DR and TV3 have produced situation comedies which follow the conventions of the genre, to a great extent.

DR has broadcast *Madsen og Co.* (12 episodes in 1996 and new episodes in the autumn of 1998), set in a traditional family with two teenagers. The series contains serious problems with, among the other things, the acting style. Peter Schrøder, one of Denmark's best actors in the field of revue and satire, plays the part of the father, Mogens Madsen, in revue style in which only one stage is used – the above-mentioned second stage – direct to the audience and thus the interaction with the other characters is imperfect. This means that the fine balancing act of situation comedy between the two stages does not work, which makes the actors look like extras who lack comic timing.

Moreover, there are considerable problems in the manuscripts. The series is a Danish version of a Swedish series, *Svensson & Svensson,* and the translation completely lacks imagination. In one episode where the father has great sporting ambitions for his son, ice hockey is used as the sport involved, but the differences in the cultural importance of ice hockey in Sweden and Denmark are too great to allow of a literal translation. It is, however, even more problematic that the central axis of conflict of the series seems out of date and un-Danish.

Kaos i opgangen (15 episodes in 1997-98) on TV3, a translation of the classic American situation comedy, *The Honeymooners*, of 1995 suffers from the same problem concerning the acting style and the matter of thematic authenticity.

In summary, it can be concluded that the problems of the popular cultural series have undergone a paradigm shift. Formerly, the problem was connected with the circumstance that the relics of a romantic view of art meant that the series first and foremost had to be original in form, preventing a serious development of the popular cultural aspect, which precisely subordinates form to content. At present, the popular cultural genre is in the process of liberating itself from the romantic view of art and in the comedy genre, problems arise instead from the lack of professional ability, which is true right from the decision-makers, through the manuscript to the direction. There is also the obvious problem that it is not just a question of copying the genre conventions, but that foreign series are being translated instead of authentic Danish TV fiction being produced.

Bibliography

Adams, J. (1993). "Yes, Prime Minister: 'The Ministerial Broadcast'". In G. W. Brandt (ed.): *British Television Drama in the 1980s*. Cambridge: Cambridge University Press.
Barker, D. (1994). "Television Production Techniques as Communication". In H. Newcomb (ed.): *Television. The Critical View*. New York: Oxford University Press.
Bondebjerg, I. (1993). *Elektroniske fiktioner*. Copenhagen: Borgen.
Cleese, J., & C. Booth (1977). *The Complete Fawlty Towers*. New York: Pantheon Books.
Marc, D. (1989). *Comic Visions. Television Comedy and American Culture*. Boston: Unwin Hyman.
Mayerle, J. (1994). "*Roseanne* – How Did You Get Inside My House? A Case Study of a Hit Blue-Collar Situation Comedy". In H. Newcomb (ed.): *Television. The Critical View*. New York: Oxford University Press.
Neale, S. (1989). *Genre*. London: BFI Books.
Nielsen, P. E. (1992). *Bag Hollywoods drømmefabrik. TV-system og produktionsforhold i amerikansk TV*. Aarhus.
Nielsen, P. E. (1994). *Tre ludere og en lommetyv – En analyse af dansk seriedramatik*. Working paper from the research project "The Aesthetics of television", no 4. Aarhus.
Rowe, K. (1995). *The Unruly Woman. Gender and the Genres of Laughter*. Austin: University of Texas Press.
Rowe, K. Roseanne (1994). "Unruly Woman as Domestic Goddess". In H. Newcomb: *Television. The Critical View*. New York: Oxford University Press.
Søndergaard, H. (1992). "Fra programflade til kontaktflade". In: *MedieKultur nr. 17*. Århus.

CHAPTER FOUR

Crime and Gender in the Provinces
– an Analysis of *Island Cop*

Gunhild Agger
Department of Communication
Aalborg University

> *"There's a picture missing ... A little tern which I photographed the other day here on the main street. It has this typical way of jerking its neck. I don't understand."*
> Keld in Island Cop, episode 3.

Beloved and Missed

When *Island Cop (Strisser paa Samsoe)* was screened on TV2 during spring 1997 it filled a national gap as far as genre is concerned. The latest Danish-produced police series was *Station 13* from 1988-89; there had also been a few crime serials. In terms of ratings reception was overwhelming. The series attracted an exceptionally large number of viewers. The genre had obviously been missed as there was a viewing public of between 1,9 and 2 million, which is between 39 and 41 percent of Danish viewers.

The lack could have several causes. Firstly, police-related themes during this period, were presented as reconstructions on a drama-documentary basis. Inspiration for this was found primarily in English and American productions. Secondly, the supply of police series from abroad based on heavy action and violence increased during the period, making it more difficult for smaller nations to compete due to larger budgets for stunts, special effects and computer-simulated action. Thirdly, the roles and functions of the police have been under constant debate during recent years, and severe criticism has been launched against the police, questioning its methods and solutions both within the criminal and the civil sphere.

All this might have influenced the deficit in the production of police series. It is part of the genre, as it has been elaborated on an international level, that at least some of the representatives of the police should stand for justice, that there should be a certain degree of sympathy for those representatives, and that the crime should be solved. In Denmark, however, there has been no tendency to place the police in a heroic role, neither on film, nor on television. Traditional, internationally used role models such as Sherlock Holmes and Maigret have not really been translated with any success lately. And Danish popular comedy has repeatedly pictured the police force as ridiculous, ineffective, bureaucratic. In this respect the films about the Olsen gang are models of caricature. On this background it is more surprising that there has been a Danish tradition of criminal serials since the 1960s and for police series since the 1970s. The pauses in between are not difficult to explain.

It is common to criminal fiction and police fiction that they make a theme out of both crime and the attitude to crime, which at any time is negotiated in a society. Criminal fiction works within a broader frame because the detective can represent unofficial layers and special environments. Still, police fiction can represent contrasts and conflicts which extend the axis of crime and law, typically between different levels within the police, orientated towards gender, or internalised within the single policeman or -woman. The genre is of course well-suited to an examination of the state of our sense of justice and to the description of central social problems in a moral narrative form: "Television crime stories play out fundamental social moralities before a national audience" (Paterson, 1995: 109). The social importance of the genre is confirmed by almost all the articles in the anthology by David Kidd-Hewitt and Richard Osborne, *Crime and the Media* (1995). Richard Sparks also looks at the genre from this point of view in his *Television and the drama of crime* (1992), which bears the significant subtitle *Moral tales and the place of crime in public life.*

Island Cop can be seen as a reopening of the dialogue between citizens and state about violations of norms and sanctions. It puts a human policeman with a strong sense of both justice and humour and an ability to act immediately as its front figure. In this way the debate is placed down to earth, obviously carrying a sense of 'no more fuss', of the traditional clearly legitimating function known from classical police series. In the same movement it rediscovers and renews themes and angles from former Danish productions, the theme of the provinces, the relationship between big fish and small fry, the lonely detective. It renews the series by mixing a serial in the different episodes.

Island Cop is both traditional and renewing. The most important purpose of the analysis derives from this. It is to place it in its relationship to international and Danish traditions within the genres of crime and police series to discover in which way it is traditional and in which way it represents a renewal.

Especially in genres based on crime it is important that the plot is well done. Every plot involves two levels. The reconstruction of the plot – or, in the terms used by the Russian formalists, the development of 'fabula' in 'sujet' – has a special importance in the criminal genre, because the pieces of a good plot must finally fall into place. The ending is decisive both in the hunt for 'who' and when we already know who did it and attention is thus concentrated on 'how'. A similar distinction has been elaborated by Tzvetan Todorov directed at criminal genres. Todorov calls the 'fabula': 'l'histoire du crime' and the 'sujet': 'l'histoire de l'enquête' (which corresponds to 'investigation' in English; Todorov, 1971: 57).[1] These concepts can be useful to characterise the narrative levels in the different plots both in the classical detective story and the suspense story, showing where the plot fails from a genre viewpoint. In *Island Cop* there are good plots as well as less successful ones.

Personnel and Facts

It was the editor of TV2, Mogens Kloevedal, together with the film producer, Per Holst, who provided the idea for the police series *Island Cop* 1-6, broadcast on TV2 on six Mondays from 17 February to 25 March 1997. Six new episodes have been broadcast on six Saturdays from 17 October to 21 November 1998. According to Eddie Thomas Petersen, the director, this will conclude *Island Cop* in spite of its extreme popularity as he does not want it to become mere routine. The series has been sold to Norway, Sweden, Finland, Slovenia and Ireland, which shows that it has not only had a national appeal, and that it has primarily appealed to smaller nations in Europe. Eddie Thomas Petersen was also a scriptwriter in collaboration with Hans Mortensen, Hanne Vibeke Holst, Flemming Jarlskov and John Stefan Olsen.

Eddie Thomas Petersen received his training at the Danish Film School and has previously produced short features: *Toesedrengen (The Cissy Boy)* 1984, *Salamandersoeen (Newt Lake)* 1986 (about the relationship between children and death), *Nanna og Pernille (Nanna and Pernille)* 1988 (on children of divorced parents, which won a 'Robert' award as the best short film of the year) and the award-winning *Eksamen (The Examination)* 1993. He directed *Springflod (Spring Tide)* 1990 and *Roser og persille (Roses and Parsley)* 1993. The last-mentioned was also made into a TV version in five parts with the title *Tango for tre (Tango for Three)*, broadcast on TV2 in October-November 1994. This production has also been screened in a number of small European countries. *Island Cop* was filmed on location on the island of Samsoe in August 1996.

The casting is characterised by a mixture. It makes use of young, newly-trained actors not previously seen on screen, as well as good old popular actors who have played many roles in film, on stage and in TV fiction. The three main roles were played as follows: Christian Torp, the cop: Lars Bom, who has previously played a part inside the costume of a popular teddy bear character for children, and has appeared on the stage of the experimental Dr. Dante Theatre in Copenhagen, his daughter Cecilie, called Sille: Amalie Dollerup, the police secretary, Ulla Snedker: screen newcomer Andrea Vagn Jensen, recently trained at Aarhus Theatre. There is a return appearance from one episode to another in the roles of the female pastor, Dorthe Bloendal (Lotte Arnsbjerg), her unemployed husband, the amateur bird-watcher Keld Bloendal (Finn Storgaard), the taxi driver, Taxa Ejvind (Folmer Rubaek), and the doctor at the little hospital (John Hahn-Petersen). The cameraman was Tony Forsberg and scenographer Palle Arestrup.

The Traditions of the Crime and the Police Genre

The serial is the dominant form of Danish TV fiction and this is also true of the crime genre. Up until 1988, when the Danish Broadcasting Corporation (DR) still had a monopoly, the TV fiction series format was the exception which proved the rule; the rule was the single play or TV film and serials of varying lengths. Of course, this did not mean that Danes lacked series. Especially American, English, German and French series were shown and became established as the convention of the genre, models to be copied and/or to be dissociated from by Danish serials and series.[2] Which is what was done.

Thus, the first Danish police series proper, the very popular *En by i provinsen* (*A Provincial Town*) 1-17, 1977-80, was to a certain extent inspired by the almost as popular American *McCloud*, transferred to an anonymous, but easily recognised, Danish provincial town with a police station, pub and social worker. Right from the start, the provinces as place play an important role. Whereas in the prototype, as in most international police series, the city was the favourite location for crime, it is typical that in the Danish context, the provinces are regarded as a well-suited location for crime. In the provinces, secret links between politicians, local businessmen and various forms of shady affairs and sharp practices can be exposed. The relationships – or more often the lack of connection – between the official facade and the less glamorous, unstable private life can be displayed. And there is always someone who knows something about someone else which the latter doesn't think is known. Inquisitive observers and people in the know abound and their powers of observation are extremely well developed. This cocktail is familiar from the works of Agatha Christie amongst others, especially when her female detective, Miss Marple, is involved. However, while the element of social criticism is totally absent from Agatha Christie, it often plays an important role in *A Provincial Town*.

In *McCloud*, country and city meet, the main character, McCloud, being a western sheriff stationed in New York. As a constant ingredient in every episode, his down-to-earth drive is contrasted with the working methods of his superior officer, marked as they are by routine. The relationship is mirth-provoking and these stereotypical figures are used but not allowed to develop. There is a corresponding clash between the provinces and the city in *A Provincial Town*, where it is worked out in the relationship between the local detective inspector, Samuelsen, and detective superintendent Eriksen, who comes from Copenhagen. The point here is that the two need each other. In spite of the differences in rank and language, they form an excellent pair of partners.[3] Logically enough, it is the characters of the two policemen which are concentrated upon, at least as much as the plot. The genre emphasises mores, including those of the police force, as much as crime and the solution of crime.

The team of writers which had been formed before and during the production of *A Provincial Town* came to have great importance for the later shaping of Danish crime fiction, in the form of novels and films as well as TV serials: Leif Panduro, Johannes Moellehave, Poul-Henrik Trampe, Poul Oerum and Anders Bodelsen. Casting came to have a certain importance: Jens Okking was so convincing in the role of Samuelsen that he could, without difficulty and with even more physical and psychological weight, go on to play the main part in Anders Refn's film *Stroemer (Cop)* in 1976. Correspondingly Henning Moritzen, known as Eriksen in *A Provincial Town*, went on as detective superintendent in *Station 13*.

Among the script writers, Leif Panduro was the veteran ideas man. He had an eye for both psychological and social realism and this he used to provide a diagnosis of the problems of the middle class in the 1960s and 1970s, in their efforts to find their place privately and socially. This he did in the form of novels, TV plays and, to a certain extent, in crime serials. Leif Panduro's first crime serial as a script writer was *Ka' De li' Oesters? (Do You Like Oysters?)* 1-6, 1967. This was followed by *Smuglerne (The Smugglers)* 1-6, 1971 and the Danish-Swedish co-production *Strandvaskeren (Body Washed Ashore)* 1-6, 1978, both with a critical purpose: the 'bosses', the men behind organised crime, escape while the 'small fry' – ordinary people and petty criminals – have to pay the price of crime as victim and jailed, respectively. This theme was further developed in two of the leading crime serials of the 1980s: *Anthonsen* 1-6, 1984-85 and *Een gang stroemer (Once a Cop)* 1-6, 1988, while the provincial theme was carried on in *Rejseholdet (The Flying Squad)* (1983: 1-6 and 1985: 1-6). Let us look at the last first.

The provincial environment and the contrast between a local and a central level played a main role in the police series, *The Flying Squad*, produced by a branch of the national TV system in the city of Aarhus. Director was Bent Christensen. The fictive provinces Svanbjerg were here replaced by authentic milieus. Larger towns in Jutland such as Fredericia, Kolding and Silkeborg provided the provincial atmosphere together with rural settings around Randers, Horsens, Aalborg. Places and crimes changed, but the sense of the provinces was everywhere just as the flying squad. One renewal was that a female detective inspector was a member of the team. In spite of the good intentions of a broad representation of provincial milieus and a certain political weight as gender is concerned the series was not as well performed as *A Provincial Town*. Characterisation and plot development in *The Flying Squad* were too stereotyped and the genre fell below its accustomed level.

The script of *Anthonsen* was based on an idea by Henning Bahs and Erik Balling, the stylistic and genre-conscious team of Danish film and TV fiction, who have cooperated and shared various tasks on productions over a long period.[4] Erik Balling directed *Anthonsen*. The series is peculiar in that it is a parody of a genre which has not received any special expression in a Danish context – the hard-boiled, American private eye genre, as seen in Raymond Chandler's novels and their film versions. But this was not the first time that Balling had made a parody over something which in itself had not previously found convincing expression in a national context. The same was true of the film *Slaa foerst, Frede* (*Strike First, Freddie*), 1965, which was a parody of the action film genre done by transferring it to Copenhagen and district. The recipe for the parody was, in brief, to alienate the codes of the genre – by bringing them close to home.

To have a private detective as main character and at the centre of a Danish crime serial seems, in itself, quite strange. By far most areas of Danish society are strongly marked by public institutions. From child minding to care of the elderly and from education to social care, there is only a very limited tradition of private organisations. A private detective is thus in itself a joke, a marginal phenomenon in a society where the conception of justice requires that it is the police who take care of public safety. And if the police failed the choice would certainly not be a private detective. It is characteristic that the function of detecting in *The Smugglers* and *Body Washed Ashore* is not performed by a private detective but by a sports journalist and a medico-legal expert, respectively, and that Dan Turèll uses a journalist in *Mord i moerke* (*Murder in the Dark*).

Accordingly the out-of-date, decayed and perhaps, to a certain extent, nostalgic element is emphasised. Ove Sprogoe's Anthonsen is in his sixties, his office is threatened with being pulled down, only with difficulty can his secretary keep creditors from the door, he is himself treated again and again in the most humiliating way by clients and not least, by society's big shots – and by the police. Anthonsen earns his keep as an expert in the kind of surveillance that is a preparation for a divorce case. But during this surveillance he always catches sight of something else, just as important, usually with broader perspectives, which leads to the powers-that-be in society and the places frequented by them – leading banks, insurance companies, fashion houses, finance and investment companies, lawyers' offices. Even without being asked, he cannot help pursuing major criminals and arranging matters so that an exposure is made possible. Anthonsen never receives recognition from anyone, but at least he derives his own pleasure from being proved right – and so does the audience.

The location is Copenhagen in the 1980s, marked by the new conservative optimism following the Conservative taking of power in 1982, The industrious Copenhagen of Poul Schlüter, served both sweet and sour. But the approach is provincial insofar as it is based on a dated type, a genuinely old-fashioned, eager and honest detective, not really understanding what is going on but definitely determined to find out. Anthonsen is, in a way, a parody of his American prototype. He catches cold during his surveillance work, he is no great success as an action hero and he keeps silent when confronted with the insults of his tormentors. Whether he is insulted by criminals or the police, he is unable to respond with the impertinence of a Philip Marlowe. This produces many embarrassing and amusing situations. But he conforms to the pattern in that he is incorruptibly loyal to his self-chosen tasks.

Anthonsen is thus the 'little man' who, in spite of everything, often succeeds in exposing the 'operators', even though no one knows he is responsible. Old-fashioned morality thus becomes the operator in the fight against crime, the counterpart to the modern, stream-lined operators who went free in Panduro's 1970s serials. In Anthonsen, there is a certain portion of poetic justice, ironically presented in the fact that while the criminal is exposed, it remains a matter between Anthonsen and the audience how it has happened.[5] The parody works again through the codes of the genre being exposed by being transferred closer to home, which demonstrates the provincialism that may be present in the awareness of tradition and the outside world found in Copenhagen.

Whether justice can be fully done is at issue in the genre as it presents itself in the course of the 1970s and 1980s. The problem is treated in the film *Cop* (1976) and again in the TV series *Once a Cop* 1-6, DR 1987 with the same director. Like *Anthonsen*, *Cop* takes place in the setting of Copenhagen and northern Zealand. But as the title indicates, the main character, detective inspector Karl Joergensen, played by Jens Okking, is a policeman. He has a not unfamiliar problem, which is that his indignation about violence and crime sometimes leads him to be just as violent as those he is struggling against.

The conflicts are so great that, following the introductory confrontations of the film, Karl Joergensen is admitted to a psychiatric sanatorium and the film ends with him asking to be admitted again to the same institution. In the crime genre, being committed or shut away is something which usually happens to the criminal, not the policeman. Karl Joergensen has uncovered the links between minor and major criminals but this insight when combined with powerlessness is frustrating.[6] The resolution and relief at the crime being solved are absent, the minor criminals are dead and the real operators, a contractor, a mayor and their mutual financier and go-between, a stockbroker, can continue their lives at the summit of society as usual.

The social accusation and criticism consist in that it is always the 'minor' critics who have to take the blame, both from the criminals and from their superiors, who are deeply in collusion with each other. The obvious nature of the social collusion is amusingly demonstrated visually when the corrupt mayor and the understanding chief of police, each with his wife, meet as they are walking their dogs in the park. Conflict between the top and the bottom in the police force is not unusual in police series. It is often resolved by the little policeman defeating his superior, but here he has to give up. Realistic but disillusioned. Logically, the film makes a comment on the criminal genre as seen in the version provided by the media and thus involves a level of genre self-awareness.

This happens clearly in a scene where the widow who rents a room to Karl Joergensen is watching TV with him. In contrast to him, she has a colour TV, a trait so typical of the depiction of time. The sound of gunfire is heard. From the soundtrack, it becomes apparent that the series is German. The two people comment on the genre from a realistic and a consumer perspective. She: – "What does a series like this look like through the eyes of a policeman? Is it truthful or mere imagination?" He: – "It's a little exaggerated. But at least it's better than an American series". A formulated critical attitude to the realism of the series and a clear dissociation from the American model. But the consumer perspective is also more important. She: – "After all that death and killing it's nice to have a bit of company". Against the background of comfort and togetherness created by the unpleasantness on TV, this is a clear invitation to Karl Joergensen. He is not yet ready to accept it, but he will.

The quality of genre self-reflection is introduced into the plot through the tabloid newspaper *Ekstra Bladet*. In the 1970s, the paper had a campaign against string-pullers, slum landlords and speculators. For a long time in *Cop*, it looks as though the newspaper and the policeman can help each other, but the need for sensation and the editor contribute to the newspaper proving itself to be completely ineffective. The media exploit the stories of violence and do not contribute to the promotion of truth. Again there is disillusionment.

The harsh criticism of police, press and the social order in *Cop* was renewed over ten years later in the TV serial *Once a Cop*. The contrary and difficult Karl Joergensen has now settled down at the passport control office of Copenhagen Airport. In his leisure time he fishes from a boat and drinks beer (which he also does while on duty, although from a vacuum flask). A new, young generation of police personnel has arrived, providing hope for the future. There is a new woman, an airline stewardess, in the offing and he gets on well with his now adult daughter, even though he does not like her boyfriend.

But the boyfriend gets murdered and Karl Joergensen can continue where he left off in 1976 with the solution of crimes such as murder and violence which unerringly lead to the real big-shots at the top of society. The latter are not afraid to use dirty tricks. The young constables are effective allies for Karl Joergensen. Nevertheless, the odds are unfair and the serial ends with Karl Joergensen being liquidated by the bigshots. The hero is dead and the young are disillusioned. The scene in which Karl Joergensen's body is to be identified is constructed exactly as any other such scene: the white sheet is lifted from the face and the camera dwells for a moment on the victim. With this farewell, the director is also saying farewell, in a way, to the genre: its main character can no longer survive in a society like ours. The vigorous, strong man at odds with the police system and middle class society is dead.

The big-shots are charged but the evidence is not strong enough. This is not so strange, for the witnesses have systematically disappeared. From a bird's eye view, perhaps indicative of an even higher justice, we look down on the central court in Copenhagen with its inscription "Med lov skal man land bygge" (The Land Shall be Based on Law). The accused, a shipowner, a politician and a financier walk away without a word to the press – or with the single ironic remark: "Fortunately we live under the rule of law!"

In its narrative style, *Once a Cop* is in stark contrast to *Anthonsen*. It is well told and quickly cut in a narrative rhythm which corresponds with its strong elements of action and it clearly aims at an international standard of camera work and aesthetics. The journey through Europe and the exposure of the international nature of the crime harmonise well with this tendency. On the other hand, the message of the death of the genre goes against international currents. But it turned out to be true for Denmark, in the sense that the following years saw only a few decisive attempts at using the genre and renewing it.

It was precisely in 1988, the year in which the monopoly was broken, that DR prepared itself to meet new competition, often by taking up forms and genres that it expected a competitor to make use of. Partly as a continuation of this trend and partly as a lack of belief in the genre in its serious form, DR launched a comedy version of the genre, *Station 13* 1-8, 1988-89. The format was the typical half hour comedy format. *Station 13* can be characterised as *Hill Street Blues*, transferred to Danish circumstances and with the cosy atmosphere of the Danish tradition of popular comedy.

At the centre was life at the police station with all its ups and downs and conflicts both vertically between leadership and the rank and file, horizontally between former lovers and present colleagues, between various types of policeman, e.g. the seriously working policeman versus the 'eager notebook user'. The series captured the atmosphere and conflicts, including that between the two sexes, in the miniature community of the police station, in a way that everyone could transfer to any other workplace. The police were presented as very human, more interested in sex, flirtation, love, comradeship, career, and a drink rather than in the great questions about crime and society.

Against all expectations at DR, their competitor TV2 made only slight effort to take up the challenge. A single crime serial was produced by the new national channel, *Blaendet (Blinded)* 1-3 in 1992, with the series experts, Peter and Stig Thorsboe, as script writers. The psychology was heavy and the characterisation overdone. DR continued to produce serials with a little more success. *Moerklaegning (Blackout)* 1-4, also in 1992, was a psychological and atmospheric crime story taking place during the wartime occupation and had Anders Bodelsen as scriptwriter.

The Danish-Swedish production *Frihedens skygge (The Shadow of Freedom)* 1-4, 1994 about a retired policeman who turns to murder for the sake of love was a demonstration of talented camera work and cutting with a sense of timing and visual narrative but the plot creaked at the seams. Neither the scriptwriters, Birger Larsen and Joern O. Jensen, nor the director, Birger Larsen, succeeded in making the main story sufficiently relevant.[7] On the other hand, there was a series of sub-plots that worked well, and thus the production contributed to the development of using several subplots in crime fiction.

A relapse in terms of genre, though in a cut-price edition, was the last attempt of the provincial branch of DR in its *Vildspor (Wrong Track)* 1-3, 1996. Like *The Shadow of Freedom*, *Wrong Track* was produced on the basis of a novel, this time by Poul Oerum. The aim was clearly to catch once again the special atmosphere of the provincial town, but the result was lower than *The Flying Squad*.

This brief survey of genre shows that two tendencies within milieu and plot can be discerned. One is to develop the provincial setting and the silent characters, often with a touch of humour and a way of stressing mores instead of action, both at the police station and in the homes, as in *A Provincial Town*. In the other tendency, large cities and an international setting are connected with a stressing of action, importance of plotting, and a human and sympathetic character as action-minded policeman. *Once a Cop* is the main representative of this tendency. Elements from both types can be recognised in *Island Cop*.

The genre has been difficult. It has given rise to a dilemma. On the one hand, the national public service programmers and producers have felt a certain obligation to maintain it on the national level; this is seen in the fact that it has turned up, from time to time, in new forms. On the other hand, many of the international police series – with the Americans in the lead – have included a significant element of violence and action, that may have increased the appeal of the genre, both on commercial and on public service channels but which, at the same time, has been considered as deeply dubious by programme planners on the public service channels.

The dilemma of the genre has been tackled in various ways in different countries. But none has been able to avoid facing the new conventions of the genre. In Denmark, the challenge was taken up mildly in *The Shadow of Freedom*. But the attempt at a new orientation was here on the technical side rather than in terms of the basic material of the genre or of the field of ideas. *Island Cop* makes an attempt at renewing the genre by combining the two main tendencies, the provincial, that makes everything close and within scope, and the action-minded which demands that something should be done. It represents an attack on the basic message of *Once a Cop* that crimes are always connected with the top of society and persons you cannot hit. Instead, *Island Cop* focusses on concrete crimes played out before everybody on a level where they can be handled. In this way it follows the pattern of *A Provincial Town*. The protagonist in *Island Cop* successfully deals with crime whereas his counterpart in *Once a Cop* failed. However, they share traits such as individualism, stubbornness, masculinity, sense of action. How the tradition is treated is to be shown in detail during the following sections.

The Chief Character, Format and Genre

That an action hero connected with the police can be both masculine and half-bald, we had seen from the Swedish Carl Hamilton. That a policeman could be a single father and have some problems with the role of child minder, daily care and the legitimate demands of a daughter, we knew from the French Navarro. In *Island Cop*, the two types are combined and mixed in with the cop's human commitment and his good citizenship, as the role was played by Jens Okking in *A Provincial Town* and the *Once a Cop* serial. The result is a very sympathetic policeman, a stubborn loner who is not always right, but is so when it really matters.

In 1981, Geoffrey Hurd pointed out that most screen policemen are either divorced, separated, widowed or unmarried (Hurd, 1981: 60). This emphasises how difficult it is to combine a well-functioning or simply normal private life with a police career. The disadvantage was that this made the characters more "flat" than was necessary. Throughout the 1980s and 1990s, it has become more usual to include the private lives of detectives and policemen as a more or less noticeable ingredient in fiction that can make the character more "round" and operate as an extra tension-creating aspect in relation to the main plot.[8] Even Wycliffe, who otherwise represents the ultra-classical police detective, phones home to his wife from time to time in 1994 and asks how the children are. However, it is still the fact that a harmonious family life with children is seldom seen. It is perhaps too alien to the world of crime.

In this regard, the policeman on Samsoe is both typical and atypical. Christian Torp's marital status is that of the widower and thus in keeping with the genre's mainstream. More atypical is the importance which the influence of his past is given, the story of how it is to live on after a traumatic experience and try to come to terms with it. Torp's tragic past is sketched in the compressed picture narrative of the introductory sequences (episode 1) and is resumed in clips included in the introduction to the following episodes. It is thus given a central position in terms of an understanding of the situation and psychology of the main character.

In this background story, the happy family is represented in a point-of-departure, everyday situation familiar to us all. It is night, father and mother are driving in their car along a main road; mother is pregnant, the daughter is asleep on the rear seat and the two adults want to get home to sleep. But the fuel tank is nearly empty and this circumstance leads to a catastrophe. When the policeman sees a robbery at the petrol station, he can't avoid getting involved in spite of his wife's "Don't do it!" and the daughter's "Are we home now?" – There is a struggle, Christian Torp is in difficulties and his wife wants to help him. As she raises her arm with her stiletto-heeled shoe as a weapon, a shot rings out and she dies as the arbitrary victim, in the first instance of the armed robber's gun, in the second instance of her own husband's intervention.

This introduction characterises Christian Torp as a man of action, who does not distinguish between his work and his private life and whose spontaneous involvement overshadows cold deliberation. At the same time, we see the reasons for the feelings that characterise him: sorrow and protest at the arbitrariness of existence, expressed in a cry to heaven as he carries Sille around the deserted forecourt of the petrol station after the acknowledgement that his wife is dead. The point-of-departure situation also explains why Christian Torp is transferred to the island of Samsoe: he wants to get away from memories and a tiring daily life in the big city, out to a more peaceful existence as a village policeman on Samsoe.

The location of the island is ironically commented upon by the pompous lawyer, Lillian Lyttke, in the fourth episode: "The island in the middle, isn't that how you advertise it?" Like any island, Samsoe can be regarded as the ultimate province, defended on all sides against invaders by the sea, as is pointed out in the transition between the introductory sequence and each new episode, when the sea and the title text fill the whole screen. But as it turns out, the sea not only separates, it also joins together. People from Sweden, Germany and Brussels come by boat to Samsoe – as well as all those from Aarhus and Copenhagen. The island itself also contains a mass of conflicts that are eventually exposed. This will be treated more fully in the following sections.

For Christian Torp, the loss is the starting point – the loss of his wife and the unborn child, the loss of the city, the loss of the normal company of colleagues. The first loss is seen as the decisive one, through the insertion of a bridal picture of his wife in the introductory sequences of 2-6. But all the losses are included in the part of the plot which touches on Torp's personal development, his gradual adjustment to the norms and morals of the island and his situation as the solitary village policeman, who only has a secretary, albeit a very knowledgeable one. The loss of family is not a complete loss: he still has his very bright daughter with whom to share the ups and downs of his life.

The stress laid on private life has consequences for the treatment and structure of the genre in this series. On the one hand this is a series in the sense that each episode has an independent plot in traditional crime terms: a crime or crimes are committed and have to be solved. The institutions of law and order, the courts and prisons, are absent from the beginning and instead we get "the moment of capture", "the moment of conviction" or the movement "trial – truth" (Hurd, 1981: 57) as the culmination of the process of crime solving. Each episode can be viewed separately.

On the other hand, the producer cleverly provides us with more enjoyment if we see all or most of the episodes. This is because there are a number of developments in the private lives of the policeman, the secretary, Sille, the pastor couple and others. These developments cut across the single episodes and are often woven into the plot of the individual episode by giving rise to doubt, misunderstandings, hasty reactions or simply parallel actions that throw an oblique sidelight on each other. When, for example, the policeman exhibits sexual behaviour on the edge of the acceptable in relation to the secretary, who should she turn to? This will be treated further in the following sections. These individual stories mean that we here have a serial. The format is thus that of a series-serial.

The title indicates the genre to be a police series – possibly with an acknowledgement to Sjoewall and Wahloeoe's filmed novel *Strisser, strisser (Cop, Cop)* (in Swedish: *Polis, polis, potatismos!* 1970) and the *Stroemer* film. But where many recent police series emphasise the collective, the police station environment (on the *Hill Street Blues* pattern) or the working partners (*Miami Vice*), the Samsoe police station is of such a minimum size that it only consists of the village policeman and his secretary. Authority is on the mainland in Aarhus. The manning is thus reminiscent of that of a detective story, where the standard cast list is that of a male detective and a female secretary, cf. *Anthonsen*. This genre identification fits well with Christian Torp's individual attitude, to the fact that he avoids wearing uniform or police badge (which means, though, that he and Ulla are beaten up by a gang of bikers in episode 5) and that he does not clearly distinguish between his private life and his work. His official residence is, logically, above the police station and from the staircase between them, Sille is fond of observing and commenting on what is happening. The associations with the private detective are obvious and the western sheriff is almost brought to mind, cf. *McCloud*. But there are differences. The secretary, Ulla Snedker, is a very independent type, as is the daughter. From time to time, events, as well as the basic circumstance that the police station is so small, introduce a comic tone, which also comes to expression in characterisation and situations. In some ways, *Island Cop* is not far removed from traditional Danish popular comedy. Just as the format is a mixture of series and serial, the basic police crime genre contains a number of mixed elements – taken from the detective crime story, from everyday realistic fiction and from popular comedy. This is a help in the ambition to unite the two main traditions of the genre.

There are three basic levels in the presentation: 1) daily life on Samsoe, 2) the independent episodes about crime and detection, which usually contain several dependent plots or sub-plots; there may also be plots that happen to run together, 3) the personal and connected stories of the relationships between, first and foremost, Christian Torp, Ulla Snedker and Sille but also a number of other characters, both major and minor. The various levels are mutually linked. What happens on one level has relevance for the understanding of what happens on another. Cause and effect relationships are also established – and, of course, false trails. In the next section, I shall comment on each individual level whilst showing some examples of how they are related and using the 'fabula'/'sujet'-distinction to indicate how the plots work (or don't).

The Places and Times of Everyday Life

Back to clearness is essential as a point of departure. Samsoe is the perfect setting for this purpose. Everyday life on Samsoe is shown in the many pictures of everyday places: the harbour, which is the entrance to and exit from the island; the sea surrounding the island and which one can swim and fish in, sail on or simply look at, the harvested fields separated by the few roads; the main street; the houses and public places, the police station, church, pub and hospital.

But the rhythm of everyday life is also represented temporally by the daily rhythm, which is mimed. Each single episode occupies three to four days, where the daily rhythm is clearly marked in several ways. First and foremost, light plays a great part – the light in the sky at dawn and dusk, often caught in a symbiosis or contrast between sea and sky; the more sober light of morning and afternoon and the darkness of night. Several activities typically take place at the times of transition – for example, Torp's long jogging tours that mark times of rest, time for reflection. Viewers are helped also by linguistic indicators such as "Good morning" and "Good evening", "Go to bed" and "Eat your fish", as well as the sound of church bells ringing the sun up and down. The temporal indicators of everyday life are ever present, not primarily through the media, which are otherwise very widely used as temporal indicators, both in real life and in fictional representations, but through nature and culture. Even though Sille sometimes watches TV in the evening, it is the old-fashioned time indicators that are dominant. Again a sign that we are in the provinces.

In addition, time is also used to characterise persons. How the village policeman really finds time to sleep is something of a puzzle, for his job is a 24-hour one. At night he has to keep an eye on what is happening and try to prevent the worst, by day he has to solve crimes, and at dawn and dusk he has to ponder them. At the same time, he has his own life to live. No wonder that he says at one point "Sille has begun to wash her clothes herself".

The same conditions apply to Ulla, who has her 24 hours occupied with being a secretary, informer, practical helper, spiritual adviser, lover and substitute mother to Sille. No wonder that in the last episode, she makes a fatal mistake and demands time off in lieu of wages. Against the background of this marking of the daily rhythm and work ethics, it is cause for suspicion when someone behaves differently. In the first episode, the big-shot criminal and paedophile from Copenhagen doesn't start his morning shave until after the grocer and the pastor, the policeman and the secretary are in full activity. This brands him as a villain.

In keeping with the fact that it is the old-fashioned and not the media-based time indicators that count, it is not only the times of everyday life that are scanned. The ceremonies and ritual turning points in the lives of individuals are also accentuated and their stories are thus inscribed as part of the more long-term perspectives of a life or a generation. A wedding (episode 1), the preparation for confirmation and confirmation itself (episode 4), death and burial (episode 6) are mediated through the presence of the pastor.

At the police station, everyday time corresponds to the normal rhythm of police life, as seen when the only two employees discuss the police report. The morning after Torp's arrival on the island, Ulla sums up: "Four illegally felled birches – burglary at a summer cottage – a lost wallet ...", and next morning another case turns up – a wife who has been beaten by her husband but will not report him. Nothing very much is ever reported on Samsoe, people prefer to solve problems themselves, possibly with the help of the policeman. He thus has several functions in addition to his own. He gets clothes from the pastor's surplus store for the wife who has run away in her underclothes from her violent husband (episode 1), he mediates between and reconciles the lovers Kesse and Britt (episode 5) and he looks into the matter of Mrs. Bluhme's disappearing cat – albeit with an ulterior motive: Mrs. Bluhme is a neighbour to the criminal couple Bente and Peter Soenderholm and is sure to have seen something or other (episode 6). At the little police station, trivial everyday cases form a vibrant background to the whole series. In episode 2 there is "The theft on the car deck of the Hou ferry, the dog run over in Nordby, the meeting with the social services ...".

On the one hand, the firm rooting in everyday places and times is used to emphasise the provincial theme. On the other hand, it is also known in urban contexts, where in every local newspaper one can read about weddings, confirmations and funerals, thefts, lost dogs and household violence. All these things are the stuff of everyday life but it would not be a police series if everyday life was not disrupted by cases which disturb the surface of normality. Still this happens in a way which keeps the proportions of clearness.

Dark Deeds – the Closing Episodes

On the basis of a number of American, British and a single Italian, police series, Richard Sparks has extracted the basic features of the genre (Sparks, 1992: 115). As far as theme is concerned, his conclusion is that murder is the leading and most common crime, often for personal gain and related to a number of criminal ramifications, in the course of which the murder or murders take place (Sparks, 1992: 140-141). It's not like this in *Island Cop*. Here, attempted murder and suicide are more usual. There are two murders, but in both cases it is the victim who has been subject to an attack or attempted murder who strikes back and kills the criminal. There are two basic patterns for the development of the crimes.

The one is that evil, coming from the outside, arrives sailing to the island in the person of a paedophile drug dealer from Copenhagen (episode 1), a couple of Swedish bank robbers on the run (episode 3), some officials from Brussels (episode 4) or non-resident estate agents in the time-share business from Aarhus (episode 6). But evil cannot flourish without a counterpart among some permanent residents or new arrivals and this happens in all the cases mentioned, when the former drug dealer Kim, the verger Gilbert, the chairman of the arts council Bent Boegh, and the doctor Joergen Skaenk, respectively and through various degrees of active effort, assist the criminal activities.

The other basic pattern sees the crime arising within the island's own closed society. This happens in episode 2 where the Jehova's Witnesses are shown as an evil, life-threatening environment, both as a congregation and in the conflict-filled families in episode 3, which presents the hypocrisy of the leading figures of the island as well as the voyeuristic tendencies of the optician and, not least, in episode 5 where the ancient peasant society shows its face in a mother's persistent possessiveness towards her son.

Crime is thus seen as something which comes, more or less equally, from the outside as well as the inside and with mutual interaction. Only exceptionally, is there a deeper analysis of the psychology of the criminal. As is the rule in this genre (cf. Sparks, 1992: 141), motives are usually merely outlined. The most interesting from a psychological point of view are those cases where the hero and the villain are reflected in each other, or where they confront each other and where it is not completely clear which is which. The two basic patterns operate as continuity-creating factors. Another continuity-creating factor lies in the special relationship between the episodes.

Throughout, the individual episodes complement each other successively and thematically. The theme of episode 1, *En ven af familien* (*A Friend of the Family*), is the linking between ten-year-old girls, sexuality and death in a staging in which the concept of normality is examined. Briefly, the main plot is that the ten-year-old Maj, living with her mother and the latter's new lover Kim, is assaulted by the paedophile drug dealer, Kim's former employer, who has a hold on Kim and wants him to work for him again. Maj is an unusual girl. She is very fond of Kim and her feelings are returned. He almost seems more ready to marry the daughter than the mother. Maj mistreats her dolls, hanging them up on a string. She also has knowledge of poisons and makes a witches' brew of henbane. One evening after her future stepfather and then her mother have left her, she is alone at home – with the paedophile. His slow run-up to an assault she meets resolutely with a game in which they are to take turns at swallowing drinks of various colours – on the third turn, he chooses the witches' brew.

The episode thus continues the problem posed in the introduction: who can be held responsible for what? Does the victim, in a way, invite the criminal? Is it reasonable to defend oneself against rape by committing premeditated murder? Can a ten-year-old child be called to account? And what is to happen to Maj afterwards – is she to experience an incestuous relationship with her stepfather or will they become a happy family? For the time being, her mother saves Maj by the use of violence – she hits the drug dealer hard with a spade. But the look which Maj sends to Torp in the wedding situation shows that she, of course, knows better.

Episode 1 concentrates on death and sexual perversion. By contrast, the theme of episode 2, the title of which is *Jomfrufoedsel (Virgin Birth)*, is life. But not a life without problems. A new-born baby is left with the pastor and the first question is: who is the mother? And then: who is the father? In fact, viewers have known it from the start. The camera catches the guilty-to-be, and 'investigation' thus begins before any 'crime' has happened. A young girl, Karina, weeps while the preacher fulminates: "If the Lord wants a child to live, it will live. If the Lord has decided that it shall die, then you must not interfere". A young man, Simon, is watching her. The lines of conflict are drawn as we see the serious, aloof looks of condemnation on faces that clearly belong to the parent generation. Another form of perversion is at work, a misanthropic sectarianism which makes an enemy of every individual if he/she behaves humanely and against the norms of the religious society. The 'fabula' can be reduced to the following: Hans Beyer, the father of the newly-fledged mother, tries to kill both mother and child, but Torp and Ulla prevent it.

The hand of the female scriptwriter can be sensed. Blood plays an important role in this episode. However, it is not the blood of a murder victim as would be normal in this genre, but the blood from a clandestine and premature birth. Karina's father tries to wash it away but there are traces outside the house, which is also a reminder of how old the theme of unwanted life is. It is therefore logical that the girl, who in the first shot is seen running through the fields with blood running down her legs, in the next bird's eye view is seen quite small against the field, with shadows dominating the picture right up to the horizon.

The first episode concentrates on the main plot. In the second episode, the sub-plot slowly begins to develop. The relationship between Ulrik and Ditte is a less brightly lit parallel to the relationship between Karina and Simon. Apparently, the female pastor and her husband do not have an especially harmonious relationship; she receives threatening letters accusing her of murder (she has had an abortion). Expelled from Jehova's Witnesses, the fisherman, Fisker Jens, is living alone in the hills and is seen in an ambiguous relationship with the pastor.

In continuation of the reflections on the functioning of crime seen in episode 1, the importance of various standards for the definition of what constitutes crime is underlined in the theme of this episode. That which is legitimate in society in general, is a crime among the sect – such as having sexual relations and giving birth outside of marriage, having an abortion as has the pastor and having blood transfusions. And vice versa: what is legitimate within the sect is a crime in society, such as trying to kill one's own daughter. Suspense and thus concept of time is crucial: will Ulla and Torp know what the viewers know in time to prevent catastrophies?

The unwanted baby places the relationship between Ulla Snedker and Christian Torp in sudden relief. The previous night they had been to bed together for the first time and Ulla is satisfied with the night but certainly not with the morning after, when Torp indicates that it is business as usual. Her comment is: "Not every child is conceived in love, is it Christian Torp?" – His prompt reply is: "You are taking precautions, aren't you?" Here is a good example of the interplay between two levels, that of private life and the plot of the episode. This is visually emphasised by a sudden shot of a little new-born baby immediately after Torp's worried remark. A graphic illustration of possible consequences!

In episode 3, *Kiggertsyn* (*Peeping Tom*), there are even more sub-plots and a viewer must wonder what connection there is between a photographing voyeur, a dead man on a bench, the beaten-up prostitute, Jeannette, attacks on Taxa Ejvind and on the verger, Gilbert, a Swede in a boat, Keld Bloendal's nocturnal bird-watching – and a church concert at which the blind organist, Elisabeth, is to play Bach? The surprising connection is that all these situations can be linked to the hunt for 260,000 D-mark that have disappeared – and that the voyeur has captured it all on film, except for one situation where he himself has been unwittingly captured by the camera of another observer.

The plot of this episode is very-well constructed. The title and the many layers of observation lead to speculation about the relationship between seeing and being seen, what is not seen, not being able to see and seeing with the distance created by a camera – to photograph and be photographed. The point is that the audience is forced to try to understand the relationship between subject and object, who sees what and with what kind of eyes, in order to follow the plot. At one point, the audience only has the simple clicking sound of photographs being taken in the darkness of the middle of the night. It is the decisive image that is supplied in this way and the enjoyment consists, of course, in the reconstruction of this moment later, when we know what it means. It is Keld, who photographs a little tern on the main street of the town and unknowingly catches a picture of the optician, Frederik, who also photographs birds, but is especially fond of focussing on the intimate moments of other people. The observer becomes the observed.[9]

The ending is a tour de force of exposure. It seems that most of the officials on the island have been visiting the island's prostitute, Jeannette, and many have also been involved in the hunt for the missing money. It is therefore very suitable that the pictures and the money rain down over the audience at the scandalous church concert. The private and the financial are made public in real style.

Thematically, it is striking how the interplay between several levels is made to work. Torp, who as a policeman should be able to find out the identity of the voyeur, has to put himself in the criminal's place and lie in wait outside the window of the lovers, who had been photographed the night before. He falls asleep at his post during the lovers' argument and wakens to the sound of their lovemaking. But when the real voyeur fails to turn up, he hurries home – where Ulla is looking after Sille. He carries Ulla to bed and rips the clothes off her whilst she, half willing, half resisting, talks hectically: "Do you know the feeling that there is someone watching you ... sometimes you feel as though you are being used ...". Here the situation of watching is rubbed off onto the watcher, which is visually expressed in his raffish smile. This small example shows how the sujet gives food for thought, before the viewer can see through the underlying context in the fabula.

As the title shows, the theme of surveillance is given special attention in this episode. But again it is a matter of a theme that is repeated with various stressings. By definition, the role of the police is that of surveillance. The pastor's husband, Keld, is another watchful surveillant who, very conveniently, can also take on the role of suspect in various situations. In general, people in the island society keep an eye on each other: "That's the wonderful thing about this island. Just as you think you are alone – you're not" (Christian Torp at the end of episode 5). In this part the connection between fabula and crime, investigation and sujet, is highly developed. The camera presents one little bit after another to the viewer who can then reconstruct the crimes. The different subplots have the effect that the reconstruction can easily fail – which is the point.

That the local politicians on the island are hypocritical is revealed incidentally in episode 3. Episode 4, *Besoeg fra Bruxelles (Visit from Brussels)*, connects with this theme in a plot that once again mixes main plot with sub-plot. The subplot about the 14-year-old Heidi, who runs away from home because she is unhappily in love, leads Heidi and thus the viewers around the island. This wandering leads her directly into the main plot, the theme of which is power and the cliquishness of the power-seekers: the local politicians have joined with an EU politician to get a convention centre for Samsoe, paid for by the EU Fund for Development. It is hinted that the municipal interest in this project is to get rid of a plot of polluted ground and the possibility of personal gain is what drives the EU Commissioner, Joergen Sivertsen, and his lawyer partner, Lillian Lyttke. Everyone connected with the project is presented as more than usually unsympathetic and the project collapses with the disclosure of their human failings. Sivertsen and Lyttke can look forward to a charge of assaulting their female companion; Lyttke has wounded her and together, they try to smuggle her off the island, hidden in the boot of a dark blue Audi. Bent Boegh, chairman of the arts council, can expect a charge of attempting to rape Heidi.

This plot shows what happens when external forces are united with internal forces in business that is financially and morally improper. The problem is, though, that the characters are almost caricatures and even though the problems as such may be topical, the plot is not very exciting. It is obvious from the start that an enterprise run by such villainous characters is bound to fail. Fabula forces itself too much upon sujet, with a resulting loss of tension.

The symbolism is similarly heavy. Sivertsen and Lyttke behave literally like bulls in a china shop, when the super villain and lesbian, Lyttke, shoots at plates which Sivertsen casts into the air, without thinking that the line of fire points directly at her female partner. The local chairman of the arts council is presented as ridiculous in his pandering to his partners and is also drunk, corrupt and selfish. The caricature turns finally into coarse comedy when, during a public hearing, Bent Boegh suddenly sits down on the model of the proposed convention centre. Characterisations and situations like these mean that, from time to time, the episode has more the character of a popular comedy than that of a criminal story. This episode is thus borne along not by its plot nor by an elegant relationship between sujet and fabula but by the serial structure.

Popular comedy is also present in episode 5, *Den sjove mand* (*The Funny Man*), but in a more melodramatic version. The archetypical theme in a rustic country like Denmark is the farm and inheritance. This theme is here taken up in a clear reference to the popular novels of Morten Korch, which are nearly all concerned with the relationship between property, national sentiments and succession, with an admixture of melodramatic and merry staging.[10] In this version, the merry element is represented by a rather amateurish stand-up comedian from Copenhagen who tries to throw a humorous light on everyday situations. The melodramatic element is introduced by the farmer's widow, Telma Oester, and she is almost as un-professional. Her attitude to her daughter-in-law, Lotte, is indicated by the following line: "When you come from nothing and marry into one of the largest farms on the island, then ...". Once again the relationship between fabula and sujet fails, the fabula being too predictable and the sujet thus too easy to see through.

Lotte and her husband Johan are sorrowing over the death of their five-year-old daughter. Lotte is depressed. The plot now is that everyone who could help Lotte fails her because of chance and unfortunate circumstances, while the mother-in-law systematically drives her towards the apparently unavoidable suicide. Telma Oester is an old-fashioned fanatic of the same type as Hans Beyer in episode 2, to which this episode is thematically linked. She is a symbol of the fact that the ancient rural society, in which mother, son and daughter-in-law live under the same roof, still has a destructive power of the same character as that of the Jehova's Witnesses. She is the very incarnation of the decadent consequences of convention.

The unambiguous characterisation, the theme of property and the alternation between comedy and melodrama fit very well into the Morten Korch pattern. The association is also strengthened by the visual and audio aspects. The camera dwells on the countryside and the farm, just as the church and time are emphasised more than is usual. There are two sunrises and two sunsets with the related bell ringing.

On the other hand, Morten Korch's novels, the films based on them and popular comedy in general usually end happily with reconciliation and the willingness of the young generation to follow in the footsteps of the old. This is not true of this episode, where the crime consists of wanting to own another person's life and fate: Telma Oester wants only the best for her son and thus spoils his life. Viewed from this point of view, the ending also contains an accusation against the local community for being silently privy to the destruction of a human being – and a criticism of the genre which has especially pictured such local communities positively, the harmony-seeking popular comedy. Thus, it is not just the old, fanatical, self-opinionated community that is displayed but also the new one, in which people are too superficial or too busy to get involved.

The linking of genre inspiration and genre criticism, pastiche and exposure doesn't, however, seem to be quite clear. The crime of the mother against her daughter-in-law and her son is followed by the fact that the son strips himself naked and burns down the farm. An action which is more in accord with the melodramatic than with the criminal. The plot is thus more inclined to drama than to the crime genre.

Again there is a link to the next episode, *Rebet* (*The Rope*), this time the suicide theme. Episode 6 opens with a classic shock effect – a boy in pyjamas swinging from a tree – it is full moon – a wandering, mentally disturbed person cuts down the body. It is Fisker Jens, whom we remember from episodes 2 and 3. Even though suspicion can be directed against Fisker Jens, it is clear to viewers from these introductory shots that he is a witness rather than a murderer. But this is just an approach to the main theme, child abuse, which has been treated earlier, in episode 1, and which was followed up by the physical and mental abuse of Karina in episode 2 and the attempted rape of Heidi in episode 4. The child abuse theme is also linked with a local corruption scandal of the same type, seen in episode 4. The threads are drawn together in the series/serial's last episode.

The local doctor is more interested in the selling of timeshares and shady loans than in attending to his practice. He is thus part of the general misuse of public office. As a mediator he makes use of the Soenderholm couple who, in their turn, use any means to earn money to pay for their drug addiction. This includes fostering children, who are abused so badly that one of them has hanged himself. The two others live mostly tied up in the cellar, hungry and frightened. That the doctor does not especially inspire confidence is indicated from the beginning, when he is called to Sille, who has a sore throat. He seems uninterested and superficial and Sille's comment is "He was very quick, dad".

Later the doctor turns up at the pub and the harbour. The persistent rumours that the Soenderholm's foster child has hanged himself he opposes with violence. He tries to kill the witness, Fisker Jens, with cylinder gas in the boat's galley. Jens is saved by Torp and has his revenge. He sees to it that it is the doctor who dies instead. Of course, this is done by hanging. Here we have a new version of the theme of episode 1. An obvious victim, respectively a child and a simpleton – as well as being known as 'Fisker Jens' (Fisherman Jens) he is known as 'Tosse Jens' (Crazy Jens) – reacts against an abuse by committing murder or suggesting suicide and in both cases, the taking of the law into their own hands is sanctioned by the fact that the representative of the law, Torp, conceals his knowledge. It must, though, be noted that neither we nor Torp see exactly what happens. It might be a matter of yet another suicide. What we – and Torp – see is that Jens approaches the Soenderholm house with the rope, Joergen Skaenk comes out and is then seen hanging from the tree that we saw the boy in pyjamas hanging from at the beginning.

The moral of this repeated story is that not all crimes are solved and that some of the unsolved are best hidden in the category of silent knowledge. Child abuse is seen as an injustice that gives the right to take the law into one's own hands in self-defence or revenge. This aspect is emphasised by Sille's function in the same context. Torp says to the Soenderholms: "I have a ten-year-old daughter myself, so ...". Just as in episode 1, she is a parallel to, and a mirror image of, the victims. There, she becomes friendly with Maj and might thus offer her a more normal childhood. That she succeeds in this, we see briefly in episode 2 when the two girls splash around in the water with a bathing ring. Here, it goes even further, since Sille plays an active part in the lives of the children. When Torp has been forbidden to work on the case and Ulla claims that the doctor is a respectable person and since she is also involved with an old flame, there is only Sille to help with the solution. The awful Soenderholms and the doctor are presented just as unattractively as the villains in the other episodes. That the plot doesn't quite fail, is due to the serial structure and Sille's role in it. The fabula is relatively quickly discovered which is also due to the missing sub-plots.

Analysing the episodic stories has exposed several features. Firstly, the crimes and the police environment that are shown are atypical of the mainstream of this genre, whilst quite clearly making use of the conventions of the genre. The list of crimes includes injustices rooted in sexual instincts and religious beliefs as well as the maintenance of status and political or financial gain. The crimes are either related to existential categories like death-life or child-youth-adult or to social and political categories and thus range relatively wide. The concept of clearness is kept through all possibilities.

Secondly, the plots of the episodes comprise complete stories but they follow upon each other in a complementary structure in which the individual plots supplement and fill out each other thematically in continued attempts to clarify the questions of crime and guilt. Crime originates both internally and externally: from abroad and the rest of Denmark as well as from the closed communities of Samsoe; from external accidents of a more or less random character and from internal human urges such as lack of concern for others, egoism, lust for money and power, various kinds of religious or sexual extremism.

Thirdly, not all episodes are equally successful. The best contain several subplots or work on a conception where the sujet offers the viewer different possibilities, suggested by different camera angles and forms of tacit knowledge. If there is a lack of tension in the relationship between sujet and fabula the plot inevitably suffers.

Forthly, if the mixture of genres is weighted too much towards the pattern of popular comedy and – combined with this – if the characterisation is too simple, problems arise again. Either the sub-plots or the on-going stories of the lives of Christian Torp, Ulla Snedker and Sille must compensate for this. In which ways will be analysed in the following section.

The On-going Life Stories

As suggested, one of the pleasures of *Island Cop* lies in the serial structure and thus in the on-going stories, large and small, which the structure involves. I have already provided examples of successful relationships between the episode level and the serial level. I want now to establish the type of the on-going stories and then characterise the qualities that are found in the three chief characters and the relationship between them. The on-going stories can be divided into several types.

First, there are the little, amusing stories. These may well be inspired by popular comedy but, as such, are more successfully integrated than when major sub-elements of the genre are found in the context. An example can illustrate this. On his arrival at the police station in Tranebjerg, Torp meets his predecessor's dog, Frede. He does not like dogs and wants it put down. Already in episode 2, he has accepted it, without anything special having been said about it. In the rest of the episodes, Frede appears indispensable to both father and daughter. This little story is used here as an amusing comment: the dog-hater is turned into a dog-lover, at least as far as Frede is concerned. The moral is that one has a point of view until one adopts a different one.

Similarly, there is a little on-going story about cars. The policeman's first official act on the island is to declare the pastor's old car to be illegal and to remove the number plates from it. In episode 2, she has got a new and more beautiful, silver coloured car. The irony is that Torp's own official car, a large Volvo, is not in very good condition. The island's mechanic does not seem very keen to repair it. Torp has problems and it ends with him getting a new car more acceptable to the mechanic.

Sometimes, a whole context is contained in a few lines. In the last episode Sille asks: "Ulla, have you eaten much fish?" This is because Sille thinks that Ulla is very beautiful and the question refers to a previous scene showing Sille sitting in the pub picking at her fish and Torp remarks that girls become beautiful from eating fish.

Another way of making use of the on-going stories is more person-orientated. It consists of minor characters in one episode having a more prominent position in another one. This provides a certain continuity and context without it interrupting the episode structure very much. Thus in episode 2, Fisker Jens is seen in his isolated house, where we see a photograph of him with his family: father, mother and two children. In episode 3, he is seen in church at a time inconvenient for all of them involved in the affair of the missing D-mark. He takes communion and is given absolution.[11] In episode 6, he is seen as the chief witness and main character in the story which unfolds around the rope. Here, again, we see his family, this time as names on a gravestone in the churchyard. We are never told why they are dead but must guess at a possible connection between their membership of Jehova's Witnesses and their deaths. Jens represents the hidden drama that never comes to the surface.

The prostitute, Jeannette, is another character who similarly takes varying positions throughout the episodes. First we see her in black as the punishing 'mother', ordered and paid for by the paedophile customer. Then we see her in church as the friend of the pastor. In episode 3, she achieves a more prominent position. A bank robber is holding a newspaper in which we get a glimpse of her presentation of herself in a newspaper small ad: "Sweet Jeannette available for activities mild and hard in comfortable surroundings, Monday to Friday 5 – 11 pm, Strandstien 7, Tel. 8659 2913". The advertisement casts a sidelight back to her behaviour in the scenes shown in episode 1. She is the victim of a violent attack and an indirect cause of the public scandal in the church. But in episode 4 she is again seen with a customer in a suit: in spite of violence and exposures, life goes on as usual.

The same can be said of the taxi driver, Taxa Ejvind, who carries people, information and rumours with equal energy. He also appears in episode 3, where the point is that, like all the men of the island, he goes out of his way to please Jeannette. This model can be applied to a number of other persons, whose characters or circumstances are elucidated in a particular episode, e.g. the pub waitress, Bodil, the pub regular and mechanic, Kesse etc.

A third type marks the further development of this person-centred form in relationship to the characters who continue throughout all episodes. First and foremost, there is the female pastor and her husband. Dorthe and Keld do not have a very happy marriage. He has not found work on the island, she has plenty to attend to. He watches over her – "the little blackbird" as he says in episode 2 – as well as his other birds. She is annoyed by his jealousy and his clinging to her and she is also a little in love with the policeman, even though he has condemned her car.

From a traditional gender role pattern, it is an example of role reversal. She is a modern, self-supporting and independent woman.[12] She has chosen – at least for the time being – not to have children. She earns money and has taken over traditional male activities such as playing billiards at the pub, swearing and drinking beer. Her performance of her religious duties is based on a very literal interpretation of the words of Jesus. She spends time with those on the fringes of the small community, e.g. the prostitute, Jeannette, she visits the ostracised Fisker Jens, she has appointed the former criminal, Gilbert, as verger. As her husband says to the policeman in episode 2: "Our pastor is very good at combining spiritual work with social work". At the same time, she also attends to the more traditional subsidiary tasks of a pastor such as coffee and cakes combined with needlework for the elderly ladies of the parish, collecting used clothing for charity and church concerts. Finally, she is also seen attending to her functions proper as a pastor: wedding preparations and the wedding ceremony, confirmation preparations and confirmation, church services. We also hear about funerals.

The relationship between Dorthe and Keld is one under development. It is extremely unsure at first. He believes that she is unfaithful to him. She first suspects him of voyeurism: "Where were you last night?" (episode 3), then she attacks his whole life: "Your restlessness drives me mad. Damn it, there must be some birds you can go and look at ... and then there's your perpetual jealousy" (episode 4). In the public bar of the pub, she gets drunk and makes passes at the policeman, after Keld has told her that he is going away for a few days. We see no reconciliation, but the relationship has clearly improved in the last two episodes. To a certain extent, Keld has changed his role from that of observer to policeman's assistant. Dorthe has always been an informant and thus there is now a degree of cooperation. Correspondingly, Keld now expresses more recognition than scepticism of her work as a pastor: "I know that she is young and a woman and all that. Maybe she's too young for me. But she's not so bad" (episode 5).

The fourth and most important type of on-going story relates to the three main characters and is partly about their personal development and partly their development in relation to each other. Christian Torp's and Sille's past histories are presented in the introductory sequence and the question raised is, of course, how can one continue one's life after such a traumatic loss. There are several answers.

One answer is connected with work. It soon turns out that it is not just an easy job being a policeman on Samsoe, but a meaningful occupation, which soon comes to fill all twentyfour hours. At the same time, it is far from problem-free. It is typical of every small local community to regard newcomers sceptically and reluctantly, and on an island, this attitude can be even more marked. At the same time, it is naturally important to have good relationships with the local policeman, in other words to integrate him into the special rules and regulations that apply on the island. This is thematised in the introduction, from both points of view. Torp and Sille are looking from the ferry across the nondescript, blue-grey waters towards the land and Torp says: "There's something about an island, isn't there? Something special". At the same time, the locals at the pub are discussing the new policeman and recalling how it was when his predecessor came to the island: "He was easy to handle".

The local community is suspicious but is prepared for a policy of integration in the interests of both parties. This involves turning a blind eye to minor infractions such as, primarily, cheap, rusty, and therefore illegal, cars with their bad brakes, the grocer's illicit sale of drinks and the flourishing black market, where fish and vegetables are exchanged for various services.

The integration policy succeeds in a minor way but fails in its major measures. Torp, who in the beginning forced the pastor to get a new car, refused to accept a bucket of plaice every Tuesday, demanded the guest list from the hotel and a bill from the car workshop, ends by accepting vegetables and letting the mechanic have the old Volvo. The problem is the obvious one that things won't work if he doesn't accept the rules, e.g. the car will not be properly repaired. But it's a long way from minor corruption to the corruption which some of the other officials on the island are involved in. This, Torp continues to fight against, which is especially stressed in the final episode where almost everyone, even Ulla, is mistaken with regard to the doctor's trustworthiness. On the other hand, he endorses the islander's tradition of managing things for themselves without interference from the mainland and, to a certain extent, the accompanying tradition of taking the law into their own hands. Torp who initially asserts that Samsoe abides by the same laws as the rest of Denmark, thus accepts a certain amount of unofficial, unwritten, local legislation. Therefore, he is accepted by the island community. That integration has also succeed from his point of view is seen in the fact that Torp, who is finally offered a transfer, chooses to stay on Samsoe.

Another answer is provided by his family situation and his relationship to Ulla which, of course, mixes his private life with his work. Even though the family has become smaller, it is still there and father and daughter need each other. They both miss the motherly and womanly element. Even though Torp is a loving and humorous father he is not always aware of his daughter's basic needs. A special problem is that of feeling secure at night: "I don't like to be alone at home" (episode 2). Sille has nightmares about the killing, shown visually by her seeing images of her dead mother's face with a little streak of blood suddenly running out of the mouth. At the Soenderholm house, where her father has sent her to spy, she imagines that she phones to her mother: "We miss you". The remoteness is illustrated visually by the frosted glass, through which we see Sille. Nevertheless, Sille develops to be almost more mature than her father. She sees through her father's hesitation about becoming emotionally involved with a new woman and she challenges him again and again about his attitude to it, thus disclaiming any actuality of the stepmother myth.

Sille develops into her father's companion, adviser, secretary and finally, partner. She asks in a friendly and somewhat frivolous way about developments in his relationship with Ulla: "I think she fancies you a bit. That's something we women notice!" Following her father's hesitation, there is the following dialogue: Sille: – "You're sleeping with her". Torp: – "Once!" Sille: – "Twice!" Torp: – "Well maybe twice. That's what happens. When it's hot". Sille: – "You are using her" ... Torp: – "I'm only in love with you, I suppose?" (episode 3).

Torp's expression is deprecating and surprised but he refrains from the traditional parental protest at the precise language used by children and accepts the friendly attitude which lies behind it. There is thus a clear female alliance directed against Torp.

In continuation of this friendly relationship lie the roles of adviser, secretary and partner. Here, too, Sille and Ulla are on the same side. The most amusing expression of this is seen in episode 4, where Ulla characterises Torp in a situation where she has decided to put a brake on his usual, no-nonsense approach to sex, while she strokes his stomach: "A bit callous. Reactionary. Old-fashioned. Struggling against the dog". Torp: ... ? – "The beast within". In the meantime, Sille has taken on the role of secretary and has received the message that the runaway Heidi has been found, and has sent an ambulance for her. At home on the staircase, in the space between the public and the private areas, she makes a comment which is a reflection of Ulla's: "I don't understand why you run around like a dog every night and ... why in hell don't you marry her?" Torp: – "Well that's where the shoe pinches – but I won't". Sille: – "No because you daren't". Torp: – "I am married". In the final episode when Torp has a rival, Sille, quite logically, advises her father to leave Ulla alone a bit. In episode 4, Sille begins to take on the role of secretary, when none of the adults are present. This continues in episode 5 and she ends as his partner during the solution of the mystery of the Soenderholm's foster children.

Sille's life on Samsoe is, then, a development process with an increasing measure of independence, responsibility and authority. She never takes on the role as mother for her father, even though she protects him in a situation when he is with Ulla and she claims that his absence is due to influenza. She moves more and more from being depressed and dependent to being an active partner. Of course, independence makes her more vulnerable, as the ending shows. Both as a potential victim – parallel with Maj – and as an active helper – parallel with Ulla – the Sille figure contributes tension to the story.

Torp's basic emotional attitude – "I am married," – (cf. above) must, of course, create problems in his relationship with an attractive woman like Ulla. Their relationship undergoes a number of changes. It starts with his demonstrative rejection of her scarcely hidden invitation in episode 1. Their attitudes here are in opposition. – She regards him as being both a knowall and uninformed in relation to the island and its traditions. He regards her as "a little, corrupt police secretary". At the same time, there is attraction in the air, on both sides.

Throughout the following episodes there are two sequences where pictures and music express the emotional relationship between them, as they go to bed together. The attraction is immediate and violent, so violent that it creates problems for them both. Ulla feels herself used, as she herself says, and this is repeated by Sille. She misses foreplay and the subsequent affection, tenderness, understanding, interest. Torp is ambivalent, his body has the reflexes of a dog (see the description above), but his mind is burdened with guilt and can't keep up.

The silent sequences where it is only the bodies which speak, emphasised by music, soft lighting and the lingering camera work are followed by vocal sequences. Here again, it is a matter of teaching the language of love and the language of womanhood, which is what Ulla attempts to do. The first time is in the morning after the first night together, when the surly Torp immediately throws himself into his work and Ulla forces him to repeat what they had done during the night: "You were so wonderful last night!" (Torp repeats it) ... "And soft and warm and willing". Torp: – "And soft and wet and willing". The slip of the tongue reveals to her that for him it is a matter of sex more than love.

This does not prevent Ulla from trying again, this time by talking about women's problems. Sitting over a beer on the harbour in episode 4, Torp tells her about his thoughts concerning Sille's growth to womanhood, including when "it starts". Ulla: – "Do you mean menstruation?" – Torp: – "mmmm" ... Ulla: – "Not yet. I'll talk to her about it. If you promise me one thing. Say the word yourself!"

She gives him another chance to learn the language of love in episode 4. In a situation where he visits her late at night, she tries to replace his urgency with slowness, his dark with light, his clichés with something he really means. She finds it difficult to get him to look her in the eyes, he looks down most of the time with only sideways glances at her and he is foolish enough to say, "Yes, and you don't remind me of anyone I have met before," as he switches off the light.

In the last episode, Ulla has given up trying to get any further in their relationship and she abandons it in the full light of publicity, on the dance floor with her old boyfriend, Henrik, when Torp barges in and she says: "Ever since you came to the island, I have had to be secretary and mother substitute and get you off the hook and be your secret lover when it suited you! ... I'll fetch my things tomorrow". But the fact that Torp had been right in the matter of the foster children means that Ulla finally changes sides. At least, the policeman gets a kiss on the shoulder from behind, in the final situation.

We can summarise by saying that the various types in the on-going stories support each other in many different ways. Longitudinally, both contrasts and parallels can be seen in Dorthe and Keld's relationship and in Ulla and Torp's. Passion is the contrasting element. There is not much of it in the pastor's home but enough at the police station. On the other hand, both relationships have their ups and downs. In this they resemble each other. Transversly, there are always various kinds of mirrorings in relation to the plots of the episodes (see the examples mentioned earlier). The chief on-going actors are powerful enough that their stories continue to be interesting, even when the plots of the episodes are less convincing.

The analysis of the episodal and serial plots and the many relationships between them has shown that there are three superordinate themes, around which Island Cop revolves: 1) crime, 2) gender and 3) the provinces. Above, I have called attention to a number of general and specific features to be seen in the treatment of these themes. In what follows, I shall suggest an interpretation which takes in these themes as well as the narrative style and the relationships to the genre which I outlined initially.

Crime, Point of View and Mirrorings

In *Island Cop*, there are a number of mirrorings, not especially demonstrative or thematically emphasised, but rather as a natural part of the scenography of everyday life which characterises the series in general. In episode 1, for example, we see Ulla applying her lipstick, on the morning after her arrival. Torp is looking at her, first in the mirror and then direct. Later in the same episode, we see the paedophile shaving, the door behind him opens and Kim enters. All this is seen in the mirror. A mirror is not even necessary for this mirroring effect to arise. Thus, Torp is captured in episode 2 as he leans in over his car and the roof of the car reflects a distorted miniature picture of him. Similarly, the sea around Samsoe is a macro mirror for the sky and the clouds, the weather and the seasons – and, from time to time, for people. As already pointed out, the whole of episode 3 is concerned with the relationship between experiencing and being reflected – in the pictures produced by the concealed camera – with the relationship between activity and registering, open and concealed.

The basic rule in crime story plots is to present the information in measured portions at the right time and place, to organise the distribution and supplying of knowledge, to arrange the sujet so that the underlying fabula is reconstructed in the correct tempo. In *Island Cop*, viewers receive a great deal of information, including some which Torp has to work hard to obtain. Purely visually, the viewer often has superior knowledge, cf. the examples reviewed above. Sometimes, Ulla or Sille knows something which Torp does not yet know (on the basis of a newspaper cutting, Sille identifies the paedophile as the drug dealer, before her father knows). And if we are unobservant on the visual side, there is the sound track, the music of which often underlines the visual aspect and through its leitmotifs makes the viewer aware when something worth noticing is happening. A specific sinister theme, borne by a double descent in the strings, warns of danger. At the same time, information is withheld on the visual side and the cutting between the various plots means that we move from one context to another. We are mystified. Similarly, the danger theme of the music may be wrongly placed in order to lead us on false trail (as when the descent in the strings is linked with Fisker Jens).

Always within the framework of everyday life and the conventions of realistic aesthetics, the various forms of mirrorings quietly indicate that here are perspectives, and especially varying perspectives, where we do not always know what the others are seeing and understand by what they are seeing. The mirrorings emphasise the elementary fact that we only ever see part of the truth, that the narrative exists within a framework, as a segment of a whole which we only eventually become aware of. The recurrent mirrorings pose the question: how do we see ourselves and others? And in the last analysis: who are we? What are we capable of?

This is where the mutuality of the mirrorings can be drawn into play. We not only see things and each other from various points of view, but we are also reflected in each other. This applies to individuals and groups of individuals reciprocally, as already mentioned, but it also applies in larger contexts. The Jehova's Witnesses have a Bible quotation hanging in their assembly hall: "They being knit together in love, Col. 2:2" (episode 2). Their relationships to each other and their actions make a mockery of the quotation. But their miniature community also casts a sidelight upon the slightly larger community in which they live: in reality are not the same forms of intolerance, superiority, and hypocrisy found among the leaders of this community as they are among the sect? And perhaps this is true not only of the leaders of Samsoe. From time to time, even the charming and tolerant police secretary suffers from narrow-mindedness and prejudice. The problem of those who take the law into their own hands is present, even among those who administer justice. When Ulla organises a group to escort the bikers who have attacked her and Torp to the ferry, this is amusing (episode 5). But is it discretion or corruption when Torp ignores an incitement to suicide or murder?

This problem is close to the classic mirroring between detective and criminal. The detective has to know something of crime in order to be able to recognise, discover and prevent it. He has to be able to reconstruct a crime and the psychology of the criminal, to put himself in the criminal's place. Christian Torp is far from being a demoniacal type. His strength lies not in being an observer, supervisor and thinker – his assistants are far better at that. His strength lies in action aimed at preventing crime or at redressing its consequences. But it is precisely in this respect that he resembles the criminals who, with few exceptions among the professionals, do not work on the basis of careful plans which can be reconstructed but who, to a much greater degree, act instinctively.

Gender: a Half Somersault with Twist

Christian Torp has, then, some of the characteristics of the action hero. In *Single White Male: tv-actionserien i 90erne (Single White Male – the TV action series in the 1990s)*, Rikke Schubart says that, irrespective of type, the action hero in international TV is a single white male between twenty and forty (Schubart, 1997a: 65). This is true of Torp. According to Schubart, it is typical of the action series that the hero's past history is told in a compressed version at the beginning. The same type of visual history introduces *Island Cop*. Furthermore, Torp shares with the action hero the fact that he starts marginalised. By marginalisation I mean that the hero is in crisis, socially, psychologically and in terms of his career and that precisely this combination characterises the initial situation.[13] Henrik, Ulla's former boyfriend, calls Torp a halfwit thus emphasising what he regards as the primitive in the policeman's character. Torp shares other characteristics with the action hero: he is emphatically masculine with a clear attractiveness for women, he ignores all emotional and practical considerations in pursuit of his goal, he is a workaholic with very little need of sleep and his crime solving success rate is quite high.

Even though all these qualities are present, they are not shown unrealistically, either because Torp can suddenly deny them ("Let's sleep on it!", episode 2) or because he also represents opposite tendencies. He may be 'single' but he is also a father, and his daughter has not been sent to live with her grandmother, even though, on one occasion, there is a move in that direction. He may be a loner and an individualist but he is also caring and loving (towards Sille) and in love and jealous (towards Ulla). Despite the action orientation, the picture is not unambiguous. The action hero has performed a half somersault with twist and has landed with a human face.

Contributing to this partial conversion is the context in which Torp finds himself. He may be surrounded by women who, in principle and based on traditional concepts and situations, ought to be easy to associate with: the dependent daughter, not yet in puberty; the secretary who is dependent on him as her immediate superior; the pastor, herself married and with the welfare of the human soul as her main task. The problem is that the structure of authority is shown as being unsteady. Even though Taxa Ejvind calls him "the sheriff", Torp lives, in the police station and his home, in a female world rather than a male world, the ideals of which would better match those of an action hero.

Some of the traditional power structures are thus turned on their heads: the women too turn a somersault. Sille has more and more influence and with good reason. Like her father, she has an instinct for who is guilty and who is innocent. From her first meeting with the paedophile, she shudders and turns away from him, whilst denying, on the other hand, that Fisker Jens could be a criminal. She has greater insight into her father's psychological mechanisms in his relationship with Ulla than he has himself and she is not afraid to tell him what she perceives to be the truth.

In her work, Ulla, who knows the local community inside out and who is coloured by both her knowledge and her prejudice, can boast, sometimes justifiably, of the fact that she already knows what Torp knows. She has only visited the baker's. At the same time, in her private life she is willing to teach him the language which he has repressed, even though he tries to avoid it. That a woman is willing to teach a hero in crisis about the life of the emotions is a common feature not only of action series but also in the genres of popular culture. What distinguishes Ulla's reactions is her insistence, her lack of respect. She challenges the policeman instead of adjusting to him. She is not satisfied with the nocturnal outbreaks of passion, she wants a relationship in the daytime, too. Even though she is his subordinate, she is an independent woman with her own integrity and it is this that Torp disputes.

The ending seems though to re-establish the main male and female characters in a traditional pattern where he – after having made enemies of all and sundry – wins her back by simply being right in his assessment of the nature of reality. She has to submit to his correct judgement and this implies that she also submits to him. So it is still only a question of a half somersault but on the other hand, there are many twists.

Formally, Dorthe is the most independent woman in relation to Torp and superficially she is the most self-contained and masculine. However, at one point, she clearly has the ambition to have a closer relationship to him. Torp depends on her information and he continues to visit her. She obviously finds him more attractive than her own husband: Torp is more direct and sexually appealing; Keld lacks both a work identity and a sexual identity and there is no obvious spark between the married couple.

None of the women is passive, on the contrary they are initiators and insistent in everything they want. At the same time, it must be said that the female world sketched here is also marked by traditional female virtues in the form of much implicit knowledge and the desire to concern themselves with how people are and to talk about it: i.e. a tendency to talk rather than act.

In this connection, it is striking how many of the episodal plots are concerned with sexual infringements and with the power status of adults and their opportunities to abuse children. Not even here, however, is the picture quite unambiguous. It is true that the men and women who commit sexual infringements are pictured one-dimensionally and clearly negatively and the children and young girls affected take on the role of victim. But this theme is also distorted, cf. the ten-year-old Maj, who as victim makes a radical counterattack. Again, a half somersault with twist.

The Provinces: Idyllic and Threatening

As my introductory section on the tradition of genres shows, Danish crime and police fictional series are played out in two locations. Either in a city (always Copenhagen), often focused on the similarities and contrasts between the surroundings and criminality found in the Copenhagen districts, working class Vesterbro and upper class Strandvejen. Or in the provinces, where a minor provincial town became the norm through the series *A Provincial Town*. *Anthonsen* combined the traditions by occasionally focusing on the provincial aspects of the big city. A rural environment was used in *The Flying Squad*; as far as location is concerned this series was special by paying attention to major recognisable provincial towns of Jutland. *Blinded*, the first crime production of TV2, was set in the country, but on the whole the city and the provincial town have been dominant. To a certain extent, representations of the country have been left to popular comedy, especially in the version by Morten Korch, whose favourite setting is the farm at the heart of a smiling Danish landscape with waving corn, green meadows and preferably, the blue of the ocean nearby. Against this background, Samsoe is a radical choice for a police series.[14]

The countryside is presented in two different ways: as landscape and as a small community, marked by transparency and clearness, but also by the fact that, occasionally, people get a bit too close to each other.

In his *Television and the Drama of Crime*, Richard Sparks gives a description of the countryside as a location for crime. He points out as a general feature that the country often has two aspects: the idyllic landscape and the landscape of fear (Sparks, 1992: 127). The same ambivalence is seen in the presentation of the landscape of Samsoe and not least, the sea surrounding it. At the beginning, we see the landscape from the point of view of someone arriving and expectations represent both extremes: "Winnie-the-Pooh Land" says Torp reassuringly, thus over-explicitly establishing the idyllic aspect, while Sille is more aware of the disquieting side. It is still the landscape by day that meets them, also as they drive past the already harvested fields. The transition is marked naturally by sunset and the coming of evening. We see the nocturnal aspect of the landscape: the elements of air and wind, sky and sea blend into each other, thus underlining the elusive character of things otherwise stable. The camera pans across water and land following a large flock of birds in flight and the music indicates that the nocturnal aspect is, perhaps, less pleasant. Quite logically, images of the dead mother occur to both daughter and father. An analysis of the rhythm of everyday life, shows how clearly day, night and the transition between them are presented. But it is not only a question of the accentuation of the twenty-four-hour rhythm, but also that the shifts between idyll and threat are always present. It is precisely the ever-present ocean that emphasises the doubleness: just as idyllic as it can look, just as lethal can it be.

Images of the landscape become thus images of a state of mind. Just as the mind has its aspects of day and night, so the landscape has its harmonious, inviting and beautiful sides whilst also hiding its secrets. As already mentioned, the mirror construction applies here, too.

As far as rural characters are concerned, Sparks finds that they are usually honest farmers as well as violent red necks, religious sects, rich eccentrics and corrupt sheriffs (Sparks, 1992). He maintains that evil in the country arises from corruption and intimidation, more than it does in the city. These observations can also be applied to the presentation of the community on Samsoe, even though the sheriff here resists the temptation to any serious corruption. It is thought-provoking that, at least on a certain level of abstraction, there is apparently a great degree of harmony between the conventions of the international genre and this Danish version of a rural police series.

A clearly marked feature in the Danish context is the close relationships among members of the local community. In *Island Cop*, there is one short sentence that is repeated in all episodes, said by various characters in various tones of voice – complaining, stating, accusing. It is: "People talk". Christian Torp says it, Ulla Snedker says it, the organist says it, Johan and his mother say it and the gossip, Mrs. Bluhme, varies it with "Between you and me!" That it is not just something people say, we can see for ourselves: people are constantly sitting or standing in small groups and chatting, in the pub, on the harbour, in the churchyard, in the pastor's garden, at the mechanic's.

The representation of the provinces is linked to the tradition familiar from the genre of popular comedy: everyone in a small community knows everything about everyone else – except perhaps precisely the main character in a drama under development. The talk has its positive side: it is necessary to know what is wrong before one can do something about it. Torp also has to gain his information by talking to people. The negative sides are presented just as clearly: vague ideas soon become 'facts' and then it is a problem of distinguishing between them. Or even worse: the fact that people talk can be the direct cause of tragedy. In popular comedy, it is naturally the humorous version that dominates.

It comes into play several times in *Island Cop*, e.g. when the seriously injured Ulla and Torp stagger home on foot, after the unfortunate encounter with the bikers. The reason is that Torp will not phone for help – because people will talk. Nevertheless, a little later he is confronted with gossip about their idyllic picnic – at the mechanic's. But the tragic version is also present, for example, when gossip leads indirectly to Lotte's suicide.

In spite of the criticism implied in "People talk", the local community is marked by a clarity and transparency in relationships that are presented partly with irony and partly with nostalgia. Just as the police station, when all is said and done, consists of policeman, secretary and daughter/extra secretary, so are other communal institutions easy to grasp. The pub, church and hospital all have extremely human dimensions: they appear less as institutions than as persons. When the public cultural administration and the mayor try to exaggerate their roles, the attempt fails hopelessly. Likewise, prostitution is represented by a solitary individual. All institutions are personalised. This helps to convey the closeness and clearness which otherwise is lacking in modern society.

The attitude to the provinces is thus a mixture of sympathetic intimacy and aloof criticism, of nostalgia and irony. In other words, here too, there is the striking of a balance that examines and rejects some elements in the typical representation of rural life and retains others. Accordingly, the genre mixes elements from various types of police series, both Danish and foreign, from Danish popular comedy and from realistic, everyday TV fiction. First and foremost *Island Cop* accomplishes combining the two main traditions from the Danish police series, the provincial tradition providing a representative and close milieu, with the action hero who is represented both as a professional and as a private person.

Reasons for Popularity

Island Cop was unusually positively received, both by reviewers in the daily press and by the general public. In this analysis, I have shown how it constantly balances and mediates: between the episodal and the serial structure, between crime and detection, between the reversal of gender roles and the revocation of the reversal, between intimacy and distance, nostalgia and criticism. In many ways this seems to correspond well with some typical tendencies of the 1990s. If, in conclusion, I have to suggest other reasons for the success of the production, I would do so as follows.

Firstly, Danes were glad to renew an acquaintance with a popular genre, long missing from the screen in a national version. Secondly, this was a successful attempt to renew the Danish tradition of the genre in a way that mixed various genres and thus contributed to reinstating the genre in a dialogue function. This dialogue works both in relation to the surrounding community and the latter's general discussion of norms and changes of norms, and in relation to problems of a more existential and ethical nature. Thirdly, the updating of, and commenting upon, well-known foreign versions succeeded in a way which, within the ironical framework – the one-man police station – in most respects was able to satisfy the present technical and formal requirements to the genre. The audience was indulgent of the fact that some of the plots in the episodes failed. Finally, there were the convincing performances of the actors, Lars Bom, Andrea Vagn Jensen, and Amalie Dollerup.

It is not surprising that DR decided to go on with the genre. In spring 2000 the Danes were offered *Edderkoppen* (*The Spider*), a historical crime serial in six episodes, made in film noir style. And from October a new and more successful *Flying Squad* was launched, combining a *female* detective superintendent with various provincial settings.

Notes

1. These concepts of the Russian formalists were introduced by Victor Sklovskij in *O teorii prozy*, Moskva 1925, and Boris Tomashevskij in *Teorija literatury*, Moskva & Leningrad 1928, both of which contain previously published contributions. Tzetan Todorov makes a useful distinction between 1) the classical 'roman à énigme' where the crime story is in focus, 2) the American police novel which mixes the two levels by suppressing the 'fabula' and giving life to the 'sujet', and 3) the novel of suspense which tries to balance the two levels (Todorov 1971).
2. For example *McCloud* 1971-77, *Columbo* 1971-77 and again 1994-97, *Kojak* 1973-78, *Der Alte* 1979-88, *Miami Vice* 1986-88, *Inspector Morse* 1987-98, *Taggart* 1986-98, *Maigret* 1970-73, all DR, and *Hill Street Blues* 1990-94, *NYPD Blue* 1994-97, *Navarro* 1994 and 1996, *Prime Suspect* 1991, 1993, 1996 and 1998 with Jane Tennison, all TV2 – to mention just some of those which have set the standard for the genre. Swedish criminal films and TV series have presumably had a special effect on the conventions of the genre in a Danish context, for example, the Martin Beck films based on the novels of Sjoevall and Wahloeoe and the Carl Hamilton serials *Jagten paa fjendens fjende* (*The Hunt for the Enemy's Enemy*) 1991 and *Vendetta* 1997, based on the novels of Jan Guillou, and the Kurt Wallander serials *Mordere uden ansigt* (*Murderes without a Face*) 1994 and *Hundene i Riga* (*The Dogs in Riga*) 1996, based on the novels of Henning Mankell.
3. See Schmidt, 1981, for a short description of the relationship between the two series.
4. The best-known include the TV comedy series *Huset paa Christianshavn* (*The House in Christianshavn*) 1-84, 1970-77, the film comedies about the Olsen gang 1-13, 1968-81, and the historical serial *Matador* (*Monopoly*) 1-24, 1978-82. They have a legendary status, both have been rerun on DR during 1997-98.

5. In the middle of the 1980s, there was a clear fascination with the Marlowe figure in the Bogart version. As a private eye with an especially cynical attitude to criminality and a tough vocabulary, the Marlowe character is reflected in the criminal novels of Dan Turèll and the film versions of them. At the same time, there are good parodies, such as the *Tonny Toupé Show* by Michael Wikke and Steen Rasmussen, DR 1985. The recurrent detective character in this series "Klap-i-Olsen" was presented in black and white and as the first person narrator with a typical Bogart intonation. It is interesting to note that the film magazine programme on DR, a one-man show by Ole Michelsen, is called *Bogart*.
6. Edwin Kau analyses these mechanisms in Kau, 1980.
7. It was produced on the basis of a novel, Erik Otto Larsen's *Manden der holdt op med at smile (The Man Who Stopped Smiling)* 1990.
8. The concepts of "flat" and "round" characters are borrowed from E. M. Forster: *Aspects of the Novel*, Harmondsworth, Penguin 1974. The tendency can be followed earlier in Sjoewahl and Wahloeoe's ten-volume work with the overall title of *Roman om en forbrydelse (Novel about a Crime)* 1965-75, where Martin Beck's personal situation is made even more clear.
9. Not an unknown theme in criminal films, think of Hitchcock's *Rear Window* (1954).
10. Morten Korch (1876-1954) became popular with his novel *Guldglasuren (The Gold Glazing)* 1912. He wrote a long series of novels, which were printed in large numbers even after his death. From 1950 many of his novels were made into films and these films set the standard for the concept of popular comedy in Denmark. Cf. Troelsen (1980: 235 ff) and Bruhn Jensen (1997, vol. 2: 112 and 251). A serial 1999-2000 called *Silent Waters* TV2 is based on a selection of his novels.
11. A reviewer who had obviously not followed the case from the beginning asked: "Who was it, by the way, who received absolution?" (the Danish newspaper *Politiken* March 4, 1997). This could be taken as a demonstration of the importance of the element of the serial.
12. For a woman to be a pastor is not unusual in Denmark. During the last 15 years, the Danish state church has seen the advent of a new generation, which means that there will probably be more female than male pastors in the future. The female pastor in *Island Cop* thus represents a general trend. Neither is it the first time that a woman pastor has been seen in TV fiction. It happened in *Johansens sidste ugudelig dage (The Last Ungodly*

Days of Johansen) DR 1989 (scriptwriter: Steen Kaaloe; directors: Michael Wikke and Steen Rasmussen).
13. In "Syndabock och haemnare" ("Scapegoat and Avenger") Schubart, based on the narrator structure in *Rambo: First Blood* part two (1985), proposes four features of the action hero that can be regarded as fundamental 1) marginalisation, 2) being chosen, 3) self-sacrifice, 4) revenge (Schubart, 1997b: 64 ff). Of these four features, it is only the first that can be used meaningfully about Torp.
14. A choice which is quite logical in relation to the profile of TV2 as the TV station of the regions.

Bibliography

Agger, Gunhild (1991). "Dansk naar det er bedst og værst – om traditioner og genreforvaltning i dansk tv-fiktion". In Jens F. Jensen (ed.): *Analyser af tv & tv-kultur*. Copenhagen: Medusa.
Agger, Gunhild (1995). *TV-fiktionens realisme*, Working paper from the research project "The Aesthetics of Television". Aarhus.
Agger, Gunhild (1997). "The 'Sideplays' Aesthetics': On Popularity and Quality in a Danish Film Maker's Television Success". In Martin Eide, Barbara Gentikow & Knut Helland (eds.): *Quality Television*, Report No. 30. Bergen: Department of Media Studies.
Bondebjerg, Ib (1993). *Elektroniske fiktioner*. Copenhagen: Borgen.
Bondebjerg, Ib, & Francesco Bono (eds.) (1994). *Nordic Television – History, Politics and Aesthetics, Sekvens*. Copenhagen: Department of Film & Media Studies.
Fiske, John (1987). *Television Culture*. London & New York: Routledge.
Grodal, Torben Kragh (1996). "Glamour, Ghetto, and Wasteland. Los Angeles as Film Backdrop". In *Sekvens* 96. Copenhagen: Department of Film & Media Studies.
Holmgaard, Jørgen, & Bo Tao Michaëlis (eds.) (1984). *Lystmord. Studier i kriminallitteraturen fra Poe til Sjöwall/Wahlöö*. Copenhagen: Medusa.
Hurd, Geoffrey (1981). "The Television Presentation of the Police". In Tony Bennett et al. (eds.): *Popular Television and Film*. London: British Film Institute.
Jensen, Klaus Bruhn (ed.) (1996-97). *Dansk mediehistorie* 1-3. Copenhagen: Samleren.
Kau, Edvin (1980). "Strømere og stoddere". In Anders Troelsen (ed.): *Levende billeder af Danmark*. Copenhagen: Medusa.

Kidd-Hewitt, David, & Richard Osborne (eds.) (1995). *Crime and the Media*. London & East Haven: Pluto Press.

Larsen, Peter (1985). "Fra Los Angeles til Valby". In Ralf Pittelkow (ed.): *Analyser af TV*. Copenhagen: Medusa.

Paterson, Richard (1995). "Drama and Entertainment". In Anthony Smith (ed.): *Television: An International History*. Oxford: Oxford University Press.

Schmidt, Kaare (1981). *TV i 70erne* 1-2. Copenhagen: Politikens Forlag.

Schmidt, Kaare (1995). *Film*. Copenhagen: Gyldendal.

Schubart, Rikke (1997a). "Single White Male: tv-actionserien i 90erne". In: *Kosmorama* nr. 219.

Schubart, Rikke (1997b). "Syndabock och hämnare. Maskulinitet i actionfilm". In: *Filmhäftet* nr.1-2. Stockholm.

Sparks, Richard (1992). *Television and the drama of crime*. Buckingham & Philadelphia: Open University Press.

Stigel, Jørgen (1997). "The Aesthetics of Television, the Quality of Television". In Martin Eide, Barbara Gentikow & Knut Helland: *Quality Television*, Report No. 30. Bergen: Department of Media Studies.

Todorov, Tzvetan (1971). "Typologie du roman policier". In: *Poétique de la prose*. Paris: Éditions du Seuil.

Tulloch, John (1990). *Television Drama. Agency, audience and myth*. London & New York: Routledge.

CHAPTER FIVE

Distinctions in Documentary Television

Rasmus Dahl
Department of Information and Mediascience
University of Aarhus

My aim in this contribution is to suggest a framework for discussing, and making distinctions among, television documentaries. The framework I am outlining is based on a theoretical platform, and I will not enter very much into specifics with regard to the variances between different audio-visual media, channels, or institutionalised contexts (film – television – computer network – video; independent cinema – mainstream television – short film/video; public service – commercial). My primary goal is to advance parameters for an analytical engagement in documentaries,[1] but the theoretical approach suggests that it is also appropriate to non-fiction aesthetics in general, because the 'textual' considerations are of widespread relevance, and because the components taken into account here are shared by all non-fiction, or at least appear right across the non-fiction spectrum. I refrain from the challenging task of going into a more subtle definition of documentary, although some of the considerations I have pull in that direction. To use the label of documentary is always risky. It has shown itself to be very slippery to handle, theoretically and at the textual level, partly because it has had such a wide and diffuse area of application, dependent on the empirical context. Even so, my second objective is to fertilise the documentary field, with some reflections on the fundamentally different ways of functioning, of the documentary text, in order to make more clear what we are discussing.

The Documentary between Clarity and Confusion

Documentary is a term frequently used, sometimes without much controversy, as a self-evident description of a television programme, genre or film, and sometimes, whether in academic situations or more everyday surroundings, as a starting point of discussions and often a great deal of confusion. Because what, after all, is a documentary?

In my eyes, the unproblematic usage of the term stems from the simple fact that we all know what a documentary is. The best account of this kind of clarity, I think we find in the writings of Carl Plantinga (Plantinga, 1997). In this book he dares to define a documentary as one which – "assert a belief that given objects, entities, states of affairs, events, or situations actually occur(ed) or exist(ed) in the actual world as portrayed" (Plantinga, 1997: 19). As a matter of fact this is a distinction meant by Plantinga to fit all kinds of non-fiction material, but for the moment I will simply accept that since a documentary must also be a non-fiction, the definition also applies, even when we look more narrowly at documentaries. So, watching a documentary means watching something that the makers of the programme, the 'speaking' agency, claim is based on events that were actually happening at the time of production, or that had actually happened at some time in the past. And this is why we can continue using the term much of the time agreeing on what is meant, because the assertive stance as described by Plantinga, the claim to refer to reality, is accepted by the viewers. Watching a documentary means engaging in an act where you accept that the content of the programme is directly connected to real circumstances.

If we then turn towards the more problematic usage of the term, and try to figure out why discussions of documentaries might end up with confusion and perhaps even controversy, it could be that one thing is missing when the talk is about the documentary, compared with other kinds of television (the news, the soap, the talk show, the game show, etc.). I believe that the missing link is a shared and obviously marked prototypical kind of programme. This view of a missing common denominator among documentaries will be strengthened and illustrated, if we take a look at the academic literature on the subject. Here we find, from the very outset, a tendency to deviate from, and classify, different modes, schools, voices, subgenres or whatever we wish to call them.

Eric Barnouw's well known historical book on documentary (Barnouw, 1974), is divided into chapters based on the kind of position or occupation the documentary and/or documentarist seeks to fill – the documentarist as: explorer, reporter, poet, advocate, and so on. Bill Nichols (Nichols, 1991) also feels the need to make from the outset a distinction between what he calls 'modes of representation'. These modes are partly based on what kind of "organisational pattern" (Nichols, 1991: 32) he finds is the prevailing one, at given periods in the history of film: the expository, the observational, the interactive and the reflexive. As a third and final example, I would choose Michael Renov's 'modalities of desire', which he takes to be, in his own words, the "four fundamental tendencies or rhetorical/aesthetic functions attributable to documentary practice" (Renov, 1993: 21). These four tendencies are: to record, reveal, or preserve; to persuade or promote; to analyse or interrogate; to express.

Another way to focus on this conception of a missing common denominator is through the question of genre. Is documentary a genre? It has now become the predominant understanding that genres cannot solely be constructions made by the researcher in his or her effort to categorise. To have explanatory power, the concept of genre must reflect a way of functioning that has resonance in the actual circuit of consumption, from production over distribution and promotion to reception, in the broadest sense of the word. It is my contention that in this respect we cannot talk about documentary as a genre. We cannot find a shared way of functioning, we cannot find a mutual resonance among all documentaries, whether we look at textual structures and conventional ways of narration, at intentions and purposes, at social functioning, at institutionalised ways of production or at patterns of reception. Whether we look at these aspects as a whole or in isolation, we hardly find grounds to call the documentary a genre.

If we take a look at the fiction/non-fiction distinction it seems quite obvious that it mirrors some significant differences in respect of the aforementioned aspects. But we cannot call non-fiction a genre, it is much too broad a category. We might call it a super genre or master genre and from there move a level down and expect to find the real genres, which possess some kind of shared discursive functionality among their members, like the television news programme. The question is if we take this step downwards from non-fiction, do we then find the documentary within one single category? It should be clear that my answer is no, we do not find one category, we find several. What I will try to show is that in my opinion instead of one genre we find three different kinds of categories, modes, prototypes of documentary – whatever the right term might be.

Some would find it very awkward or futile to try to get entirely rid of the genre-notion in relation to the documentary. As a generic label it has proved quite vigorous since at least the 1930s. To employ the distinction from Todorov, we can say that the documentary has proved its worth both as a 'historical' genre – as one which has been empirically described or derived by observing its 'actual' workings at a given period in history, and as a 'theoretical' genre – as one which has been significantly characterised through the application of the existing body of theory within film- and media studies.[2] However, I find that our conditions for making definitions, both historical and theoretical, are in some trouble. My intention is the opposite: to bring life to the theoretical thinking surrounding the documentary notion. But by momentarily sidestepping the questions of what constitutes the documentary, what it is that all documentaries have in common, and of how this uniformity stands out as compared to other forms of non-fiction, we can jump straight to the essential task of making distinctions among, and hopefully of getting a better hold on, the different aesthetic potentials resting within the notion. Thereby coming closer to an understanding which eventually can promote the development of thought surrounding the documentary as a 'theoretical' genre.

Intervention

Making distinctions among television documentaries raises the question of what kind of parameters to use in the search for differences. Since we cannot include all aspects at once, we have to start the search at a place where there seems to be some apparent and significant signs of separation. John Corner has proposed a model which is very helpful and illuminating in this respect, and it looks like this:

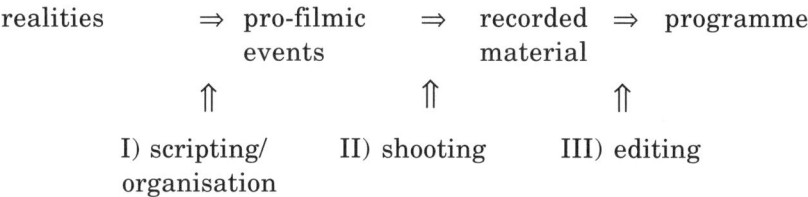

Figure 1: Documentary production as a series of transformations (Corner, 1995: 79)

What is illustrated here is the process of creation of a documentary passing through four stages, interspersed with three production phases. These phases are the room left over to the creators for deciding what to do and how to do it, in order to make up the finished programme. The phases also depict the conjunction between stages, where a sort of transformation inevitably must occur. Going from the muddy, baffling field of reality, or realities, to the focused and limited space of the pro-filmic – the events observable by camera and microphone – involves necessarily a sort of transformation, and the nature of this transformation is dependent upon the decisions made by the producing agency. The decisions determines what Corner calls a "strategy of representation and of visualisation" (Corner, 1995: 79), and we can add that even deciding to try to intervene as little as possible is taking a decision – choosing not to have a strategy is also a strategy. A second inevitable transformation takes place between the pro-filmic and the recorded material, when audio-visual traces are stored by means of the recording equipment, and where the makers have a range of possibilities to support their 'strategy of representation and of visualisation'. Finally, the move towards the final programme as it appears on the screen constitutes the last transformation. It might of course be argued that we can skip the editing phase entirely and let the programme consist of one single long shot with the appropriate diegetic sound, thereby making no transformation at all. However, this would be a very unusual and I think quite unfruitful strategy. So I will merely remark that the editing phase is where different recordings are put together and additional material eventually incorporated – sound effects, music, graphics, titles, etc.

My point here is to show that in the process of intervention in the three phases of production, in the carrying out of a strategy of intervention, and in the strategy itself, we do find a parameter of significant differences. The degree of intervention will be determinant in relation to the kind of aesthetics found in the programme. It might be helpful to visualise this parameter as a continuum stretched out between a low and a high degree of intervention.

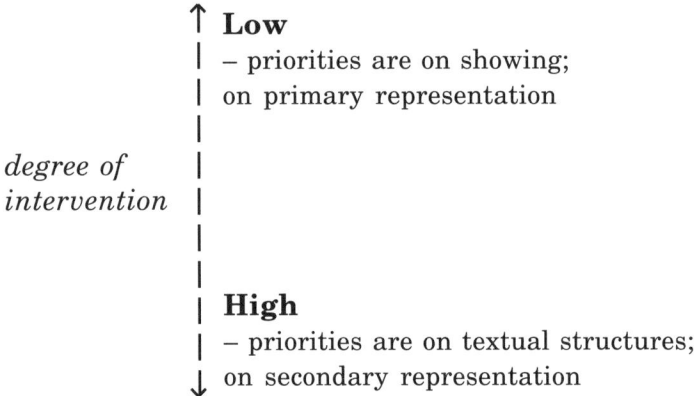

Figure 2: *Degree of intervention as a way of making distinctions between different strategies of representation*

The arrows indicate that this is principally an open-ended scale, where we can never reach the point of no intervention, since that would leave us without any programme. Neither can we talk meaningfully about total or sole intervention, at least not if this means leaving no room at all for some kind of manifest or explicit reference to reality.

Carrying out a strategy of low intervention means giving high priority to the pro-filmic in itself. Doing as little as possible in terms of intervention means trying to catch reality out there as it unfolds without disturbing it too much. It means using the available light, recording the actual sounds, and registering the events as they occur on the spot. It means using as long takes as possible in order not to disrupt the continuity of real time and space, and it means excluding the additional material of voice over, music, etc. in order to let the actual occurrences speak for themselves. The aim of this strategy must be to give priority to the evidential value of filmed reality.

If we take a step further to look beyond the strategy of intervention, visualisation and representation and toward aesthetics, and even further toward the viewer, we can ask what the principle of low intervention means to the reception of the programme. It means that the viewer is offered a certain kind of experience. This experience takes its outset in what Corner calls "'second-hand seeing' which seems like 'first-hand'" (1995: 30). It seems like first-hand seeing in at least two different but related ways. Firstly, because what is experienced is a kind of direct and intimate nearness to the events. The presence of the medium is at times hardly recognised and perhaps sometimes even forgotten. Secondly, because the withdrawal of the producing agency is also a withdrawal of expression in terms of textual cues, which I will return to soon. The viewer is left alone with a very concrete manifestation of the real, and must find the necessary clues towards meaning-making and interpretation in the actual occurrences themselves.

Returning to the strategy of visualisation and representation, we find that there might be something the producing agency wishes to say and is eager to express about reality, which cannot be conveyed through the simple showing of things themselves. The interventional phases constitute the area of possibilities in respect of this kind of telling and expressing.

It is necessary now to complicate the matter a bit, and make a distinction between what we could call primary and secondary representations. Following John Corner (Corner, 1996), we can say that primary representation is the kind of representation exercised when the degree of intervention is low, it is based on the recorded sounds and images as we have just seen. Secondary representations then can, as Corner puts it "encompass abstract propositional/argumentational matters. The whole textual system of the film or programme, its expositional organisation, forms of argument, modes of adducing visual and verbal evidence and the lines of causality indicated in the narrative scheme are all implicated here" (Corner, 1996: 18). Secondary representation has to do with talking about and referring to reality without showing it. But it also has to do with making representations of more abstract and general themes, problems and features within reality which can't possibly be rendered through a straightforward primary representation. A high degree of intervention can be used in a variety of ways, using the means of expression known from audio-visual communications and aesthetics in general. The kind of programme we find in this end of the intervention spectre carries out a strategy of visualisation which has as its priority the use of textual structures in the construction of representations, expressions and interpretations. To put it another way, the programmes rest upon the level of textual structure and organisation in their effort to convey meanings and references, and this even opens up the possibility of using a more metaphorical, associative and indirect mode of relating to reality.

If we once again take the viewer into consideration, it seems plausible that watching a programme with a high degree of intervention triggers a somewhat different experience than when intervention is minimalised. Here the process of meaning-making and interpretation becomes directly influenced by the traces of mediation and construction, manifest on the textual level. The metonymic relationship between programme and reality is at times declining, is perhaps even forgotten, leaving room for metaphorical reflection and abstraction.

To sum up, the parameter of intervention takes into consideration the degree of intervention as an overall strategy carried out in the programme. It might be possible to place programmes in relation to each other along the scale. In our search for differences we here seem to find a key, based on strategic, aesthetic and receptional considerations. The distinctions we can make is stretched out between programmes with a low degree of intervention giving high priority to primary representation, and programmes with a high degree of intervention giving high priority to secondary representation.

Rhetoric

The degree of intervention as a parameter misses one central aspect within documentary television. To complete the picture we have to include this aspect, and to do this we need a second parameter. The aspect I am thinking of can best be understood in terms of rhetoric, in terms of argumentation, in terms of making probable, in terms of proving and of convincing. What I am talking about, is the effort incorporated in the programme to get a grip on the viewer and to guide and control the viewer towards a specific conception of the states of affairs, advanced by the programme. Any television documentary establishes a view of the world, a certain perspective or interpretation of at least a part of the world. But the way it insists on its own interpretation, its efforts to make its points convincingly, may differ, and likewise the weight put upon the argumentation. Before pinpointing the indicators of rhetorical strategy, we need to straighten something out. In my usage of the degree of intervention as a parameter there is no necessary connection with this kind of rhetorical configuration. Increasing the degree of intervention does not necessarily result in a tighter and heavier argumentation. The intervention opens a path for textual structuration but this structuration can take different directions. A conspicuous use of staging, of camerawork, of lighting, of montage, of sound editing might very well be used to create a room for the interpretative work of the viewer, which is confronted with a redundancy of expressions. The particular interpretation and meaning-making can in this way, to a large degree, be left to the viewer to seek out. What is at stake, then, in the rhetorical perspective, and accordingly not necessarily in the interventional perspective, is argumentation, authority and mode of address.

Following a line of thought comparable with that of Umberto Eco, we can think of documentaries as open or closed texts. An open text is one leaving plenty of room for the receivers' own interpretations, while a closed text is the opposite in insisting upon a close tie with the receivers' conclusions. I suggest using a distinction based on the degree of 'closedness' to outline differences in a rhetorical perspective, and to visualise it in a way similar to the first parameter.

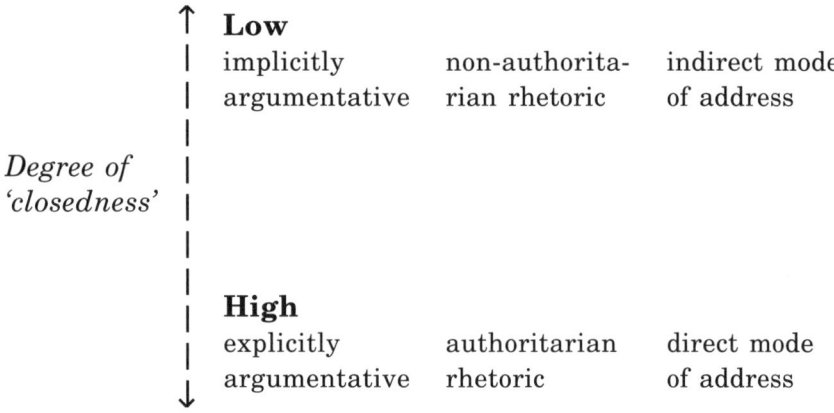

Figure 3: Degree of closedness as a way of making distinctions between different strategies of representation

The position on this scale will indicate how insistent a programme is on its own interpretation. An open programme could then either be the non-interventional type, or the interventional type relinquishing the rhetorical tools of explicity and authority and the propositional advantages of the direct mode of address. A programme of the closed type will typically use an argumentative logic in the building up of an exposition, and will explicitly announce its arguments and line of proof. It will use an authoritarian rhetoric, meaning that it will use the shown material in order to support, prove and insist upon its own interpretation. Finally, the voice-over is frequently used to create a direct mode of addressing the viewer, thereby controlling and directing our way through the exposition. An example is the hard-hitting journalistic type of programme, often carried along by the desire to make accusations, to point out injustice, and to place guilt or blame.

Voices

Having reached this point, it is possible for me to explain why I find three categorical or prototypical forms of documentary. The three prototypes can be found at the extremities of the parameters. The first is the minimum-intervention kind of documentary with its eagerness to show and its unwillingness to explain or express. Moving up along the interventional axis we can take two directions. One leads toward openness and the formation of the second prototype, the one with an expressive outlook and a denial of exclusiveness in its interpretations. The other direction is toward rhetorical manifestation in the form of authority and explicit argumentation, constitutive of the closed kind of prototype.

I will later conclude with some reflections over the applicability of this kind of categorisation and its coherence with an analytical perspective. But before doing that, I want to work through some of the presumptions presented this far by touching on one central issue. As can be seen, my findings look very much like the ones Carl Plantinga suggests (Plantinga, 1997), and my 'prototypical forms' are almost identical to his three 'voices', the formal, open and poetic. Although I am closely inspired by and very much indebted to his work, it might be useful to elaborate on a point which I see as a problem in his distinctions. It is not that I essentially disagree with him, on the contrary, but I want to avoid some possible misunderstandings, and a bit of pedantic fiddling in the use of notions is illuminating in this respect.

Plantinga rightly shows a concern for including the poetic-aesthetic aspect in the investigation of potential means of expression within non-fiction depiction. While discussing Bill Nichols' modes of representation, he calls attention to the problem that these modes are not able to take the poetic dimension sufficiently into account. As he writes:

> "We need a category of the poetic non-fiction film to recognise the fact that some non-fiction films are concerned not primarily with argument, or with the assertion of propositions about the world, but have an aesthetic function that serves as their primary organisational principle." (Plantinga, 1997: 103)

We could then expect to find a concern to include such a category within the more systematic and principal pattern, underlying Plantingas distinctions among voices. The strange thing is that we do not. He does include the poetic voice as a possibility, but he somehow manages to direct it out onto a side-track:

> "These types [of poetic films (R.D.)] correspond not to logical alternatives to the formal and open non-fiction films; they fit no symmetrical grid designed to exhaust the possible different sorts of films. The sole rationale for discussing these films here is that they present the major empirical groupings of alternative non-fiction films at this historical juncture. Although these films constitute four separate subgenres, it is not misleading to call them instances of the poetic voice in non-fiction filmmaking." (Plantinga, 1997: 172)

It can of course be argued, as he does, that not all documentaries are argumentative and therefore we need a poetic-aesthetic category, but that this is a peripheral and remote voice compared to the mainstream of non-fiction. Somehow this seems very unsatisfying to me, because I think it implies the unfortunate risk of underestimating the poetic dimension of documentary depiction on the microlevel – on the level of more confined stylistic and aesthetic expression within all types of non-fiction – and because I think these forms of expressions should be seen as integrated within the more general principles of potential non-fiction meaning-making.[3] But why is it Plantinga ends up isolating the poetic voice from the logic/systematism underlying his categorisations?

To answer this we have to take a closer look at his agenda, which for the sake of clarity, I will here outline.

1) First he argues that we must consider the non-fiction/documentary as a discourse framed within an assertive stance and indexed as a 'text' concerned with reality. The fundamental characteristics of non-fiction must somehow be sought and found 'outside' the text itself, on a broader contextual level.

2) Secondly, "Non-fiction films are not imitations or representations, but constructed representations" (Plantinga, 1997: 37). What we witness is not the real thing itself, and not even an attempt to replay it, but a construction made up to direct our attention towards real-world issues. An essential point here is that this constructedness does not at all imply that we are now automatically dealing with fiction. The proper understanding of this constructedness can be found within the boundaries of rhetoric. The representation is rhetorical, it is based on research and investigation, it is arranged and organised both in the process of construction and in the structuring of the final presentation for the audience.

3) The next step is to deal with differences within this framework. To form a basis for making distinctions among different voices or organisational patterns, and among different epistemological goals or claims offered by the different voices.

To fulfil this task, Plantinga takes the crucial decision of suggesting a rhetorical parameter as the basic one. The logic seems to be that since we are dealing with a rhetorical discourse, the basic distinction must be made between voices whose epistemological functioning is founded on the promotion of certain knowledge, on certitude, and voices which are hesitating and open ended in their way of treating and promoting knowledge – the formal vs. the open voice. But in the movement from (2) to (3) Plantinga takes the rhetorical aspects into somewhat different considerations. In (2) where he wants to promote a rhetoric perspective, in opposition to the misunderstood conception of 'construction equals fiction', the understanding of rhetoric is broad and general:

"Nor do I mean by "rhetoric" merely the realm of persuasion. I take the word in a broader sense, as the study of the richness, complexity, and expressiveness of non-fiction discourse, and the means by which it is structured to have influence on the viewer." (Plantinga, 1997: 3)

Rhetoric becomes in this understanding a matter of stating the case abundantly, not necessarily of persuasion, arguing and proving. It becomes equal to construction and structure, and it is the aspect within the discourse which separates it from mere imitation. This conception of rhetoric as the domain of structuring the means of expression on a general level, seems to me to be a very fruitful approach to non-fiction discourse,[4] but it differs from a more constrained conception.

In a more narrow and strict understanding, rhetoric comes very close to the argumentative and the persuasive. It is this understanding which prevails in Nichols' definition of documentary (Nichols, 1991), and which Plantinga seems to fall back on in (3), even though he elsewhere has reservations about the comprehension of non-fiction as essentially argumentative. The strict, narrow sense of rhetoric stands out as the determining parameter:

"The formal voice explains; it teaches and directs. It maintains a hierarchical relationship with the viewer, such that the viewer is taught by a discursive presence that assumes a position of knowledge ... It argues about, categorises, and gives canonical narrative structure to events and topics. The formal voice makes sense of its subject and passes on that sense to the spectator ...

The open voice is always implicitly rhetorical, but it does not take the overt rhetorical position of the formal voice. This epistemological position, basically an unwillingness to claim full knowledge on its part, results in representational strategies markedly different than those of the formal voice. One sees a meandering, open, unpredictable structure ... It is content to observe or to explore; it lets the viewer draw her own conclusions." (Plantinga, 1997: 115-116)

Plantinga seems to imply that there are two fundamentally distinct types of voices, recognisable by the degree of rhetorical harshness, and then there is the third voice – the poetic – which cannot be described or considered within the same terms, but stands out as an isolated exception from the rules.

My proposal to somehow avoid or solve this unfortunate disintegration is that we follow what I have referred to as Platinga's agenda down to (3). But to answer the questions there, of voices and epistemological offerings, we should initially stick to the broad and comprehensive conception of rhetoric. This means that we do not immediately raise the issue of whether the voice appears with persuasive certitude, or rather reveals reserved hesitation, but that we ask whether or not the voice gives high priority to interference at all.

The aspect of interference or intervention as a matter of degree, only makes sense if we hold the position that something can be gained from a strategy of minimum intervention. Or in other words, that to a certain extent, the contours of reality can be represented and preserved through the recording-displaying process.[5] If we do think that a representational strategy resting heavily upon primary depiction can constitute a distinct epistemological space, a particular way of knowing and experiencing, that can be acknowledged as a proper fashion of looking into the world, it also becomes reasonable to make a comparison within this constitution, and say that some films or programmes are more dependent on minimum intervention than others. But to think in terms of minimum intervention is misleading, if it is understood as minimising the obstacles on the road towards the viewer's mind, as the possibility of creating a road which can make way for the passage of "pure reality" or "the truth". We must instead think of intervention as an interruption in the rudimental road of visual documentary in its most basic manifestation. Where basic is meant in a non-normative detached sense, as one way of doing things, which is not necessarily the true or most adequate one, but simply the one that relies substantially and as far as possible on the photographic technique of moving images. If there is a road in this sense, and even if it is rudimental and straight, someone has planned and constructed it. Someone made it happen, it did not come out of the blue. Someone had a purpose in bringing it about, and that is why it is rhetorical. There is a purpose, a voice, and an effect and subsequently a rhetoric.

So, we must stay within the broad rhetoric conception, and ascertain that even a withdrawal of intervention constitutes a voice, but a voice with a distinct rhetoric and with characteristic epistemological implication. The next step will then be to deal with different sorts of interferences. If the voice shows an explicit eagerness to interrupt and take advantage of the possibilities that are resting within the realm of secondary representation, there must be a motivation for doing so. A loud, marked occurrence will exert an influence on the epistemological offering, and will help determine the distinct construction of the field of experience and knowledge, accessible by the viewer. It is my assertion that this must be the right place for integrating the poetic aspects of documentary depiction, and also to draw in the more narrow rhetorical perspective. Because here we can make a distinction between two fundamentally different offerings, and correspondingly two oppositional motivations. On the one hand, that which is closed, exclusive, and embracing in its dealing with knowledge. Which is argumentative, persuasive and heavily concerned with proving its conviction of certainty. And on the other hand, one which wants to expand and open up the territory of signification by triggering off metaphorical, associative, emotional or poetic reflections. Which is hesitating in its conclusions but conspicuous in its means of expression, and thereby leaving room for an epistemology of poetic aesthetics.

Why Distinctions?

Here, towards the end, it might be relevant to outline some of the benefits, but also the limitations, I find in the reflections presented this far. The most rewarding payoff is perhaps that the logic of the parameters supplies a coherent framework, suited for analytical considerations. The analytical importance lies in the description of aesthetic extremes; in the potential communicative consequences and advantages which can be strived for through the structuring of a documentary programme. The important thing is not so much the possibility of deeming programmes as either non-interventive, argumentative, or poetic, as to detect the striving in itself and use it as a source of insight into the destination of the programme in question. Where is it heading? What kind of receptional patterns and epistemological rewards is it aiming at, through the specific structuring it makes?

Of course it would be wrong always to consider the striving as a means of reaching a unified, stereotyped output. The concept of the framework is not least to enable us to catch more isolated elements in their specific workings. To make distinctions among tendencies and strivings gives us the possibility of estimating different functions and effects. I have been eager to integrate the poetic dimension as a logical alternative not least in this respect. The poetic aspects are essential to reach places that are not attainable otherwise. And these elements appears over and again, also in programmes which otherwise must be considered as exemplars of the formal voice. They can be there to support and intensify the argumentation and the logic behind it, through the representation of feelings and moods within the depicted reality which are of rhetorical importance, and by providing weight to the exposition itself. But they can certainly also be there in their own right, resulting in an integrative breakaway from the formal ordering, and a consequential opening up for associations and interpretations which can take not so controllable directions. As an analytic device, the parameters might be more useful in the detecting of means than in the drawing of conclusions, although these matters, of course, are connected. The richness, complexity and variety of documentary aesthetics are exactly due to the unique combinations and mutual influences among elements, which it is up to the analyst to try to reveal.

It must be stressed that a lot of important analytical aspects are beyond the reach of this framework. Of course it has its limitations and cannot reveal everything of importance, it must be thought of as a way of breaking the ice. First of all it is a tool for looking into the aesthetic or formative aspects, leaving most of the content and subject matter untouched. But also the narrative/dramaturgic administration of information is an important factor which is partly left out. Besides that, several contextual influences have analytical value, but are not accounted for here. When we are talking about television it seems evident to look at the way a programme is promoted – what are the 'directions for use'; at the way it is scheduled – is it a single feature, part of some kind of serial, or linked thematically with other programmes. These are all aspects which can and should be incorporated dependant on the analytical aims, focal points and perspectives.

Another rewarding perspective has to do with the basis for making categorisations, although also here there must be some reservations. In order to comprehend and in order to communicate, we are dependent upon categories being perceptive schemas and intersubjective understandable labels. To base categorisations on a strict theoretical logic, like the one I have advocated here is not enough, it cannot stand alone. It does point at some possible clarity and coherence, but must be supported otherwise, in order to make real sense as a generic explanatory device. To research and explain the functionalities catalysed through the different prototypical forms of documentary, we need the support of critical investigation; of a historical perspective to look at specific developments and traditional anchorage; of psychological studies in receptional patterns and cognitive structures; of research into productional routines and the institutionalisation of the media systems.

In such a broad perspective, it is my assumption that we find a division of labour between the three types of documentary. They can be seen as more general discursive functionalities filling out different and fairly well-defined roles: in relation to an institutional perspective, in terms of socio-cultural purposes and as centre of a television experience. On the one hand, a distinction between the three sorts of discourses can in no way be airtight or bullet-proof, in-betweens and mixtures are common features. On the other hand, it is often possible straight away to consider the specific television documentary as an example of one of the tendencies, and I find that all programmes can be fruitfully described, analysed or explained on the basis of these tendencies, and that is precisely the idea of the suggested parameters.

Notes

1. I have presented a similar line of thought in (Dahl, 1997).
2. Cf. Tzvetan Todorov (1975): *The fantastic: A structural approach to a literary genre.*
3. I don't think Plantinga disagrees as his stressing on the diversity of different uses of pictures shows, and also his general concern for the 'unlimited' possible means of expression in non-fiction underlines.
4. In Denmark, Søren Kjørup has been an eager advocate for the benefits of this approach; in terms of the relation between factual and fictional texts, and between reality and representations of reality; and in comparison with a semiotic/structuralist approach.
5. "In contemporary theory and practice of the documentary film, embrace of the idealist/nominalist theory of cinematic representation has led to questions about the legitimacy of the documentary form itself. Such writing draws upon the ontological and epistemological assumptions of idealism/nominalism, with sometimes an admixture of the philosophical theories of Jacques Derrida" (Casebier, 1991: 137). Nichols, Renov and Brian Winston can, among others, be said to follow the post-structuralist/-modernist questioning described in the quotation. In opposition to this, there are scholars who believe in a qualified realism of the photographic image, and a realist theory of cinematic representation, among them Plantinga and Casebier (and also myself, as should be clear).

Bibliography

Barnouw, Eric (1976, orig. 1974). *Documentary. A history of the non-fiction film.* Oxford: Oxford University Press.

Casebier, Allan (1991). *Film and phenomenology.* Cambridge: Cambridge University Press.

Corner, John (1995). *Television form and public address.* London: Edward Arnold.

Corner, John (1996). *The art of record.* Manchester: Manchester University Press.

Dahl, Rasmus (1997). *TV-dokumentarisme. Fra virkelighed til seer.* Working paper from the research project "The Aesthetics of Television". Aarhus: Aarhus University.

Nichols, Bill (1991). *Representing Reality*. Bloomington: Indiana University Press.
Platinga, Carl (1997). *Rhetoric and representation in nonfiction film*. Cambridge: Cambridge University Press.
Renov, Michael (1993). *Theorizing Documentary*. London: Routledge.
Todorov, Tzvetan (1975): *The fantastic: A structural approach to a literary genre*. Ohio: Case Western Reserve University Press.
Winston, Brian (1995). *Claiming the real*. London: BFI.

CHAPTER SIX

TV Sport and Aesthetics
The Mediated Event

Preben Raunsbjerg
Department of Communication
Aalborg University

In portraying an imagined instrument that would be able to transmit pictures telegraphically, much in the same way that Alexander Graham Bell before beginning exhibiting his telephone in 1876 described his invention as an apparatus for transmitting sounds telegraphically, in 1879 the artist and writer *George du Maurier*, in the magazine *Punch* depicted a so-called *telephonoscope* – a telephone transmitting sound *and picture.* Du Maurier's picture shows a couple by a fireplace, *watching a tennis match on a screen on the wall* (Barnouw, 1990: 4). Although not realised at the time, and even later never realised in full – in du Maurier's vision the viewers are not only able to watch the tennis match, but able also to communicate with the players – this may well be one of the first attempts at televised sports.

George du Maurier probably wasn't particularly interested in TV Sport as such – it can hardly have been the case, since no such thing existed at the time – but nonetheless it is interesting that he chose sport in the attempt to depict his telephonoscopic vision. Reasons for this particular choice may well be linked with subjects considered in this article. They have to do with sporting events and, indeed, with TV sporting events as events taking place in a confined space and within certain given temporal limits. Even more so, they have to do with sporting events and TV sporting events being events that are easily recognised and categorised in comparison with other types of events and TV events. They have to do with televised sporting events as a TV genre.

Most television programmes are not easily categorised, programme formats are often fluid, and categories tend to overlap. For this reason, many articles and treatises on television start out with a definition of the kind of programme or genre to be discussed. The subject of the present article is televised sport. A good proportion of the texts on this subject do not address the question of what precisely television sport is, or how this particular kind of television programme or genre differs from other kinds of programmes and genres. Perhaps because what television sport is seems as obvious as the question is banal. For, even if one may often be in doubt as to the genre a given programme belongs to, few if any have trouble deciding whether or not they are watching sport. In fact, characteristic of televised sport is the fact that what passes across the screen seems to proceed so 'naturally', is so self-evident, that it seldom raises any major questions.

Whereas analysts and critics of the medium (and to a lesser extent those who write reviews) frequently discuss the formal language or 'grammar' of fictional programmes, the forms of expression of sports programmes are only discussed when something has gone wrong, when something has interfered with the 'natural' representation of the event at hand.

The literature on televised sport is not totally devoid of definitions and delimitations, but the vast majority concentrate on the content of the programmes rather than the form of expression. Thus, the area is characterised in terms of content rather than format inasmuch as definitions take their starting point in 'sports', and anything and everything on television that deals with sport is tossed into the same bag. In other words: sports programmes are television sport because they are about sport, and not because they have the appearance of sport and have the format of television sport. I do not mean to reject this traditional definition but I do intend to proffer an alternative to the genre problematics of television sport with a view to gaining a better understanding of television sport as a phenomenon.

Here I propose a generic delimitation of television sport which takes its prime point of departure in what might be called the nature of (televised) sport as an event (Dayan & Katz, 1992). That is to say, a delimitation that relates to sport, both as an object of media intervention, and, secondly, as a media event and television text. The point of departure is Dayan and Katz' theory of media events: it is in connection with live transmissions of sporting events that one finds the most characteristic features of TV sport, while such transmissions also elicit the greatest degree of fascination – both on the level of reception and in purely aesthetic terms. Ratings around the world are unanimous: live transmissions of sporting events attract by far the largest audiences. They are mainly international contests, e.g., the Olympics, World Cups and European Championships. On the aesthetic level, too, it is these same events which set the standard which other sports programmes emulate, and which national channels' sports departments are judged by. In extension of the delimitation of sport as a field, this article will also examine the aura of 'naturalness' which seems to surround television sport. Or, more precisely: I shall examine the seemingly extreme degree of codification in the semiotic structures of television sport, and the extent to which this codification can be said to involve a specific 'rhetoric of TV sport', and what such a rhetoric might consist of.

TV Sport and Genre

Efforts to situate television sport in relation to other, more thoroughly described, television genres often point out that television sport contains elements from many other television genres and thus occupies a position 'somewhere in between'. (These exercises may well be a kind of apology for having shown interest in such a low-status subject as sport in the first place and TV sport still is low-status in many respects.)

In his book, *Fields of Vision*, Gary Whannel proposes a triangular model of television genres, the points of which are labelled drama, journalism and light entertainment (Whannel, 1992: 61). He then argues that television sport occupies a position somewhere in the centre of the triangle. That is to say, it contains elements of all three. This, Whannel proposes, is the reason television sport is so popular. Margaret Morse expresses a similar point of view in her article, "Sport on Television", one of the few decidedly aesthetic approaches to the subject. Among other things, Morse discusses what happens to an American football match when it is televised. Before going into the process of mediation, she tries to pin down the source of the fascination sport-on-television exerts. Sport, Morse argues, is special because it occupies a position between news and entertainment:

> "Sport thus enjoys some of the privileges of instant-breaking major news stories as well as some of the authenticity of the news. Indeed, sports do make the news shows, after the political reports and before the weather. Thus the position of sport in the television flow raises it, like the news, above genres which specialise in mere entertainment. The aura of scientificity of sport, its news-value, and its perceived realism protect its extraordinary status." (Morse, 1983: 60)

Despite an aesthetic interest, which is developed in extenso in the rest of the article, Morse's approach to the problem of genre and television sport is largely content-based. The programme format is defined in terms of the subject treated and is found to be interesting because it occupies a special position – in relation to news and the weather.[1] This observation is most valid in relation to sports magazine programmes, however.

In her doctoral dissertation on sports journalism, Danish media researcher Kirsten Frandsen (1996) differentiates between two main formats in televised sport: the magazine and 'live' transmission. The former category includes sports news, interviews, reportage, and documentary journalism – in short, everything that is not a live transmission. Whether this distinction adequately covers the television output of today – with show-like programmes such as the British Gladiators, programmes offering bookmaking odds and advice on forecasting soccer results, and, finally, what might tentatively be called 'activating' sports programmes, viz., work-out programmes, tai chi, etc., where the intent is to get the viewer to participate in one or another form of physical exercise – is open to question. Nonetheless, the distinction between magazines and the live transmission is a handy tool, affording a means by which to remove all the derivative forms, leaving the central and original form of television sport, which is also the form which has the most well articulated aesthetics and rhetoric, namely, the live transmission.[2]

The essay "The Super Bowl: Mythic Spectacle", written by Michael R. Real, provides a case study of the 1974 Super Bowl. In it, Real treats the TV event as a databank of cultural indicators and a para-literary text for exegesis, whereafter he interprets this data with a view to explaining the inner structure and the social function of the Super Bowl as a totally mass mediated cultural event (Real, 1982). On a theoretical level, the essay tries to establish a balance between the traditional Anglo-American focus on empirical data and a more European, or continental, philosophical interest. Apart from containing an interesting analysis of the 1974 CBS-produced Super Bowl transmission which reveals that in this particular four-hour-long telecast (including all pre- and post-game coverage) the ball was in motion for approximately seven (7) minutes, Michael R. Real tries to narrow down what makes the marriage between sport and what Real calls 'the electronic media' a happy one. According to Real, there are three main qualities that makes this union fruitful:

- The physical nature of sport meets television's need for events capable of colourful visual representation and/or aural description.[3]
- TV sport offers a sequential and cumulative dramatic structure that divides the actors into heroes and happiness, losers and tragedy. Herein lies, according to Real, that which distinguishes spectator sports from participatory exercises and therefore also that which makes televised sporting events able to attract and hold large number of viewers.
- Sports are self-determined and take place in real time. Furthermore, unlike the formal drama, it is impossible to predict the result of the sporting drama. Thus, the viewer in front of his or her television is as qualified in making predictions of the eventual outcome of the sporting event as the organiser and broadcaster. Because of the event taking place in real time there is no such thing as a privileged or more or less qualified or competent viewer.[4]

In an attempt to develop a new conception of television sport in relation to other genres, I shall try to avoid regarding TV sport as something chiefly defined by its content, where format is treated in the same terms as are commonly applied to newscasts and magazines. Instead, I shall try to specify the aesthetics of television sport and take that aesthetics as my point of departure in defining 'television sport'. Aside from a latter day tradition of festive studio decor and more or less glamorous studio hosts and hostesses, accompanied by brassy musical and graphic vignettes, etc., it is essentially an aesthetics of the live transmission. Consider the model below.

News	Sports news	Other news
Events	Sporting events	Other events

Figure 1

Figure 1 shows the rationale behind a content-based definition of the genre. The most salient distinction is that between sport and non-sport, indicated on the vertical axis. It is, however, the horizontal distinction which interests us here: a distinction in which the definitive criteria are a specific form and aesthetics of production: the live transmission. In this sense, the 'horizontal' genre definition takes its starting point in the characteristic features of the programme; it is media specific and operates in terms of the aesthetics of the medium. The point is this: even if the live sports transmission might easily be defined in terms of its content and be lined up alongside other representations of TV sport, on an aesthetic level it bears greater resemblance to other live transmissions that do not necessarily have anything to do with sport.

The live transmission is the form of television that is most characteristic of the medium, mainly because it capitalises on what the other major visual medium, film, cannot achieve: simultaneity. In his book, *The Open Work*, Umberto Eco discusses the possibility of defining a television-specific aesthetics – or poetics, as he puts it. In Eco's view, the starting point for such a discussion should be the live transmission:

> "The aspect that would seem most interesting and fruitful to our research is also its most characteristic, unique to the medium: namely, live broadcasts." (Eco, 1989: 107)

Umberto Eco's view is shared by Danish media researcher, Jørgen Stigel, who in the text *The Aesthetics of Television, The Quality of Television* mentions *the aesthetics of the instant* as something that is unique for television:

> "This aesthetics of the instant I would claim is one of the primary qualities of television and a kind of quality which is quite different from most other media and traditional aesthetics in general or at least conceived as work-of-art-aesthetics. This quality is closely connected with the qualities of the 'here and now', the qualities of simultaneity, the qualities of nearness (this is happening (almost) right now) and yet being at a safe distance." (Stigel, 1997: 7; and in this volume 25ff.)

The issue at hand being a combination of 'the aesthetics of the instant' and transmissions of televised sport enables us to remove Stigel's phrase *almost right now*, because the televised sporting event is first and foremost a *live* event. Transmissions of sporting events are generally simultaneous with the represented events themselves. And, as pointed out by Michael R. Real, a central aspect of televised sporting events is the suspense of not knowing the outcome of the contest; here the coincidence in time between the event and the media event is crucial.[5] The term 'the aesthetics of the instant' furthermore offers, in a more precise and less generalised way, an entrance to a way of understanding what happens in the *special moments* of sports. These moments are the ones which, partly via slow motion replay, become subject to special attention in an attempt to capture and enlarge them. More about this later.

The reason simultaneity is so important is that televised sport, more than anything else, is a representation of a sporting event. In what follows we shall examine the transformation (Whannel, 1992) which takes place in the mediation of events. Our point of departure, however, is that in relation to media events television primarily (but not exclusively) serves as the "channel" – in Jakobson's sense of the term – which makes communication possible. The event takes place first outside the medium, then in the medium – a circumstance which to a considerable degree dictates how the medium forms the event. Eco:

> "... a TV narrative represents autonomous events which, though they can be approached from different angles, have a logic of their own that demands to be respected." (Eco, 1989: 110)

> "...a kind of narration which, despite an appearance of causality and coherence, relies primarily on the mere sequence of events, and in which the narrative, even though it might have a thread, is constantly spilling beyond its margins, into the inessential, the tangential, the gloss, where for a long time nothing may happen, and the camera remains focused on the curve of a road waiting for the sudden appearance of the first runner, or, weary, wanders to the facades of the surrounding houses or the expectant faces of the spectators, for no other reason than that this is the way things go, and there is nothing else to do but wait." (Eco, 1989: 116)

Thus, television is dependent on the event that it transmits. The medium is not in control; rather, the event lives a life of its own, largely independent of the medium's intervention. Given the importance of live sports transmissions in relation to other sports programmes on television, one would expect the form to have been the subject of frequent analysis. Surprisingly, this is not the case. One reason for the relative lack of such studies is the degree of 'naturalness' or 'self-evidence' associated with sports transmissions: What is there to analyse? TV only shows what is going on. It is primarily a question of representation, and no amount of camera effects and graphic design can change the basic factors which make up the focus of interest: Who will be the winner? If nothing happens, there is nothing to show.

> "What cameras can never do, of course, is legislate for drama that is not there. If a match is tedious, or a race is all but won with fifteen laps to go, even the most sophisticated camera work cannot install drama where none exists." (Barnett, 1990: 156)

I shall return to some of the factors which distinguish the mediated sporting event from the actual event, for, even if television is dependent on the chain of events as they develop, it would be naïve to assume that television has no alternative but to "wait and see". The event and the media event do not coincide totally, they are not identical. But first, let us consider the points of similarity between the two, which are regarded as the distinguishing characteristics of live sports transmissions as a genre. It is this similarity which is indicated on the horizontal axis in Figure 1, and in the following, we shall base our discussion on Dayan and Katz' definition and discussion of media events.

The Media Event

> "If festive viewing is to ordinary viewing what holidays are to everyday, then these events are the high holidays of mass communication." (Dayan & Katz, 1992: 1)

In *Media Events: The Live Broadcasting of History*, Dayan and Katz (1992) specify the definition of a media event in terms of a series of criteria regarding conditions that must be present in the event itself. In the first place, a media event is never routine; it breaks the routine and "pre-empts" the ordinary programme tableau; the biggest media events are those which occupy all channels simultaneously. By appropriating the programme tableau, the medium accords the event importance and underlines its character of event. Secondly, the event is transmitted 'live' and takes place in remote locations (Dayan & Katz, 1992: 5); the event occurs, furthermore, independent of the media organisation. Finally, in contrast to a news event, the media event is planned in advance. It is this combination of live and distant and exceptional but planned which Dayan and Katz considers the prime feature of the media event as an independent genre.

In the early days of television, the entire programme schedule (brief as it was) was a media event – an event about the medium itself. Programme scheduling was fluid; there was no formal tableau to be changed or pre-empted, only a series of programmes.[6] There has to be a fixed programme tableau for there to be any meaning in the concept of media event. For example, the weekly British soccer match on Saturday afternoons on Danish television was a feature of the fixed programme tableau until a couple of years ago; it was not a media event. On the contrary, it was part of the programme tableau which can be pre-empted by an event.[7] *Tips-Lørdag*, the Danish equivalent of the British Grandstand, was a 4- to 5-hour sports programme, typically with a soccer match or the like as its main feature. In November 1995, it was pre-empted by a live transmission of HRH Prince Joachim's wedding.

It is, of course, not always easy to determine when a programme is part of the programme tableau. Over the past few years, it has become a tradition for Danish TV2 (corresponding to British ITV) and many other European television channels to carry long transmissions from the Tour de France bicycle race for three weeks in July, and we know already that we will be seeing a 14-day transmission from Beijing in the late summer of the year 2008. The typical event must therefore be singular or unique, a once-in-a-lifetime occurrence. The degree of an event's 'event-ness' will decline in direct proportion to the frequency of its occurrence. The borderline between event and non-event is not precise, but the circumstance that an event, unexpectedly delayed for some reason, will pre-empt programmes later in the schedule constitutes a sure criterion. If delayed, say, for one hour, the Saturday football programme would not be transmitted, whereas a national team soccer contest would be, no matter when it finally got under way.[8]

That the event is planned in advance is another characteristic feature. 'Planning' should be understood as being known in advance to occur at a given time and place, not as being regularly scheduled. This, too, is a definitive criterion that excludes a number of similar types of programmes. 'Special bulletins' and coverage of major accidents, etc., which break into the normal flow of programmes, concern events which were not planned in advance or foreseen. They are generally news related.[9] As in the case of pre-emption, there is no firm definition of the degree of planning and how far in advance the event must be known.

A media event is always 'live', and it is this directness which gives it the quality of something happening 'here and now', plus a sense that 'anything can happen'. Thus, directness lends the situation an element of suspense. This feature is the media event's most palpable characteristic, and indeed, it is hard to find examples of media events which are not transmitted live.[10] In the case of deliberately delayed transmissions, the programme will not fulfil the pre-emption criterion. In such cases we have an event which is not considered important enough to break the programme tableau for, and therefore it does not qualify as a media-event.

Finally, there is the criterion of 'remote location'. In Dayan and Katz' simplified model, a programme can originate in one of two places: in a studio or outside one. The medium has to go to the event, which takes place elsewhere – otherwise, it is not a media event. This criterion is closely related to the secondary differentiation into three levels of events, which Dayan and Katz operate with.

They distinguish three levels of actors: organisers, broadcasters, and spectators. The organiser is responsible for the event in reality, that is, whether it receives media coverage or not. The broadcaster (producer) is the actor who arranges the transmission of the event, which occurs apart from the transmission. In the terminology of traditional communication theory this actor corresponds to the sender or the media sender. Audiences (viewers, spectators) are the actors who receive the transmission, in whose eyes it is an event. On this level it is important to conceive of the three actors as being distinctly separate or independent, and as interacting via a "process of negotiation" (Dayan & Katz,

1992: 55).[11] Cases where the organiser is also the producer are, by definition, not media events.

In many respects, this trichotomy corresponds to the trichotomy, reality, text and reception. As in all textual relationships, transformation occurs between reality and the text, viz., encoding, and another occurs between the text and reception, viz., decoding. In the present article, it is mainly the former transformation that will be examined, with a view to gaining text-based insights into the process of decoding. In other words, our focus rests on how the real-world sports event is interpreted by the producer and presented as a textual representation to the viewer. Before considering the levels of the producer, let us first briefly orient ourselves concerning the levels of the organisers and the viewers, respectively.

The Level of the Organiser

Before looking at the media sports event in greater detail, we should consider certain aspects of the (real) sports event, i.e., the sport itself. Every sport has its own set of rules; these may be said to provide the script for the event in question. The rules say which person(s) will play, where the event will take place (locus), and when, or in what time frame, it shall take place (time). Thus, the rules provide a synopsis or storyboard which is then filled with concrete spatio-temporal phenomena and actors. The storyboard is the framework in which the event takes place; it is a temporally and/or spatially inviolable framework: the locus of the sport is artificially, but definitely, limited. Any transgression of the rules which apply within this framework is penalised. If, for example, a soccer player takes the ball over the sideline, he or she forfeits control of the ball.

Needless to say, the event involves any number of scripts. Some derive from cultural myths; others derive from the manifold character of the sport itself. Here I have no ambition to characterise various sports, but it is obvious that a three-week bicycle race differs considerably from the execution of a five-minute figure skating programme. This 'phenomenology of sport' frequently figures in discussions of what sports make 'good television' and what sports do not lend themselves to the medium. In this context let us be content with making a distinction between aesthetic and pragmatic sports, or qualitative and quantitative sports. Any sport, as opposed to games played for the pleasure of the player, contains a quantitative dimension in that the result of the exercise is some sort of measurable ranking order. In the here so-called aesthetics sports this ranking order is established from somebody's (usually one or more judges) subjective judgement (marking), while in the pragmatic sports, an objective measurement (score, point, time, height, or length) is decisive. This does not mean that pragmatic sports do not have an aesthetic dimension but in establishing a ranking order it is always completely inconsequential which team played the best or the most beautifully; who had the best technique; it is always only the objective result that matters at the end of the day. Also in sports, as opposed to games, we have, at least potentially, a spectator, i.e., the sport is exercised or performed towards somebody else, and therefore directed towards others than the performer himself. Thus, the sport in question is in this way *agôn* rather than *ilinx* in that it has the extroverted activity as its distinctive mark.[12]

Meanwhile, there is also a sociological aspect. Various organisations, committees, leagues, etc. organise the sport and arrange the events. Tournaments and cup contests are the archetypical forms on this level. On the one hand, we have forms in which the various events are essentially of equal status (e.g., golf tournaments, league matches); on the other, structures in which the events form definite hierarchies, culminating in a championship or 'cup final' (e.g. elimination tournaments like Wimbledon or the World Cup).[13]

Thus, already on the phenomenological plane, we find a range of semi-textual and narrative entities, which on this level in the concrete execution supplies the sporting event with a discursive determination of the actors in the context of a spatio-temporal framework.

The Level of the Viewer

On the level of the viewer, we have the viewer, obviously, but also to some extent the spectator, as well. In a study of television aesthetics it is only natural that the viewers be in focus, but the presence of a spectator role on the phenomenological level makes it necessary to examine the two roles more closely. The viewer role is often filled by an individual with knowledge and experience of the spectator role. As a spectator, one can find oneself missing the slow-motion instant replay; as a viewer one can miss the spectator's control of his gaze.[14]

In the process of defining the event in terms of organisational structures, we touched on the sociability of sport and that the observer which this quality implies is primarily the spectator, and only secondly the TV viewer. It is not particularly productive to rank-order the two categories like this inasmuch as the number of viewers nearly always outnumbers the number of spectators attending the event. It is commonly assumed that the spectator's access to the event is more authentic than the viewer's, and it is also typical that the idea of having 'been there' is a hallowed emblem of the sports audience.

The Level of the Producer
– the Rhetoric of the Sporting Event

As we have seen in the foregoing, using Dayan and Katz' typology of the media event, one can conceive of it as consisting of three levels: the organiser, the producer/sender and the viewer. This trichotomy corresponds in a number of ways with a conventional model of verbal utterances, viz. 'someone (1) tells something to someone (2)'. The producer (someone 1) relates an event (something) to the viewer (someone 2). At the same time, it is quite clear that the event-as-told is not identical with the event-as-it-happens. We are dealing with two levels or perspectives here, a textual level and a referent level. The latter casts light on how what is told relates to the occurrence related; the former on how the message related is related to the other person.

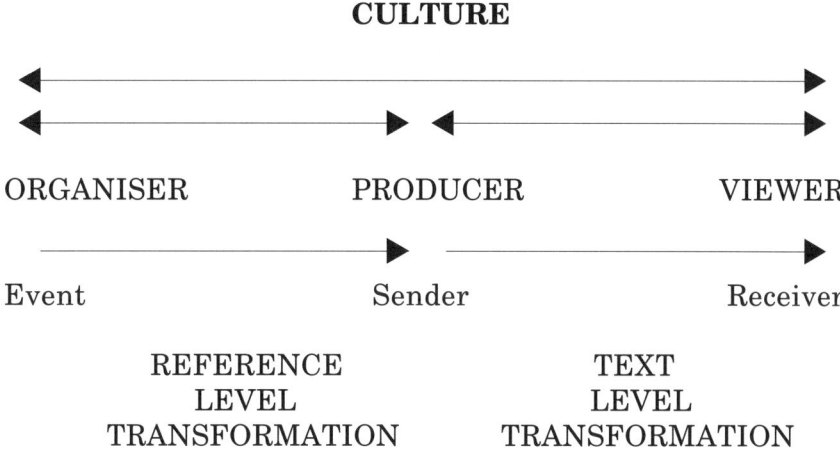

Figure 2

Figure 2 shows the processes of transformation that take place in connection with a media event, where communicative and cultural levels are differentiated. The model is general, covering all kinds of textual contexts, including those which in concrete textual contexts are to be regarded as derivative forms. Within the fictional register, the sender level will also prevail over the actor level in the event; fictional reality is totally steered by the sender, who creates the text. In the case of non-fiction, sender and actor operate on different levels; indeed, this dual relationship to the factual register is constitutive of non-fiction.

Meanwhile, there is also a metacommunicative level: the various actors know how other actors, as well as the relationships between the various actors, normally work. These relationships are non-textual, but they are cultural. This means, first of all, that the different levels can act on this knowledge and plan their actions accordingly. Actors on the level of the event can either ensure lack of coverage or increase the likelihood of coverage, i.e., textualization of the event by using what they know about the sender and the receiver and their behaviour and preferences. A striking example was the 'invasion' of Somalia by U.S. military forces in 1992. The sender level was commissioned to cover the event 'live', and the invasion was scheduled to suit 'prime time' on the Atlantic coast of the USA: Within the world of sport there is a recurrent discussion of when matches should be scheduled in order to reach the maximum number of viewers.

Viewers, meanwhile, generally know enough about the circumstances of the event so that they can, if they wish, wait until the climax – the last quarter of an hour, for example – before tuning in to see the most exciting part. Any number of examples of this metacommunicative or contextual knowledge present themselves, and the implications such knowledge has for the textual level are quite fundamental. However, on the textual level they are, and remain, contextual and in many respects secondary as something which exists, but only materialises itself in the textual representation. The text is also the focus of our attention here.

The transition from the realm of opportunities associated with the event to the text is simultaneously a transition into the level of discourse; a text is always uttered from an utterance position (the sender) and in this sense becomes the perspective on the open phenomenological event which, through objectifying it, closes the event.

> "A TV-transmitted soccer match is such a narrative: It is a discourse, because it – in contrast to the match itself – can be attributed to an utterance subject, to a narrating party (the producer, the collective behind the audio-visual production itself). It is this utterance subject, who creates the match. The discourse is closed, inasmuch as every televised soccer match has a beginning and an end (and a middle, I am tempted to add – homage Aristotle)."
> (Schantz Lauridsen, 1986: 27, author's translation)

The text specifies the discursive entities, I-HERE-NOW, or, more generally, a perspective, a place, a time, which together organise the closure of the event, which defines a textual process in a finite space. Every textual presentation is subject to this discursive logic, this verbal Origo,[15] and, through its textualization, sets out a set of entities. At the same time, the discursive utterance positions the receiver in relation to the event. We must therefore operate with three sets of Origo entities: Thus, the text – quite in keeping with the model, someone says something to someone – sets out three discursive levels, each of which consists of three logical relationships. The figure shows one of many possible configurations of them; the time is constant here, but could as well be a variable.

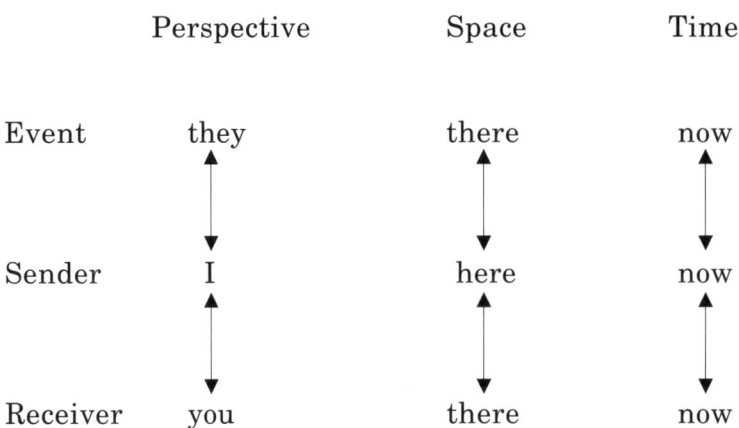

Figure 3

Returning for a moment to Dayan and Katz' definition of the media event and the four definitive criteria: planned, pre-emptive, distant and 'live', we find that these two pairs of relationships correspond well with the two levels indicated in Figure 2. The qualities of being planned and pre-emptive have to do with the overall contextual relationships, where the three actor-levels know about the event in advance and are familiar with normal scheduling, which can be set aside. The qualities 'live' and distant, on the other hand, have to do with the textual representation. The media event represents a concrete case of there-here-there and now-now-now. In the following, we shall take a closer look at how these relationships are concretely expressed in the transmissions, but first we should consider another important communicative element.

As we see in Figure 3, the actual perspective is situated as a distinction between different perspectives. We may assume that the sporting event is ever trying to offer opportunities for identification on this level, and, furthermore, that sport is a very suitable framework for sympathies and antipathies, which on the textual level means that there is a constant rhetorical effort to link perspectives of the three levels together through the utterance of a transcendent 'WE'. It is this level which means that events are related through a fundamentally actantial identification of villains and heroes, winners and losers. And it is on this level, too, that the producer stands between an essentially communicative inhibition and a narrative necessity. It is these narrative scenarios which are in focus in the following.

Four Levels of Meaning in the TV Sport Text

The television sport text may be divided into two main categories: picture and sound. Each of these in turn may be divided into two levels: in the case of picture, photographic image and graphics, and in the case of sound, wild sound and commentary. An early treatment is Edward Buscombe's now classic monograph, *Football on Television* (Buscombe, 1975), which consists of structuralistic essays on various aspects of BBC's and ITV's coverage of the Soccer World Cup in West Germany in 1974. The Danish literature offers scattered analyses, particularly of the visual aspect of televised sports, all of which are indebted to Buscombe. Among these contributions, Palle Schantz Lauridsen's "A Football Narrative", an analysis of DR TVs coverage of the World Cup contests of 1986, is seminal.[16] In this article, Schantz Lauridsen describes how a soccer match is narrativised through ritualised sequences of shots, which are repeated in certain situations throughout the match, thereby forging the contest into a narrative whole. The article focuses exclusively on the sequence of shots that occurs when teams score, but the author also notes that similar "rituals" may accompany throw-ins and corners (Schantz Lauridsen, 1986: 49). Analyses of individual transmissions will not be considered here; instead, we shall treat the subject more generally, describing the four levels of meaning in the texts of televised sport in relation to the factors specified in Figure 3: perspective, space and time.

The Image and Perspective

A television transmission requires one or more cameras. Even if modern television transmissions nearly always use more than one camera, the viewer can orient him/herself in the space of the sporting event thanks to the fact that the primary camera maintains (what has become) a codified position which does not alter during the event. This position, which may be regarded as the primary position of the sports transmission, is the point of view which becomes established as the viewer's point of view, and it is returned to time and again throughout the transmission. It is the 'normal' position, the point of departure or the basic point of view. According to the conventions of the genre, the primary position coincides with the best seats in the stadium.[17] This rule is especially applicable to most televised sport in Europe and other countries outside the USA.[18] Thus, a firm point of view is established at the start, but it is a point of view from which one departs and then returns. One of the most common observations regarding perspective and televised sports versus non-mediated sports is that the many cameras in the former case provide a broader and more comprehensive perspective than is available to the real-life spectator. This is partly true, but the opposite may be argued, as well. For even if the many cameras from many angles, plus their ability to zoom in and zoom out, to be very close and very distant and all points in between, give the viewer an omnipotence which is specific to the media sports event, it is nonetheless a chosen position, one of many possible at any given moment.

"The live spectator will be free to move, to turn the head, to absorb many different pictures, sounds and smells simultaneously, and will therefore stay master of his or her own interpretation." (Barnett, 1990: 155)

The placement of the cameras and, thus, the chosen perspectives define and delimit the space of the televised sports event. Whereas the use of zoom-lens close-ups gives the viewer an illusion of 'here' (cf. Figure 3), the at once comprehensive and delimited overall images of the transmission are a deixist reference to 'there', i.e., to the locus of the sporting event. A place which the cameras have made accessible to the viewer.

Television transmissions of soccer matches have evolved considerably since 1986 and 1974 when Schantz Lauridsen and Buscombe, respectively, described them. On the visual front, the greatest change is due to a tremendous increase in the number of cameras used to cover matches. When German ZDF transmitted the World Cup tournament in 1974, they used five cameras per match (Buscombe, 1975: 50). Twelve years later, in Mexico, eleven cameras were used in the most important contests. Today, eleven cameras is standard procedure, and if a match is of extraordinary importance, up to twenty cameras may be used. In the World Cup tournament in Italy in 1990, RAI used 16 to 18 cameras per match from the quarter-finals on (Seifart, 1990: 86).

The Tense of Visual Images

The time frame is the same in all three levels in Figure 3. But time is also a dimension on which direct sports transmissions differ from other direct transmissions, such as openings of Parliament, royal weddings and jubilees. Running time and real time coincide in all live transmissions; in the cases mentioned there is a 1:1 relationship between telling time and told time. Live transmissions of sporting events differ in that the running time is regularly interrupted with brief pockets of suspended time. Most such pockets are filled with play-backs ('action replays') or slow-motion repeats of the play just completed, etc. Episodes which the producer deems more or less crucial.

In his article, "Chance and Plot", Umberto Eco (1989) likens what happens in the producer's televised text to jazz improvisations; he conceives of the production of the televised text as an instantaneous piecing together of information within the framework of knowledge of previous texts of the same kind, television texts which make use of the same code. The amount of raw information in a soccer transmission is tremendous: images from as many as twenty cameras, wild sound from about ten microphones, the words of the commentators (one or two in most cases), and various kinds of graphics at the producer's disposal.

> "Filming, editing, and broadcasting, three phases that in cinema remain perfectly separate and distinct, are here fused into one – a fact which certainly warrants the identification of real time with televisual time, since no form of narration can condense the autonomous duration of the represented event." (Eco, 1989: 107)

In addition to giving the producer a 'second chance' in case he/she has missed something important in the running account, the 'pockets of time' have the more significant function of punctuating the account, preserving and embellishing crucial junctures. These unpredictable moments, their preservation through the 'instant replay', and the almost erotic – at once intimate and analytical – aesthetics which characterises them make up one of the prime characteristics of the live sports transmission. It is an aesthetics which reflects a desire to make the most of the highlights, the most exciting moments of the match. The aesthetics of sports journalism is, as touched upon previously, an "aesthetics of the instant", and the endless repetition of the most exciting moments is a visual celebration of both the aesthetics and the moment.

Graphics

The increasing use of computers in modern television production has had a palpable influence on live sport transmissions, particularly on the graphics used in them. Graphics are primarily used for two purposes: to package and present the transmission, and to provide various kinds of information during the course of the event being covered. Here, we shall concern ourselves with the latter. Computers are mainly used to collect, store and process data and information, and they give broadcasters access to much more information than they might have otherwise. It is both information that producers may have had access to earlier, albeit less readily – the names of players, officials, coaches and managers, playing time, and the score – and information that is available thanks to the computer alone. This is information which, typically, is of a more analytical nature and which is the result of 'collaboration' between camera and computer.

It is, for example, information about the distance between the ball and, say, a defensive 'wall'. The computer analyses the data registered by the camera and, on the basis of that data, calculates the distance and a graphic representation of the play at hand. Other examples include graphic representations of the configuration of players over the field and the use of paintbox (to analyse key plays in retrospect). Other computer-aided information includes the age, weight and 'track record' of individual players, the number of warnings (yellow cards) received, and so forth. It is all presented visually and not, as earlier, by the commentator. Characteristically, information once provided by the commentator now originates with the producer – superimposed over the picture of the field, the ball and the players. As the source – or sender of the concrete graphical image – increasingly often is the producer or other person on a higher level of utterance than the commentator, the authoritativeness of the information provided in the graphics is greater than that of what the commentator says. (More on this point in the section on the commentator, below.)

This leads to situations in which the commentator speaks on the basis of the graphics, i.e., orients himself to them, rather than having the graphics illustrate what he says. There are quite practical reasons for this: major international events involve far more commentators than there are producers, and each covers the event in his own language to his respective audience. In most cases, the pictures (and thereby the production) are supplied by a team from a broadcasting company in the country where the event takes place. (Consequently, it occurs that viewers can hear a commentator complain that the producer has not supplied the 'right' pictures, but hardly ever when producer and commentator come from the same country, or rather: the same broadcasting organisation.)

In addition to descriptive and analytical information relating to the event, graphics may also be used to identify the station producing the pictures, i.e., the station which owns the rights to transmit the event. Here we have the logotype of the company, commonly placed in a corner of the screen, but in the case of televised sport also different kinds of station identification worked into the informational graphics; the station and (often) the manufacturer of the computer program, the time-taking device, etc., used in the production may be integrated into the presentation of the commentators, information about players entering and leaving the contest, the remaining minutes of play, match statistics, and so forth. Or in the graphics which more and more frequently accompany the instant replay: the blinking 'R' of yesteryear is increasingly replaced by three-dimensional, framed images, where the station's name and logotype and identifying typography are included in the frame. This visual effect, which represents a new, computer-animated intermediate form between graphics and picture has a corresponding hybrid on the sound front, as well: a whistling or 'swooshing' sound that accompanies the 'photographics'. On a metonymical level the sound mimics the movement of the framed picture as it sweeps onto the screen, while it metaphorically signals a jump (back) in time.

'Wild Sound'

Television productions normally involve three kinds of sound: 'wild sound', speech and music. In the present context, we may largely ignore the latter category, inasmuch as the only music present in televised sporting events occurs as wild sound, music as heard in the arena or room of the event. In the case of soccer matches, for example, music is most prominent in the case of contests between national teams (albeit an increasing number of clubs have anthems of their own, which are played when the players take the field and perhaps after the match when the 'home team' has won). In sports like gymnastics, where rhythmic music plays a key role, significantly, the music viewers hear in their loudspeakers is nearly always acoustic sound from the venue of the event, i.e., wild sound, rather than background or 'mood' music.[19]

'Music as heard in the room of the event' has an ambient, spatial quality which signals that it has been 'picked up' by a microphone on the scene. One might say that in addition to the music, we hear the room itself – consider, for example, the characteristic acoustics of a handball court or gymnastics hall. In this sense, wild sound is the sound of the event itself; it is not a parallel tape or CD recording of whatever piece of music the gymnast may have chosen to perform to. That the output, in purely technical terms, may be (and usually is) the result of mixing the uptake of several microphones in the room is irrelevant; the point is that the sound viewers hear sounds 'like' the sound which spectators who are physically present in the room are experiencing (even though it in fact is a mix of sounds from different sources in the room). Wild sound includes the voices, breathing, puffing and groans of the players; they, too, are experienced by viewer and spectator alike.

It is important that we hear sounds from the venue of the event; it is, we will recall, a definitive characteristic of the media event. The ambient, spatial and, in some senses, less-than-perfect wild sound is a sign that the sender/producer level does not control the actor level. Consequently, viewers experience the televised event as an event that has a life of its own, above and beyond the intervention of the medium. One might say that wild sound is the fingerprint of the event on the media event, or a stamp of authenticity. The distinction between the sender and the actor which the sound of the television text marks thus plays a part in the aesthetics of realism in which television wraps the event.

Commentary – Speaking about Pictures

Of the four levels of meaning, the picture is paramount; the primary information is carried in the picture. Be that as it may, the commentator's speech is a prime characteristic of televised sport, and sports commentary is one of the most studied features of televised sport in the literature on the subject. The analyses to date have mainly concentrated on the commentary divorced from the pictures; interest has mostly revolved around what is said without any particular relation to the accompanying visuals, let alone how words and pictures might interact. (Not infrequently, the purpose of the analysis is to reveal one or another kind of 'chauvinism': considering the sparseness of the literature, one finds surprisingly many examples of commentators talking about "exotic foreigners", "good-looking handball lasses", and so on.) Here, however, we are interested in the interaction between the commentary and other levels.

The role of commentary in the case of televised sport is special inasmuch as the interaction of sound and picture in sports transmissions is quite different from that in newscasts, for example. In the latter case, the greater share of the information is imparted via the speaker, and the visuals serve as illustrations.[20] The newscaster/reporter is a speaker – one who speaks – and not a commentator, i.e., someone who talks about something which we, too, can see. The TV sports commentator mainly plays a verifying, clarifying and corroborating or anchoring role. He speaks to the pictures and generally speaks about something we can see. Consequently, the role differs from that of the news anchor, who talks about things we do not know, what is more, things that often either have not been or cannot be visualised. The function of the commentator is fourfold; he/she speaks about

a) things viewers can see: "… Number Ten, Michael Laudrup enters the field …"
b) things they may not necessarily be able to see: "… all three substitutes are now warming up …"
c) things they may or may not know: "… Thirty-seven-year-old Peter Schmeichel, who hails from …"
d) things they cannot know: "Michael Laudrup warmed up before the match, but is not in the starting line-up."

It is in the first case, a), that the commentary has the most corroborating function, i.e. where the commentary anchorages the pictures. In the second case, b), the commentary may have an anchorage function, or it may be diverting, i.e. have a relaying function. If the commentary arises out of something the commentator alone can see, thanks to his physical presence at the scene, in the room of the event, it is diverting and relaying; if, on the other hand, it refers to something visible on the screen, something viewers, too, can see, its function is anchoring. Thus, the nature of the function depends on whether the commentary has its origin in the event or the media event. In the third case, the commentary is that of relay since we cannot see on the screen that Peter Schmeichel is thirty-seven years old, nor what club he hails from. Even here, however, the commentary bears a fairly close relation to the picture inasmuch as such comments usually are made when the player in question is on camera. This may also be true in the fourth case, d), but such information is more likely to be offered when the referent is not on camera (the example above might be elicited by a reflection on what Laudrup might have done in the situation at hand, had he been in the game). The comment contains an implicit desire to change the referent's absence into presence. Commentary of the fourth kind may, for that matter, be entirely explicit since it need not bear any relation to the game or what appears on the screen: e.g., comments on the behaviour of the crowd before the match, or 'insider' gossip about purchases, sales and firings.

As we proceed from a) to d), we note a gradual tendency away from the corroborating or anchoring function. At the same time, we experience an increasing freedom from the requirement of simultaneity between picture and commentary. This has to do with the nature of the game itself. The primary object is the ball. The commentary follows the ball, not the players, because the commentary follows the camera (the picture is paramount), and the camera follows the ball. The symbiosis between ball and camera remains unbroken as long as the ball is in play. As soon as the whistle sounds and a pause ensues, the focus can shift, and the focus of the commentator generally shifts from the ball to the players.[21]

In addition to the anchoring and relaying functions, sports commentary is also instrumental in channelling and conveying sympathies and antipathies. Commentators are supposed to be non-partisan, but they seldom are. In transmissions from domestic (national) matches, where two athletes or teams from the same country oppose one another, a commentator's impartiality/fairness to both can be a source of considerable irritation to viewers. The opposite holds, however, in international contests or if one of the teams has the same nationality as the commentator and his audience. When players in one way or another are the extended or vicarious agents of a national audience, that is, their actions and feats are metonyms for an ideal or sense of community, the commentator's role will essentially be to mediate a transcendental 'we' (Fig. 3). His very use of the word, 'we', reduces the distance between the viewer and himself and by virtue of his position on the sidelines of the field, to the players. The players, who were originally the objects of the viewers' sympathy are rendered, so to speak, identical with the viewers, so that sympathy no longer flows only from the viewer or commentator toward the players, but from the commentator toward the viewers, as well.

The Partner

Whereas it once was uncommon for a match to be covered by more than one commentator, today it is the rule rather than the exception. Naturally, the two commentators do not say the same things. The commentator is the one who corroborates, who reinforces and anchorages the events; his role is to impart the sense of immediacy, simultaneity, and he has the right to speak in the present tense at the very moment events transpire. The co-commentator or 'partner', on the other hand, has to wait until there is a pause or a lull in the match. Just as the studio host or hostess gives the floor to the commentator, the commentator gives the floor to his partner, either by asking him his opinion or simply by stopping to give him a chance to speak. Should, however, something unexpected or exciting happen, the commentator has both the right and a duty to break in and take over, since both cannot speak at once. The here and now is the province of the commentator.[22]

Thus, the commentator is the one who anchorages the events in real time, whereas the partner mostly does this in connection with replays, whereby he also contributes to an auditive embellishment of the moments which have been deemed worth repeating. The partner may, however, contribute relaying comments at will, but only when the commentator has given him the floor. Nor is the partner allowed to let himself get carried away.

The partner is (nearly) always a retired star player. This lends him credibility, especially when he talks about behind-the-scenes happenings. Since his function is primarily relaying, he needs to know things we (and the commentator) do not know. This information can be of many different kinds, but basically falls into one of two categories: tactical information and insider information. The tactical information is analytical in relation to the match at hand, yet relaying: it does not relate to what is shown in the picture, but to the background. Insider information does not necessarily relate to what is on the screen or to the background. It may consist of gossip which the partner has picked up thanks to his privileged status as an ex-star; belonging to the inner circle, he is privy to information. But the partner may also contribute simple fillers – anecdotes and references to his own career, which besides helping to maintain the aura and mythology that surrounds the sport, serves a vital function: filling the time in lulls in the game. The partner is an important figure in that he, regardless of what takes place on the field, can always contribute something of interest to the televised event. And this something is totally independent of the real event. Thus, the partner helps differentiate the media event from the event itself in that he is part of the system which means that a dull sporting event need not necessarily be a dull media event.

The Commentator's Perspective

The commentator is located not in the 'there' of the event, but in his capacity of on-the-scene reporter, he establishes his own 'here', which coincides with the 'here' of the event, but different from the 'here' of the sender.[23] The 'here' of the sender is the studio or the medium, from which the commentator has ventured to cover the event.[24] The producer and the camera crews have been sent to the scene, as well, but they lack significance in this context; in fact, an effort is made to ignore their presence and to reduce the results of their efforts to a 'given', to something 'natural'. The commentator is 'our man on the spot' par excellence, and typically we only hear mention of the producer and crew when something goes wrong and prevents us (and the commentator) from seeing what we want to see. Often, all these co-workers are reduced to 'the hardware' which underlines that it is the privilege of the viewer and his ally, the commentator, to interpret the event – not the cameraman, engineers, etc., whose job it is merely to bring the pictures to us.

One of the purposes of the rhetoric of the transmission is, to the extent possible, to make the 'here' of the event and the 'here' of the viewer coincide. At the same time, it should be clear that the sender/station's normal 'here' is not the place where he, for the sake of the event, is stationed. This last point is of importance in establishing the autonomy of the event, that it would have taken place (in the same way) regardless of whether television had shown an interest or not. Interestingly, however, in relation to Dayan and Katz' criterion, that the event generally take place outside the studio in remote locations (Dayan & Katz, 1992: 5), the sporting event establishes an intermediate position inasmuch as not infrequently, not only does the commentator, but the entire studio, with studio hosts/hostesses, guests, and so forth, move out to the venue of the event.

Concluding Remarks

In this article I have proposed a genre approach to televised sport with a focus on form, rather than content. I have found televised sport to share certain characteristics with other kinds of television which – applying Dayan and Katz' definition – may be called media events. The concept of the media event represents a point of departure for the study of how television sport on an aesthetic level transforms the sporting event from an event into a media event. I have shown that the sports transmission is the result of a transformation which takes place in both sound and picture components. The aesthetics of televised sporting events draws to some extent on the aesthetics of the sporting event, an aesthetics of realism, so that the sports transmission has an aura of 'naturalness'.

But the aesthetics of the televised sporting event is equally an aesthetics of the instant, and a characteristic feature of that aesthetics is a tendency to try to preserve and embellish the decisive moments in the event. This is done on multiple levels: in the narrative, through repetition of the moments in question; visually, for example, through the graphic framing and enactment of the repetition and the graphically designed analysis of the moments; auditively (and narratively), through a doubling of the commentator function by the addition of a co-commentator or 'partner'.

The commentator function is, furthermore, crucial to the striving of the media event to establish a transcendental 'we', which is a key to understanding the rhetoric of major national televised sporting events. This 'we' comes into play in establishing/imparting the antipathies and sympathies which arise in connection with international contests, while it also shortens the distance between the viewer, the mediator (here: the commentator), and the actors. It may be conceived of as a verbal analogy to the camera's intimate study of the event and its actors – particularly in the most intense moments, but it also extends beyond these individual moments, and even events, to be a model for the entire medium in its approach to major national sporting events.

Notes

1. Much of Morse's article is devoted to identifying certain aesthetic characteristics of television sport, and in the course of that pursuit she does indeed move beyond the content-related approach signalled in her more general introduction.
2. This article, parts of which were written in collaboration with Henrik Sand, Aalborg University, and presented in a working group at the 13th conference of the Nordic Association of Mass Communication Research in Jyväskylä, Finland, in August 1997, is written with mainly soccer in mind, but the more general observations in the beginning of the article apply to all kinds of sports, and even the more concrete examples in the latter part of the article may be more or less readily transposed to other kinds of sports (see further note 17). The first 'live' images of a soccer match – England vs. Scotland – were transmitted on 9 April 1938. Thus, the tradition of live sports transmissions is virtually as old as the medium itself.

3. Michael R. Real here uses the term *athletics*, but does not make any further distinction between sports and athletics. Later in a sentence on the same page (1982: 210) he goes on to describe one particular play from the 1974 Super Bowl, thus, entering into an area that within the framework of this article is *sport* more than it is *athletics*.
4. It is therefore quite interesting why so much of the time of 'Sport on TV' as such is devoted to pundits trying to do exactly that: Predict the outcome of the sporting event. It is a shame; it cannot be done. But it still makes good TV.
5. Thus, in a sense, the simultaneity of the representation points toward the future, which is unknown to everyone – the producer, the players, as well as the spectators – an uncertainty which applies to both the event and the media event. Not knowing the outcome is the key to the programme's fascination, an important aspect in the phenomenology of sport as well as of the aesthetics of televised sport. Nonetheless, the aesthetic expression of delayed transmissions is often identical with the truly 'live' transmission – perhaps in order to maintain the illusion of simultaneity. Only in the case of sport news and 'wrap-ups' is the aesthetic expression remarkably different.
6. Paddy Scannell (1995) describes fixed programme scheduling as a key to why television is perceived to have the character of "routine" or "everyday". Viewers have to know when and what they can expect to see on television so they can get excited about it! Media events require, quite dialectically, the everyday, the routine in order to be the "holiday" Dayan and Katz conceive them to be.
7. Even though the weekly soccer match in itself is not a media event, in an attempt to resemble a 'real' event as much as possible, it borrows much of the aesthetic praxis of major TV sports events. Thus, on a purely aesthetic level most of the characteristics of television events are transferred over to weekly/daily non-events. The aesthetics is applied on the rhetorical plane so as to convince the viewer that this weekly event – on the rhetorical plane at least – is equivalent to an exclusive media event.
8. It is common knowledge that channels are commonly besieged by irate viewers when events unexpectedly pre-empt other programmes. Viewers are angry, for example, when a sports transmission is broken off in the middle of a key play, and parents are angry because a women's handball match has pre-empted a children's programme.

9. Dayan and Katz offer an illustrative example of the distinction: "Thus, we are interested in the Kennedy funeral – a great ceremonial event – and not the Kennedy assassination – a great news event" (Dayan & Katz, 1992: 9).
10. When saying 'live' or 'direct' here, the physical delay inherent in the transmission itself is ignored. The moon landing was a direct transmission, even if it took six minutes for the signal to reach Earth; similarly, live interviews are direct, even if we hear a slight delay in the voice transmission.
11. In the real world (of sport) they are not actually distinctly separate. Due to the sums of money involved, particularly money deriving from the sale of distribution rights, the sender (broadcaster) has more and more say in the organisation of the event itself, i.e., more influence over the organiser.
12. This typology stems from Caillois classification: agon, mimicry, alea, and ilinx (Caillois, 1979). See also Andersen (1995) for a short introduction to these categories.
13. In some elimination tournaments, such as the FA Cup football tournament in England, this hierarchic organisation of meaning also takes place on a spatial level. The final (match) is here played in a special stadium – in this case Wembley Stadium – where only very important events take place (Wembley Stadium is not the home ground of any team other than the English National Team). Thus the cup tournament in this case takes on the shape of a crusade, where the spatial recognition that is involved in obtaining the right to play at Wembley is very important. This is expressed not at least by the supporters of the various clubs, and can, among other places, be observed in their chanting at cup matches: *"... we're the famous Ar-se-nal, and we're going to Wem-ber-ley"*. The situation surrounding Wembley is at the time of writing somewhat confused as the stadium is currently closed for refurbishment, which, due to various political and economical developments, may never take place! Thus, the last F.A.-cup final to be played there (at least for the time being) was the final of the year 2000. Similarly, Wembley does not host the home games of the English national soccer team any more. However, it still remains a sacred place in English and international footballing history and several forces in England are battling to restore it to its former glory for exactly this reason.
14. In addition to the experience of being a spectator, many viewers also have the experience of being players. This is particularly true with respect to the most popular sports, ball sports, cycling, etc., and may contribute to the great popularity these sports enjoy.

15. The concept of the linguistic Origo originates with Karl Bühler (1934, orig. 1965). Bühler's linguistic model is most widely known through Jakobson's (1967, orig. 1960) model of the text, in which Jakobson's three fundamental functions reproduce the Origo concept.
16. Other Danish contributions include Henrik Jagd and Benny Warning's "TV Soccer and Nationalism" ("TV-fodbold og nationalisme") and Mogens Schmidt's "The Armchair Stadium?" ("Et stadion i stuen?"), which, besides being the first, is also the treatise which contains the deepest reflections on the role of the commentator. Nearly all the Danish literature on mediated sports concerns soccer, and it is characteristic that a peak in the interest in televised soccer may be noted around 1986, when the Danish national soccer team attracted (Danes') attention to it, and to the sport in general. Since then, academic interest in soccer (and other sports) has gradually subsided, and not even the Danish European Championship in 1992 could revive interest among the research community – perhaps because analysts failed to find much of interest on the aesthetic level in the 1992 version of Danish football itself. Be that as it may, one of the more recent analytic works on sport and television, Kirsten Frandsen's dissertation, *Sports-journalistik (Sports journalism)*, is not about men's soccer, but about women's handball. References to 'the real world' seem in many ways unavoidable when it comes to sport.
17. As mentioned earlier, soccer is the focal sport in this article. Most observations are applicable to other stadium sports, i.e., sports which take place in a confined space and which involve one or more objects or players operating in a well defined arena. Such sports include most ball games, boxing, swimming and so forth. Other conditions apply in the case of sports which are less spatially confined: bicycle races, cross-country races, etc. In order to achieve satisfactory coverage of such events, the camera must be mobile in order to follow the object, and several cameras will be necessary inasmuch as several objects are of interest, and the objects are often relatively far apart. Cf. the individual starting points in the Tour de France cycling race. As part of a forthcoming ph.d.-dissertation an article trying to develop a comprehensive typology of sports and televised sports is under way.
18. Writing with reference to Edward Buscombe's *Football on Television*, Margaret Morse (1983) makes this observation in a comparison of English and American football. English coverage, she notes, expresses a basic agenda-setting desire to report, to repre-

sent the event at hand, whereas American coverage evidences a desire to entertain.

19. In the 1994 Winter Olympics in Lillehammer, Norway, non-ambient music was added to slow-motion reviews of episodes from cross-country skiing races. This was – and remains – an exception, however.
20. For more on newscasts, see Peter Larsen's "Analyse af TV-avisen" ("Analysis of the evening TV news"), 1974.
21. This is the back cloth to the Monty Python sketch depicting a soccer match between teams of Greek and German philosophers: The camera follows the various 'players' who absent-mindedly wander about on the field, when suddenly the ball is seen in the picture, still placed on its initial spot in the middle of the pitch, and the commentator exclaims, "... Oh, and there's the ball!"
22. The first and most famous commentator in Denmark, Gunnar "Now!" Hansen, is a case in point. His nickname "Now!" is a veritable ode to the medium which makes simultaneity possible (first radio, then television) and a fairly exact expression of the fascination of the aesthetics of the instant.
23. Cf. Peter Larsen's (1974) remarks on the hierarchy of utterances, which is largely applicable to televised sport.
24. This is one of the features of transmissions which has changed in recent years. Although the transmission of the match itself is largely the same, activities which previously took place in the studio have been moved out to the 'here' of the event in order to achieve coincidence between the 'here' of the sender and the 'here' of the event. The absence of the 'here' of the studio from the textual level in no way damages the sense of 'event-ness'. On the contrary, it tells us that this event is so important that even the manager of the Sports Department himself has gone out into the cold for its sake. In a metaphorical sense this is a step back toward the days of the rosy-nosed, bundled-up reporter who, pencil in hand, braved sleet and hail to fill us in on the latest scores.

Bibliography

Andersen, T. (1995). "Chancekultur – Sport og spil i skæbnens tegn". In: *Alebu* no 1. Aalborg: Aalborg University.
Barnett, Steven (1990). *Games and Sets: the Changing Face of Sport on Television*. London: BFI Publishing.
Banouw, Erik (1990). *Tube of Plenty. The Evolution of American Television*. Oxford: Oxford University Press.
Bordwell, David (1985). *Narration in the Fiction Film*. London: Routledge.
Buscombe, Edward (ed.) (1975). *Football on Television*. London: British Film Institute.
Bühler, K. (1965, orig. 1934). *Spracheteorie. Die Dastellung der Sprache 2*. Stuttgart: Gustav Fischer.
Caillois, R. (1979). *Man, Play and Games*. New York.
Dayan, D., & E. Katz (1992). *Media Events: the Live Broadcasting of History*. Cambridge: Harvard University Press.
Eco, Umberto (1989). *The Open Work*. Cambridge: Harvard University Press.
Eco, Umberto (1989). "Chance and Plot". In Umberto Eco: *The Open Work*. Cambridge: Harvard University Press.
Frandsen, Kirsten (1996). *Sport og journalistik (Sports journalism)*. Ph.D. Dissertation. Aarhus: Department of Journalism.
Jakobson, R. (1967, orig. 1960). "Lingvistik og Poetik". In: *Vindrosen* 14 (7).
Jantzen, Christian, & Verner Møller (1994). "Marginaloplevelser og tærskelværdier. Til installering af begrebet vanvidsidræt". In V. Møller, J. Poulsen & K. Lyders (eds.): *Hooked*. Odense: Odense Universitetsforlag.
Larsen, Peter (1974). "Analyse af TV-avisen". In M.B. Andersen & J. Poulsen (eds.): *Mediesociologi*. Copenhagen: Rhodos.
Lauridsen, Palle Schantz (1986). "En fodboldfortælling". In: *Sekvens. Filmvidenskabelig Årbog*. Copenhagen.
Marriott, Stephanie (1996). "Time and Time Again: 'Live' Television Commentary and the Construction of Replay Talk". In: *Media, Culture & Society*, vol. 18.
Morse, Margaret (1983). "Sport on Television: Replay and Display". In A. Kaplan (ed.): *Regarding Television: Critical Approaches*. Los Angeles: American Film Institute.
Real, Michael R. (1982, orig. 1977). "The Super Bowl: Mythic Spectacle". In Horace Newcomb (ed.): *Television: The Critical View*. Oxford: Oxford University Press.
Scannell, P. (1995). "For a Phenomenology of Radio and Television". In: *Journal of Communication* 45.

Schmidt, Mogens (1981). "Et stadion i stuen? Om fodbold i fjernsynet". In Frands Mortensen, Jørgen Poulsen & Preben Sepstrup (eds.): *Underholdning i TV*. Viborg: Nyt Nordisk Forlag.

Seifart, Horst (1990). "Vom Rekord zum technischen Ritual". In: *Brennpunkte der Sportwissenschaft*, 4.

Stigel, Jørgen (1997). *The Aesthetics of Television, the Quality of Television*. Working paper from the research project "The Aesthetics of Television".

Whannel, Gary (1992). *Fields in Vision. Television Sport and Cultural Transformation*. London: Routledge.

CHAPTER SEVEN

The Aesthetics of the Television Talk Show

Hanne Bruun
Department of Information and Mediascience
University of Aarhus

On stage there is a mother and her 17-year-old daughter. Today's problem is mothers who can't stand their children's partners. Mother and daughter tell the studio host about the conflict, and the studio host and the studio audience ask questions and make comments. Finally, the apple of discord – the boyfriend – is let into the studio. There now follows an extremely violent verbal clash between the mother and the boyfriend. They scream and shout at each other, and the studio audience applauds, jeers, and shouts comments. The emotional climax is reached when the tearful daughter declares her love to both mother and boyfriend, and calls upon them to make a reconciliation. The studio host rounds off, and, in a close up shot, she praises the maturity of the daughter to the applause of the studio audience. A commercial break follows.

We are witnessing the American talk show, *Ricki Lake*[1] and the sequence with the mother, daughter, and boyfriend is one of the day's three stories. *Ricki Lake* is a talk show which is specially organised with the aim of capturing a segment of young, female viewers who, in marketing terms, are the most interesting in the American commercially based TV system. The series is a success in the USA, and it has made Ricki Lake one of the most highly paid talk show hosts in American television. The series is also broadcast on a number of TV stations across Europe. In Denmark, at the moment, we can see the series on TV3 and 3+.

As a TV genre, however, the talk show is neither exclusive to the last decade nor to commercial television. In the USA the genre is as old as the medium of television itself, and today, talk shows comprise no small percentage of available programmes on commercial as well as non-commercial TV stations. Talk shows are cheap to produce and popular among viewers, and the ability of this genre to attract viewers is no new phenomenon either. It is, of course, no new phenomenon in Danish public service television either. For example, at the end of the seventies the talk show *Kanal 22* (DR, 1979-82) was able to attract 36% of the population. This type of programme was developed into the series *Lørdagskanalen* (*Saturday Channel*, DR, 1982-86) which had a viewer quota of 68% of the population. The programme type survived after the ending of the television monopoly in Denmark, in *Eleva2ren* (TV 2, 1988-96). In spite of viewers having a wider choice of channels, *Eleva2ren* was able to reach average ratings of 27% of the population.

In short, we are apparently dealing with a TV genre which has qualities attractive to viewers. I will offer an explanation of what these qualities are with an angle of approach in audience-oriented critism.[2] The reason why the talk show is a popular form of TV, and generally becomes so with relative ease, can be explained theoretically by a closer examination of the special relationship that the talk show attempts to create with its viewers. We are, in other words, placed in a special position of experience, which makes the talk show different from other TV genres.

In addition, I will emphasise that the relationship of the genre to the viewers would seem to contain four dramaturgic models in which actual talk shows are staged. Finally, I will return to the subject of *Ricki Lake* and examine how this talk show can be discussed from the theoretical angle of approach to the genre.

Three Fundamental Characteristics

Although it may be difficult at first to see what traits *This is Your Life*, *Ricki Lake*, and the Danish, *Mors Hammer* (a talk show in which various moral and social issues are discussed) share with each other, the three shows do, in fact, have three elements in common. These are, the TV studio, the host, and the interview.

The TV Studio

In the talk show the TV studio is the space of the programme, and in this genre the unity of time and place are observed in the same way as in classical drama. If the unity is broken, it is only momentary. The role of the TV medium in the talk show is to be both the event *in itself* and to be *the place* of the event at one and the same time.

Consequently, the talk show becomes different from other TV genres, even at this stage. In this genre TV is not a reporting medium, in which the medium primarily tells of a reality outside the medium itself. Neither does it have the role of a transmitting medium in which the medium is a visitor and, in principle, is not responsible for that which is shown. Transmissions of national sporting events and concerts are examples of TV in this role.

The planning of a talk show in terms of time and space has the character of a 'now and here', i.e. the aim is first of all to give viewers *an experience of* simultaneity between the time of the programme and its transmission. Secondly, the aim is to create an experience of mergence of space between the programme and the viewers, in such a way that the viewers feel as if they are participants in the programme as opposed to spectators. The scenographic arrangement of the studio is an important element in creating the experience of being a participant. As well as this the studio audience is able to function as a mental bridge between the *place* of the programme and the place of the viewers. The talk show is 'now and here', whereas the time and space of TV reporting is 'there and then', and the live transmission is 'now and there'.

The Studio Host

What is offered by the 'now and here' of the talk show is a form of togetherness. The studio host is the central dramaturgic element who functions as an intermediary between the programme and the viewers. For this reason, unlike the staging of an anchor person in a news broadcast, the talk show attaches great importance to the television personality of the host, as this is an essential part of the *content* of the talk show. On the other hand the anchor person in a news broadcast is, to a much greater extent, an institutional representative, partly for the TV station, and partly for the phenomenon 'news'.

The talk show is, to a great extent, the studio host's programme – and the programme is the host's 'world'. First of all the studio host has a variety of guests, depending on the nature of the programme. The guests are invited on to the host's programme, they are welcomed, and the host expresses his gratitude to them for coming on the show. He also has other guests on the programme, however. They are present, but unseen and silent. These are the viewers. For this reason the talk show is punctuated with many vitally important remarks directly to the camera in which the viewer is addressed directly.

The talk show host is, therefore, performing on two scenes. One of the scenes is in the talk show itself, and the host performs to the participants of the show and the studio audience, if there is one. The other scene exists between the programme and the viewers, such that the viewers are given the impression that the show exists for their benefit. In this way the viewers are recognised as participants in the programme and are addressed as such, as opposed to the position of voyeurs in relation to what is being shown. The position of voyeur is where viewers are generally placed in the TV documentary and in TV fiction.

The Interview

The interview is an important method of creating the content in the talk show. It is also the way in which a great portion of the content of the genre is presented, and consequently the focus is on people and conversation between people. This is what is on offer to the viewers. Because of this focus on people and conversation, the talk show differs from the TV-quiz show and the TV game show in which the emphasis is on a game governed by a set of rules. The talk show is like the performance of a theatrical improvisation, and the way in which this performance is set up with regard to interview style, the role of the interviewer, and the role of the participants, has a vital significance for the viewers' perception of actual talk shows.

The TV studio, the studio host, and the interview are the basic common elements in the various forms of talk shows. Other elements which are vital in deciding how each talk show is perceived and experienced, are the scenographic set-up, camera techniques, the use of sound and the entire audio-visual dimension. The fact that the talk show can attract viewers when what it has to offer is relatively minimalist, is due to the fact that the talk show embodies basic qualities of the TV medium itself. These features are to a very great degree so apparent, that they are considered natural for both producers of talk shows and viewers alike. That is why they are important.

Uncertainty and Sociability

Two basic qualities of the TV medium are central to the talk show. First of all the medium's ability to broadcast live non-fictive pictures. It is this quality, which separates television from radio and cinema. Secondly, television is mass communication, addressing a mass audience, but it is broadcast directly into the private sphere of the viewer. The medium is a part of our everyday routines, but is a medium primarily used in our leisure time when we want to relax. This means that TV programmes must find a mode of address suitable for a situation which is both collective and individual – a situation which is at once public and private for the home viewer.

In the talk show these two qualities of the TV medium play a vital role resulting in textual features in the genre which I describe with the concepts *the uncertainty factor* and *sociability*.

The Uncertainty Factor

Television was born as a live medium, i.e. there is simultaneity between the spoken statement and its reception, and has its technological origins in radio. Broadcasts were live because in the early childhood of television, facilities for storage and editing were unavailable. If anything other than simultaneous editing was required, recordings were made on film. Not until the end of the 1950s – CBS in 1956 and the BBC in 1958 – was video tape used (Tusa, 1993: 11), and in 1959 the ampex video tape recorder was used for the first time in Denmark. In addition moving out of the studio, which Danish radio had begun doing as early as the mid-1930s, proved extremely difficult when applied to television.[3] Although the BBC, as early as 1937, began using the first OB (Outside Broadcasting) unit, and thereby was able to broadcast live from the coronation of King George VI, both TV cameras and recording equipment were heavy and unreliable. For this reason pictures were limited to the area around Westminster Abbey.

If recording equipment were to be moved, it was necessary here too, to record events using film cameras with the consequential time lapse. It was not until the end of the 1970s that ENG (Electronic News Gathering) equipment began to be used in western Europe (Hjarvard, 1995: 266).

Because of the technological circumstances, a great many television programmes in the early period were unmarked by the aesthetic norms of the film genre. Instead, television was, in terms of organisation, and to a certain extent aesthetically, considered as a visualisation of radio – radio with pictures. That television could show live pictures, and broadcast these as they happened, was considered the most important aspect of the new medium.

Live broadcasting and the limitations of Outside Broadcasting, combined with the lack of experience of production teams and unreliable technology, meant that programmes were often studio productions full of technical errors. It was impossible to edit out unsuitable remarks or behaviour, as the technology was non-existent. Anecdotes from this early phase are often characterised by an almost Monty Python-like eye for the farcical scenes these production conditions could produce. A good example of this is found in *En danmarkskrønike (Chronicle of Denmark)* by the Danish journalist and author Paul Hammerich:

> "A tour de force was the performance of Aladdin in 1952 with Henning Moritzen in the title role and Helle Virkner as Gulnare. An unintentional dramatic effect was achieved when the genie of the lamp appeared and Aladdin exclaimed: "Oh, how hungry I am, dear spirit! Were you to provide me with a meal, then I would gladly serve you at other time, should you need my help." Then, just as the gastronomic wonder was about to appear, thanks to the magic of the genie, the camera caught a little stage manager crawling across the set with sweat on his brow and wearing a set of earphones. He placed Oehlenschläger's favourite dishes on a silver platter at the feet of the astounded Moritzen." (Hammerich, 1976, vol. 3: 249)

Television's take-over of many radio programme types and its organisation of transmission areas, combined with conditions of production, has undoubtedly acted as a socialisation factor for viewers and producers alike. 'Real' television was live television, and still is for many people today, not just when the broadcast is news, sport or events, but also when it is studio production such as a talk show: that is to say, when topicality is not the reason for broadcasting live. An exemplary expression of this attitude among producers of television is to be found in the article by the Danish journalist Poul Trier Pedersen in *Levende Billeder (Live Pictures)*, 1979 in which he writes the following based on the programme *Kanal 22*.

> "A television genre had almost been forgotten, at any rate in Denmark, when "Kanal 22" made its appearance on our screens on Monday 5$^{th.}$ February – *the live talk show*. Usually it is the case that a talk show with some degree of topicality, either with or without guests, and broadcast live, is indispensable and included as a matter of course in the repertory of every television company. It is something that just has to be there, to be included without the need for debate ... Attached to the genre there are qualities which in some way make TV genuine, i.e. television that is *itself* and not merely an imitation of, or a substitute for other media. When a programme in this genre is a success, it contains an excitement factor of "here and now" which is also experienced by the viewers." (Trier Pedersen, 1979: 23 and 25)

In spite of the development of technology, some of the qualities of production and the experiences connected with live production are still sought after as a normative point of departure. It is found desirable to maintain these qualities, either in the form of truly live productions, or in the form referred to as 'live on tape'.[4]

There would seem to be an overriding reason for maintaining a production form which is live or simulates a live production: *The Uncertainty Factor*, or TV without a safety net, in which one can get close to the qualities in face-to-face interaction of actual reality. The Danish TV producer and author John Carlsen describes the intensity of this adrenalin-producing live form in the following way:

> "The risk of a planned mini-interview developing into a boring exercise in futility, which you can do nothing to change, is ever-present. And the danger that an actor will freeze, the sound disappear, or that the camera will swing aimlessly around before capturing a picture is always lurking in the background. All these risks, of huge blunders and small cosmetic blemishes, could be re-

moved. So what causes us to choose the live transmission? It is probably the same thing that causes a risk of errors, because the element of unpredictability which is built into the live transmission also creates the opportunity for the unexpected bonus. A participant in a discussion can suddenly get excited and say things that he had really intended to keep quiet about, a member of the audience might actively intervene, or an entertainer might begin to improvise, take over the programme, thereby breaching time limits, plans, and other arrangements." (Carlsen, 1984: 120-21)

For John Carlsen, the possibility of the live experience, and thereby the possibility of a completely different experience than the cinema film can offer, is one of the principal reasons why the sequence, the pulse and the rhythm in television are crucial as opposed to the aesthetically perfect. Carlsen compares the possibility to edit television programmes with the effect the talking film had on the aesthetics of film. The heavy, unreliable recording equipment caused a setback in the development of film because it once again took on characteristics belonging to the theatre. For television this:

"also meant the edited programme's opportunity for perfection, which in some respects was a step backwards in relation to the live programme's unpredictability, incalculability, and fortuitousness which has a certain amount in common with 'life itself'. The sequence, by definition the element which carried the live transmission, has to be re-learned in the edited TV programme." (Carlsen, 1984: 126)

When the sender adheres to an actual or a narrative immediacy in the unit of space of the talk show, it means that this type of programme is situated on a fulcrum with the organised, tried and tested, and predictable on one side, and the uncontrollable on the other. The interaction is not scripted exactly (as opposed to theatre drama in which we are dealing with a fictive universe) and the chance of something going wrong, or taking an unexpected turn is always present. It is this degree of unpredictability which might conceivably be one of the talk show's strong points in relation to viewers. This also applies to the live on tape form, where editing opportunities are limited, and the experience of unity in time and place can thereby be achieved. Re-taking all, or part, of an interview is a difficult task because the changes have to be contextualised into a unit, and at the same time the 'nerve' of the live transmission has to be maintained for participants, host and audience alike.

In addition to this, real simultaneity can be utilised so that contact with viewers becomes an element in the programme by using different kind of phone-ins. This can, for example, be in the form of questions to the guest of a show from viewers, or in the form of a quiz in which viewers participate by phone. Thus the show depends on there being an empirical receiver in order to exist at all, but this also functions as a part of the unity of the programme for those viewers who do not participate directly, and is perhaps a decisive factor in the appeal of the genre.

Sociability

Immediacy as a priority in the production of the talk show, and the experiential qualities sought through it, for both the sender and receiver, should be seen in the context of the 'here' which is created by the scenic character of the programme type. The programme type attempts to deny, with every means at its disposal, that television is dominated by one-way communication. Only in short sequences, and with a limited number of selected viewers, can television actually be two-way communication in which it is possible for a receiver to answer. The fact that this insistence of contact is such an emphatic trait of television is not merely the result of commercial TV's anxiety about ratings, but is also, to a great extent, connected with the user situation that television is a part of. The reception of the TV mass medium takes place predominantly in the viewers' private sphere, and what TV has to offer is a part of everyday life. Television is still, however, the leisure medium unlike radio which is increasingly becoming the medium of non-leisure time. Radio is heard as an accompaniment to work and in transition periods between work and leisure time. Radio 'keeps the beat' in the part of our lives which is governed by the clock (Dahl, 1991: 13). The crossfield between public/formal and private/informal is, therefore, the basic communicative 'area' of television. The many anonymous receivers must be 'talked' to, but in the private surroundings and individual life of each.[5] This has consequences for the mode of address and the structure of broadcasting, which influences TV generally, and the talk show in particular.

John Ellis' analysis (Ellis, 1982) of the aesthetic form of television relative to that of cinema film is still the most extensive bid at a maximal description of the communicative characteristics of television in relation to the user situation. Ellis emphasises that the combination of reception situation, screen format, the audio-visual factors, and the daily presence of television, give it, its programmes and its personalities the tinge of everyday familiarity and intimacy which radio to a certain extent also achieved with the auditory form alone. Finding a form of communication which suits the cross-field between public/formal and private/informal is an art which was not automatically mastered when television was born. It takes time to assimilate the legacy of other media forms as the British media researcher Paddy Scannell has shown in his examination of the historical changes in what he calls the BBC's "communicative ethos". In his micro-sociological, Goffman-inspired angle of approach to the analysis of media products, Scannell emphasises that awareness of the fact that the sender has no control over the reception situation, which takes place in the receiver's private sphere, is increasingly evident in television's mode of address in general. Intimacy, both in expression and content, the person-orientated, the schematised structure, and the focus on contact, should be seen as the sender's attempt to motivate an interest on the part of the receiver by talking to him in a form that reflects reception in his private sphere and in everyday domestic situations. As an example Scannell uses the BBC's Talks Department which recognised this at an early stage:

"Quite quickly, older public models of speaking (the lecture, the sermon, the political speech) were rejected and replaced by more direct, intimate, personal styles of speech (Matheson, 1933). In short, broadcasting learnt that its expressive idioms must, in form of content, approximate to the norms of ordinary, everyday, mundane conversations, or talk. In talk-as-conversation participants treat each other as particular persons, not as collective. So too with broadcasting. The hearable and seeable effect of radio and television is that, "I am addressed"." (Scannell, 1995: 10)

In the book, *Radio, Television and Modern Life* (Scannell, 1996:28) Scannell distinguishes between two forms of contact-making which can be recognised in the talk show. According to Scannell these two forms could be observed as early as the 1930s in radio, and he uses two forms of entertainment programmes as analytical examples:

- In the first type the receiver is 'invited in' to a studio which is the place of the event. Here the studio audience plays a crucial role as a stand-in for the absent audience who are at home. This is an attempt to establish the 'invited in' element. The function of the studio audience, along with the host is to convey an experience of togetherness which includes the receiver.
- In the second type the studio audience is absent. With the help of the TV host's verbal, and in the case of television, audio-visual planning, the receiver is addressed in his private sphere by a process in which the programme simulates a private sphere, thereby seeking to give an experience of spacial simultaneity between sender and receiver:

"The classic entertainment programme, from this period, which deliberately sought to enter into the "fireside world" of listeners, and to invoke "the pleasures of privacy" was "Monday Night at Seven"." (Scannell, 1996: 28)

According to Scannell, it is the contact itself between programme and listener which is the dominating feature in the content of these programmes. Here he uses the term *sociability* to describe intimacy-creating mode of address, and atmosphere of togetherness sought by both types of programme. The German sociologist Georg Simmel describes the phenomenon sociability as "a special sociological structure" that is a significant trait of living in society in general. It is based on people's need to join together with other people for the sake of unity itself (Simmel, 1910: 128). Sociability in its narrower sense – being together with others as an activity in itself- emphasises form as opposed to content. Sociability, according to Simmel, is "the play form of association. It is related to the content-determined concreteness of association as art is related to reality ..." (Simmel, 1910: 130). Thus, sociability is almost a ritual activity, has no aim apart from its own being, and is, at the same time, "oriented completely about personalities" (Simmel, 1910: 130). Sociability is created by personalities, which means that sociability emphasises human qualities.

There are, however, limits to the kind of human qualities allowed. In order to establish and maintain sociability it is necessary for participants to restrain certain aspects of their individuality. If too much emphasis is put on individuality the experience of sociability will disappear

> "The most personal things – character, mood, and fate – have thus no place in it. It is tactless to bring in personal humor, good or ill, excitement and depression, the light and shadow of one's inner life." (Simmel, 1910: 131)

This means that personality must be exhibited, but not private, personal things which can form the basis of strong emotional outbursts and serious confrontations, among other things.

Paddy Scannell considers sociability as a trait which is, or ought to be, common in the mode of address in the electronic media across the more manifest content, such as the wish to inform or convince. In the talk show the spacial insistence of a collective 'here' – a virtual meeting place – combined with the talk show's actual or narrative 'now', or immediacy, means that sociability is at the centre of the communicative relationship between the programme and the viewer. The roles and expectations associated with sociability are an indispensable part of the talk show's substance. Individual programmes can, however, be produced with varying degrees of emphasis on sociability. The use of the studio audience is the decisive, definitive factor. By involving the studio audience in the production, sociability is emphasised as a dimension of the programme's contents. Irrespective of the degree to which sociability is emphasised as a dimension of the contents, there will be consequences for the way in which communication takes place in the programme type, and what is possible in terms of contents, if sociability as a factor is to be maintained.

In the essay "Hosts and Guests" (Arlen, 1997), the American author Michael J. Arlen focuses on a particular form of role play which is characteristic of American television and the talk show in particular. He characterises the interaction between TV hosts, guests and viewers, with a point of entry in the original Latin root *hospes* in the notion 'hospitality', which contains an ambiguity of status in the term used for host, guest and strangers alike. Every instance of participant interaction has a double status of both host and guest, which Arlen illustrates with an example from *The Barbera Walters Special*, in which she visits a number of celebrities in their homes. This gives rise to a certain amount of turbulence in their roles and thereby making them more apparent:

> "... the programme opened with Ms. Walters standing in her New York apartment, all dressed up to receive company in the accepted manner of a television hostess, but informing us that she was going to take us *out*, so to speak, "into the private homes and private thoughts of two couples." Then the Streisand-Peterses were shown acting as hosts to Ms. Walters. Then, there was an intermission of shots, during which Ms. Walters – transported back to her apartment and her original hostess role – proceeded to take us, as her guests, on a tour of her various art objects and souvenirs. Then, we were off to Georgia, where the Carters were clearly now the hosts and took Ms. Walters through *their* house. In conclusion

we returned to New York with Ms. Walters, who signed off by saying, "I'm so pleased you could join us in your homes. Good evening from mine"." (Arlen, 1997: 309)

Arlen considers the host-guest dramaturgy in the talk show as a ritualised acting out of the hospitality that comprises a significant part of conversational structure of this type of programme (Arlen, 1977: 310). The talk show must act out hospitality as a ritual in order to relieve or avert the hostility that viewers might have by being 'invaded' by strangers in their private sphere. In other words the programme type is subject to certain communicative norms that exist in social, informal, face-to-face forms of interaction between people who do not know each other very well. In connection with this one might expect that in the talk show rules of politeness (Argyle & Henderson, 1985; Drotner et al., 1996)[6] and the handling of others' "face" (Drotner et al., 1996; Goffman, 1967)[7] become particularly important, because they have influence on the interaction in the programme type and how the programme type is experienced "behind the back" of what is probably a more explicit aim of the communication.

Dramatic Excitement

The two dimensions – the uncertainty factor and sociability – mean that the unpredictable and the unplanned, become important in the talk show, and it means that form, rules of politeness, and the treatment of others' 'face', become extremely important in the talk show. Both dimensions are essential *elements of content* in the genre. For that reason they are present no matter what the more manifest content of the show might be, e.g. a discussion of Danes' attitude to immigrants and refugees, or people's experiences of taboo subjects from the private sphere.

At the same time, however, the elements of uncertainty and sociability are incompatible qualities, and because of this a form of tension exists between the two dimensions in the genre. This tension exists between the tendency towards chaos, danger, unpleasantness, and loss of face found in the uncertainty factor, on the one hand, and, on the other hand, the tendency towards impeccability, politeness, and pleasure of sociability. How this tension is administered depends on the actual use of the genre. In addition, the way in which this tension is administered by the individual programme will have experiential consequences for the viewers. Here one might expect too, that what constitutes the experience of uncertainty and sociability in actual programmes depends very much on who the viewers are. This means, for example, that if one wishes to produce a talk show directed towards young people, the production of the two dimensions must be thought out in relation to this specific target group. Therefore, the estimation of the individual talk show's degree of success and the experiential consequences of the viewers is inseparable from considerations of whom the show is directed at.

Because of the accentuated textual features of the talk show, I believe that there is reason to consider the talk show as experientially different from other types of television programme. The talk show can be expected, theoretically, to be 'closer' to the interactional and behavioural framework which is characteristic of informal face-to-face communication.

Anthropologist, Donald Horton, and sociologist, R. Richard Wohl, have defined the special communicative relationship between the programme type and its viewers as para-social interaction (Horton & Wohl, 1956). It is precisely the non-fictive TV-personalities ("personae" Horton & Wohl, 1956: 216) who are focused on, whose existence, "is a function of the media themselves" (Horton & Wohl, 1956: 216). Their ideas are based on the assumption that the viewers' relationship to these personae, who act as both hosts and interviewers, can be described as a para-social relationship. According to the authors the relationship differs in *degree* but not in *type* from genuine personal relationships between people. It is the degree of reciprocity which is the decisive factor, but, on the other hand it gives the viewer the freedom to withdraw, to experience from a distance, and not to get involved, which face to face situations of this nature would otherwise render impossible. An important factor in establishing the para-social relationship is the stability of the TV personality. Depending on how often the actual programmes are broadcast, these programmes can offer weekly, or often daily, 'meetings' at an appointed time which can be integrated into the routines of daily life. In addition these programmes are to a great extent, representatives of security in a world which is insecure:

> "unlike real associates, he has the particular virtue of being standardised according to the "formula" for his character and performance which he and his managers have worked out and embodied in an appropriate "production format" ... The persona is ordinarily predictable, and gives his adherents no unpleasant surprises." (Horton & Wohl, 1956: 217)

Horton and Wohl describe, in addition, how the illusion of intimacy and participation is created in the talk show by means of four central devices:

1. The host duplicates the gestures of informal interaction, conversational style, and milieu.
2. The host attempts, verbally, to give the impression of camaraderie and personal knowledge of the production team, who are addressed and brought into the programme.
3. The host moves physically among the studio audience, and for short periods he can become a spectator to the performance of others, along with the studio audience.
4. Focus is put on the hosts method of communication, i.e. the medium itself and its technology.

The conclusion of Horton and Wohl is that stability and these four devices help to create and emphasise the main values of the programme type in relation to the viewers. These values are predominantly orientated around how this form of togetherness is characterised by sociability, courtesy, friendship and close contact. However, unlike theatre drama in which secondary identification is probably a relevant feature in the way the audience relates to what is shown, Horton and Wohl emphasise that the situation is different in personality-centred programmes

"The "personality program", unlike the theatrical drama, does not demand or even permit the esthetic illusion – that loss of situational reference and self-consciousness in which the audience not only accepts the symbol as reality, but fully assimilates the symbolic role." (Horton & Wohl, 1956: 218)

The role of the viewer in these programmes is fundamentally different and the psychological attitude must generally be assumed to be different too:

"When the persona appears alone, in apparent face-to-face interaction with the home viewer, the latter is still more likely to maintain his own identity without interruption, for he is called upon to make appropriate responses which are complementary to those of the persona. This "answering" role is, to a degree, voluntary and independent." (Horton & Wohl, 1956: 219)

Horton and Wohl consider viewers to be extremely competent players who have no difficulty in separating the various forms of symbolic universes from actual reality. Furthermore the authors are particularly cautious in drawing conclusions of a socio-psychological and societal nature. This caution cannot be said to characterise Carsten Y. Hansen's use of the theory. In his article from 1988 he uses the theory as the basis in examining the talk show in Danish public service television. The article points out that the talk show is the form of non-fictive television entertainment which began to appear on the Danish state television service, "DR" at the end of the 1980s. On the basis of a comparison of a number of Saturday entertainment programmes, Hansen draws conclusions which are far more radical with regard to the dangers of the para-social for viewers en masse:

"It is the everyday, person-to-person conversation [which, H.B.] makes these programmes popular because they fulfil one of the most important viewer needs of entertainment television: to purvey material to the para-social interaction process with which viewers substitute actual interpersonal relationships." (Hansen, 1988: 102)

Horton and Wohl, on the other hand, consider the para-social as a *supplement*, and only in the case of individuals who are already socially and psychologically isolated can it develop into a substitute for self-created relationships in reality. And only if the para-social in *these cases* becomes a substitute can it be considered pathological. Hansen concentrates exclusively on the part of the argumentation concerning the para-social theory of interaction, in which the general validity of the principles are illustrated with the support of extreme, and possibly pathological cases.

Four Dramaturgic Models

It is within the area of tension between the uncertainty factor and sociability, that the dramaturgic arrangement of the talk show would seem to revolve. The emphasis in the individual programme can therefore be placed differently in relation to the two dimensions, or each element can be given equal priority.

In my work with the talk show I have contrived four prototypical models of how the tension between the uncertainty factor and sociability is arranged. I have termed the four dramaturgic models the Debate, the Research, the Therapy, and the Consultation.[8] Each of these elements gives a particular type of progression in the programme as a whole, or in sections of the programme, and they give differing roles to the host and participants. Differences and similarities can be illustrated thus (cf. figure 1).

It is therefore a question of how the individual model prioritises and arranges the chaos potential and the danger to sociability contained in the uncertainty factor. All four models have a potential for chaos, but it is especially prominent in the Debate, the Therapy, and the Consultation. I will briefly describe the various characteristics of the individual models

Dramaturgic model:	Debate	Research	Therapy	Consultation
Course of the programme:	The possiblity to take sides	Process of exposing different aspects /narratives	Insight making the personal narrative public	Solving a problem by giving advice
Host:	Provocateur & moderator	Involved & hero	Therapist & friend	Advicer & friend
Participant(s): 2 or more:	Conflict and confrontation between positions	Different aspects	Different aspects	People with problems & co-advicers
1:	Party in the case	A riddle to be solved	Narrator with a special story	Representative of the problem

Figure 1: Four dramaturgic models

The course of the programme: The Debate model is characterised by a course of the programme that will focus on the possibility to form an opinion. The Research will, on the other hand, focus on the process of discussing in itself, and getting as many aspects/narratives as possible brought into the discussion in order to shed light on as many dimensions of an issue, or a person, as possible. The Therapy will aim for insight by making the personal narrative public, and finally, the Consultation will aim to solve a problem by giving advice.

The role or function of the host: In the Debate the role of the host is to be a provocator, but also the moderator. In the Research the host's role is to be personally involved, and the role is similar to the role of the hero in the fairy-tale. The host has to use all his/her personal and professional skills to get a topic or a guest's personality described. In the Therapy the host is staged in the role of something in between a therapist and a close friend. And in the Consultation the host's role is, again, something in between an adviser and a best friend.

The role of the participant or the participants: In the Debate you can either have two or more participants and they will then be cast as opponents and confronted in the show. If there is only one participant/guest in the show, the host will act as the opponent, and this kind of model is rare in the talk show, because the host will have to be unpleasant towards his or her guest. It can be done, but the examples show that it takes a special kind of host, and the sympathy of the viewers will very easily turn in favour of the guest, who has been invited. The only exception is politicians, who are professionals, and therefore we do not feel sorry for them so easily! In the Research, participants represent different aspects of a problem discussed. And with one participant the guest will be the riddle the host has to solve using all his or her skills. In the Therapy, participants have the same role as in the research, and if there is only one participant he or she is cast as narrator with a special story to tell. In the Consultation, the participants are a mix of people with problems and co-advisers. If there is only one participant, he or she is cast as a representative of the problem.

As it can be imagined the Debate, the Therapy and the Consultation are dramaturgic models where the uncertainty factor has high priority, and these models will often go to the limits of sociability and beyond! In the Debate, the temperaments of the participants and the conflict between positions in the debate can boil over – even the host can get aggressive towards his or her guests.

In the Therapy and the Consultation the problems, the stories told, and the emotional disclosures, can result in emotional breakdowns by the participants and even the host. The Research is the most harmless, and this model is the dominating model in late-night talk shows with famous guests, and in breakfast television – at least in Denmark.

Ricki Lake

Ricki Lake is an example of a use of the talk show genre in which a mix between the Debate, the Therapy, and the Consultation has been chosen. At the same time the chaos potential of the uncertainty factor in both dramaturgic models is prioritised equally. For that reason we get a programme in which it is desirable that the participants e.g. burst into tears or break down, and in which it is desirable for the participants to get involved in violent verbal, and sometimes physical, confrontations. In other words, it is intended that private lives are exhibited in *Ricki Lake* and so, sociability is intended to go to its limits, touching on whatever kinds of personal details it can.

However, in spite of the emphasis on confrontations and emotional outburst, sociability still plays a significant role in this series. It is through sociability that consensus is reached in the debate, and the 'therapy' succeeds. First of all, the studio host is never challenged and is never part of the conflict. Secondly, each programme in the series has *reconciliation* as its aim. In many programmes this happens by means of a reassertion of the positive, almost mythological status of the family. As with the description of the mother, daughter and boyfriend at the beginning of this article, all the other programmes in the series are brim-full with stories of moral guidance. The result then is usually that the solution to all manner of problems is to be found in traditional (nuclear) family values.

Along with the talk show's fundamental efforts to create 'here and now' experiences and an experience of togetherness and community among people, the set of values in the series might also be part of the explanation as to the popularity of the programme. The viewers witness a discussion of a number of serious emotional, and common human problems, and at the same time they are presented with a solution to them.

There is no doubt that *Ricki Lake* is an example of the effective use of the genre characteristics of the talk show, but the effectiveness with which emotional and other human problems are dealt with, is open to debate. The talk show is not a fictive genre, although as in all forms of television of course, there is a high level of construction. The fact that we are dealing with factual television is significant not only for those who appear in the series, but also for those who watch it. As fiction the programme would be unable to survive.

An important question which can be directed towards the series concerns the possible consequences that exceeding the limits of sociability might have. Is the effect that the programme contributes to creating social dissociation and hardening of attitudes, or does it on the other hand encourage empathy and tolerance i.e. diametrically opposed values? Are the participants in the show exploited in a host-centred freak show that offers five minutes of fame to anonymous ordinary people? Or is the series, on the other hand, one in which the problems of ordinary people are taken seriously and in which the personality of the host is the driving force? And does the programme provide a public forum in which these problems can be thematised and discussed?

It is important to emphasise that *Ricki Lake* represents only one of various ways in which the talk show genre can be used. It is therefore a good idea in discussing the talk show, to differentiate between the genre and the *use* of the genre in actual programmes. This could also be a point of departure for criticism, in which, one can, with relevance, begin to examine the nature of the uncertainty factor and sociability, and what the experiential consequences might be for the viewer. Such an approach would also mean that it is not the talk show genre itself which is the object of criticism, but rather how different TV stations put the genre to use. As it has been my intention to emphasise in this article, the talk show is popular among viewers because it is a genre based on fundamental qualities of the TV medium; a medium that is an important cultural and political forum in contemporary daily life.

Notes

1. The sequence is from a *Ricki Lake* programme broadcast on Channel 4 on March 30, 1995.
2. The article's theoretical angle of entry and points of view are based on my book on the TV talk show and the use of the genre in Danish public service TV: H. Bruun *Talkshowet. Portræt af en tv-genre* (*The Talk Show. Portrait of a tv genre*), Borgens Forlag, 1999. In the book I discuss, among other things, the sparse theoretical literature on the genre. The boundaries of this article, however, do not allow for a more protracted argumentation of my theoretical angle of entry. The book focuses on the talk show in Danish public service TV and contains five analyses of Danish talk shows, viz. *Kanal 22*, *Lørdagskanalen*, *Eleva2ren*, *Damernes Magasin*, and *Højlunds Forsamlingshus*.
3. In 1934 the so-called mahogany cart was used for the first time. It was a mobile recording unit which connected a microphone to two lacquer-plate sound-recording machines, each of which could record approx. three minutes of sound. This technical development had a great influence on radio's aesthetic and linguistic development. See Bondebjerg (1990: 22) for a detailed description.
4. Live on tape – also called delayed live, is a production form in which the producers attempt to re-create the live element by simulating a live recording. It involves a chronological and con-

tinuous recording which, when finished, is edited only marginally. The main emphasis in production lies in the pre-production process, i.e. concept development, research and briefing. As a rule the recording is made one or two days before the date of transmission, which means that if anything goes wrong with the recording itself it must be transmitted in any case. There is no time to make a new programme even if it is not a success. According to the Danish TV journalist Michael Meyerheim who was host of TV 2's talk show *Meyerheim at Eight* for a number of years, this is exactly what happened when a well-known politician was to guest one of the programmes. In the research phase NN had been amusing, talkative and courteous. It seemed certain that the politician in question would "deliver the goods". When it came time to record, however, NN, for reasons unknown, closed up like an oyster. He answered in monosyllables, and the prepared jokes seemed lost on him. Meyerheim described this show as one of the longest in his career as a talk show host! (Source: own interview with Michael Meyerheim, May 16, 1994.)

5. The realisation of television as a much more individualised medium which the fusion of the computer, telephony, and TV makes possible is still some time away. It is also open to debate whether a technological possibility will, in reality, change our conception of the TV-medium and the way in which we use it, in a short space of time. There is, perhaps, good reason for skepticism as, apart from the financial outlay necessary on the part of users, this involves an adjustment in the habits and expectations to the TV-medium on the part of the individual. That expectations to the medium are surrounded by a certain tardiness is shown by the fact that the 'live' production form as used in the talk show, for example, is still maintained in spite of its being made unnecessary because of technological advances.

6. Drotner et al. (1996: 148) gives an account of the communicative principle of politeness which is presented by philologists as a supplement to Grice's principle of effectivity. According to Drotner et al. the principle of politeness can be put into practice in five communicative rules of politeness. These were presented thus by John E. Andersen (1989): 1) Be considerate to others and avoid being troublesome to others. 2) Be generous in fulfilling the wishes of others. 3) Be positive. Avoid criticising or expressing dissatisfaction with your partner in conversation. 4) Be modest. Avoid praising yourself. Be self-critical. And 5) Agree. Seek the greatest possible area of agreement, e.g. by

declaring yourself to be in partial agreement although you totally disagree.
7. Goffman's 'face' concept is based on the notion of how we all – individually and in co-operation with each other – attempt to preserve our subjective and socially-created self-image. This image of self is bound together with our self-esteem and thereby our dignity and honour. Loss of face is, therefore, extremely dangerous for the individual, and one tries in many different ways to avoid this e.g. by being polite and tactful when dealing with other people's 'face' in order to avoid their attacking one's own. In addition, we often attempt to help each other through situations which could give rise to loss of face. If, in spite of these attempts, the situation occurs anyway, one can attempt to 'pay back' so that face is re-gained by the loss of someone else's. Drotner et al. (1996: 113) give an account of the linguistic ritual into which the re-gaining of face can be divided in an interaction, if the situation has been accidental. Thus: 1) Challenge: the break takes place and is recognised. 2) Sacrifice: atonement, apology and punishment. 3) Acceptance: the offender is forgiven. And 4) Thanksgiving: the healing of the break.
8. The terms debate and therapy are borrowed from Sonia Livingstone and Peter Lunt. In their extensive reception research they examine the type of talk shows which they term, "Audience discussion programmes" in the book *Talk on Television – Audience Participation and Public Debate,* 1994. In the study the authors concentrate exclusively on talk shows that resemble *Ricki Lake*. However, it is primarily the reception of British programmes they investigate.

Bibliography

Allen, Rod, & Nod Miller (eds.) (1993). *It's Live But is it Real?* London: John Libbey.
Andersson, Anna Maria, & Olof Hultén (1995). *Det svenska tv-utbudet 1987-1994*, Institutionen för Journalistik och Massekommunikation. Gothenburg: Gothenburg University.
Argyle, Michael, & Monika Henderson (1985). *The Anatomy of Relationships*. London: Wm. Heinemann Ltd.
Arlen, Michael J. (1981). "Hosts and Guests". In Michael J. Arlen: *The Camera Age*. New York: Farrar Straus Giroux.
Bondebjerg, Ib (1990). "Den sociologiske og visuelle lyd". In: *Mediekultur*, No 14, Aarhus.
Bruun, Hanne (1998). "Talkshowet som tv-genre". In *Kvan*, No. 50.

Bruun, Hanne (1999). *Talkshowet. Portræt af en tv-genre*. Copenhagen: Borgens Forlag.
Carlsen, John (1984). *Det gode fjernsyn*. Tønder: Centrum.
Dahl, Henrik (1991). "Danmarks Radio – mellem enhedskultur og pluralisme". In: *MedieKultur*, No. 15.
Drotner, Kirsten et al. (1996). *Medier og Kultur*. Copenhagen: Borgen.
Ellis, John (1982). *Visible Fictions*. London and New York: Routledge.
Goffman, Erving (1986). *Frame Analysis*. Boston: Northeastern University Press.
Goffman, Erving (1992). *Vore rollespil i hverdagen*. Norwegian Edition, Hans Reitzels Forlag.
Hammerich, Paul (1976). *En danmarkskrønike*, vol. 2, 3, & 4.
Hansen, Carsten Y. (1988). "Talk-showet som fjernsynsunderholdning". In: *MedieKultur,* No. 8.
Hjarvard, Stig (1994). "Intimitet, Autenticitet og Kvindelighed". In Peter Dahlgren (ed.): *Den mångtydiga Rutan*. Stochholm.
Hjarvard, Stig (1995). *Internationale TV-nyheder*. Århus: Akademisk Forlag.
Horton, Donald & R. Richard Wohl (1956). "Mass Communications and Para-Social Interaction". In: *Psychiatry*, vol 19, No 3.
Kozloff, Sarah (1992). "Narrative Theory and Television". In Robert C. Allen (ed.): *Channels of Discourse, Reassembled*. The University of North Carolina Press.
Larsen, Peter (1989). "TV: Historie og/eller diskurs?". In: *EDDA*, hæfte 1. Oslo.
Larsen, Peter Harms (1991). "Den iscenesatte snakkemaskine – når tovejs skal ses i den envejs". In: *Kvan*, No 3, November.
Larsen, Peter Harms & Lotte Lindegaard (1990-92). Arbejdspapirer til udviklingsprojektet *Fakta og fascination*. DR's uddannelsescenter 1990-92.
Livingstone, Sonia & Peter Lunt (1994). *Talk On Television – Audience Participation and Public Debate*. London.
Matelski, Marilyn J. (1991). *Daytime Television Programming*. London: Focal Press.
Meyrowitz, Joshua (1979). "Television and Interpersonal Behavior: Codes of reception and Response". In Gary Gumpert & Robert Cathcart (eds.): *Inter/Media*. New York: Oxford University Press.
Meyrowitz, Joshua (1985). *No Sense of Place,* New York: Oxford University Press.
Meyrowitz, Joshua (1994). "Medium Theory". In Crowley and Mitchell (eds.): *Communication Theory Today*. Polity Press.

Morse, Margaret (1985). "Talk, Talk, Talk – The Space of Discourse in Television News, Sports Casts, Talk Shows and Advertising". In: *Screen* Vol. 26. No. 2.

Morse, Margaret (1986). "The Television News Personality and Credibility: Reflections on the News in Transition". In Tania Modleski (ed.): *Studies in Entertainment*. Indiana University Press.

Munson, Wayne (1993). *All Talk – The Talkshow in Media Culture*. Philadelphia: Temple University Press.

Nielsen, Poul Erik (1996). *Comedy Series in Danish Television for Better or Worse*. Paper for IAMCR-conference, Sydney.

Pedersen, Poul Trier (1979). "Det direkte snakkeshow". In: *Levende Billeder*, No 2. Copenhagen.

Poulsen, Henrik (1993). *It's Showtime*. Copenhagen: Gyldendal.

Priest, Patricia Joyner (1995). *Public Intimacies. Talk Show Participants and Tell-all TV*. Hampton Press.

Rose, Brian G. (ed.) (1985): *TV Genres. A Handbook and Reference Guide*. Greenwood Press.

Scannell, Paddy (1994). "Kommunikative intentionalitet i radio og fjernsyn". In: *MedieKultur*, No. 22.

Scannell, Paddy (1995). "For a Phenomenology of Radio and Television". In: *The Journal of Communication*, vol. 45, No. 3.

Scannell, Paddy (1996). "Sociability". In: *Radio, Television and Modern Life*. Blackwell.

Shattuc, Jane M. (1997). *The Talking Cure – TV Talk Shows and Women*. Routledge.

Simmel, Georg (1971, orig. 1910). "Sociability". In: *On Individuality and Social Forms*. The University of Chicago Press.

Timberg, Bernard (1994). "The Unspoken Rules of Talk Television". In Horace Newcomb (ed.): *Television – The Critical View*. New York: Oxford University Press.

Tusa, John (1993). "Live Broadcasting: The Keynote Address". In Rod Allen & Nod Miller (eds.): *It's Live But is it Real?* London: John Libbey.

CHAPTER EIGHT

Journalism as Company

Stig Hjarvard
Department of Film & Media Studies
University of Copenhagen

TV journalism is changing. As a language and as a method, journalism has spread to a range of other TV genres: to weekend, show-like entertainment programs such as TV2's *Eleva2'ren* and *Colourful Friday*, to more intimate weekly TV magazines such as DR1's *Ladies' Magazine* and TV3's *No men allowed*, to mildly informative and exciting criminal magazines such as TV2's *Station 2*, and TV3's *Wanted*, and last but not least to breakfast television, TV2's *Good morning Denmark* and TV3's now closed *Good morning*. In these programs, journalistic elements are combined with other, typically more entertaining elements. Journalism's area of coverage – real world events – is used increasingly as the raw material for TV entertainment. The journalist's tool, *the interview*, is not only used in pre-program research, but has to an increasing extent become a central form of presentation in the mixed and entertaining factual programs. The staging of the journalist's conversations with people, well-known as well as unknown, about their lives, experiences and opinions has become a widely used aesthetic form in TV. Programs in which such conversations constitute the main element are normal classified under the common heading of "talk show" (Bruun, 1997).[1]

Journalism has not remained unaffected by this trend. In order to become part of the mixed TV genres and, thus, to serve programming aims other than those of the traditional genres such as news and topical programs, journalism has had to change character and combine with other elements. The characteristics of this mixture of programs and its consequences for the contents and form of journalism constitute the theme of the following analysis of a program genre that is rather new in Denmark: Breakfast TV.

The analysis will focus on two circumstances surrounding the mixture of genres: First, on how coherence, continuity and transition are created in a program that consists of apparently incompatible elements such as cooking, interviews with top politicians, musical performances, etc. Whereas it could be expected, on the face of it, that such a combination would give the program a heterogeneous and kaleidoscopic character, producers are frequently able to create a reasonably coherent program with apparently 'natural' transitions. The question is how such coherence is established.

Second, the article aims at shedding light on the consequences of this type of program mixture for more traditional journalism when it becomes a part of this mixture. Which aspects of traditional political journalism must be made less prominent, and which aspects stand a greater chance of coming into focus? It should be noted that breakfast TV is one of the few established television program formats in which politicians are allowed to appear and speak for relatively long periods (typically 5-10 minutes) and in which they are not subjected to strict editing and constant interruptions; this makes it particularly relevant to investigate the type of political journalism that is mediated.

The History and Structure of Danish Breakfast TV

In December 1985, breakfast TV was launched in Danish television by Channel 2, a local TV station in Copenhagen. This was during the trial period in the mid-1980's for local radio and TV. Breakfast TV was known from the United States and England. However, Channel 2's edition was not consistently modelled on any foreign concept, but had a rather home-made touch. This low budget program was called *Morningflicker* and it combined news bulletins with weather forecasts, studio conversations with guests, animated cartoons, quizzes, live music, morning work-out, etc. The program was originally planned to run only during December in order to attract viewers around Christmas. But since the program was relatively successful, it was made permanent on Channel 2. *Morningflicker*'s characteristic features, the strongly repetitive program structure, the informal mode of address as well as the mixed program contents are central characteristics of the genre, and they were taken up in later renditions on other Danish channels.

The other Danish TV channels waited quite a long time before attempting to produce breakfast TV. After the TV monopoly was abolished in 1988, eight years passed before breakfast TV appeared on the nation-wide channels; many channels had breakfast shows for children, mainly with cartoons, but they did not have breakfast TV for an adult audience. When breakfast TV eventually became a reality on nation-wide TV, the initial competition was tough. On November 1, 1996, the commercial channel TV3 owned by Modern Times Group, began sending *Good morning*, a program produced by Nordisk Film. One month later, on December 2, 1996, the advertising financed public service channel TV2 went on the air with *Good morning Denmark*. This program was produced by the Skandinavisk Film Kompagni, which was founded in 1996 by a number of TV people who had left Nordisk Film. After about one year of broadcasting, TV3 gave up its breakfast TV program, and TV2 was alone in the area. During most of the period, TV3 had had considerably fewer breakfast TV viewers than had TV2. Since TV2's *Good Morning Denmark* was, thus, in sole control of the area, the following analysis will almost exclusively consider this breakfast TV program.[2]

TV2's *Good Morning Denmark* has a very repetitive and schematic design. Program duration is approximately two and a half hours and it is structured in half-hour blocks. After the final news broadcast at 9 and the following weather forecast and commercials, slightly more than half of the program is rebroadcast. Thus, it occupies the time interval from 6.28 to 10.55 every weekday, i.e., more than four hours. Of course, a program of this duration is not supposed to be followed by the audience from beginning to end. Instead, it is designed to allow viewers to watch intermittently, without problem, during the morning hours while they prepare for the day's other chores.

The schematic structure and repetitive character of the program enable viewers to establish an 'internal' program scheme.

For one thing, such an 'internal' scheme makes it possible for viewers to anticipate the types of features that will appear, and when they will appear, without having to orient themselves in the TV program or sit idly by and wait for certain features. It also makes it possible for viewers to use the sequence of program features in order to structure their own mornings: When the cartoons are over, the children are to come and sit down at the breakfast table; or, when the news comes on at 7, there are 20 minutes left before the bus leaves, etc. But not only people who are on their way to work watch breakfast TV. A qualitative analysis of breakfast TV viewing suggests that the program is watched by non-working people as well (students, pensioners and the like), and that these people use the program to get started with their chores at home (Alsted, 1997).

Scheme 1 represents the schematic structure of the program. The program flow contains two types of elements: On the one hand, there is the actual breakfast TV that is led by the two program hosts Cecilie Frøkjær and Michael Meyerheim and that is broadcasted from a home-like studio; and, on the other hand, there is a sequence of program elements such as news, weather forecasts, commercials and program trailers, whose common characteristic is that they clearly mark TV2's identity and that they are also found in the general program selection of TV2. Thus, on the whole, the program is marked by a regular switching back and forth from being 'at home' with Cecilie Frøkjær and Michael Meyerheim and going 'back to' TV2 Denmark in Odense, from which the program is mainly broadcast and the identity of which is particularly established through the news element. In this way, the news has the function of being a kind of public and 'hard' framework for the homespun and 'soft' breakfast TV. The hard and soft elements are also reflected in the time structure: the news comes each half hour; the material from the homey universe fills up the time between these sharp strokes of the clock.

Bracketing the actual breakfast TV with news at each half hour contributes to creating a fixed repetitive structure that takes advantage of breakfast TV's character as a continuous program flow. With its news, TV2 provides a continuous update of the news picture. At the same time, the news editorial staff has the opportunity to get started with their news re-

6,28: Introduction by hosts in kitchen
6,30: News
6,35: Weather
6,36: Commercials
6,39: Trailer: coming programs on TV2
6,40: Going through the morning newspapers
6,43: Children's movie: Garfield
6,50: Bubber: Interview with young people
6,57: Announcement of coming items
6,58: Commercials

7,00: News
7,08: Weather
7,09: Trailer: coming programs on TV2
7,10: The "morning chance"
7,13: Children's movie: Bananas in Pyjamas
7,18: Interview in the sofa: well-known people in/out of politics
7,26: Announcement of coming items
7,27: Commercials

7,30: News
7,35: Weather
7,36: Trailer: coming programs on TV2
7,37: The "morning chance" via telephone
7,39: Interview with parachute instructor

7,48: Interview i sofa: Art exhibition
7,56: Music on stage
7,59: Announcement of coming items
7,59: Commercials

8,00: News
8,09: Weather
8,10: Commercials
8,12: Interview in sofa: refugee politics
8,17: Children's movie: Locomotive Thomas
8,23: Interview with guest about health campaign
8,28: Announcement of coming items
8,28: Trailer: coming programs on TV2
8,29: Commercials

8,30: News
8,35: Weather
8,36: Commercials
8,37: Interview in sofa / "speaker's platform"
8,46: Interview with film reviewer
8,54: Music on stage
8,58: Goodbye from hosts in kitchen
8,59: Trailer: coming programs on TV2
8,59: Commercials

9,00: News
9,13: Weather
9,15: Commercials
9,16: Repeat of "Go' morgen Danmark"

Scheme 1: Program structure of TV2's Go' morgen Danmark, *30.9.1997*

ports and thus gain an advantage over the morning newspapers which must finish editing the day before, and over DR and TV3 which do not begin their news broadcasts until late in the afternoon.

A further and very essential reason for interrupting breakfast TV each half hour with other program elements is that this makes it possible to send commercials. Danish TV legislation prohibits commercials within programs. Thus, if breakfast TV were broadcasted as *one* program, TV2 could only send commercials at the beginning at 6.28 and at the end at 9.00. This would obviously endanger the financing. TV2, therefore, marks each half hour segment with an initial and a final jingle and introduces news in between. However, it is, in fact, one coherent program, as is also clear from the continuous announcements in each half-hour block of features that will appear in the next block. It is, thus, not at all clear that TV2's actions are in accordance with the Danish advertising laws.

The various fixed program elements of breakfast TV consist of the studio hosts' summaries of the morning newspapers, children's movies, interviews with well-known and unknown people, cooking, film reviews, music or other stage performances, and the "morning chance". The major portion of this program material is presented in the studio that makes up the frame of breakfast TV: the studio hosts' 'home'. Only cartoons, film clips in connection with film announcements, and, rarely, stories tied to interviews with people in the studio break the uniformity of the set. It is almost as though the areas in the fictitious home structure the program. The different program elements take place at four locations defined by the scenography: the kitchen, the drawing-room, the kitchen floor, and the small stage.

Rather than changing types of contents or people, the variation and repetition of the program consist of a steady alternation between the areas of the home. Features succeed other features through changes of place. Thus, the scenography is not supposed to be adapted to the particular program contents (with the possible exception of some simple and topic-appropriate props). Instead, the places created by the scenography segment the program into fixed units: first, we are in the kitchen, then on the sofa, after that on the kitchen floor, and so on. As will be discussed below, the different places contain specific features that favour certain types of content or people and, thus, changing places gives a rhythm to the flow of program contents. The fixed structure of room changing in the 'home' is also related to production conditions. The very high productivity demands – several hours of TV every weekday – require a considerable degree of industrialisation and standardisation of production. Thus, the production framework, including scenography and camera placements, structures the flow and contents of the programs rather than *vice versa*.

Mastering Variability and Continuity

Breakfast TV constitutes a kind of miming or mirroring of the viewers' social situation during the broadcasting of the program. In the universe of breakfast TV, we are at home in the localities of the sphere of intimacy even though there are also a number of openings towards the outer world. Considerable efforts are made to make breakfast TV parallel the viewers' morning situation. When we look through the windows of the scenes, we get the impression of being in an apartment in the middle of Copenhagen, and the light in the windows is adjusted to simulate the sun rising. These adjustments are made according to the weather reports that appear each half hour. The studio hosts' interaction with guests and viewers also thematises this parallel world: there is coffee and bread on the tables, the viewers are greeted good morning, we know the hosts by their first names, etc. The producers have even considered it important that the cameras are concealed so that the illusion of visiting a home is not broken.

However, breakfast TV is not a duplication or mere reflection of the viewers' morning; had that been the case, the program would not have been as attractive. It is a weekday morning with a little extra spice, during which the walls of the home are opened towards a recognisable but nevertheless bigger and more interesting world. This extra quality starts with the scenography. Furniture and interior decoration are chosen to give a nice and homey impression but, at the same time, this home is slightly more attractive and exciting than the typical viewer's. The former producer Henrik Zachariassen explains the decoration of the 'home':

> "We belong after all to a higher social group than our average viewer. There is a big room and a big kitchen, and the kitchen is not the cheapest one available from Silvan [a "do it yourself" store; SH]. It is an expensive kitchen, there are some expensive sofas and that sort of thing; but on the other hand, there are no gilt water taps and that sort of thing. It is very important that it doesn't stick out, that it is just nice ... Like if someone had won 250,000 kr. and wanted a new kitchen, and would say, okay, rather than buying the one for 50,000 kr, we'll buy the one for 80,000 kr."

The steady stream of guests passing through the studio creates variation in relation to the otherwise somewhat routine and static quality of the program. Through the guests, sociability and a sense of togetherness – of having company – is added to the morning. At the same time, there is a systematic change of different kinds of guests such that the social tone of the get-together is varied. Cooks perform in the kitchen, showing their professional competence; their cooking skills function not only as an instruction on how to cook, but, for the most part, the cooking is just a background for humoristic dialogue between themselves or with the hosts. On the kitchen floor, there are typically guests who are there to show something, or to demonstrate some ability, and also to participate in the game "The Morning Chance" which is sponsored by Dansk Tipstjeneste [National Pools Agency]. On the stage, there are music performances by well-known and unknown artists. It is a rather small stage, an intimate one, one might say, so the transition from the home environment to the stage is not perceived as a style clash.

While the kitchen floor is the place for active guests, the sofa is the place for speaking guests. Following an everyday habit of positioning talking guests on the corner of the sofa and those dealing with practical matters in the kitchen, a rough social sorting of the guests takes place on breakfast TV. People of social importance in society (politicians and other decision-makers, experts and well-known media people) are typically placed on the sofa, since their most important performance quality is talking. More average people are, on the other hand, mostly placed on the kitchen floor or at the kitchen table, since they are interesting by virtue of something that they can demonstrate or achieve; their points of view *per se* are rarely interesting or essential. Instead, they show their athletic talents, their funny pets, and the like. In the kitchen, participation is motivated by knowledge of or an ability to do something slightly unusual, but mostly these unusual things are related to recognisable, everyday activities. However, when average people's participation is motivated by their involvement in and stories about unusual or tragic events, they are also allowed to sit on the sofa.

The four areas used in breakfast TV motivate the presentation of different kinds of guests. In this way, during the course of the program, variation is created that runs through a sequence of poles: There is the change between everyday people, problems and experiences, on the one hand, and the world of the well-known people that is dominated by essential themes, on the other. In the universe of the program, what is 'essential' may refer to society as a whole (in terms of politics, power or the like), but also to 'big' issues (such as life, death and love) as opposed to the 'small' themes and events of the everyday world. Another thematic variation in the program, that creates an atmosphere of pulse and balance, is related to seriousness and work, on the one hand, and entertainment, on the other. The successive change between the four sets guarantees that seriousness (e.g., politics, personal experience) will be replaced by amusement (e.g., musical performances, small talk in the kitchen, film reviews).

Scheme 2 presents a graphic display of the thematic universe of breakfast TV and the positioning of the single places within this universe. A typical half hour program block will bring the viewer through 2-4 of those localities. Thus, a one hour broadcast comprises the whole spectrum of themes and atmospheres. The steady transition between the places in the 'home' guarantees a continuous oscillation between the thematic and mood-related axes of this universe.

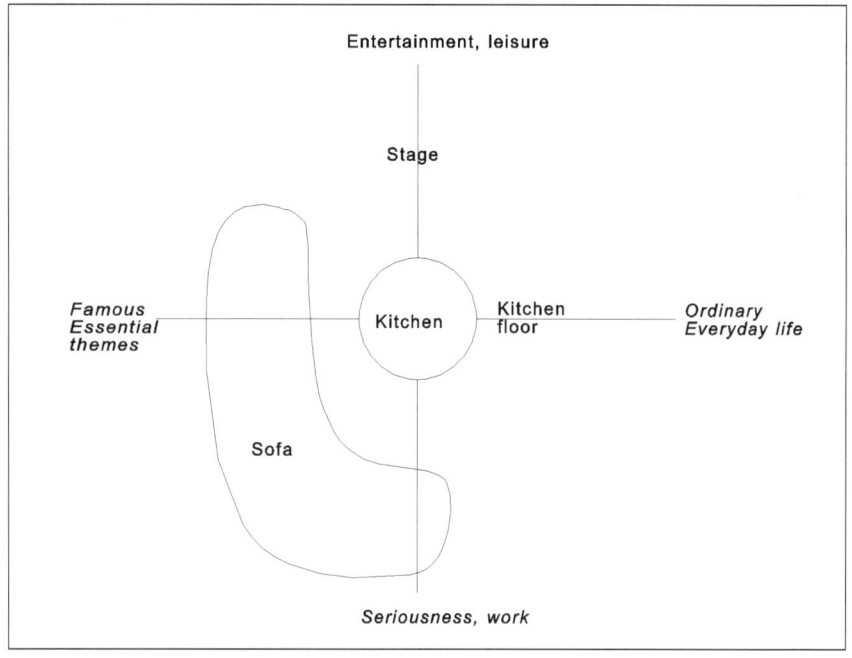

Scheme 2: The four locations in the thematic universe of
Good morning Denmark

This regular shifting of scenes guarantees variation. The question is, then, what it is that creates continuity and coherence in the program? An important element of the program's unity is that the variation takes place within a thematic and a mood register, but that the extreme poles are never attained, let alone crossed. The program has a homespun and personal quality, but the tone or the topics very seldom involve intimacy or confession that creates embarrassment. The program brings up many political topics, but while complicated, technical problems are avoided, efforts are made to bring to fore the people behind the political game playing. There is supposed to be entertainment such as music and competitions, but only the kind that can take place inside the home.

This downplaying of things extreme and extraordinary is evident in, for example, "The Morning Chance". This is a very quiet game, a kind of dominoes largely without the use of technology or other conspicuous props that are otherwise characteristic of TV game shows. Rather than a show-like game dramaturgy including coloured lamps, blinking score tables and fanfares, the "Morning Chance" is meant to be associated with a cosy family game at home at the kitchen table, providing the opportunity for a chat between guests and hosts. This guarantees that the game can be smoothly replaced by other activities in the home.

The program's orientation towards a normal, middle-level in terms of topics and atmosphere is visually supported by camerawork and editing. The camera moves between half total and half close, it never gives a picture of the entire home at once, and never goes close or ultraclose to the people. There are no zooms in or out during the interviews, even though zooming in is almost standard in interviews in order to engage the viewer's attention and empathy. Considering the relative length of the interviews, this fixed editing is quite marked. This approach is taken in order to preserve a certain distance in terms of atmosphere and empathy. The editing is accordingly very slow and motivated by people's interactions while talking and acting. Apart from stage performances, editing *per se* does not add a dynamic component to the program. During musical performances on stage, camera work and editing are more varied and autonomous, but still limited. The small size of the stage, the fact that fixed (not handheld) cameras are used and the lack of time for rehearsing camera glides and angles all set limits for the visual support of musical expression.

The real responsibility for holding the single program elements together is borne by the two studio hosts. Coherence is partly achieved at a general level, in that the hosts' presence creates continuity across the single program events. Irrespective of what is happening and who the guest is, the studio hosts guarantee a basic stability: we are always 'at home' with the hosts and they control people and activities regardless of the topic. Coherence is also achieved at a more specific level in terms of the concrete transitions between program features. To avoid an overly sharp break when transitioning from one feature to the next, both hosts are involved in most transitions: one of them finishes the feature that he or she has been responsible for, and the other announces the next feature even though he or she might not be responsible for it. In other words, the host who concludes a feature is rarely the one who announces the next feature. It is precisely through this division of labour that gliding transitions are achieved in the program.

Erwin Goffman's (1959) microsociology provides some relevant thoughts on the explanation of this division of labour between the studio hosts. In a limited social interaction, the individuals involved are responsible for winding up the interactions, and this requires acceptable introductions and terminations. In particular, interactions involving a host put the responsibility for an acceptable flow on the participant playing the role of the host. If a host wishes to change the character of a social interaction in a given situation, a great amount of persuasion is typically required to avoid appearing offensive or inappropriate in the eyes of the participants. There is seldom a change from great seriousness to nonsense without social interludes. If, on the other hand, an external person announces a shift in a social situation, the transition will typically appear to be less problematic since that person is not responsible for the interaction that has just taken place. This social mechanism is utilised by the two hosts (as well as in many other programs with two hosts) in order to achieve shifts that would otherwise appear offensive. For example, the former producer Henrik Zachariassen, explains the transition from a political interview on the sofa to a cartoon in the following way:

> "From a production point of view, it would be much, much ... easier if the host who has just done the interview said "now it's time for a cartoon" ... Then we wouldn't have to cut over to the other host or move a camera. BUT: ... we have obligations to the adult viewers who are watching ... a political story, and we also have obligations to the children, to whom we have promised a cartoon, and it is much more difficult to say, to interrupt the two politicians who are arguing about something that is very, very important to Denmark, and say, "now it's time for a cartoon". Then people will say, "no, wait a minute, let's make it clear whether there is going to be an election or not". But if we switch to another host, it won't be the same host saying "time is out", who then says "now for a cartoon" ... It is much easier to sit and talk seriously, and then cut

to another universe, which is after all the same, where the other host is doing something fun..."

In programs that contain a number of different features that are basically incompatible when viewed as social situations, the two-host system is an efficient solution. The two hosts take turns at being external and, thus, the situations may shift without breaking general rules of politeness. However, this social 'technique' does not guarantee smooth transitions. The difference between certain types of situations can be so great that linking them may appear offensive and provocative under all circumstances; but the combination of a general orientation towards normality in topics and atmosphere and an homey setting allows *Good Morning Denmark* to create unity and congruence out of the variation. In comparison, TV3's *Good Morning* had some problems in combining variation with continuity. For example, the same hosts presented the news and all other material. This made the hosts seem overly diffuse in the eyes of the audience (Alsted Research, 1997); the host was, in other words, forced to span social roles that were too different. Also, the very large proportion of cartoons during the first hour of TV3's breakfast TV edition caused decreased interest in the program among adults. Thus, attaining the right control over variation and continuity is quite decisive in mixed journalistic entertainment programs such as these.

Politics with Your Morning Coffee

Political interviews have a high status in breakfast TV even though they constitute a modest proportion of the program. Although there are seldom no more than two interviews on political topics during one morning, the political interviews are always emphasised in the program's introductory announcements and in the continuous announcements of the contents of the upcoming program block. The status of the political material is also underscored by the successful efforts made to bring top politicians to the studio.

The choice of political guests is made by the breakfast TV editors themselves, but there is a certain degree of coordination of the political material with the TV2 news editors so that the short news blocks and the political interview will support one another. Thus, TV2's breakfast news typically contains items that relate to one or more of the following interviews in breakfast TV; and while the news is being broadcast from Odense, it is monitored in the breakfast TV studio so that the studio hosts can follow up on what has been said in the news. To the extent that interviews on breakfast TV contain relevant political statements, these are later quoted in the breakfast TV news. In this way, breakfast TV supports TV2's ambition to use breakfast TV to start the day's news. At the same time, breakfast TV borrows some of the prestige and identity that are associated with regular news programming.

As part of the division of labour between the hosts, it is Michael Meyerheim's responsibility to conduct the political interviews. This is, thus, a traditional gender-based division of labour: the female host stands primarily for the softer topics while the male host presents the political material, including interviews with politicians from Christiansborg and political commentators. Michael Meyerheim also takes part in the softer features but, on the other hand, Cecilie Frøkjær rarely interviews men in positions of power.

In order to understand the particular form of breakfast TV's political interviews, it is necessary to consider the double host role played by Michael Meyerheim – a role he plays simultaneous to his journalistic role as an interviewer. In comparison to traditional journalistic genres such as news and topical programs in which the journalist's role is primary, the role as a breakfast TV host is at least as essential. The consistent framework for interaction in the program is the host-guest relationship, and this relationship is a double one: the studio hosts are hosts for the visitors to the studio, but they are also hosts for the viewers who are, during the program, 'visiting' Michael Meyerheim and Cecilie Frøkjær. These divided duties as a host imply that consideration for the actual studio guests must constantly be balanced with consideration for the viewers. The studio guests must be treated in a friendly and polite manner, but their behaviour has implications for how the host's other responsibility can be executed. Thus, the host may be forced to interrupt and change topics if the guest does not contribute anything that is socially acceptable to the other guests: the viewers. In general, since the framework of this type of interview consists of conversations adapted to the fact that they are heard by others, consideration for the viewers as guests is primary, while consideration for the actual studio guests is secondary. When, in practice, no major problems arise in balancing these two considerations, this is mostly due to the fact that the studio guests have accepted this premise in advance and are able to play the role of a performing guest with relative ease. On the whole, guests' ability and willingness to play the appropriate role in both radio and TV programs seem to be quite high (Scannell, 1991).

The role as a journalist and the role as a host are not necessarily incompatible, but they entail a different definition of social interaction and thus of the very goal of the conversation taking place. When a given person accepts the simultaneous dual role of host and journalist, a modified social role must be created that includes some aspects of each of the two roles, and that plays down or completely excludes other aspects.

Scheme 3 presents a typology of the two social functions that are to be united in breakfast TV's political interviews. On the one hand, there is an interview being held in a public or political context and, on the other, the conversations are also taking place in a private or social context. Both are central aspects of the situation: the political element is not only a thin layer of varnish on top of a private conversation, and the familiar tone of the conversation is not only a temporary form that has no influence on the contents. In breakfast TV, these two types of situations are combined, but to understand the interaction between them it can be useful to first look at them separately, as two different ideal types of communicative interaction.

	Interview in a public, political context	Conversation in a private, social context
Definition of situation	Politics	Sociability
Purpose of conversation	Dissemination of information	Get-together, confirm social relations, entertainment
Division of roles	Fixed interviewer-source structure	Fixed host-guest structure
Power and control of conversations	Asymmetrical. High degree of control on the part of the interviewer	Symmetrical. Loose, mutual control
Permitted reactions	Personal reactions not allowed	Personal reactions required
Considerations in conversations	Consideration for essentials is more important than consideration for participants. Principles of efficiency dominate	Mutual consideration for preserving 'face' is more important than objectivity. Principles of politeness dominate
The role of the host in relation to several guests	Chair, moderator, judge	Catalyst, initiator, reconciler

Scheme 3: Features of conversations having the character of interviews in a public, political context as compared to conversations in a private, social context

In political journalism in general, the objective of an interview is mediation of information. The receivers are to gain knowledge about political events and opinions. This implies that consideration for the essentials of the information, and thus for the public, must be more important than consideration for the participants in the conversation. A journalist is supposed to ask questions even if they embarrass the interviewed politician. The interview should also be relatively efficient. Everything that does not contribute something new or informative is perceived as idling or, even worse, as mere mic holding. Attending to the substance also means that personal reactions are not permitted; emotional outbreaks or reference to personal information is considered to be a genre break. Since the journalist has a responsibility to a political public, his or her control of the conversations will typically be strict. The journalist sets the agenda and asks the questions; the interviewee is supposed to take the role of information source and answer as fully as possible.[3] In an interview with several people, the journalist will also have the role of chair and moderator, and in some situations he/she even gives the verdict or draws the conclusions from the conversation. In cases of disagreement, it is not the journalist's role to avoid an open controversy; on the contrary, the intention behind interviewing several people at the same time is often to provide an opportunity for (great) disagreement. The journalist must only guarantee that the controversy is to the point and not personal.

In the private, social context, the most essential objective of conversation is often the get-together *per se*. The goal of sociability is to confirm social relationships between people; but these relationships are not to be used for other social purposes in the context of the sociable situation itself; the company *per se* is the objective and it may, therefore, only have an entertaining or pleasant character. Here, too, there is an established role structure between the host and the guest, but it is typically of a more symmetrical character; control of the conversation may well be exercised, but the right to speak and the division between interviewer and interviewee is more loose; it typically shifts continuously, and the role of the host is solely to guarantee the start, breaks in and termination of the conversation at some central points during the ongoing social situation. In a private, social context, more attention is paid to the participants' personal dignity and status than to objectivity. If the conversation begins to threaten the pleasant atmosphere or even makes it likely that a participant will lose face in the presence of others, there will most often be some repair and diverting manoeuvres. The re-establishment of social harmony must be safeguarded, even if it means that the conversation is moderated: disagreements are downplayed, contradictions are accepted, etc. In a social situation, it is the host's task to act as a catalyst, to get the participants talking to each other, but also to reconcile the parties if there are signs of conflict between them.

Furthermore, another requirement is that participants in a private, social situation should contribute certain personal reactions; typically, these should not be very intimate reactions or information, but a certain amount of personality should be brought to the fore. In a social context, the sole use of objective questions is usually considered to be incorrect. In the same vein, politeness principles dominate over efficiency principles; for example, even if a participant tells a long, rambling story, everybody listens politely; in a political interview, such long-windedness typically leads to an interruption and a new question meant to help the interviewee come to the point.

As noted, the typology surveyed here is an ideal one and thus, in practice, each of the two social situation types is characterised by great variation. Also, both types can be subdivided into a considerable number of sub-genres: for example, the private social context can be semi-official in, e.g., representation situations, or it can be more familiar or have a more friendly tone, etc. Furthermore, sociability can be subdivided in a number of ways depending on social, gender, class and lifestyle factors. Similarly, a political interview can be analysed in terms of several modalities or sub-genres with various degrees of objectivity, efficiency, asymmetry between journalist and source, etc. (see Sørensen, 1989, for a more detailed description of different sub-genres of interviews and interpersonal conversations). In practice, the most interesting observations in an analysis will often be made at the sub-genre level; it is there that the specificity of the program in question or the social interaction is typically found. But sometimes it is important to emphasise the two superordinate ideal types because they constitute very different institutional anchorings of conversations: on the one hand, the political institution and, on the other, social communication that is bound to the interface between the private and the public. A social conversation is not public in a political sense, but it is also not private: it is found in the intersection of the intimate, social and public spheres. When a form of conversation is created that cuts across these institutions, the communicative rules of the game are changed and so is the behaviour that is expected from politicians.

Some of these changes in demands on political behaviour will be exemplified in the following analysis of a breakfast TV interview. It is part of an interview with Anne Birgitte Lundholdt, who was foreign policy spokeswoman for the Konservative Folkeparti [Conservative] at the time, but who chose to leave this post for a position as a director at Danske Slagterier [Danish Slaughterhouses]. The interview was part of a double interview in which Ole Andreasen, vice director of the Carlsberg Brewery, was the other participant. The reason for the interview with these two politicians was the shifts they had made in their political carriers. Ole Andreasen was about to become member of the executive committee of Venstre [the liberal party]; with her job change, Anne Birgitte Lundholdt gave up her political career when the Konservative Folkeparti changed party leader (Hans Engell had resigned and Per Stig Møller had become the new party leader), thus putting that post out of her reach. The analysed interview excerpt is presented as an appendix to this text.

The interview takes place on the sofa group and surrounding furniture, and the two politicians are seated on the same sofa facing Michael Meyerheim (MM). After having talked to Ole Andreasen, MM faces Anne Birgitte Lundholdt (ABL). MM begins with a congratulation and a short flashback to the beginning of the interview when the theme was introduced: her way out of politics. Next, the conversation takes the form of four sequences of questions and answers, all focusing on revealing ABL's personal motives for leaving politics for a position in the private sector. This conversation is characterised by a typical question-answer structure: MM controls the conversation by keeping the initiative, but some of the questions have a rather open character, so it is possible for ABL to steer the conversation according to her preferences. Analytically, the conversation can be broken down into the following 5 sequences:

Opening (1):
MM's reference to the previous opening. Congratulation.

Carrying out (2-4):
   MM's first question: Asks for confession
   ABL's first answer: Gives confession

   MM's second question: Invitation to deepening
                                       of confession

ABL's second answer:	Sets limits on confession – generalisation of argument; repair of face
MM's third question:	Re-invitation to deepening of confession in humoristic form
ABL's third answer:	Apparent acceptance of invitation, but then rejection of statement; repair of face

Closing (5):

MM's forth question:	Invites deepening of resignation from politics and signals conclusion of conversation
ABL's forth answer:	Deepens resignation. Consolidation of face

MM's first question is what in speech act analysis is referred to as an utterance with strong initiative, i.e., he explicitly requests an answer to the question of whether ABL's leaving politics is caused by an earlier struggle for power in the party. The request is made even stronger by MM's insisting addition: "now if we can just be a little bit honest about this". This initiative makes it very difficult for ABL to avoid answering as requested, because this would explicitly jeopardise her trustworthiness. Thus, she responds with the requested confession: the party's decision and renunciation of her are behind her leaving politics.

This confession is followed up in MM's next question in which he invites ABL to deepen her personal motives for leaving politics: that she felt she had been badly treated and therefore felt like slamming the door. This time, however, MM's initiative is weaker. The question is just an indirect one; using his tone of voice, MM invites ABL to confirm his statement. This time ABL only appears to comply with MM's request. Instead of talking about her possible experiences of being badly treated, she generalises MM's door-slamming metaphor. Not wanting to slam doors has nothing to do with the matter at hand, but instead reflects her general code of behaviour and morals. Only her concluding reservation that she "after all" has had 8 good years in politics reflects an implicit restatement of her previous confession.

In a third question, MM also tries to get her to follow the thread from the first confession, this time using a rather sharp characterisation of her political fate ("the slaughter phenomenon"). The choice of words underscores the fact that this characterisation constitutes a risk that she will lose face, but the acuity of the words is modified by the humoristic metaphorical association with her coming work in the Danske Slagterier. The initiative is less strong since it contains a humoristic component as well as a question. The question is a relatively open invitation, and it gives her the chance to both talk about her former defeat and her future work. ABL first appears to accept MM's premise: that she was politically slaughtered. She laughs dutifully, but adds a certain distance by commenting that his wording is "a little funny so early in the morning". Then comes her counter-move which is to mention her qualifications for the director position; in this way, she is able to emphasise that her job change is a positive choice rather than a result of defeat, which is otherwise a strong implication of the slaughter metaphor. She now avoids the potential loss of face associated with appearing in public as a political loser. In the forth and concluding question, she has the opportunity to continue this 'rehabilitation'; she is now on her way into something new and positive which is underscored by the personal declaration: "And I am rejoicing".

This conversational flow emphasises the essential role played by the personal factor in the treatment of political topics in breakfast TV. The main theme of the discussion is simply the personal experiences and motives in ABL's political and professional life. ABL's confession of at least a certain measure of personal defeat is not only possible within the framework of the program, but almost a requirement on the part of MM; otherwise she runs the risk of appearing dishonest. MM's questions to ABL are not intended to reveal the political aspects of her previous career (for example, what she has achieved during her many years of work in the party) or her professional qualities; the latter is something that she brings up herself while repairing the damage inflicted on her face. MM's request for honesty does not involve a sober and comprehensive political analysis of the struggles in the party. When MM requests honesty he invites a form of personal confession indicating that *sincerity* is a very central norm when participating in breakfast TV's political interviews. Politicians' trustworthiness is created not only through the solidity of their arguments, but equally by the sincerity of their speech and personal appearance. In this half private, half public context, personal experience and motives create trustworthiness behind the political statements.

There is also a limit to this sincerity. However, this is not set as much by the program itself as by the political actors' own need to preserve another type of trustworthiness based on professional qualifications and expertise. This can be seen, for example, in ABL's third answer in which she insists that her political experience and expert knowledge are the reasons why she is now going to be a director. Even though breakfast TV's sociable, homey atmosphere encourages sincerity, she must motivate her social roles outside this situation where her trustworthiness is based on more than personal sincerity.

The relationship between host and guest is marked by politeness. As soon as ABL has provided the confession that MM requested, she is given relatively great freedom to carry out the face repair necessitated by the confession and the (partial) defeat. MM's approach is not aggressive, but adheres to the code that is applied to all guests on breakfast TV; the relationship between host and guest must adhere to norms of sociability and must never become negative. Guests may well disagree with one another, but host and guest have a basically positive attitude toward each other, irrespective of point of view. This very polite relationship between host and guest reflects the fact that practically all political interviews on breakfast TV (and other guest interviews as well) belong to the sub-genre of talk shows that Bruun (1997) calls "the research". The objective of this type of interview is not to create conflict, e.g., strong arguments, or to reveal things through inquest-like forms of interview. The objective is to provide coverage of a topic or a person, and the host's role in this context is to be a kind of midwife; his or her questions are intended to help the interviewee tell a story, and therefore sufficient time is allowed so that the interviewee can give a full answer. As pointed out by Bruun (1997), "the research" is, from the point of view of journalistic criteria, often a relatively risk free genre in that the host functions primarily as support for the interviewee. The journalist is neither critic, judge nor antagonist. In return, this "research" genre allows for more subtle coverage of a person or a theme because, among other things, the polite, personal style may help the participants to relax and avoid getting into defensive positions, thus talking more freely and personally.[4] The price, however, is that politeness requirements on the part of the host dominate completely over journalistic demands for efficiency and a critical approach.

On the whole, it can be concluded that breakfast TV's political interviews illustrate in an almost exemplary way some general features of the development of modern political communication. Jamieson (1988) has, in an analysis of the development of American presidential rhetoric, pointed out three interdependent characteristics. First, a change is taking place under the pressure of the electronic media in which the political speech is leaving room for the political *conversation* as a central form of political communication. Whereas in the past, being able to speak to a big crowd was important for achieving political office, if one is to be elected today, the ability to master a conversation between just a few people is essential. Second, the *visualisation* of politics has changed political communication. In breakfast TV, there is no visualisation in addition to the portrayal of politicians themselves, but this is essential enough. Visualisation of politicians while they speak implies that it is impossible to separate what is said from non-verbal cues, i.e., the political statement is always accompanied by the talker's gestures, mimicry, clothing, etc., that constantly reveal things about lifestyle, mood, reactions, attentiveness etc. In other words, as a consequence of visualisation, it becomes more difficult to separate the political aspect from the personal aspect. Third, and consequently, there is, according to Jamieson (1988), a tendency towards intimacy in modern politics. Basing one's statements on personal experiences and motives creates political trustworthiness. This is, as we have seen above, a crucial element in the treatment of political topics in breakfast TV: giving politics a face.

Breakfast TV's way of making politics personal is a clear example of a general tendency in modern political culture. The distinctive feature of breakfast TV's treatment of politics is its *combination of the personal with the everyday*. The political conversation does not only have a personal character, it also takes place in the sphere of intimacy, over a cup of morning coffee, and is, as such, far removed from its usual, parliamentary and public arena. Scannell (1996) has described how radio and TV create a particular coupling between sincerity and intimacy in which one forms a prerequisite for the other. In radio, the microphone's ability to tie speech to a characteristic voice created an association between speech and person that has become even more exaggerated by TV's live pictures. This association has made intimacy a mediator of sincerity. People become sincere by being personal and perhaps even intimate. A person's political moral standing will also be judged by the camera's unveiling of a quivering in the facial muscles, a hearty smile or a short swallowing before answering a question. In breakfast TV, politicians or other guests seldom become intimate, but they become everyday people with a personal face. In this way, their mastery of general everyday and informal behaviour becomes an index of their trustworthiness. Politicians authenticise their political occupation through their personal and everyday appearance. Their ability to demonstrate social competence at the level of everyday life, i.e., to join us viewers at morning coffee and be pleasant, becomes a representation of their political sincerity.

Conversation and Company

Breakfast TV is a program format that has the marked ability to establish what Horton and Wohl (1956) have called *para-social interaction*, i.e., radio's and TV's ability to create a "simulacrum of conversational give and take" (Horton & Wohl, 1956). However, parasocial interaction is not limited to electronic media. For example, Berelson's (1949) classic study of what "missing the newspaper means" showed that the printed word can also give recipients a sense of an almost continuous relationship with people whom they only know through the newspaper. But TV's special ability to simulate interpersonal communication by directly turning to the viewers makes reception of the people on the screen feel like having company. As I have described elsewhere (Hjarvard, 1997), interpersonal communication – in the sense of face-to-face, verbal and non-verbal communication between two or more people located in the same room – can be said to constitute an important matrix for the general historical development of the media and genres. Thus, there is a general tendency toward attempting to re-establish central characteristics of interpersonal communication in new media forms. Breakfast TV's marked use of simulated interpersonal interaction in the form of social get-togethers is yet another example of this development.

Breakfast TV also utilises another characteristic of the TV medium: its ability to broadcast an uninterrupted program stream continuous with and parallel to the viewer's everyday life. Breakfast TV does not have a traditional time structure. Both duration and structure break with the conventions of the typical TV broadcast. Breakfast TV is both a single program and an entire program schedule and, as such, is not produced to be seen in its entirety. The entire structure of this form of programming is intended to adapt to the viewer's own weekday morning. Scannell (1996) has pointed out that the most general social effect of radio and TV has been to "re-temporize time; to mark it out in particular ways, so that the time of the day (at any time) is a particular time, a time differentiated from past time-in-the-day or time that is yet-to-come" (Scannell, 1996: 149). In this light, breakfast TV helps to give the beginning of the day a particular significance: it is never just any day, but precisely today that we are visited by these people, hear these news features, see this dish being prepared, etc. And through this fixed time structure (see scheme 1), each point in time in the morning is given its particular weight in that it receives an extra, marked meaning that is different from those of other points in time.

As mentioned above, it is characteristic of breakfast TV that what is significant is never particularly deviant or conspicuous. Breakfast TV as a whole does not differ greatly from normal, everyday life. The kitchen is just a little more expensive than that of the average viewer, most guests' abilities and experiences are typically just a little more advanced and unusual as compared to those of the viewer. The choice of themes, forms of conversation and camera angles never approach the extreme. In this way, breakfast TV can be incorporated into the viewer's everyday life as something that gives it an extra lift. However, the price of this orientation toward the commonplace is that breakfast TV may become both predictable and harmless. But this is precisely the intention; as the producer Mette Lage says about, for example, the role of the TV hosts:

> "They are our guides through a state of awakening for most of the audience, and should therefore be nice and, if not private, at least a bit predictable. The viewers must feel assured that nobody with a knife up his sleeve will attack somebody else, not even in a journalistic sense."

Breakfast TV is able to efficiently utilise the TV medium's capacity for making parasocial company and re-interpreting time in everyday life. But to achieve this goal, a number of more traditional journalistic functions must be downplayed. In any case, predictability and pleasant company can not easily be reconciled with the journalistic institution's duties to prioritise mediation of information and to reflect upon objectivity, substance, the function of criticism, etc.

TV2's *Good Morning Denmark* has taken the consequences of this incompatibility by placing pure news and the breakfast hosts' soft, get-together journalism under different management: TV2's news editorship and breakfast TV's talk show. Abroad, other solutions to this problem can be found. For example, the BBC has chosen to make breakfast TV much more traditionally oriented towards news and current affairs issues than has been the case with some of the Danish breakfast TV editions. There are, thus, many ways around the contradiction between political journalism and the TV medium's possibility of being an extended drawing room. Irrespective of current methods of combining the two elements, however, there has been, from a historical point of view, a shift between the two elements in Danish TV (Hjarvard, 1994 and 2000). When the former public service monopoly institution DR began its newscast *TV-Avisen* in 1965, the point of departure was the journalistic institution's premises for selection of material, presentation, etc. The consequence was, among other things, that *TV-Avisen* was accused of being "contrary to the nature of the screen" (Prehn, 1980); in spite of the criticism, DR adhered to a strictly journalistic approach for many years. Today, in a multi-channel and commercial TV environment, it is no longer unequivocal that the medium works in the service of journalism. The increased emphasis on journalism's service to the parasocial togetherness between hosts and viewers indicates that journalism works more and more in the service of the medium.

Notes

1. In Bruun (1997: 25ff.), a talk show is defined on the basis of three characteristics: it is broadcast from a TV studio, either directly or live-on-tape; the studio host(s) is/are the central link between program and audience; and the (journalistic) interview is the central form of presentation. Given this definition, the breakfast TV editions dealt with here are all talk shows. For an analysis of particularly early examples of Danish talk shows, see Bruun (1997).
2. As part of my research on breakfast TV, I have followed production and broadcasts of TV2's *Good Morning Denmark* and also talked to the former producer Henrik Zachariassen, who participated in the development of the program concept, the present producer Mette Lage and the editor-in-chief Anna Vinding, all from the Skandinavisk Film Kompagni. Their interest and cooperation in this investigation are hereby gratefully acknowledged.
3. The agenda for and the contents of an interview are typically the result of a negotiation between journalist and source, and as such the interviewee may in practice have considerable influence over what is said. However, during the actual interview, the journalist has a great deal of control.
4. Many breakfast TV staff-members emphasised this as an essential quality of this type of journalism. The interview with Anne Birgitte Lundholdt was explicitly emphasised as a good example of how this form of interview can enable politicians to make confessions that would not have been made in more traditional interview formats.

Bibliography

Alsted Research (1997). *Kvalitativ undersøgelse af seervaner. TV2's Morgen-tv* [*Qualitative investigation of viewing habits. TV2's Breakfast TV*]. Analysis carried out for TV2 Reklame, June 1997. Copenhagen: unpublished.

Berelson, B. (1949). "What 'Missing the Newspaper' Means". In P. F. Lazarsfeld & F. N. Stanton (eds.): *Communication Research 1948-49*. New York: Harper & Brothers.

Bruun, H. (1997). *Snakkeprogrammet. Portræt af en tv-genre* [*The Talkshow. Portrait of a tv genre*]. Ph.D. dissertation, Aarhus University: unpublished.

Bruun, H. (1999). *Talkshowet. Portræt af en tv-genre*. Copenhagen: Borgens Forlag.

Drotner, K., K. B. Jensen, I. Poulsen & K. Schrøder (1996). *Medier og Kultur* [*Media and Culture*]. Copenhagen: Borgen.

Goffman, E. (1959). *The Presentation of Self in Everyday Life*. New York: Doubleday.

Hjarvard, S. (1994). "Intimitet, autenticitet og kvindelighed ["Intimacy, autenticity, and femininity"]. In P. Dahlgren (ed.): *Den Mångtydiga Rutan*. Stockholm: JMK, Stockholm University.

Hjarvard, S. (1997). "Simulerede samtaler: Om forholdet mellem interpersonel kommunikation og medieformidlet kommunikation" ["Simulated conversations: On the relationship between interpersonal and mediated communication]. In: *MedieKultur* nr. 26, Aarhus.

Hjarvard, S. (2000). "Proximity. The name of the ratings game". In: *Nordicom Review*, special issue, no. 2. Gothenburg: Nordicom.

Hjarvard, S., & H. Søndergaard (1988). *Nærsyn på Fjernsyn* [*A Close-up on Television*]. Copenhagen: C.A. Reitzels Forlag.

Horton, D., & R. R. Wohl (1956). "Mass Communication and Parasocial Interaction: Observations on Intimacy at a Distance". In: *Journal of Psychiatry* 19. Reprinted in G. Gumpert & R. Catchcart (eds.) (1986): *Inter/Media. Interpersonal Communication in a Media World*. New York: Oxford University Press.

Jamieson, K.H. (1988). *Eloquence in an Electronic Age. The Transformation of Political Speechmaking*. New York: Oxford University Press.

Prehn, O. (1980). "Idag er det TV-Avisens Føs'dag" ["Happy birthday to the tv news"]. In: *Levende Billeder*, October 1980.

Scannell, P. (ed.) (1991). *Broadcast Talk*. London: Sage.

Scannell, P. (1996). *Radio, Television & Modern Life*. Oxford: Blackwell.

Sørensen, T.B. (1989). *Talehandlinger [Speech Acts]*. Aarhus: Forlaget Gestus.

Appendix

Excerpt from Michael Meyerheim's (MM) interview with Anne Birgitte Lundholt (ABL) in TV2's Good Morning Denmark, *September 30, 1997.*

MM: Now I would like to hear from Anne Birgitte Lundholt, first of all, congratulations on your new job. You have kept your spirits up, it would seem at least, during your setback after Hans Engell's fall. But, if we can be just a little bit honest about this, would it have happened at all, the shift you are making now, if you had not experienced such adversity?

ABL: Ah, if I had been sitting either as leader of the Konservative Folkeparti today, or still as number two with Hans Engell at the helm, I would of course have both a responsibility and an inclination to lead the party further to the next election campaign and back into government. So, of course, it has had an effect on whether you say yes or no when such a good offer comes up.

MM: Yes, you have said that you will not slam the door, uh, now. But that seems to indicate that you do have a good reason for doing so.

ABL: I am always of the opinion that irrespective of whether you leave for a particular reason, or because something else has come by that is more interesting – as in my case – you should always close the door behind you in a nice way, so that you can come back, even though I have not considered returning to politics, I like to bid a fond farewell to things I leave. After all, I have had 8 good years.

MM: Is it fair to say that you are well prepared for your new job because you understand the phenomenon of slaughter?

ABL: Ahr (laughter), I guess yeah, if we are going to be a little funny so early in the morning; but, uh, I would like to say that the reason I got this offer and accepted the job is that I have a past as a director of a branch organisation, and of course it also counts that I am now a little familiar with the political system from within, and it is rather important for a branch organisation to be able to move in elevated circles.

MM: Is this a definite goodbye to politics? It sounds like it from what you are saying here.

ABL: Yes, it is a definite goodbye. I am 45 now, which means that I have another 15, maybe 20 active years left, and I feel it is very appropriate to spend them in the private sector. And I am rejoicing.

MM: Yes. Ole Andreasen, you are moving...

CHAPTER NINE

So – That's Your Life?
Authentic Forms of Television Talk

Tove A. Rasmussen
Department of Communication
Aalborg University

This article will deal with parts and potentials of everyday talk and behaviour portrayed on television. For the last 10 to 15 years, media studies have been preoccupied with the concept of talk on and about television. This attention is mostly related to talk shows and simulated forms of contact between host and viewer. Also the situated contexts of television viewing and viewers' talk about TV-programmes have been discussed. In reception studies and media ethnography, the viewers' talk produces the basic empirical data. The phenomenon of the viewers' talk about TV has been conceptualised as a "third intertextuality" by John Fiske (Fiske, 1987).

My textual objects are two Danish programmes sent autumn/winter 1996. I aim to propose a framework for the theoretical understanding of the importance of the 'situation' in television studies – both in relation to actual programmes and with respect to the reception of television as a communicative mode. I have been inspired by computer research concerning concepts such as interaction and interactivity but, most of all, I have been wondering about the 'user-interface' of television – and asking myself whether there is such a relationship and what it may look like.

One of the programme formats is internationally known, as it is a Dutch concept called *Taxi*, where several candid cameras are hidden in a taxi during its normal routine. In Finland, the programme was hosted by the taxi-drivers themselves while the Danish concept introduced a 'proper host' in the shape of a young yellow press journalist named Anders Lund Madsen. At the time, Madsen was not a well-known TV-personality but the programme made him one. The other programme is a Danish concept called *Pizzamanden* (*The Pizza Man*) where a well known and popular talk show host goes for a ride with a local pizza man – delivering pizzas to people in very different domestic situations – big parties, watching TV, painting the apartment or the like.

In both programmes we follow the conversations of 4 to 6 different kinds of 'customers' and the host – travelling by taxi or having ordered pizza. By means of authenticity, spontaneity, contact and personality, we are invited to take a glance at different lifestyles and different modes of interpersonal communication. At several points, our observational 'glance' is transformed into something more – a kind of interest in, and sympathy for, the participating persons which is best known from involvement in interpersonal contact – moments of just being glad that you met this person.

The programmes are quite differently produced and comprise different intentionalities. At a general level, they can both be said to experiment with the form and content of television talk. Four important comments to be made at this point are: 1) the programmes are ex-studio; 2) the subject of talk is neither pre-defined nor determined by a producer; 3) the roles of interviewer and interviewee are not given in a traditional sense; and 4) talk is processual and momentarily dialogic.

Does Small Talk Count?

Creating authentic situations on television is hard work. As for the programme *The Pizza Man,* the visual and auditive codings of authenticity are very strong. The viewer has to be convinced that the pizza customers are really surprised when Camilla Miehe-Renard rings the door bell. The pizza bar is the home base of the programme and we follow Camilla and the 'pizza man' by hand-held camera – from the pizza bar, into the car, out of the car and into the doorway of the customer. Camilla makes eye-contact with the camera – smiling and waving as she invites us on the ride. The role of the camera is primarily to follow Camilla from behind in total or half total figure until we reach the entrance door. When she rings the bell and the door is opened, the camera moves closer and catches the surprised customer/participant in half total figure with Camilla's microphone pointing at the 'victim' (cf. Fig. 1).

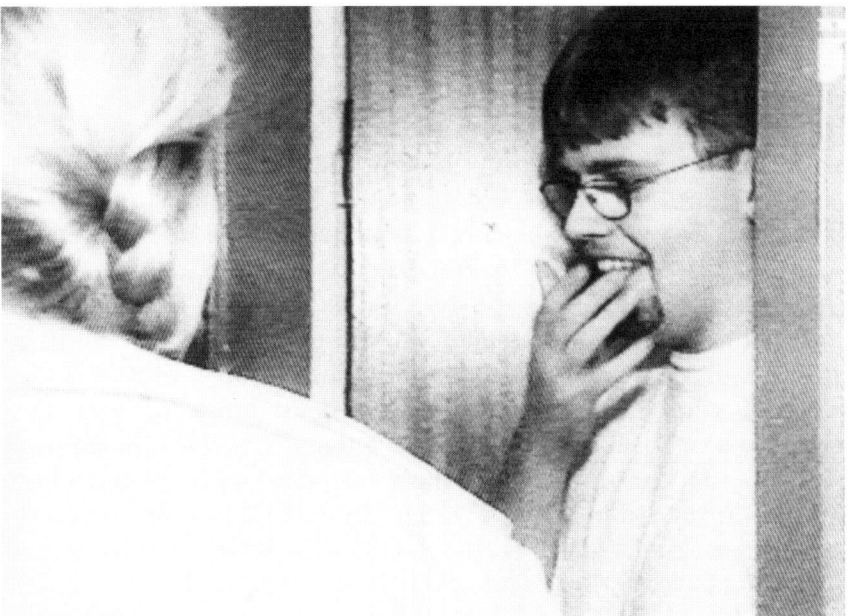

Figure 1: Camilla: (photographed from the back): "Hi, are you Gert? Then you have ordered pizza". Gert: "Yes". Camilla: "We are from Radio Denmark, we would like to ask if we may disturb you, while you are eating your pizza". Gert: "Well, well ...", Gert takes a look at the mess in his apartment and then he invites Camilla inside

The visual codings of the authentic visit are supplemented with a more deictic and interpretative camera in the conversation sequences which last approx. 6 minutes. To a certain degree, Camilla instructs the camera what to focus on in the deictic function, but during the concentrated conversational sequences, the camera tries to support the dialogue by interpretation – by zooming in at specific important utterances or by focusing on the hands or feet of the participant. (I have analysed the programmes in greater detail in Rasmussen: 1998.) Camilla's qualifications as talk show hostess are demonstrated under very difficult circumstances. She has to adapt to and interpret the home situation as well as the participants almost immediately and by means of small talk about the pizza, she starts to focus the conversation spontaneously by following up on very few 'testing' questions: "Are you living alone?" or: "Have you been together for a long time?", "What are you celebrating?" – or whatever the actual situation of eating pizza at home may be.

The participants then engage in conversation – most importantly the subject of the talk is produced in the process and through mutual understanding. Even the style and mode of conversation is very quickly adapted to the actual situation and to the mood of the participants. When the conversation works best, it has some of the characteristics of an open ended life-world qualitative interview because of Camilla's ability to give feedback, show empathy, follow up and focus. At the same time, she leaves space for the participant's line and she is constantly aware of the potential loss of face. Metacommunication and humour are also important traits of conversation. So participants are taken by surprise; – the spontaneous conversation combined with the authentic coding of the whole set up of pizza-delivering provide an expectation of ... exactly the unexpected where participants seem to be very open and interested in telling about their lives, without instruction.

The focus of interest is primarily: How do ordinary people react when confronted with the well-known television 'personae' Camilla Miehe-Renard? Secondly, a fundamental interest in seeing other people's private homes. Thirdly, an interest in the line and life-world of the participating person. And finally, the possibility of involvement and interest in the person as a human being. It is an involvement based on the authentic mode of spontaneity, simulated viewer-contact and the dynamic interaction potential of the authentically constructed situation itself.

The programme *Taxi* does not have to work so hard at establishing the authentic framework. It is a candid camera programme where the premises of the unexpected and the spontaneous are already given. Yet the interpersonal coding of the taxi-interaction is very important. The 'host' Anders Lund Madsen is not, at the time of the broadcast, known to the public and he plays the part of the taxi-driver. In the intro-sequence of the programme, we see how he achieves his taxi-drivers' licence and throughout the programmes, he explores the limits of conversation in the context of a taxi ride. In contrast to more traditional candid camera shows, the 'plot' is not the exposure of the victim: "You have been on candid camera". On the contrary, the taxi functions as a kind of social laboratory as Madsen plays his part as a very lively, talkative and provocative taxi-driver.

Only on a few occasions, do the passengers notice the hidden cameras; they all try to adapt to the rather strange kind of conversation and they also contribute by giving very positive feedback to Madsen. As opposed to *The Pizza Man*, the conversation does not take the form of an interview – even though Madsen asks a lot of questions and follows up and provides a lot of feedback. But as the overall framework of 'television' is lacking in the conversations, the passengers act within the framework of an ordinary everyday conversation with a stranger. Besides the verbal talk, we observe the non-masked non-verbal language and behaviour of taxi-passengers. After the trip, the passengers are told about the hidden cameras, but this does not usually take place in front of the camera.

The programme is humorous as Madsen is very self-ironic. He mocks the passengers in a gentle way and keeps a very close simulated contact to the viewer by means of the rear-view mirror. A great deal of metacommunication takes place and the topic of conversation is mutually constructed during the process. Roles of speech are free but not totally equal as Madsen is the one to take the floor and follow up by questioning. Conversation never gets directly problematising and the participating persons usually do not risk losing face. So the content of the programme can be said to be small talk made entertaining by the host's capacity for humour, irony and not least his ability to maintain contact – both with the present interaction partner and with the distant viewer. The question is then how we, as viewers, come to enjoy the observation of interaction under those circumstances.

Figure 2: The customer – Vicki – is telling a great story about her former life in the Middle East. By laughing, Madsen makes her go on telling – and a bit later he makes eye contact with the viewer by means of the rear-view mirror

First of all, we have the fundamental interest in watching other's non-masked behaviour, secondly, the excitement of the set up – do people recognise the 'unnaturalistic' situation and how far do they accept the very talkative and provocative taxi-driver? The quality of the programme lies most of all in the demonstration of the possibilities of the social interaction between strangers: The unpredictability of the situation provides an experience of how much effect small changes in ordinary talk may have. When the programme works at its best, the passengers faces and body-language simply 'light up' and the expression: "You are the nicest taxi-driver I have ever met", is heard several times.

The intentions of the programme are not as clear-cut as those of *The Pizza Man*, yet the intensity of interaction and dynamics of social being point to the endless possibilities of changing human life by means of the micro-dynamics of interpersonal interaction. In the course of a short taxi-trip, you may make a new friend, write a brand new poem as payment for the trip or gain a lot of new self-esteem provided by the positive feedback from Madsen in the conversation. In fact Vicki is going for a job interview at one of the most expensive department stores in Copenhagen and she is confirmed by him when leaving: "You could sell me anything, I am sure", Madsen says and the camera then follows Vicki as she mingles with the city shoppers on her way to her job interview (cf. Fig. 2).

Conversation and Rules

What makes this kind of programme interesting to me is primarily that they challenge the traditional authoritative relationship between talking parties on television. Hereby, we come to question the fundamentals of genre codings seen from a linguistic and micro-sociolocical perspective. The question is a basic one: Are the methods we apply for analysing television appropriate for the actual programmes at hand? The traditional journalistic genres seem to be less and less appropriate for understanding reality-oriented television such as talk shows, game shows, some documentaries and different kinds of reality television. The journalistic notion of 'a good story', the dramaturgical plots of the story, the whole point of telling the story and the story's relevance or importance to the public sphere are fundamental for the traditional sub-genres of journalism: News, documentaries, magazines.

The interviewing form itself implies certain strictly distributed roles of speakers. That goes for both the social and the linguistic roles of conversation:

> "An interview in a Western society is a clearly defined and quite common speech event to which a formal style is appropriate. It generally involves dyadic interaction between strangers, with the roles of the two participants being quite clearly defined. Turn-taking rights are not equally distributed as they are in conversational interaction between peers. Rather, one participant (the interviewer) controls the discourse in the sense of both select-

ing topics and choosing the form of questions. The interviewee, on the other hand, by agreeing to be interviewed has accepted to answer these questions co-operatively." (Milroy, 1987: 41)

The more or less unprepared context of conversation brings about new possibilities for so-called 'ordinary people' and their access to television – ex-studio, non-prepared and non-problemising talk. As a matter of fact, this kind of conversation is very much like the kind of talk of everyday life's "speech events" known from Erving Goffman's work. Goffman has been much used in recent media research and what I find most motivating in relation to the new media roles is his concept of "line":

"Every person lives in a world of social encounters, involving him either in face-to-face or mediated contact with other participants. In each of these contacts, he tends to act out what is sometimes called a line – that is a pattern of verbal and non-verbal actions by which he expresses his view of the situation and, through this, his evaluation of the participants, especially himself. The term face may be defined as the positive social value a person effectively claims for himself by the line others assume he has taken during a particular contact." (Goffman, 1955: 213)

In this quotation, Goffman talks about the "line" as the position you claim for yourself with due respect to the others' perception of you and your person. To put it very directly, the journalist's "line" and perception of his or her own role in relation to the public has traditionally been the role of the viewer's advocate – having a story to tell, a story of news, relevance and/or human interest. This role itself implies a very limited position for the participating interviewed person – performing the more or less instructed line of e.g. the expert, the humiliated mother, the war victim or the politician to be hunted down in the predisposed story of the journalist.

The discussed programmes – which may be called 'reality television' or 'video-realism' as I prefer to call it, set up a framework of openness in relation to the content and context of conversation – and to a certain degree in relation to the social and linguistic roles of interviewing. What is most important is of course that the programmes work in the field – the participating people do not have to worry about the perfect studio 'performance', etc. They do not have to adapt to television as an institution. They are taken by surprise – either by the very 'aggressive' camera's investigations in *The Pizza Man* or by the candid cameras in *Taxi*. Breaking down some of the traditional patterns of communication in television conversation is somewhat of a challenge, if we accept Milroy's definitions of the interview, but what about the qualities? Are the programmes just 'small talk' about 'nothing' since the story is not given in advance? Or might we talk about programmes involving cultural observation of other people's lifestyles and communication – a kind of phenomenological curiosity of the kind that we researchers often take as a starting point for our analysis?

Quality

How is it that there may be a certain standard of quality in this kind of programme? – And what about the ethical limitations? First of all, I must confess that I have picked out programmes which, to me, involve ethical considerations. I do not take into account the whole range of programmes labelled "reality television" (Søndergaard, 1995; Keppler, 1994), where slap-stick, drama, reconstruction and sentimentality are constitutive components – e.g. *Rescue 911*, Blind Date programmes, Home Video, Docu-soaps and different kinds of Candid Camera shows. In order to establish a proper framework for understanding the programmes, I have tried to use some of the advice given by Paddy Scannell among others:

> "The theory of communicative intentionality – which is not a theory of the motives of speakers (what they have in mind) but of the structuring preconditions of communication as social interaction (intentionality as a common ground between speaker and listener) – must in the

first place be presupposed as a grounding condition for
the activities of broadcasters *and* audiences." (Scannell,
1991: 6)

The close inspection of other people's situated living circumstances and their acting out of personal lines in communicating – verbally and non-verbally – seems to create some kind of interest in the television audience. That's where my more theoretical points are to be made. In microsociology, we see researchers take a special interest in the 'situation' or maybe the 'sequence' of interpersonal communication. The definitions of 'interaction' and 'communication' may be somewhat difficult to grasp. I have chosen to look at the actual programmes from the point of view of the sociological understanding of interaction: people being together in mutual space and time – acting out their personal lines in accordance with the demands of the specific situation. At the same time, I focus on the possibility of change – of metacommunication and spontaneity as a process of meaning and thereby a cultural phenomenon. So, in the first place, I look at the interaction which takes place between the participants on the screen.

The Spontaneous

The above definition is a narrowing of the sociological concept of interaction – but of specific relevance to the programmes and genres at hand. The unpreparedness, the unexpected, the spontaneous we know from social interaction with strangers in semi-public places – the park bench, the train or wherever you may suddenly meet a stranger and involve yourself in a speech event. We are certainly not used to this kind of spontaneous and process oriented talk on television – on the contrary, the smallest non-verbal reaction from the host is rehearsed and we do not expect any breakings of the predisposed lines of television participants – even in the talk shows by e.g. Jerry Springer, the reactions of participants and audiences seem well rehearsed and the formal rules of the emotional shows are very seldom broken.

In the creation of the authentic framework of experience, the very idea of the 'unexpected' is central and what is most interesting is in fact 'what happens'. Hanne Bruun claims in her Ph.D. dissertation on "talk programmes" that even in pre-recorded studio talk shows, the "unexpected" plays a central role (Bruun, 1997). How will participants then react when the famous Camilla Miehe-Renard suddenly appears at the front door with a pizza, a pizza man and a very lively camera. And how do the taxi passengers behave when observed by several candid cameras and conversed by "the nicest taxi-driver I have ever met"? The naturalistic situation provides splendid opportunities for the viewers' to observe human behaviour – verbal and non-verbal – the conversational space seems open and, to a certain degree, invites participants' own lines and life-worlds. My point so far is that the construction of the authentic framework makes place not only for the unexpected but also for the observation of non-verbal, linguistic, interactional behaviour and very different lifestyles and life-worlds.

The ethics and the 'artistic' way of conducting conversations is a spontaneous focusing on topics in the very proximate life-world of the participant. Most importantly in relation to the concept of dialogue, the participating persons take the floor, they metacommunicate and they are invited to elaborate on their own perspectives. Compared to ordinary interviews, this is very different. In traditional interviewing, the hosts do not talk about their own life-worlds and perspectives – yet, it does occur and thereby adds to the spontaneity of the programmes. The interactional possibility that persons face-to-face will change the actual situation, is thereby present in the programmes: You never know how the conversation will develop as the participants may change the subject or metacommunicate about the situation. For example, in *The Pizza Man*, a young man says to Camilla Miehe-Renard and her cameraman: "We usually take off our shoes", when they enter the apartment. In this way, the viewer may not only observe the lifestyles of other people from a distance, but also experience the spontaneous reactions familiar from ordinary interpersonal communication, may get to 'like' the person on the screen, study her viewpoint and ultimately have a more tolerant view of other ways of living.

Interaction and Communication – Preliminary Remarks

So much for my definition of interaction. Some of the same arguments are made by symbolic interactionists in relation to the concept of "communication" as a kind of "symbolic process through which reality is produced, contained, repaired and changed". I borrow the quotation from Margareta Rönnberg (1996: 213) who works on the basis of symbolic interactionism and especially George Herbert Mead. To me, the concept of communication is much broader than the microsociological concept of interaction and the above-mentioned "symbolic process". If we did not know beforehand, communication research has taught us that also animals communicate and they do so with often very strong intentions though not symbolically expressed in language. Communication may of course be of the above "symbolic" character but then we have to narrow the concept to human communication and the process of the creation of culture.

To Rönnberg it is very important to see communication as mutual – also in relation to mass mediated communication and she introduces the concept of "dialogue" and "inner dialogue" in relation to mediated communication and points out that the TV viewer relates to TV-figures and TV-persons as in a "true" dialogue" (1996: 213). In terms of children, this may be the case but when I examine the concepts of interaction, communication and dialogue in actual programmes, it strikes me most of all how much effort the producers, and not least the hosts, put into the construction of an authentic framework of conversation where – perhaps – the viewer involves herself in a process of following, understanding and maybe even adopting the other's line in a somewhat dialogic process. Yet to me it is an open question whether this may happen at a more general level.

As I have already mentioned, *The Pizza Man* and *Taxi* are both situated in non-studio environments in the midst of the participants everyday lives. *The Pizza Man* even breaks the limits of the private domain – without notice, showing up on people's doorsteps. I will call the situated interaction 'naturalistic' following the microsociological tradition where 'naturalistic' does not mean the real world with the observer acting as a fly-on-the wall but naturally occurring situated interaction. In this respect, especially *The Pizza Man* works very hard to establish authentic audio visual codings of Camilla Miehe-Renard's visits to the participants homes. So, in this sense, naturalistic means a TV-crew visiting a private home – just as a family therapy situation may be called 'naturalistic'.

What we have here is, on the one hand, programmes where the situated, naturalistic and authentic traits are very important. On the other hand, however, we have a conception of the television audience in which prominent writers advocate the situated perspective as well. Hereby, I mean the very private domains of the viewing environment and the different communicative actions taking place in this viewing context. So, theoretically, the common determinator is at this point situated communication and the meaning of this phenomenon in relation to programmes, programme intentionalities and the circumstances of television viewing as a specific activity.

The Situation at Home – Maintaining Contact

In ordinary terms, 'talk programmes' represent cheap television when compared with such things as fiction. At the same time, the talking heads on the screen seem to correspond communicatively with the viewer's home situation, since the viewing environment (the faces and talk of others) is easily integrated into the general reception situation. Jørgen Stigel (1997: 5) points to the fact that the deixis dimension of television communication is very important: "In the electronic media, enunciation plays a crucial part as everything which is said principally presents itself as framed by the present tense (in the general channel-audience relationship)". By means of the deixis – or simulated interaction in a broader sense – the talking heads of television (try to) make contact in the 'here and now' context of situated reception.

For a full and whole theory of television communication, the discussion of the relation between text, context and situated reception ought to be developed – if not on an empirical basis then at least on a theoretical basis. By taking this point, I am not claiming that the macro structures of production/reception are not important but the situated reception perspective implies the importance of a close examination of television as a communicative medium in specific time and space contexts – being both a communicatively forceful and potentially powerless media. When Umberto Eco speaks of this communication situation, he says that the viewer is in control and therefore, television has to attract and preserve this attention and interest by means of deictic and phatic communication:

> "The most important quality of neo television is that it still, to a minor extent (like palaeo television did or pretended to do), talks about the external world. It talks about itself and about the contact it has with its audience. It is not important what it says or what it talks about (in part, because the viewers decide by means of the remote control when it should be permitted to talk and when they want to change to another channel). In order to survive the viewers' power of replacement, the television attempts to detain the viewer by saying to him: "I am here, I am me and I am you". (Eco, 1989: 71, my translation)

Maintaining contact – being self-referential is the maxim of Eco's "neo television". In Eco's view, the strong potential of television for referentiality to the surrounding world is weakened by focusing on the communication process between channel/programme and viewer: Television is continuously making up its own reality. Seen from this perspective, the micro level of situated reception is not necessarily a question of scientific empirical observation of everyday practice. It is a much more fundamental theoretical challenge of understanding the specific communication and reception modes in a broader perspective than the well-known individual text/reader relationship.

The viewer's reception of television without making a visual contact may be characterised as distracted and inattentive. Yet, at certain points, the narration or the sounds attract attention and thereby (re)introduce the talking heads of television in the overall activities and communication patterns of the living room. Seen from the point of view of television producers and television researchers you may talk about a distracted reception form. In the situated context of the living room, however, television is only one of a number of communicative claims on attention and interaction. It is remarkable that the specifically situated reception of television has attracted attention from researchers but rather few new studies are being made.

The insights of David Morley (1986) and James Lull (1990) have been the subjects of much criticism – especially in Danish/Norwegian media research. The very broad concepts of technology and everyday life have been regarded as a problematic shift of focus in television research – from the text/viewer relation to the mixed practices of everyday life where the media and their specific texts are not the centre of attention. Thereby, media research has lost not only its focus but also its object, Schroeder (1993) and Fetveit (1996) claim.

The question: "Why do people pay attention to the television instead of the washing machine?" has been posed in a very polemic way to media ethnographers. Why are the rules and rituals of everyday (media) communication in families important? Perhaps these rules are not important but the point is that television by its nature represents here and now communication – warm or cold. The immediacy of the flow of communication calls for a situated understanding of reception as a kind of simultaneous communicative action. Seen from this perspective, the text/reader model only holds for details of the overall communicative action since the model was originally developed on the basis of a quite different kind of medium – the book.

The reading of the book as situated reception practice implies among many other things a solitary, linear and concentrated activity. Through the act of reading, you create a sort of free space – by withdrawing yourself into the book, you exclude yourself from the immediate surroundings. This goes for both everyday duties and interpersonal claims for attention. Your relation to the book as a medium is a private one – only by reading aloud, do you share the flow of the textual experience with other people. It may of course be argued that both reading the newspaper and watching television might also be acts of creating a private space. This is the case for the men in Morley's book (1986) through concentrated viewing of news. But, at the same time, Morley's investigation indicates that this kind of solitary practice in relation to television is itself a matter of discussion and dispute in the family. Only by demanding and actively creating a "cinematic reception mode" in relation to television, may you talk about a dominant text/ reader relationship.

A Common Framework

For the rest of the chapter, I shall pursue the themes of communication and interaction by taking into consideration the traditions of microsociology, symbolic interactionism and conversation analysis (Goffman, Bateson and Sheflen). In taking this path, I am following the advice of Paddy Scannell to look at the actual communicative intentionalities taking place in ordinary daily life. The above mentioned scholars make up a common framework for the understanding of communication – regardless of whether it is interpersonal or mediated. Joshua Meyrowitz makes a very clear point on the importance of the "situation" in communication studies. Drawing especially on the insights of Garfinkel and Goffman, he claims that "situationism" may be the missing link between media and understanding of behaviour:

> "Social behaviour and communication, then, involve much more than people bouncing "messages" off each other. To a large extent, behaviour is shaped and modified by the socially defined situations in which people find themselves. While much individual variation remains within a given situation, there is also a larger

consistency in the patterned variations people exhibit as they move from one type of situation to another." (Meyrowitz, 1985: 27)

To communication research, the 'setting', the 'episode', the 'event' and the 'sequence' are all important as focus points in the analysis of human behaviour. What happened in the ill-fated historical division of different paradigms into interpersonal communication and mass communication research was, among other things, that the sensibility of the situated communication process was lost to mass communication research. And that goes for uses and gratifications as well as for the text/reader model, cultural studies and semiotics. Re-establishing this common framework for communication studies may be vital for the further development of television theory as a situated and a cultural and a textual everyday activity.

There has been a growing theoretical pressure on the traditional sociological models of mass communication as well as a questioning of the traditional humanistic models of textual analysis. This pressure has particularly derived from television research itself. At the same time, it is striking that we also seem to need technological challenges as for example media convergence and digitisation in order to take 'old' problems such as the meaning of reception contexts and reception modes really seriously.

The Challenge

The new media and media forms point to the future of the 'game' between computer and television: which kinds of media formats are going to 'win' and produce the windows and packages of the screen? To which degree and in which ways are we to interact with the different options of the screen? Is it going to be a solitary or a collective kind of situated reception? The moment we pose these questions about the future use of the screen, we are forced to take the past into consideration. Is television to be defined historically as a forceful, communicative yet powerless social media in the sense that it is begging for attention on the communicative floor without getting any useful feedback from the users? Moreover, it will always be threatened by the power of the remote control: This will then be characterised by a very low degree of interactivity but by a very high degree of simulated interaction and parasocial interaction.

John Thompson (1995: 85) has proposed a framework for understanding media types in relation to the basic characteristics of face-to-face interaction.

Types of interaction

Interactional characteristics	Face-to-face interaction	Mediated interaction	Mediated quasi-interaction
Space-time constitution	Context of copresence; shared spatial-temporal reference system	Separation of contexts; extended availability in time and space	Separation of contexts; extended availability in time and space
Range of symbolic cues	Multiplicity of symbolic cues	Narrowing of the rage of symbolic cues	Narrowing of the range of symbolic cues
Action orientation	Oriented towards specific others	Oriented towards specific others	Oriented towards an indefinite range of potential recipients
Dialogical/ monological	Dialogical	Dialogical	Monological

It is striking that Thompson does not include the computer and the different kinds of interactivity in computer mediated communication. You can in fact say that all his three types of interaction are – or may be – parts of the interactivity potential of the computer. One of the great qualities of the book is, on the other hand, that it pays some attention to the telephone and to the letter as "mediated interaction".

Situation Revisited

Television, which is the primary subject of Thompson's book, is characterised as mediated quasi-interaction and is monological by nature. Production and reception are separate in place and time – yet the moment of broadcast is by nature the moment of reception. Thompson speaks about the producers in the "front region" e.g. the news anchor as being available to recipients in a unique and distinct way. They are "televisible":

> "The distinctive feature of tele-visibility is that it combines audio-visual presence with spatial-temporal distance. Hence, the producers are present to the recipient but absent from the context of reception." (Thompson, 1995: 98)

The televisual quasi-interaction depends on the recipient's ability to negotiate the space-time frameworks of different programmes. The anchor in news broadcasting is very much present in our mutual time-space, referring to actual persons whom we assume were present or events that took place in real space and time – but not in the time of actual reception. Given the relevant symbolic cues, we seldom get mixed up in our space-time relations with the media. The so-called 'liveliness' of television and the illusion of a 'here and now' aspect – the feeling of intensity, intimacy, simultaneousness and proximity is first of all a consequence of the technology and the organisation of television production: Programmes themselves may or may not take place in present time – but for the recipient they exist here and now – as programmes communicated into the living-room. In this capacity, the programmes – e.g. the actual talking heads are tele-present as communicators wanting to take the floor and to gain attention from the viewer. Yet the distance seen in relation to face-to-face communication makes the communication process impersonal – and the actions of the viewer do not have any consequences: The viewer turns off the talking head and does not have to worry about the distant person losing face on these grounds.

The nature of television is communication – metaphorically expressed in the above conditions of the talking heads trying to get attention and wanting to inform the viewer about events, presenting people talking about something in the real world, playing in game shows. This is what Scannell calls the primary intentionality of television – and it is one of contact and communication (Scannell, 1994: 32). Like Scannell and Meyrowitz, Thompson is aware of the importance of the situated reception. Scannell speaks about "a sociology of situated interaction" as the programme for television studies, whereas Thompson somewhat reluctantly speaks about the primary reception regions and the interactive framework of reception. What never becomes quite clear to me, however, are the characteristics of the two different reception domains.

Thompson refers to the "space-time interpolation" (1995: 92) meaning that recipients negotiate the space-time coordinates of the programmes with the time-space properties of their own everyday life. What I am looking for is how this goes on more precisely in the situated reception situation. From this perspective, one of the most important characteristics of television communication is that the programme as text runs continuously without physical interactivity – of course this is in contrast with mediated communication such as the telephone and the computer. However, the communicative flow of the text itself is fundamentally different from the reading process regarded as reception as discussed before.

Television regarded as communication is only one part of a situated communicative situation and this has effects on both of the previously mentioned reception regions – the individual interpretation and the interaction potential for combining interpersonal communication and "mediated quasi-interaction". The situated reception mode of television involves the viewer in the process of the production of the meaning of the text, within the overall context of various activities and other communicative actions in the recipient's life-world. As for the different reception modes, the symbolic cues for contact/attention making are very strong in the continuous flow of television communication. At the same time, these cues become constitutive for the programmes as part of the institutional flow as specific texts, genres and aesthetics.

Cinema and Television Reception Modes – Two Examples

The reception modes of the audio-visual media film and television are very different as pointed out by John Ellis (1982) following in the footsteps of Raymond Williams in his examination of the programmes as split into smaller and attention demanding "segments" within the overall flow or stream of television. From Ellis' point of view, the film and the cinematic reception mode is the correct and "positive" mode for visual fiction in general. Ellis' normative stand has been confirmed by a Danish study of differences between seeing films in the cinema and watching television. The project is commercial and paid for by the cinema advertising agency and the data are focus group interviews. The study refers directly to "reception modus" (mode of reception) in the cinema. Focus of attention (arousal) and excitement are illustrated below in figure 3 (Alsted & Moeller, 1996: 111):

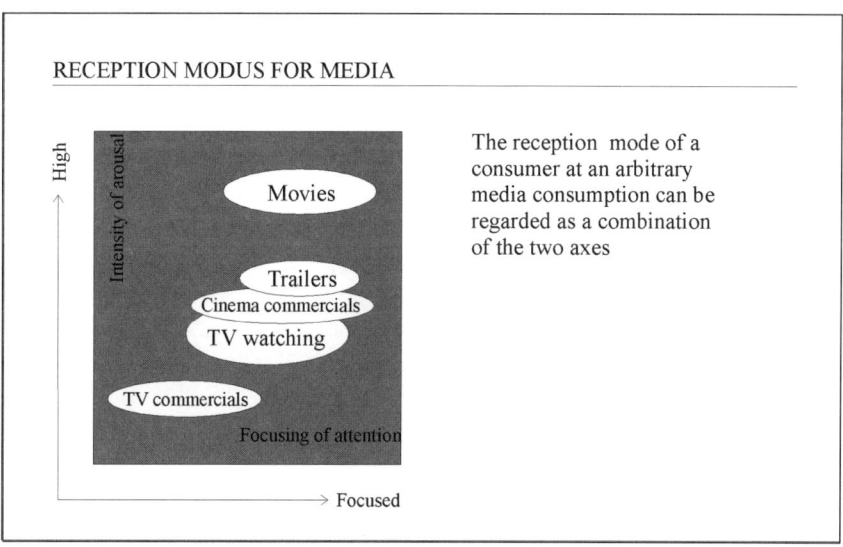

Figure 3: Reception modus for media

308 • *So – That's Your Life?*

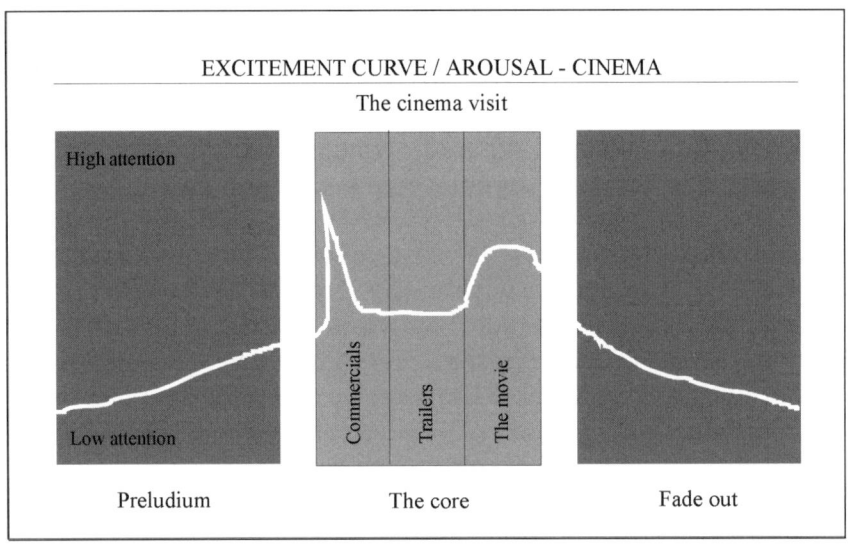

Figure 4: Excitement curve/arousal – cinema

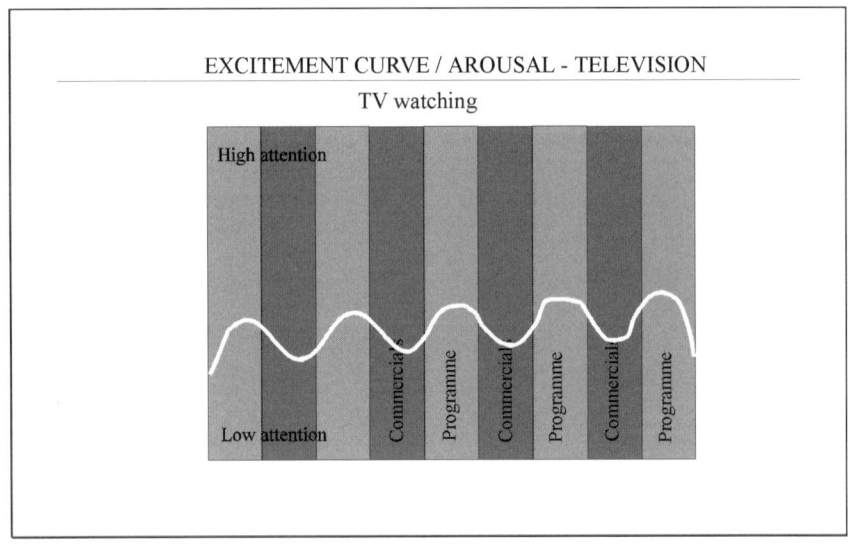

Figure 5: Excitement curve/arousal – television

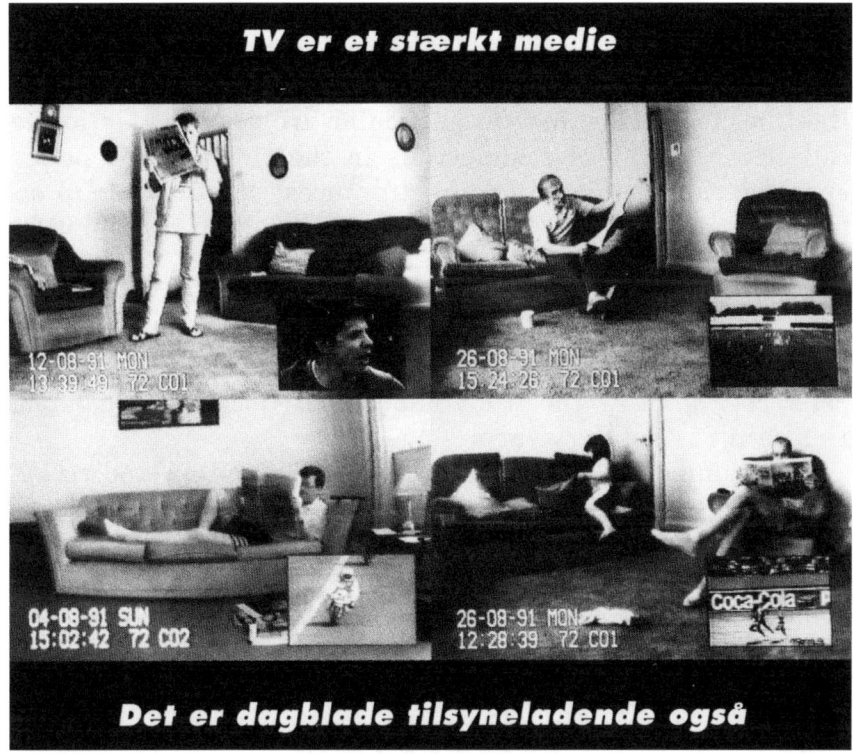

Figure 6: Oxford psychologist Peter Collett's studies of television viewing behaviour show, among other things, that 15.8% of the ads that appear on TV play to empty rooms and on average, the viewers of the remainder have their eyes on the TV screen for 43,3% of the commercial break. The illustration shows some of the home activities during breaks. Collett's data are video-recordings of the viewers' behaviour when watching television in general. Also this study is based on commercial interests and in Collett's case, the object is television seen in relation to newspaper advertising. The headline goes: "Television is a strong medium" – and below "Apparently so are newspapers". I have obtained the picture and Peter Collett's report from "Danske dagblades forening". The actual study has not been published in this form.

Before you engage in media use, you make estimations of expectations. The expectations of the reception mode of cinema going are high: You plan; you prepare; you expect an event; you have high expectations of quality; you have social expectations – going with friends/being able to talk about the film afterwards. Specific cinema attractions are: Big screen, hi-fi surround sound, rules for social behaviour, darkness, concentration (there is nothing else you can do), immersion. Specific qualities of watching films together: Laughter is contagious; you are concentrated; and you evaluate your opinions about the film. Positive values in particular are seen in relation to collective viewing of commercials in the cinema: The public space gives substance to your utterances; you are able to affect others' viewing – for example by laughing or booing or clapping. Cf. Fig. 4.

The reception mode in general is described as a kind of active interpretation and collective reception. The television reception mode brings very little positive value to the commercials, cf. Fig. 5. As the study is primarily focused on cinema, this result is not very surprising.

The commercial interests in situated reception and reception modes are highly competitive and result in negative evaluations of television and thereby of television advertising. My point here is not about advertising – yet it is striking that some advertisers see the need of investigating the television reception modes and the situated reception.

Crossing Over

In many respects, media research is at a turning point. Television talk as a subject of research has been promoted by Paddy Scannell, among others, who pointed to the limitations of the good old "encoding/decoding" model (Scannell, 1991: 10) and criticised the models of textual analysis based on literature and film studies. Scannell points to the liveliness, the here-and-now experience and to the many layers of intentionality in television, asking in fact for a communicative/pragmatic framework instead of aesthetics and textual analysis. There may be a contradiction in terms and disciplines yet the aesthetics is part of everyday life.

I claim that interaction can be understood as a domain of sociology – as a mutual copresent face-to-face exchange between human beings. Thus, I do not follow the definitions of computer science – e.g. the man-machine interaction concept. Moreover, I do not follow the widespread use of the concept of interaction in relation to cultural studies – either semiotics or reception studies where the interpretation process is often termed 'interaction' between text and reader. I prefer to use the term 'interactivity' in relation to mediated communication and text/environment and viewer/user relationships. In ordinary television production, the viewer has very little influence on the formation of the actual text – compared to the physical interactivity involved in computer communication. Jens F. Jensen (1999) claims that interactivity may be seen as a continuum where either "the information centre" or the users may be initiating and controlling the communication process. Berit Holm (1998) distinguishes between physical interactivity – where the user has direct impact on the textual formation and outcome of the text – and meaning-producing interactivity where the user involves her own framework of interpretation in the recontextualisation of the actual text. The physical interactivity is primarily connected to computer use while the meaning producing interactivity is defined as a province of textual reception in a broad sense.

Why this long paragraph about interaction and interactivity? First of all I am interested in the interaction which takes place mutually and copresent on the screen between participants. Following this, I have discussed the two programmes which experiment with what I see as very stereotyped conversational forms of especially interviewing – in both news and documentary.

Television is no longer an unquestioned authority since it seems to try to talk its way through things. "That's what we chose to bring in tonight's news" points to the framework of gatekeeping – and to the news not becoming news today. The whole process of bringing everyday life and ordinary people into focus in the news is stereotyped in, for example, consequence interviews, and the political television news discourse is – more or less reluctantly – turning from the subject of politics to the subject of politicians and their privacy.

The Remains of the Public Sphere

Media research has documented these changes in the public sphere by reference to Goffman's concepts of "front stage and back stage" (Meyrowitz, 1985; Thompson, 1995). The Habermasian notion of the decline of the public sphere has been widely accepted, also in British and American media research. Since the focus of my paper is not television news, I am mostly interested in the criteria of relevance/importance which tend to qualify different kinds of television programmes that do not operate on the basis of traditional journalism. Meyrowitz talks about the electronic media having exposed parts of the traditional backstage behaviour of many different groups of people. Especially television as a visual media represents so-called "expressive" information which was once only available in intimate face-to-face encounters:

> "Through television, each American has "access" to the personal expressions of people all over the country and the world, and he or she receives much information that was once available only to members of other groups." (Meyrowitz, 1985: 135)

The potential of observing interaction – verbal and non-verbal – of other people is a primary characteristic of television compared with all other media (the computer media and the Internet have already introduced new perspectives but I will not go further into this aspect here). Of course, this observing of others' lives can be called a "potent" merging of private and public spheres: "Through television, strangers are experienced as intimates" (Meyrowitz, 1985: 137). The discussion of time and space relations and television's institutional, technical (audio-visual) and conversational handling of the distant communicative position are very fruitful frameworks, but I lack a discussion of content and of televisual communication modes in the form of specific texts.

So, what is most interesting is "what's inside" the programmes, the possibility of observing different modes of interaction in detail – verbally, non-verbally and by means of artefacts. There is a fundamental curiosity involved in watching others displaying their rituals of interaction in distant places and strange ways – or in the form of the close inspection of everyday lifestyles in near and well-known places. Today, of course, most television is recorded and edited, so the excitement of the unexpected as found formerly in live broadcasts is no longer prominent. Yet it can be stated that, today, the professionalisation and stereotyping of important TV-genres such as news programmes go hand in hand with a strong tendency to break the rules of television perfection.

The smoothness of news as television aesthetics is paradigmatically contradicted by a phenomenon which I call 'video-realism': a conscious non-professionalism as seen in 'reality TV', 'docu-soap', 'everyday soap', 'video-diaries' and a range of documentaries. It is a quest for authenticity, spontaneity, personality and contact which is televisually and interpersonally coded. I am not quite sure that the term 'video-realism' is the best choice but I have chosen it from among several others because the paradigm of 'video' brings into mind the many private applications of the audio-visual media – and the above-mentioned types of programme make quite a point of this merging of the private and the public – 'television' and 'video'. And the concept of 'realism' brings into focus dimensions of programmes that are not predefined by the traditional genres of documentary on television. I hesitate to use concepts that have already been the subject of discourse about cultural levels of importance and value within the journalistic domain such as television documentary e.g. 'docu-soap' or the like.

In 1979, Dieter Prokop wrote a book called *Faszination und Langeweile (Fascination and boredom)*. The main point is that media – and especially television – are framed in a sort of ambivalence: On the one hand, in Prokop's terms, the programmes are instrumentalised and "modalised" in order to effectively structure and exploit common determinators of target groups. On the other hand, however, the whole business is predictable, uninteresting and boring. Fascination then in Prokop's terms lies in the media industries' clever efforts to exploit our hopes, critiques of everyday life and not least our unconsciousness.

Today, not many television critiques are based on Adorno as is Prokop's critique of the instrumentalised TV-discourse – yet the idea of the stereotyped television product as being essentially "boring" is becoming more and more relevant to me.

Is television losing not only authority but also attraction and fascination in everyday life?

But I see the new kinds of video-realism as an important step away from the predictability of the traditional television discourse. Programmes that work on the spot, which try in different ways to represent people's life-worlds and spontaneous interactive verbal and non-verbal styles, seem to fulfil a need for different models of everyday life experience. This is part of what is left of the public sphere – whether we like it or not.

The Defence

In a very illuminating article, Michael Schudson (1997) points to the fact that "there is a veritable obsession with the term" (:297) of conversation as the centre of public life. Schudson proposes to distinguish between two different kinds of conversation – sociable and problem-solving. To Schudson, democratic conversation is primarily of a problem-solving character and it is often uncomfortable to participate in this kind of conversation because it involves very different values, perspectives and solutions to the problem at hand. The democratic conversation is both essentially public and governed by formal rules which protect the discourse itself and its participants – for example by means of fairness:

> "Democratic conversation presumes not so much equality and spontaneity as a normative order that insists on equality and a social order that insists on a certain level of public-ness in talk". (Schudson, 1997: 306)

The sociable conversation, on the other hand, is seen as taking place between people in homogeneous groups. Opinions may be tested but with no consequences for the partners, who tend to confirm each other within the limits of the existing social groups: "In this model, conversation is oriented to the pleasure of interacting with others in conversation itself; it is therefore contemporaneously social" (:300). Schudson argues that both kinds of conversation are necessary in democracies but his main point is that the content substance and discourse of problem-solving is the predominator for democracy as such.

In relation to my subject on everyday talk on television, Schudson's argument goes, of course, in a quite opposite direction. When he calls for norm and rule in public conversation, my point is that television conversation might break the rules of the institutionalised discourse. I have argued that the relations between host and participant/interviewer and interviewee may be developed in a positive way by changing the power structure of the televised conversation. The unexpected and the spontaneous are some of my criteria of quality – just as they are important to Schudson in his so-called "sociable" conversation. Schudson's arguments then force me to reconsider the relevance and meaning of sociable conversation in relation to the public sphere, where the media are traditionally placed as important agents.

In doing so, I recognise the relevance of the macro perspective pointing to the importance of formal rules in political discourse. I also find a distinction between different kinds of conversation important, but it seems to me that Schudson has neglected the most fundamental cultural implications of conversation. Hermeneutics (Gadamer) and phenomenology (Schutz) may provide a different framework where interaction processes of understanding and "pre-understanding" are the premises of intersubjectivity and social being as such. According to Jürgen Habermas (1981), those premises are the characteristics of the so-called "life-world" seen as an opposition to the "system-world", where the premises are not characterised by understanding and community but rather by strategy or direct power.

The life-world is everyday communication and the creation of culture – which, from this perspective, is much more important than just being 'sociable' in conversation. You may say that Schudson chooses not to explore the domains of the life-world as he is focusing on the rule-governing of the public political discourse. So my contribution to Schudson's definition of conversation will be to see it not only as a kind of interaction but as a basic intersubjective quest for mutual understanding. Watching other people's naturalistic, situated communicative lines and private life-worlds is a question of 'curiosity' based on a need for knowledge of the different lifestyles we observe in (post)modern society. The ability of phenomenological and 'semiotic' reading of others is a necessity in relation to differentiation in terms of lifestyle and the creation of culture (Pierre Bourdieu; Mary Douglas).

From my point of view, however, understanding and tolerance must be added to the possibilities of the televised observation of others. Democracy is not determined by securing formal rules of conversation, as Schudson claims, – it is by necessity a province of the life-world, where the ability of understanding – and maybe of accepting – the other's perspective is part of the socialisation and identity formation of very early childhood. The Danish religious philosopher K. E. Løgstrup (1991), who was inspired by Kierkegaard and Heidegger among others, claims that the most fundamental aspect of human being is trust and openness of talk, and on this he based his philosophy of the sovereign and spontaneous utterances of life. In simple terms, the point is that we have to be confident and put ourselves in the hand of 'the other' when acting in the world. If we lose this basic element of trust, our options are simply 'cynical' or even paranoiac. The question is whether, and under which circumstances, we are able to commit ourselves to, and trust, the distant person in a kind of 'hyper-realistic' relationship of televised quasi-interaction to use Thompson's concept?

To some media researchers, this is probably pure metaphysics but I will claim that life-world based programmes working on the basis of openness in talk and mutual discourse may to a certain degree involve the viewer in the spontaneous utterances of life and thereby for a moment include the participant as a fellow human being in the horizon of the viewer's own life-world. Still, it is not a matter of television understood as direct interaction or dialogue, but rather a short communicative option of taking the others' perspective.

One of the obvious consequences of this development is the possibility of meeting strangers as intimates for a time. The life-world perspective seems to reflect itself from naturalistic televised situationalism to the province of the viewer and the situated reception 'at home'. As the referentiality to the surrounding world – traditionally described as the core of the public sphere – is minimised, the different televised contact possibilities and the immediate inspection/reflection of the other's life-world is growing – squeezing the 'public' between participants and viewer's life-worlds.

Conclusion

On the basis of interpersonal communication theory and a closer inspection of programmes which break the rules of televised conversation one may describe television's different communicative modes in terms that are quite different from the traditional genres: The stereotype mode, the rehearsed mode and the naturalistic mode. For *the stereotype mode*, I have used Prokop's (1979) idea of the conventional and "boring" kind of discourse where input and output seem to circulate in a never ending institutional confirmation of the ideologically correct enunciation and content. TV news serve this purpose. The stereotype mode may be criticised for its predictability (and for being boring) yet the function of the stereotype is at the same time positive in the sense that it creates a sense of belonging to a certain culture. Some kind of institutional interpretation of chaotic global life is necessary according to Schudson – the question is whether the television industry has yet provided us with proper alternatives?

The *rehearsed mode* includes both fiction and a range of documentaries. This mode is characterised by strict instruction or reconstruction where the participants act out certain roles as defined in a manuscript by the author or producer in charge. Sometimes, the rehearsed mode is a product only of the director's imagination and concept of story but in the case of documentaries such as 'nature films' – the participants seem to act naturally and not in any instructed manner – yet the personalised dramatic story of almost extinct animal species seems to be never ending. The 'rehearsal' primarily takes the form of editing by which, for example, the lions of Africa are hunting antelopes and mating all day long – yet we know that lions sleep 23 hours of the day.

Some efforts have been made to challenge the predictability of the rehearsed mode – especially concerning camera movement and editing, but also the more traditional ways of story-telling have been changed. American series like Hill *Street Blues* and *Homicide* have worked hard at the use of the moving 'reportage' camera – also in the course of the dialogue. *X-files* has brought new dimensions to an idea of a very open kind of narrative structure. Danish film and tv-director Lars von Trier together with Thomas Vinterberg have contributed with an ideological manifest of film production (the so-called Dogma 1995) in which they make a "Vow of chastity".

A quotation:

"The 'supreme' task of the decadent film-makers is to fool the audience. Is that what we are so proud of? Is that where the '100 years' have brought us? Illusions through which emotions can be communicated? ... By the individual artist's free choice of trickery? Predictability (dramaturgy) has become the golden calf around which we dance. Having the characters' inner lives justify the plot is too complicated, and not "high art". As never before, the superficial action and the superficial movie are receiving all the praise. The result is barren. An illusion of pathos and an illusion of love."

The *naturalistic mode* is most of all characterised by the new and different roles of the participating 'ordinary people'. I have chosen not to include talk shows taped in studios although there may be possibilities of producing some kind of authentic or life-world based line for the participants in some shows. Of the range of reality tv, home video, video diaries, candid camera, docu-soap and on the spot documentary, I have chosen two programmes which, each in its own manner, positively contributes to the development of televised interaction and to the ways in which authenticity may be constructed.

All of the mentioned programmes are of a quite low profile in relation to traditional demands of quality – for example there usually has to be a good journalistic story which is relevant to the audience in respect of sensation, proximity to life-world/culture, common interest of citizenship and so on. *Taxi* and *The Pizza Man* do a bit less and a bit more. They are serial, non-problematising and entertaining but at the same time their intentionalities are of a phenomenological and open investigative nature. The faces of hosts and participants are at stake in the naturalistic situation, but faces are not lost in the conversation. Reading with an open mind, one simply gets involved in the participating persons.

On the basis of interpersonal communication theory combined with an inspection of the audio-visual and interpersonal coding of televised communication, I have made a framework for describing and evaluating programmes which do not 'fit' the traditional genres very well. In doing this, I have suggested a way of understanding some of the very banal and maybe naive readings of television as communication and 'quasi-interaction' – trusting the distant person enough to enjoy his or her company for a while and at the same time enjoying the openness of the programme which allows you to include the presented person's line in the horizon of your own life-world.

Bibliography

Alsted, C., & P. Møller (1996). "A pioneer media survey – based on qualitative research and new consumer". In: *Marketing and Research today*. May 1996.

Bruun, H. (1997). *Snakkeprogrammet – portræt af en tv-genre*. Ph. D. Dissertation. University of Aarhus.

Bruun, H. (1999). *Talkshowet. Portræt af en tv-genre*. Copenhagen: Borgens Forlag.

Drotner, K. (1993). "Medieetnografiske problemstillinger – en oversigt". In: *Mediekultur,* no. 23.

Ellis, J. (1982). *Visible fictions*. London.

Eco, U. (1989). *Middelalderens genkomst*. Copenhagen: Samleren.

Fetveit, A. (1996). "Receptionsforskning og anti-essentialisme". In: *Mediekultur* no. 24.

Fiske, J. (1987). *Television culture*. London: Methuen.

Goffman, E. (1955). "On face-work – an analysis of ritual elements in social interaction". In: *Psychiatry* 18 no. 3.

Habermas, J. (1981). *Teorien om den kommunikative handlen*. Aalborg University Press.

Holm, B. (1998). *Alices nye eventyrland*. Dissertation. Aalborg University.

Jensen, J. F., & C. Toscan (eds.) (1999). *Interactive Television. TV of the Future or the Future of TV?* Aalborg: Aalborg University Press.

Jensen, J. F. (1999). "The Concept of 'Interactivity'". In J. F. Jensen & C. Toscan (eds.) (1999). *Interactive Television. TV of the Future or the Future of TV?* Aalborg: Aalborg University Press.

Keppler, A. (1995). *Wirklicher als der Wirklichkeit? Das neue realitätsprinzip der Fersehunterhaltung.* Frankfurt am Main: Fischer Taschenbuch Verlag.

Kvale, S. (1996). *InterViews.* London: Sage Publications.

Lindlof, T. R. (ed.) (1987). *Natural audiences.* New Jersey: Ablex.

Lull, J. (1990). *Inside family viewing.* London: Routledge.

Løgstrup, K. E. (1991). *Den etiske fordring.* Copenhagen: Gyldendal.

Meyrowitz, J. (1985). *No sense of place – the impact of electronic media on social behaviour.* Oxford: Oxford University Press.

Milroy, L. (1987). *Observing and analysing natural language.* Oxford: Basil Blackwell.

Morley, D. (1986). *Family television: Cultural power and domestic leisure.* London: Comedia.

Prokop, D. (1979). *Faszination und Langeweile.* Frankfurt am Main: Suhrkamp Verlag.

Radway., J. (1984). *Reading the romance.* University of North Carolina Press.

Rasmussen, T. A. (1993). "Medieetnografi og kvalitativ metode". In: *Mediekultur* no. 23.

Rasmussen, T. A. (1998). *Hverdagens samtaler i TV I & II.* Working papers from the research project "The Aestetics of Television", no. 22 & 23. Aarhus.

Rönnberg, M. (1996). *Tv-tittande som dialog.* Doctoral Dissertation. Stockholm: University of Stockholm.

Scannell, P. (1994). "Kommunikativ intentionalitet i radio og fjernsyn". In: *Mediekultur* no. 22.

Scannell, P. (ed) (1991). *Broadcast talk.* London: Sage.

Scheflen, A. (1978). "Susan smiled – on explanation in family therapy". In: *Fam. Proc.* vol 17.

Schudson, M. (1997). "Why conversation is not the source of democracy". In: *Critical Studies in Mass Communication*, vol. 14.

Schutz, A. (1975). *Hverdagslivets sociologi.* Copenhagen: Reitzel.

Stigel, J. (1997). *The aesthetics of television – the quality of television.* Working paper from the research project "The Aesthetics of television", no 18. Aarhus.

Søndergaard, H. (1995). "Virkelighedstørst eller sensationshunger?". In: *Tendens* 7. årg. no. 2.

Thompson, J.B. (1995). *The media and modernity.* Cambridge: Polity Press.

CHAPTER TEN

TV Advertising Virtually Speaking
The Invisible Voice Elaborating on the Space between Screen and Viewer

Jørgen Stigel
Department of Communication
Aalborg University

Advertising as Media-borne Communication

Advertising is a form of communication in which the special communicative intention is an obvious component of the genre. The intention to market and sell speaks through the TV commercial. And it does so, no matter how the commercial is put together design-wise and seeks to rewrite, underplay or transpose this circumstance. And the commercial knows that the public knows that this is the way things are. Thus, one of the special problems of advertising is how to transform, handle, and vary the communicative intention and simultaneously play its game with the public in a relevant and credible manner.

Like other media-borne communication, advertising also has the problem that it may well know a lot about whom it is addressing or can enter into communication with, but has a chronic lack of the same amount of knowledge about *how* to actually establish communication. It is a media-borne communication product, a manifestation which, through its gambit, hopes to establish contact by being and appearing attractive and activating the contactees in relation to a need to articulate in the *field* concerned. And so not only speak *at* them, but also speak *with* them. The latter to be so understood that the words of the advertisement acquire a persuasive effect through the recipients taking over and accepting their statement and their way of being a statement, perhaps even finding them altogether usable and irresistible within their own framework of understanding – e.g. by taking them into their own mouths. This does not necessarily mean that a (rational) argumentation is accepted at the same time and actually results in action. It may only mean that a need and a mode of expression are encountered. For the field is more than just the subject matter. It is also the speechification of the field and the subject matter and the prevalent forms of speechification.

The notion that the recipient should be able to say his piece, participate, be a partner, and actively do his bit, is a basic concept in communication. If this principle of reciprocity or interaction is neglected, then communication is reduced to little more than information. Information is something one seeks or gives, because one has either too little or too much of it. Communication is created by parties seeking to understand each other and becoming involved in and sharing something in a given situation.

It is first and foremost in this general area that advertising, as well as other media-borne communication, has a basic problem.[1] For whereas seeking to establish a relation of reciprocity and exchange is more or less a given thing in interpersonal communication, this is by no means the case in media-borne communication – if only because at least one party is absent in a physical sense during the creation of that which is to make communication possible. The possibility of exchange can only be virtually represented in the communication product and its (indirect) transformation and staging of the roles.[2]

In interpersonal communication, the parties and their physical and social context create a direct 'space' around the conversation.[3] In media-borne communication, this space has to be virtually established. And media-borne communication has to rely on doing this exclusively through symbolic and substitute effects. The recipient must be contacted and his energies mobilised. His expectations must be excited, he must be given cues, clues, and hints and altogether be 'let into' or at least relate to – a virtual world which to some extent he accepts, takes over, identifies and sympathises with, and perhaps is surprised by. The *aesthetics* of the communication product will normally be the factor, which seeks to ensure or appeals to this identification and provides the building blocks of this space. Aesthetic constructs such as the story, the drama, the poem are all entities which, by appealing to the imagination of the recipient, construct their own self-delimited worlds. But they all require that the recipient/user accepts and is familiar with the framework and premises set up, the space in which he may invest his expectations and conceptions.

Those electronic audio-visual media which are not subject to the writing, the wrapping of the writing (in letters or books/printed publications) nor contingent on a physical presence at the performance are characterised by being able to reproduce voice and body, speech and speaker and split the representation of voice from that of body and still claim that speech and address are direct here and now. They are characteristic in their fundamental claim to be simultaneous and synchronous and in their claim to be able and to want to speak and address themselves directly and fully (i.e. bodily) and not only see the recipient as audience/addressee, but also as alleged participant. And thus actualise a space for communication in a direct and interactionally realistic format.[4] The direct address from the screen with alleged eye contact via the camera lens is the most immediately tangible expression of an imitation of forms of address well-known from the interaction and presentation forms of everyday life. A person presents and addresses himself to us as if he or she was speaking directly to 'us', but without this 'as if'[5] being emphasised. On the contrary, everything is done to maintain the illusion of directness and presence. It is, above all, this simulated interaction and its similarity to everyday forms of communication which makes some people shrink from according any meaning to the word aesthetics in connection with e.g. TV.[6]

It is a general rule for media-borne communication that it must calculate on establishing a recipient who is more than just passive. This is exactly where aesthetics comes in. The recipient should be able to *do* something. This 'doing' may simply be the establishing of processes of understanding or seeing oneself as a participant in (communicative) exchanges. The communication product should not only catch the recipient's immediate attention. It should also start up the recipient and provide the recipient with a material to process, whether this is intended for contemplation or situativity. The communication product must therefore have built-in notions of a recipient and of possible actions rooted in the universe(s) of comprehension and the situational context of the recipient. As an elementary matter of course it must take into account the resistance, the barriers and blockages that the recipient may have with respect to becoming an active party in the communication.[7]

This calculation must therefore be based on ideas about how the recipient will feel that he can or cannot get a 'word in', in the virtual sense. Since the recipient is only present as a notion when the communication product is being conceived, the design, including the structure of the product, must anticipate how the recipient can be made vocal, respectively silent while receiving the product.

Like other media-borne communication, which actually wants to establish communication, advertising is an aesthetic construct, a 'set-up'. Advertising is a kick-off by a party who, through his kick-off, tries to make others party to his purpose. The chief problem is thus how to involve the absent party – make him a participant. I.e. what forms or 'modes' to utilise.

The first intention imperative in the advertising world is to lock the audience's attention and conscious activity on to specific brands/makes. An important competition parameter to the securing of this attention is thus also anchored in differences in the very method of addressing oneself to, and fighting one's way to, activity in the minds of the audience. This is especially true of the way in which one allows the audience, through a media gambit, the scope for this activity or for taking part themselves in creating this activity, making it theirs. This is governed by a more or less clear awareness that there are competitors – not only as regards the product but as to meaning as well. Just as there is competition in the market between products and brands which may satisfy (the same) needs, so there is competition in the market between forms of address and creation of attention and meaning, i.e. the ways in which one gets or hopes to get the brand to take up space and acquire meaning in the minds of the audience. Advertising is obviously a factor, which greatly contributes to the aggravation of competition in the latter area. Inversely, it is constantly the obligation of advertising to see to it that this space and meaning(fullness) are attained as cheaply as possible, i.e. on the basis of calculable financial criteria (cost-benefit). And it is the general fairly primitive, but usually effective, conclusion that once a brand has managed to occupy some space in the audience's mind, it is easier to convert this space into cash on the nail in the form of a concrete consumption choice. The exchange on the financial level presupposes that an exchange has taken place on the communicative level and that this exchange is maintained.

The roads to the attention and exchange on the desired communicative level can be many. Advertising itself has taken part in cultivating the quite elementary ones. From the tender years of advertising, the belief in repetition and argumentation has been a fixture.[8] This belief was rooted in a specific view of communication and information, i.e. specific ideas of learning (e.g. in the form of rote learning, authoritative teaching, and logic). As advertising (as well as the school system) lost its didactic virtue and realised it had to move closer to the conceptional universe of the audience in order to break through to the consumers' consciousness, advertising began to operate from fairly simple notions of motivational psychology. In more popular terms, advertising should 'seduce' by creating a wish in the audience: the wish to get something more cheaply, easily, safely or quality-like than normal, the wish to be a social success, be enviable, be generally successful or at least escape social stigmatisation, the wish to be in autonomous control of one's life and without the overbearing influence and interference of others, the wish to avoid anxiety and attain security, the wish to be a better, healthier etc. person (than others). In other words, it is a matter of an elementary play on presentations, which appeal to presuppose elementary notions of needs. These are presumed fillable by products, which are presented as being able to meet these various mental and social needs.

In a sense, the belief or tendency in advertising today is elementary, too. But it is less elementary as concerns the belief in being able to work one's way straight into the consciousness and specific needs of the audience. As a tendency it does not appeal directly to desires and wishes which are rooted in 'objective' or specific needs. To a greater extent, its appeal is oriented towards the formation or genesis of meaning, and thus in a certain sense aimed at a symbolic desire. In this connection, advertising is above all conscious of being an appeal, which is simply meant to ensure that communication becomes possible. With its appeal, it is to open a semantic field or fields to the public and try to make the public enter this/these fields in an active notional way and take part in them. The communicative problem of advertising thus becomes less advertising-specific and more general and aesthetic.

That this is so is evident partly from the circumstance that advertising travesties itself and its forms of expression to an ever-greater extent,[9] partly, and not least, from the circumstance that a great majority of the prizewinners at Cannes are mini dramas. They appeal to the public exactly by constructing those areas in the form of audio-visual narratives which play up to the public's interpretative abilities and do not (at least not on the surface level) directly dictate or direct them, but evidently leave it up to the public themselves to construct and comprehend the meaning – on the basis, however, of familiar narrative and dramatic templates.[10]

Routes to the Public. Mini-drama or Direct Address

More than 80-85% of the prizewinning commercials and TV spots at the annual Cannes Festival are tiny mini dramas.[11] They are designed as audio-visual narrative sequences, which follow a diegetic form of presentation. The viewer is situated as witness to events, actions, and interactions in the same way as when watching a typical Hollywood film: as an onlooker who is invited to watch a sequence, whose dialogue, plot etc. are designed to construct this very sequence, its characters, and peculiar world, the concluding point of which is the brand name that has paid for the fun and games.

These sequences attempt to motivate the viewer by offering him optional endings or inferences based on the design of the sequence (montage and structure). The assumption is that the viewer will involve himself in the sequence, decode its meanings, and perhaps identify with some of the characters, their 'views' and the given universe, which is constructed. The narrative is presented in the form of physical and speech actions in this universe, which is separated from the viewer and which can be received on the principle of the fourth wall. Only at the very end is it explicitly put together and stamped with the brand name. In other words, the viewer is, by what takes place in his sight and hearing, and of the decoding of the meaning in the actions played out among persons and things. The communicative intention and address are thus presented indirectly. They are presented by way of drama, the acted-out situation, the mini film.

If one takes a look at which forms of TV spots are actually presented in Denmark, it is characteristic, however, that the main format, the mini-drama which wins prizes for creativity in Cannes, does not make up 80% of the output, but maximum 30%.[12] Approximately 70% of the TV spots are characterised one way or the other by addressing (or claiming to address) the viewer directly – or as directly as possible through the medium of TV. This is accomplished through a presenter format, a testimonial format or a voice-over format. Especially the latter is predominant. In the first two, speech and speaker are typically represented synchronously and bodily present on the screen. The differences lie chiefly in varying degrees of possibility of direct 'eye contact' and the degree of unambiguity of the speaking authority. In contrast, the voice-over format is characterised by the owner of the voice either being invisible, i.e. solely represented as a voice, or represented in different ways shifted/asynchronously or metonymously on the screen.

In any circumstances what characterises these forms is an emphasis on the *direct* address and speech to the viewer. (S)he is placed as an addressed 'you', and not first and foremost as a contemplative witness to a sequence, the activities and independent world of which offer the opportunity of involvement and which translate this involvement into the brand name and thus argue the point indirectly.

However, in Danish TV advertising there has also been a quantitative growth in the drama format.[13] The trend thus points in the same direction as the Cannes prize awards. In other words, the trend points out that advertising follows in Hollywood's footsteps and – to an ever greater extent – transforms its communicative intentions into the indirect form of address of the mini-drama in accordance with Hollywood's successful and internationally dominant narrative formula, but obviously in tempos and styles of somewhat higher compression. Presumably, this tendency is partly a reflection of the intensification of the competition in the 'meaning market', partly a reflection of the fact that precisely the minidrama possesses the virtue of providing the public with an open (and entertaining) appeal. More than any other format, it transforms the advertising intention.

However, more than one road leads to Rome as the city of open appeals. The mini-drama is just one of them, and in addition, the mini-drama has several weaknesses as regards communication: for one thing, in its very format it disclaims the communicative intention (which is nowhere if not there), for another, there is a risk that the public gets hooked on the good story, the actors and the total entertainment value, but forgets or overlooks what the whole thing is finally about (the brand name) because the story has used up all its energy. To be sure, it has provided the viewer with an open field, but the viewer has, so to speak, been sucked into this field and when the total experience is then stamped with a brand name, this may be felt as an example of aesthetic coarseness or disproportion.

There is no risk of such an imbalance if the communicative intention is clearly perceived from the outset and if the play with the public is established – not by the public being 'sucked' into the plot in a fictitious universe – but by the desired universe together with the public being established in the middle field between screen and viewer. What calls this imaginary middle field into being? Among other things, direct speech and eye contact from the screen in the form of the presenter or the presenter format, but certainly also the invisible voice, the function of which is precisely to mediate and establish 'space' between screen event and viewer. The following will concentrate on this voice (position) and the various special role and acting opportunities it offers in the audio-visual universe.

A Significant and Obvious Appeal to the Viewer

A TV spot for Circle Coffee shown on Danish TV2 in the month of April 1997 (but 2 or 3 years old as a concept) bears the title "The Experiment". The spot lasts 30 seconds, and this is how it goes in all its brevity:

1) Simultaneously we hear and see, "You are now invited to take part in an experiment." The male voice is deep, pleasantly modulated and a bit monotonous. The text, which fills the screen with the same statement in 'print', is white on black.
2) The voice continues without pausing, "Here you see a glass ...
   (A flashing arrow points to a quarter-filled brandy glass placed inside an orange circle on a white background). A glass ... em ...
   Take a good look at the glass ... Concentrate on the glass ..."
3) The screen goes black and the voice continues, "A blue circle is now printed on your retina ... (which is in fact the case). Now you know ...
4) (An arrangement of a packet of Blue Circle Coffee on the left and a steaming coffee cup on the right of the picture) ... which coffee to enjoy tonight. But what you pour (hand removes coffee cup from the picture) into the glass is entirely up to you ..."

5) "Blue Circle ... collects your thoughts. Ahh ...".

As is evident, the TV spot is controlled and bound together by a voice and a speech act, a voice-over whose owner is not seen. The voice ensures coherence and continuity. This is where control of the sequence is anchored. Whereas the statements of the voice and the screen are manifestly redundant in the first phase (1), there is a somewhat higher degree of separation of the voice-over and screen statements in the later phases.

The speech is characteristic in constantly addressing and appealing directly to the viewer ("you are invited", "your retina", "now you know", "entirely up to you", and the imperatives "take a look", "concentrate") as well as by emphasising the address itself and the appeal for participation ("invited ... to take part"). Furthermore, the simultaneity is emphasised in the form of "now" ("now invited ...", "is now printed", "tonight") and "here" ("Here you see", "the glass"). It is not just the arrow that points. There is also a linguistic arrow pointing at the very event or what is being created in the demonstration and communication situation: its here-and-now-tense, its ingredients, and what in the communication situation is transformed – not in front of – but in our eyes ("the retina"). A linguist would say we have situational pointing and speech, which greatly anchor and emphasise the communication situation itself (deixis).

As already mentioned, there is a high degree of redundancy between the pictures or the visual 'statement' of the screen and the statement of the voice. To be sure, it decreases from phase 1) to phase 3). But it is fairly indisputable as the voice maintains that we see a glass and that subsequently we see or form a blue circle on the screen, by 'magic' as it were. As a matter of course, the voice attempts in phase 4) to exploit and 'cash in' on the logic and the 'value' arising from this constructed and manifest *indisputability*. Here it shifts gear from present to future. From concerning something on the screen its claims shift over to concerning something and somebody in front of the screen, the viewer and the viewer's actions. In an unchanged tone of voice, quite matter of course and with irresistible 'logic', it takes the liberty of asserting, "Now you also know which coffee to enjoy tonight". It looks like an argument of the deduction type. Into the bargain it allows itself to take the matter-of-courseness so far as to ram the point home, "But what you pour into the glass …" In other words, still more is presupposed on behalf of the viewers and their scope of action. It is quite characteristic that the whole thing is gathered together in a conclusive point, a slogan, which – implicitly – via the 'physically-visually' or perceptionally incontestable form is claimed to have been demonstrated, after which the coffee may be enjoyed. Argumentation and enjoyment, QED (Quod est demonstrandum) and "Ahh" in the same breath. The argumentation and demonstration are illuminatingly self-evident in the literal, visual and auditive senses.

In this way, nearly everything is directed towards the viewer and the communicative situation itself and towards establishing a fellowship with the viewer around something virtual and imaginary, yet manifestly a visual experience, which *is being created* on the screen in this situation. At the same time it is performed in a slightly play-acting, travestying style which lends a touch of humour to the hypnotic and suggestive argumentation: the deduction from the perceived blue circle to the absolute inevitability of the coffee brand (and the glass) in the viewer's reality.

But a trail and a pointer have been laid out to the individual world of the voice, to that 'I' which speaks and to the place from where it speaks: the hand which picks up the coffee cup and the final "aahh". At the end, the speech instance, the "I" does not only speak *about* something and *to* somebody. It suddenly interacts *with* what so far it has only spoken about (the hand that picks up the cup, the invisible, but presumed act of drinking and the final expression of enjoyment, which attach the hand and the action to the speaker). In this way it is also manifested that the voice represents a more real and emotive "I", and not just an anonymous voice speaking about and to. The speaker role is transformed from being a third-person narrator into being a first-person ditto, and there is a manifest merging of the speech level and the visual level – and (implied) the level of the public: the hand takes action from the direction of the viewer.

The voice plays in a certain register, a speech mode, a certain manipulation code: it is at once the monotonous seductive voice of the hypnotist and a paraphrasing give-away of this speech form. This happens in its semi-slip of the tongue ("a glass ... em ...") in its excessive presupposition ("what you pour into the glass ..."), and generally in its exaggerated redundancy (text = speech, 'flashing arrow pointing at glass' – "here you see a glass ..."). But the give-away probably also lies in the voice agent itself being persuaded, being unable to keep his hand off the coffee, having to reveal his 'enjoying I', and in the tomfoolery between brandy and coffee.

In the relation and action between said, unsaid, and shown, the statement of the voice plays upon a presupposed, but not directly expressed syntagma: "coffee and brandy", and the showing of the brandy, but explicit unspokenness is due to an implicit understanding: on Danish TV, the advertising of (and tempting with) liquor is prohibited.

The sequence is however so designed that the brandy precedes the coffee (brand) which then takes over from the brandy. The focus shift from what is inside the circle – which one is even explicitly asked to look closely at –, *to* the circle itself which turns out to be the very point of the exercise, expresses this shift in no uncertain terms. This is the stage magician's manipulation of, and pulling the wool over, our visual perception (the formation of after-images) as well as our immediate and almost automatic criteria of visual relevance. This takes its course in total accordance with gestalt psychology's definitions of (hidden) contextualisations between foreground and background: you involuntarily register the figure, but not the framing or background of the figure. This is overlooked. The leading role of the brandy, established visually and verbally, turns out to be an incidental circumstance in a totally different set-up, which makes its appearance to us something at once invisible or illusionary and inevitable: just as the blue circle is transferred to/is generated in our subjective vision with objective necessity, so the coffee (brand) of the same name is given with the same (objective) necessity in our subjective choice. This necessity stands out in so much stronger profile, because the teasing tag-on remark points out that what you "pour into the glass" is a subjective and in reality a trivial and incidental matter. The freedom of choice is emphasised so as to underline more powerfully the compulsiveness and inevitability. In this way, the sequence forms a narrative transformation functioning as an argumentation structure, which obviously is not made explicit by the voice, but at most elliptically expressed or touched upon by: "Now you also know ...". What is shown merges with what is said, but replaces and displaces speech right at the crucial point.

What happens on the level of the voice itself may be viewed as a parallel transformation and heavy-handed emotive argumentation: from having addressed itself factually and anonymously, the voice is suddenly associated with an intervention on the visual level and an organ for the subsequent inarticulate, subjective enjoyment. And in the visual and spatial sense, this intervention is solidary with the visual angle of the viewer. With the hand as representative, the otherwise uncertain placement of the speaker is suddenly anchored virtually (but not at random). Thus the speaker may well be interpreted as a substitute dramatic representative of the viewer, but in any case the speaker also reveals himself as the totally crucial middle field between screen and viewer.

The "Experiment" is presented as an example, because right on the surface it contains and comprises just about all the opportunities contained by a TV commercial in the voice-over format.

It thus sums up central features characteristic of a very large part of TV advertising, i.e. the part in which the allegedly direct, but disembodied, address to the viewers forms the (an) immediate principal element. But *all* these features are actually far from being exploited in a similarly sophisticated way in the average representative of the voice-over format. However, these features, including the distinctive features which separate the creative voice-over from the average one, may for the present be defined as:

1) A voice which, as a general rule, is only present as an auditive reproduction/representation (voice-over), but which is dominant and prominent by being the governing and linking factor and by using the visual side for the (il-

lustrative) purposes of his argumentation. The voice may speak in the first person (i.e. emphasis on an "I" and a subjective/emotive speaker) or as third-person narrator (i.e. emphasis on subject matter and in the character of objectively arguing authority). On this level, the main distinctive feature within the format is transformations between the first and third person.

2) Varying degrees of redundancy (semantic merging) between said and shown, and varying degrees of play upon the governing relation and the levels of statement between said and shown, but also play upon the relations between visible and invisible, said and unsaid, explicit and implicit. The distinctive feature of the format, however, is the extent to which the visual element is permitted to form or appear with its own decisive meaning which, in interaction with the sequence of the speech, has decisive consequences for the aggregate sequence.

3) A more or less directly expressed appeal and/or invitation to take part in what emanates from and takes place on the screen. What happens on the screen is claimed and pointed out as the 'common third' between voice and audience. This is the field of participation. The distinctive feature is whether anything crucial/cataclysmic takes place in this field.

4) Creation of closeness and simultaneity and attempts to realise a virtual (sense of) community in the 'here and now' of the communication situation between actors who are otherwise separated and remote: speech actor at screen level and audience actors in front of the screen. In spite of the mass-medial form of communication this is evident, partly via the linguistic forms of address, e.g. evidenced through the direct second-person address, the suggestions and the emphasis on simultaneity of the voice ('now' and 'here (on the screen)'), partly via the visual or displayed side (the common third), i.e. the sensorily perceptible situations and processes played out before our eyes and ears and in our vision. In the final instance, these may then be transferred, more or less relevantly, as points or meanings to the brand name. The distinctive feature is whether the spot really establishes some form of here-and-now; i.e. actually elabo-

rates or exploits that it is a case of communicative *situativity*, that somebody addresses/is addressing somebody.
5) Conscious attempts at argumentation, including 'short circuits' or suggestive mingling and linking of separate levels of perception, argumentation, and communication (e.g. the circumstance that the 'magic' blue circle imperatively and inevitably transposes to a particular brand of coffee, and also that the glass on the screen with the same matter-of-courseness is claimed to have the same reality status as the viewer's glass).
6) Transformations of the relations between the ingredients of the material as well as where the presumed actors' relations to it are concerned. These transformations may – separately considered – build on:
a) What is manifestly to be seen on the screen, i.e. in the visual plot.
b) The roles in which the speaker may cast himself in relation to the screen or the visual material. That is to say, the voice may mention what is happening or shown, but it may also interact with and handle with what is shown, and thus change from being outside the level of what is shown to being in (or part of) it.
c) The intended role position of viewer, who may shift from the role of addressee and contactee to the role of experiencer, the role of one who concludes something from what is presented.

The total function (and intention) of these more or less completed plays, transformations, and short-circuits is on the one hand to make room for the receiver, who (according to the extent to which the above-mentioned distinctive mechanisms are employed) should activate his imaginativeness and personally fill in and take part in creating meanings. Generally speaking, the media-borne gambit is to create a virtual space, which may create tension and *mobility* in the viewer's notions. On the other hand, this mobility is chiefly induced to seduce and persuade, in ways which acquire their persuasive substratum and power from the viewer's own acceptance and reception.

Creating virtual spaces for the viewer's powers of imagination and mobility in the viewer's notional world is obviously the main point of the mini-(micro-)dramas of the TV commercial. But in their case, the exchange between viewer and on-screen event is based on a fiction code and on the viewer's readiness to identify with the action and to consent to interact with it. The fullness is therefore created through the elaboration of the dramatically presented narrative and the presumed involvement and gradual consent of the viewer. In metaphorical spatial terms it is a question of a movement of the viewer 'into' the screen event offered.

In the voice-over format the exchange – again in spatial terms – lies so to speak further towards the surface of the screen and as a claim to direct exchange between viewer position and the screen position's doubleness of speech (from a virtual 'place') and shown picture (the 'manifest' or 'palpable' visual 'place' of the screen). That is to say, the fullness relies on tensions and mergings between these two fields with the intent to create a 'fused' expansion of the space and the (speech) field 'towards' the audience.

In what follows, we shall take a closer look at the various visual and potential qualities in this middle field of simulated interaction,[14] and its special qualities seen in relation to advertising.

The Invisible Voice as Mediating Middle Level

The invisible voice – or the voice which is not visually and synchronously anchored in a depicted speaking person – can as demonstrated (like any separated sound, e.g. background music) relate to and influence the visual, the visible on-screen sequence as well as the viewer in a variety of ways. The only feature these different ways have in common is that the owner of the voice *is not visible* as a speaker. The speaker is outside the visual field or is not (obviously) depicted as 'physically' taking part in the action in the visual field. The speaker is either on another level or (implicitly) in another space/

place, another time or another world (e.g. of the mind) than the visual sequence. Somehow or other, the voice is at a distance in relation to what happens on the screen, but at the same time one might argue that it is so in order to mediate to the viewer of the screen – to reduce the distance to the receiver of the message. The voice creates an atmosphere of familiarity, intimacy, and mediation which acts as a connecting link between screen event and screen viewer,[15] and the visual anonymity of the voice and the lack of bodily anchoring of the speech has the effect of weeding out a number of distracting bodily features – but obviously not those of the quality and modality of the voice. This is exactly why the quality and modality of the voice, i.e. what it signals or gives associations to by its way of being a voice and by its bodily indications, are so crucial.

All this establishes that this voice speaks from a privileged and concealed position, and this kind of vaguely indicated location is especially interesting and significant when, incidentally, the medium is visual and well suited to depict and present speakers in action. So here we have actors who are invisible, as a unity of body and speech, but still very much present and prominent. The point of this metonymisation of the actor to a voice and abstraction from other parts of the person is – quite generally seen – precisely that some circumstances or qualities of the communication are suppressed so that others may stand out more clearly or unambiguously. The reduction to voice equals reduction of information, including information which might interfere with the concentration on the intended message, what "it is all about", i.e. the referential aspect. So, on average, the voice-over format concentrates on informing and teaching. It is a fact format.

But which different roles can these only-as-a-voice present actors play? And what do these roles mean to on-screen action and when seen in relation to the role positions that may be adopted by the screen viewer and in relation to on-screen action? And – all in all – how does the precise fact that we are dealing with an obviously independent, 'disconnected' voice or speech level, which in the purely phenomenological sense is alleged to be located in some other 'place' than the immediately visible action plane of the screen, affect the aesthetic and creative opportunities?

In other words, the basic point of departure is

1) That whereas synchronous speech/voice from the screen (the speaker is seen as speaking directly from the picture level with 'eye contact' to the viewer) – i.e. typically the presenter format – establishes two actor levels only, that is to say the speaker(s)/actor(s) and the viewer as alleged addressee/audience and an alleged contact between these two worlds or planes
and whereas
2) Synchronous conversation between two persons on the screen (i.e. typically the drama) also establishes two actor levels, that is the visible and audible event/action between some people/things and an invitation to the audience to perceive this, but without the allegation of direct contact as in 1)
then
3) Asynchronous speech, where the person, world or place from where or wherein the speech emerges is invisible, establishes not two but three levels, between which a far more intricate and at once more ample and more economical role play can be established: the visual level, the speech/voice level, and the level of the audience/addressee.

As mentioned before, this means that the anonymous voice is located on or rather establishes a middle level, which insinuates and unfolds itself *between* what the viewer sees and the viewer-listener position. In other words, there is – or is established – a level, which often functions as a filter between what is seen and the viewer, but which may also have other functions (mediating and manipulative) by – as we have seen – transforming the roles in the aggregate system.

In spatial terms the aggregate system is made up of:

- a first level which is = the voice/speech represented without body,
- a second level which is = the visual one (i.e. the (audio)-visual screen level)

- and a third level = the viewer and the viewer's (presupposed) combination/selection via a number of codes and conventions of elements in the first and second levels so that all in all they acquire meaning.

Which level is in the foreground and actually (i.e. chronologically) comes first, may vary, but it will usually be the voice that indicates a shift of level. In order to emphasise the spatial dimension of the communication this tripartite structure might be termed the *trigonometric* addressing play of TV advertising.

The Trigonometric Addressing Play of TV Advertising via Voice-over

More than any other TV genre, the main format of TV advertising, the voice-over, cultivates and exploits the polar extremities and the acting opportunities in a trigonometric addressing play which, in a variety of ways, may create/creates a space round the very address as a communicative event. In some connections this happens in order to ensure the unambiguity of the message, but it also happens in various ways by establishing ambiguous, transformed, equivocal addressing ploys, which create a cognitive and communicative tension between the viewer's immediate perception and his virtual one. This is typically how the space between the seen and the heard is expanded for the viewer.

Furthermore, it follows logically that precisely the TV spot commercial must try to expand in this particular field because a) the time frame is so compressed that a minimum must create maximum impact, b) above all, advertising is the creation of contact (phatic communication) and the creation of attention, for which reason the cultivation and the variation of the routes to the creation of contact, and the establishing of virtual spaces and roles for contact are of crucial importance.

As previously hinted in connection with the treatment of "The Experiment", the majority of the voice-over format spots do not distinguish themselves by exploiting the opportunities of the format in a distinctive way. But regarded in a more generalised and graduated way, how does the TV spot commercial exploit and sophisticate this tension field consisting of 1) invisible speaker(s)/voice(s) 2) visible manifestations on the screen 3) audible speech acts aimed at a virtual viewer?

If we take our point of departure in the voice as voice-over, then this voice in its most elementary form will be aimed at the obvious 'you' of the screen, i.e. the viewer, and will – in the same way as a presenter – place the accent on contact, an offer, and the appeal to the receiver's 'acting' in the situation, "Good evening", "look", "imagine", "this week you can ...", "buy ... tomorrow". Likewise, a quite elementary form will be the voice controlling a sequence, while what is flashing across the screen will just be a more or less redundant illustration running parallel to what is being said: what is shown on the screen is 'subject' to the statement of the voice and has only to serve to clarify, make unambiguous, but also to amplify what is being said and make it more readily intelligible and sensorily perceptible. Using a traditional Roland Barthes terminology, one would say that voice serves as anchorage to the visual element.[16] Functionally seen, it has among other things to guard against possibly undesired and wild-flying associations. The voice is in the most literal sense voice-*over*. It speaks over and across what we see in the picture, and tries to dictate to us what we see on the picture level. This is the voice-over in its most elementary form. The speech runs its race, while a sequence – admittedly of a different – but more or less redundant character runs across the screen, which is to supply a sensorily intelligible 'added value' to what is said. In other words, the recipe is: since words are poor but necessary for purposes of information and instruction, they are provided with the additive of an experience-oriented substratum of more or less relevant or far-fetched visuality, but without the visual element being allowed to stand in its own right and speak for itself. The visual element, what happens on the screen either is subjected – or there is an attempt to subject it – to the meanings and demonstrating dictates of the voice/speech.

We find a slightly less elementary form where the voice is aimed at on-screen action and at the same time demonstratively tries to establish a sense of community with the viewer about what is shown, "here is/we see/you", "this one", "that". Here the voice places itself in an exchange relation with on-screen action. This could – again in traditional Barthesean terminology – be a case of a 'releasing' relation between the statement of the voice and the 'statement' of the screen.

This interplay between shown and said can be further elaborated to contrapuntal or contra factual circumstances and other disproportions and incommensurabilities (ironies and distortions) between the two entities/levels. In other words, it is the alternation, the distortions, the fill-ins, the contextualisations between said and shown which can be brought into co-operative interplay aimed at the active acceptance of the viewer. There is a higher degree of equal rank and co-operation between the statement of the voice/speech and the visual one of the screen, but there is at the same time a semantic tightening of the statement as a whole. The visual side is accorded an independent semantic status, which provides the audience with openings.

The exchange may – as demonstrated in the Circle Coffee commercial – be in the shape of a manifest intervention from the voice level into the visual level, so that the voice agent becomes an interfering actor on the level of mentioning or showing. Likewise, there may be attempts (pretended, of course) at intervening and presupposing on the level of the viewer (cf. e.g. "*the* glass" in the same TV spot). This represents a sliding expansion of the voice-role. It begins to become or becomes the representative of a dramatic character who is in interchange with an otherwise only mentioned universe.

Until now the 'you' addressed by the voice/speech is unambiguously identical with the viewer at the screen. This is not true of the following where precisely the gradual slides between the roles become manifest with a vengeance.

The very interchange between invisible voice and what is visible on the screen may be intensified to an exchange between more elaborated roles. The voice may use a "you"-address as its lead. On the face of it, this 'you' equals the viewer. It turns out, however, that it is addressed to an on-camera person looking directly at the viewer, so that we now have an invisible speaking agent and a visible responding agent. The voice's opening lead is thus quite clearly ambiguous. In principle, the voice actor is indicated as being on the same level and on the same imagined reality plane either temporally or spatially as the person/thing visibly present, looking straight at the screen. But the decisive ambiguity does not spring from the double "you" of the address only. It arises precisely from the circumstance that the voice actor has not been established as a figure in their visual space, which at first glance blurs the fact that it is this actor's unidentified 'look' which anchors the visual angle (via so-called subjective camera/point-of-view) and so places us on a diegetic level.[17] But the truly interesting thing is that the axis forming the exchange is identical with the axis to the viewer. That is to say, the viewer is placed in the same position as the pretended, constructed voice position. The viewer is alleged to see through the same eyes as this pretended voice position and is willy-nilly 'forced' to take over this view of things. As the voice's "you"-opening and the anchorage of the look become ambiguous, so the addressed second person's response/address on the screen becomes clearly double: partly via the look straight at the viewer at the screen (i.e. as pretended first person with viewer contact), partly via the imagined look at the invisible representative of the voice (i.e. as the second person of the first-second person interaction of the diegetic level).

The relationship between voice and screen has been reversed compared to the dominance situation of the traditional voice-over. Here the reaction of the screen picture/the person-in-the-picture to the voice is dominant. The voice creates the occasion (typically by means of a question whose direction is ambiguous). The interesting features are partly the reaction, partly the circumstance that the address/reaction of the second person (the "you") is aimed at the viewer or the "you" at the screen as well as at the imagined speaker. The interchange play can thus be understood or viewed in two ways: either as a drama or play between two persons of whom we see only one, or as representative speech, i.e. the viewer does not necessarily have to be able to take over the speaking position at once, but at least in the second round be able to realise that (s)he is in the position of addressee – because the look from the screen places him in this position whether he wants it or not. The lack of visual establishment of the invisible speaker, and the fact that the communication axis 'invisible speaker'–'speaker-from-screen' is identical with the viewer-screen axis, are the very features which create the ambiguity in the address and exchange.

What then is the expediency of this ambiguity? Obviously, partly to transfer or superimpose the invisible speaking position to/on the viewer, partly that the "you" of the screen position becomes a "you" as much in relation to the viewer as in relation to the actor of the invisible voice. The roles are blurred or confounded, and fore- and background relations are confounded in the same way as when viewers phone in to a studio programme: the programme host's look is directed straight at the viewing audience, but at the same time this behaviour pretends that the host is in exclusive contact with and only addresses the speaker on the phone. In other words, we are close to drama, because we witness a dialogic exchange and an interactional play between two persons. But all the same, the invisible (middle) field between viewer and screen event is activated and elaborated.

Whereas it is true of all cases so far that the source of the invisible voice is in fact invisible or at most metonymically represented on the visual level, this does not necessarily hold good when it is a case of an I-narrator or a third person one. 1) The person or actor may be visible as a figure on the screen, but without being presented as on-screen speaker. The actor is located at the distance determined by the invisible narrator voice. This play is typically a temporal one: the distance between narration (the statement) and the narrated (who or what the statement is about). The visual actor is typically an illustrative object dealt with by the narrator voice and shown on the screen (hence similarity to traditional voice-over), but may also be accorded subjective vision, which again brings about a deputising placement of the viewer as actor. 2) The person does speak, but is not seen to begin with. However, what he talks about is seen. While the speech is kept going continuously, the speaking person comes into the picture with direct synchronous address to the camera (this situation may obviously be reversed, too).

Regarded over a continuum, the invisible voice may thus adopt various roles in relation to screen and audience. As already stated: what they have in common purely phenomenologically is that the speaking position and direct source of the voice are simply concealed. The anonymisation is a simple device to ensure that informative energy is expended on nothing but the statement of the voice. Indirectly, however, the invisibility of the voice also gives opportunities to elaborate and transform the roles and create tensions precisely *via the invisibility*.

Another common feature is that the voice forms a middle field, a 'space' between viewer and on-screen action. On the one hand it creates a distance, on the other it makes up a mediating link of closeness. But the important thing is that it can create and widen the address-wise scope of address in relation to the viewer and endow this space with a depth over and beyond what other formats can achieve. Because it does not simply speak across the picture level as an informative mediator and 'know-all'; in a number of cases it also creates its own space via the omission, from which it may play, now to the space or plane of the screen, now to the space of the viewer.

Seen in a more constructive perspective, one has to operate with/relate to the mutually negative and complementary qualities of the three levels. Radically and quite generally formulated: that the screen level may show in action and accentuate the importance of silence and behaviour, that the speech level may act with and in words accentuate the importance of invisibility, that the opportunities of movement of the viewer level may be accentuated precisely through exchanges between said/not-said and shown/not-shown, whereby with lightning speed the audience may be whisked between their positions of genre or expectation as well as their presupposed role positions.

Conclusion

What we have here termed the trigonometric address playing of TV advertising, holds a variety of opportunities to activate the viewers with open gambits, which must be presumed at least as effective as those of the mini-drama and may be even more effective exactly by elaborating and making a point of the communication situation itself as a scope for interactivity with the viewer. Furthermore, a great deal of direct-address TV advertising does not make full use of these opportunities, but slavishly follows the beaten paths, still believing that media-borne communication is nothing but the transfer of meaning, not the *genesis* of meaning.

The voice-over format is traditionally associated with a factual and didactic form of communication in which manifest instruction and argumentation are served with a dash of audio-visual experience. Judged by the normal narrative criteria of the audio-visual media there is nothing spectacular or fascinating about it. It is the safe and trivial pre-masticated, pre-digested food of TV advertising. It is certainly not exactly this format that catches either general or professional attention. On the other hand, the majority of TV advertising expresses itself in this format. There are obvious and good reasons for this, some of which are dictated by totally trivial considerations of functionality, of course.[18] But regarded from a perspective of development, one reason is that this is where the elaboration of the communication situation itself and its I-you-here-there-now roles *may* create tension, motion, and fullness round the communication act itself.

And since we are after all dealing with advertising, perhaps this form of viewer activation is conceived as more relevant and reliable (because it is in accordance with the intention) than the indirect and contemplative form of reception that the mini-drama plays up to.

Notes

1. Attempts to cross this fundamental barrier and more efficiently bring the receiver into the picture are almost as old as the mass media themselves: genres like e.g. correspondence columns, agony columns ('Dear Madge'), horoscopes, crosswords, cooking recipes, interviews, reporting, various personalised and simulated forms of address in the public space ("Dear reader/listener", "Thank you for letting me into your sitting room") may all be seen as attempts to overcome the constraints of the prod-

uct character of the mass media product and place the receiver at the centre.
2. The view of media-borne communication is thus in accordance with the 'bottle-mail' principle in e.g. Mikkelsen, 1994.
3. Several components make up this space (dialogue = 'middle speech'). The most important components serving to constitute this middle space are the (presupposed) co-operation principle, eye contact, body distance, gesture, signals for speech turn-taking.
4. For a fuller treatment of this circumstance and how as a genre it may be viewed in relation to the total genre universe of TV, see Stigel, 1997b.
5. Concerning this simulated interactivity, see thematic issue on Media and Interaction of *Mediekultur* no. 26, 1997, especially papers by Hjarvard, 1997, and Horton & Wohl, 1997.
6. See e.g. Paddy Scannel, 1994.
7. In the advertising world this calculus with the receiver is sometimes called 'seduction' or 'induction'. In the media world generally, words such as 'manipulation' or 'suggestion' mean the same and carry the same derogative or pejorative value. One might however use the word 'compliance' to cover the same meaning, seeing that as a genre, advertising obviously operates from notions of what the receiver wants and may have a need to hear, and *how* (s)he wants to hear it or see it represented.
8. The following does not even remotely pretend to be an exhaustive definition of the tendencies of advertising, but is only an ultra-brief thumbnail sketch. For more precise definitions see e.g. Leiss, William, Kline & Jhally, 1986; and Stigel, 1997a.
9. If one wants a present-day register and a very palpable giveaway of these appeals, e.g. the 1996/97 campaign by the *Diesel* textile firm: "Successful Living" (note the title!) is one long paraphrase and travesty of the faith of advertising in visual stagings with this kind of background in motivational psychology.
10. The discussion of the inherent relevance of various formats in relation to advertising may be seen among others in Wells, 1989; Stern, 1991; and Stigel, 1996.
11. Cannes Lions '97. 44th International Advertising Festival 23-28 June. The tape contains winners in a bronze, silver, and gold category. Numbers within each category vary between 51 (bronze) and 26 (gold). Total number 113. In the gold category 90% of the spots are mini-dramas.
12. Cf. quantitative tallies of the basic formats of TV spot commercials, and an account of these basic formats in Stigel 1996 and

especially in Jantzen & Stigel, 1995. Later, as yet unpublished, tallies show a solidly increasing tendency of approx. 30% over a 7-year period for the drama format.
13. Cf. note 12.
14. See note 5.
15. About this intimacy-creating and familiarising dimension in more detail see Kozloff, 1988.
16. Roland Barthes's concepts of anchorage and release (translated from *anchrage* and *relais*) from Barthes, 1980.
17. In point of fact and without any ado we are almost at the deepest level of diegesis regarded from the traditional film criteria of narration. Because we see through somebody's eyes. The unusual circumstance is that we have not been informed (i.e. have not seen) who this somebody is. This lack of knowledge creates immediate confusion and suspense (cf. e.g. Hitchcock's famous build-up to the stabbing of the woman under the shower in the film *Psycho*), and obviously does it even more so in this totally frontal exploitation. Re. the general build-up of diegesis in e.g. movie pictures see Brannigan, 1992.

    The exchange between hidden voice and screen-actor with direct screen contact (which thus pretends to be a two-way visual contact with the voice-bearer as well as the TV viewer) may adopt various basic forms. The lead may lie either with the hidden voice or the screen-actor. If the lead lies with the hidden voice, it will typically have the character of (a) question directed at the screen-actor, who will then – in a question-and-answer sequence – answer or react in some other way (mimically).
18. These reflections on function are obviously connected first and foremost to the catching of audience attention via the sound dimension as well, since TV is inscribed in a distractive form of reception (just cf. the circumstance that the sound volume is increased when there are commercials on the channel). But they are also connected to the increasingly flexible opportunities for versioning via the voice-over format. Finally, they are also connected to the fact that many TV commercials are advertisements for the retail trade and thus advertise the week's bargain prices.

Bibliography

Barthes, Roland (1980, orig. 1964). "Rhetorique de l'image". In *Communications 4*. Paris: Seuil. [English translation, 1977, "Rhetoric of the Image" in *Image – Music – Text*. London: Fortuna.]

Brannigan, Edward (1992). *Narrative Comprehension in Film*. London: Routledge.
Hjarvard, Stig (1997). "Simulerede samtaler. Om forholdet mellem interpersonel og medieformidlet kommunikation" ["Simulated Conversations: On the Relation between Interpersonal and Media-borne Communication"]. In *Mediekultur*, no. 26.
Horton, Donald, & R. R. Wohl (1997). "Massekommunikation og parasocial interaktion: Et indlæg om intimitet på afstand". In *Mediekultur*, no. 26 (orig. 1956, "Mass Communication and Para-Social Interaction: Observations on Intimacy at a distance". In *Psychiatry*, 19).
Jantzen, Christian, & Jørgen Stigel (1995). *Reklamen i dansk landsdækkende tv* ["Advertising in Nationwide Danish TV"]. Copenhagen: Statsministeriets Medieudvalg [The Media Commission].
Kozloff, Sarah (1988). *Invisible Storytellers – Voice Over Narration in American Fiction Film*. Berkeley: University of California Press.
Leiss, W., S. Kline & J. Jhally (1986). *Social Communication in Advertising*. London: Routledge.
Mikkelsen, Jan Foght (1994). "Pragmatisk receptionsteori" ["Pragmatic Theory of Reception"]. In Lennard Højbjerg (ed.): *Reception af levende billeder*. Copenhagen: Akademisk Forlag.
Scannel, Paddy (1994). "Kommunikativ intentionalitet i radio og tv" ["Communicative Intentionality in Radio and TV"]. In *Mediekultur*, no. 22, 1994.
Stern, Barbara B. (1991). "Who talks Advertising?". In *Journal of Advertising*, Vol. XX, No.3, Sept.
Stigel, Jørgen (1996). "Minimalism in TV-commercials". In J. Beracs et al. (eds.): *EMAC Proceedings*, vol. 1. Budapest: Budapest University.
Stigel, Jørgen (1997a). "Appellen til den rationelle forbruger" ["Appealing to the rational consumer"], "Billeder på forbruget" ["Pictures of consuming"], "Reklame for velfærd" ["Advertising wellfare"]. In Klaus Bruhn Jensen (ed.): *Dansk Mediehistorie*, vol. 2 and 3. Copenhagen: Samleren.
Stigel, Jørgen (1997b). "The Aesthetics of Television. The Quality of Television: On Distinctions and Relations of Programme Form and Quality of Address". In Martin Eide et al. (eds.): *Quality Television*, Report no. 30. Bergen: Department of Media Studies, University of Bergen.
Wells, William (1989). "Lectures and Dramas". In Patricia Cafferata & A.M. Tybout (eds.): *Cognitive and Affective Responses to Advertising*. Lexington, MA: Lexington Books.

CHAPTER ELEVEN

"So, what do *you* think, Linda?" Media Typologies for Interactive Television

Jens F. Jensen
VR Media Lab
& Department of Communication
Aalborg University

"So, what do you *think, Linda?"*
'Cousin'-announcer in Fahrenheit 451

Introduction

The quote that starts this essay comes from the science fiction film *Fahrenheit 451*.[1] It is from a scene where the protagonist Montag and his wife Linda find themselves in their futuristic living room in front of a huge wall-screen television. In the film version, this medium is often referred to as 'The Family' and the TV announcers and the viewers often refer to each other as 'cousins'. Montag and Linda are in the middle of a conversation about this new TV medium.

> Linda: "I'd rather have a second wall set put in. They say when you have a second wall-screen it's like having your family grow up all around you ... Anyway, tonight is special for me. I've got a part in 'The Family' ... Oh, hurry, hurry. I'll be on in a minute, quickly, quickly!" ... Montag: "I don't understand. How can you be in a play?"

Linda: "They have written a play, you see, with one part missing, that's me. When the people look at me, then I have to speak. They ask me a question, then I have to say what I think."

Linda adjusts her hair and sits down in front of the wall-screen where in direct viewer mode the 'cousin' announcer gives the following program introduction:

"And now for 'cousins' everywhere: Our family theatre. Come play with us. Naturally in what you are about to see, any similarity with the truth or real life would be purely coincidental. Do bear that in mind. So, will you come play with us? ... You will! Good. I thought you would. Come in cousin. Be one of 'The Family'."[2]

The TV play starts and proceeds with a dialogue between two actors on rather trivial problems about the seating arrangement and the accommodation for what appears to be a future family celebration. Somewhere in the dialogue, after having outlined various solutions, the two actors turn to the camera, simulate direct eye contact to the viewer and one of them asks: "What do *you* think, Linda?" The actors gaze silently from the screen, a red lamp flashes to mark that now it is the viewer's turn to give her input, to communicate, to interact.

This is possibly one of the earliest visions of 'interactive television' of the future. In the typical dystopian future prospects of classical science fiction, as well as in the critical mid-60's horizon of the film, the new medium and TV-interactivity are clearly thematicised as surrogates, as an empty and mendacious relationship, as merely simulated two-way communication. Flustered by the situation, Linda does not answer while the red lamp is on, but the TV-actors continue, completely indifferent to her lack of input: "See, Linda agrees with me".

The thematicisation of the new electronic media's tendency to manipulate viewers, make them dumber, and turn them into zombies is reinforced by the metonymic and metaphoric connections established between the TV medium and the pills which later make Linda lose consciousness. This continues with the explicit contrast between the new TV medium's lack of content and the old meaningful book medium which, according to the authorities in this repressive world of the future, make people emotionally unstable and unhappy and are therefore banned and systematically destroyed by the fire department's autodafés.[3]

The image of the interactive television of the future here obviously appears to be a menacing, dystopian tele-vision.

Today, interactive television (ITV) is no longer pure science fiction or a distant dream (or nightmare) of the future, it is rapidly becoming a realistic form of media. Interactive television is — in a very literal sense — *'coming soon to a screen near you'*. So, it probably won't be long before you have to answer questions like, "What do *you* think, Linda?" from a screen close by.

The purpose of this chapter is to describe and discuss this emerging new media form. Firstly, interactive television will be described as a form of program and as a TV system. Secondly, a set of new categorisations or typologies of networked media will be presented. And thirdly, interactive television and interactive television services will be conceptualised and discussed in the context of these new typologies of media and services.[4]

Interactive Television: an Attempt at a Working Definition

A complication in relation to describing interactive television is the abundance of differing concepts and understandings of the concept currently in circulation. The various industrial players in the ITV field — cable operators, telcos, computer companies, broadcast networks, movie studios, etc. — all seem to have different notions of the concept of interactive television as a technology. Furthermore, the players have differing philosophies about what interactivity is and what it means to 'interact' with television, as well as varying perspectives on what services and content the consumer will want and be willing to pay for. As a result, during the past three decades a broad spectrum of services, content, and programming, has laid claim to the term 'interactive television'. Some of them include: multi-channel systems with several hundreds of channels to select from; on-demand access to movies, videos, news, sports, etc.; customisation of and control over content; interactive news; local storage of programming; real time interaction and communication between users of the system, such as text messaging, voice telephony or video-phone; access to database and online information; voting in (real-time) opinion polls; control over choice of camera angles in the transmission of sports events and the like; interactive games based on stand alone or networked applications; participation in game shows; user created content; electronic town meetings, etc. The following is an attempt at a working definition of the concept of interactive television.

Media researchers, especially those from reception research, media ethnography, and media and cultural studies, have in recent years denied the perception of television as a passive medium and have instead pointed out that the viewer's reading of TV-texts is always active (and interactive). Practically and technically, however, traditional TV claims very little activity from the users. Naturally, the viewers decide what to watch, just as they must cognitively and socially deal with, interpret, and make sense of what they watch on the screen. But apart from this, strictly speaking, the only physical requirements involve turning on the set, (perhaps) changing the channel, and turning it off again (and on the odd occasion: making small adjustments to the sound and picture).

In a negatively defined demarcation, interactive television can be understood as TV which, aside from the traditional turn-on-zap-and-turn-off interaction, and cognitive (and social) interaction between the presented text and the viewer's ability to make sense of what is seen — i.e. the purely interpretative interaction — also relies upon an actual, physical interaction in the form of choices, decisions and communicative input to the system. In a shorter, more positive version interactive TV can be considered a new form of television that makes it possible for the viewer to interact with the medium in such a way that he gains control over what to watch, when to watch, and how to watch, or directly opens up for active participation in a program.

Understood in this way, interactive TV can be considered a fairly broadly defined concept. At the 1996 world conference dedicated to interactive television "The superhighway through the home?" the conference committee used the term 'interactive television':

"... rhetorically to suggest the provision of interactive multimedia services to domestic spaces. At its most general this can mean services accessed through a variety of platforms and infrastructures. At its most specific it relates to services and content specifically designed to be used through televisions, relating strongly in appearance with broadcast style displays and presentation and even co-existing and augmenting existing broadcast programming."[5]

Correspondingly, the 'Interactive TV News' site defines the term 'interactive television' as:

"... the meeting of television with new interactive technology. iTV is domestic television with interactive facilities usually facilitated through a 'back channel' and/or an advanced terminal. Equally important, interactive television is content that users and viewers can interact with via the technical system ... There are many delivery systems, technical standards, possible uses and content. These range from the WWW to home shopping. Digital Video Broadcasting to Internet, movies on demand to video telephony. The unifying factor is the television that is central to the entertainment, education, information, leisure and social life of millions of homes all over the world." (*Interactive TV News*)

As the quotes above show, the term 'interactive television' is used both to indicate a type of program, i.e. TV as software, and a certain type of system or media technology, i.e. TV as hardware. These two versions do not necessarily always coincide. In the following, the two forms of interactive TV will be briefly described and characterised.

As a form of program, i.e. in its software aspect, interactive TV can be understood as an independent program or segment of a program involving the active co-operation of the viewer. This is the case when two-way communication takes place between the transmitting medium and the viewer, where viewer input is directly included in the text of the program or otherwise used to decide the course of the program and where viewer interaction becomes a decisive aspect of the program concept and a decisive factor for its completion.

Since most places still do not have comprehensive, interactive two-way TV systems, a kind of 'two-channel' interaction is often used to produce interactive programs or interactive features. This means that another medium acts as a 'return' or 'feedback channel' from the TV viewer to the media sender. A suitable name for this hybrid form of medium might be 'duo-media'[6] and for this form of interaction 'two-channel-interaction'.

There is a long — and apparently growing — list of so-called interactive program forms or features with considerable variation between the national TV channels, TV systems, and program formats. In most of these cases, it is a question of establishing a simple and temporary interactive two-way communication system, a 'two-channel-interaction', within a certain program by supplementing the TV's one-way communication with e.g. the telephone medium, fax, e-mail, web chat, SMS, etc. as a return channel from the viewer to the media sender.

Compared to fully integrated interactive TV systems the obvious advantage with this kind of two-channel interaction is that the so-called 'terminal barrier' is already broken down, since today almost every household has a TV-set and a phone and to some extent also a computer with Internet access, a mobile phone with SMS, fax, etc. The two-channel interaction thus does not imply large investments in hardware and software on the part of the service provider, the distributor, or the viewer. Therefore it is to be expected that these kinds of interactive programs, with two-channel interactivity, will have a much larger distribution in the short term — a fact already indicated by current trends. It is also to be expected that primarily the phone, but increasingly also the modem equipped computer (also using phone lines or cable) and mobile phones with SMS, etc. will provide the return channel. Finally, it is obvious that interactive TV programs are at a comparatively primitive and preliminary stage today. It is to be expected that far more advanced formats will be developed in the future.

Interactive TV as a TV system, i.e. in its hardware aspect, can be perceived as media technology which, *within the framework of the system itself*, is able to produce two-way communication and thus give the viewers the ability to make various interactive choices regarding programs, services, information and advertising, to obtain a larger amount of control, or to experience various kinds of direct input or feedback. Judith Jeffcoate writes e.g.: "In very simple terms we may define interactive TV as a combination of technologies that allows television viewers greater control over what they watch and when they watch it" (1995: 79).[7]

Thus, in the broad sense, interactive television as a system is to be understood as the merger of conventional television with new interactive information and communication technologies. More specifically, ITV is a technology that allows the user to receive information from the broadcaster as well as to send information to the broadcaster or to other users on the network, usually facilitated by a return channel of some kind, or allows the user to employ local interactivity via broadcasted material, applications or programs, usually through an advanced ITV terminal (set-top box, etc.). By interacting with the system, users can request content, influence the content of existing programs, and/or undertake on-line activities such as home shopping and home banking. Consequently, ITV provides the technical system that makes it possible for users to interact with or contribute content.

Such a TV system must include at least 3 necessary technological components:

1. A source of information at the service supplier, typically a multimedia server with a large disc capacity for storing digitised films, advertisements, catalogues, games and other digital data.

2. A receiver which can be operated by the viewer, to receive and decode the signal, typically a TV set provided with a set-top box with a processor, a memory, and local storage — which actually functions as a computer. Thus the set-top box makes the TV set a 'smart TV'.
3. And finally, a two-way transmission system between the source of information and the receiver, that makes communication both ways possible, i.e. downstream from the source of information as well as upstream from the receiver to the source. Thus interactive TV as a TV system is — more popularly stated — 'TV's two-way street'.[8]

Interactive TV understood as media technology is therefore in itself a rather broadly defined concept. As previously mentioned, it refers to many different platforms and infrastructures that bring interactively based communication and other new forms of interactive multimedia services to the home. The concept is thereby connected with, or often used synonymously for, a number of other terms of current interest such as: networked multimedia, broadband services, Infohighway, Internet and the media convergence between TV, computer, telephony and radio.

There is apparently no necessary connection between interactive TV as a form of program and interactive TV as a TV system. Interactive TV programs can be established without an interactive TV system, just as it is possible within an interactive TV-system to transmit non-interactive TV programs. Of course the most fully developed and most advanced interactive TV will appear when interactive TV-programs are produced within interactive TV systems. However, for both interactive TV as a type of program and interactive TV as a TV system, it is important that the connection downstream from media sender to consumer must be supplemented by some kind of connection upstream, i.e. a 'feedback' or 'return channel' which is able to carry signals from the consumer back into the network or to the media sender.[9] This return channel is integrated in the media of interactive TV systems, whereas this is not necessarily the case in interactive TV programs.

Interactive TV involves significant changes in the services that can be offered via TV, the ways in which information can be presented, as well as the ways in which television is watched and used. In order to give an indication of what interactive TV technology may pave the way for, a number of the most important services, applications and types of programs which have already been experimented with and speculated in will be briefly presented.

Pay-per-view is commercial TV that uses the 'taxi' payment principle and charges only for the programs received.[10]

Near-video-on-demand is the transmission of the same program, for example a movie, on several channels in alternative time slots so that each viewer only has a brief wait (thus the name '*near*') between ordering the program and receiving it on the home TV set. If, for example, a 100-minutes long movie was aired at varied times by ten channels the viewer would end up waiting a maximum of ten minutes from the time the movie is ordered until it is delivered.

Video-on-demand (also called *true video-on-demand* or *movies-on-demand*) is the reception of programs according to individual orders. In this case, the program is not transmitted continuously over several channels, but is delivered directly to each individual home without a wait. When the programs are movies, which is typically the case, this service can be considered a network version of video rental or sales. Similar services can be found in the music field, i.e. *music-on-demand*.

News-on-demand is a news service, which is updated continuously, where the consumer interactively selects and retrieves news items and may even choose the level of detail and type of presentation (text, graphics, narration, photos, or video). Parallel services can also be found for sports (*sports-on-demand*), weather, etc.

Games-on-demand is the network distribution of video, TV or computer games (replacing diskettes, cartridges and CD-ROMs), where the consumer either downloads the desired game from a cable network to a computer, game machine or set-top box, is given online access to the game on a pay-per-play basis, or is able to compete against other players connected to the network.

Interactive game shows allow viewers to participate directly in TV quizzes or contests interactively from their homes.

Their competitors may be in a TV studio or be other TV viewers at home.

Wagering is a gambling service, which makes it possible to play the lottery, make bets, etc. using the television. Sometimes this is done in real time, i.e. while the event being bet on is taking place.

Interactive fiction or choose-your-own-story(ending) are stories with built in options that require the viewer to actively participate and make choices (using the formula "What do *you* think, Linda?"). The choices are either based on individual or collective (majority) decisions. This is the kind of interactive fiction service or form of program being parodied by 'The Family' in *Fahrenheit 451*.

Be-your-own-editor or 'choose-your-own-camera-angle' is the simultaneous transmission of an event, a sports event for instance, on several parallel channels where each channel represents a certain camera and thus a certain camera angle on the action. By zapping from channel to channel (camera to camera) the viewer puts together his own program.

Electronic programming guides are new computer based techniques or advanced interfaces that use various menus and quick scanning of current and upcoming programs (searched by category, topic, time, actors, etc.) to aid navigation through the channels and to identify programs that the viewer may want to see. Because digitisation will make it possible for cable networks to transmit up to 500 channels, a complete 'channel surf' using remote control would take so long (even just stopping to see a few seconds of each cablecast channel) that most of the scanned programs would be over before the entire system is checked. In principle, the viewer could then start from the beginning and spend his entire time in front of the television just zapping. Intelligent personal agents, i.e. software with pre-programmed guidelines, that regularly checks for certain types of programs or registers and 'remembers' a viewer's preferences, could point out when and where something of probable interest will turn up.

Home shopping or the electronic shopping mall, is where the consumer can browse through catalogues and exhibits to retrieve information, make comparisons, order and even purchase goods and services directly, perhaps using a smart card.

Parallel services are *home banking, ticketing* (purchase of tickets to events), etc.

Interactive advertising and product information is, in contrast to traditional advertising, not necessarily sent to the consumer. On the contrary, the consumer may selectively seek it and use it interactively to inform himself.[11]

Polling involves opinion surveys that use votes from interactive TV viewers on a local, regional or national basis.[12]

And finally there are *information services*, which offer to search text, picture or multimedia data bases, *interactive distance learning services, health services*, etc.

As it should now be apparent, interactive TV is many different things, just as the degree of interactivity varies widely over many different levels.

Such radical changes in TV-media as are seen here naturally also imply changed relationships between the sender and the receiver or the media-centre and the consumer, transformations of the economic models that the media are based on, new conditions for the aesthetics of television, new modes of address, as well as changes in TV culture. In the present context, only the first aspect mentioned above will be discussed: the relationship between the media institution and the media consumer.[13]

New Typologies of Information Services

This radical transformation of television as media and the extreme complexity of the new services supported by ITV necessitates, among other things, new typologies or classifications of information services that can provide us with a general view of the modes of communication in the new media form. The purpose of this section is to give a short sketch of such cognitive or conceptual maps of interactive technologies and services.

There have been numerous attempts to create categories and typologies for communication and media technologies. The most widespread classifications have been based on technological characteristics, forms of representation, or information and media types. However, as different media technologies merge in digitisation and media convergence, classifications based on technological criteria become increasingly less distinctive; as different forms of information types melt together into multimedia, classifications based on forms of representation become increasingly less revealing; and as various content melts with multi-functional networks, classifications based on content or service types become increasingly less instructive or satisfying. They simply do not seem to catch the significant features in new media development and the significant differences in the new services. Therefore, interactive systems often require their own particular conceptualisations and formats.

Some of these typologies are based on the information traffic patterns. According to Vinay Kumar (Kumar, 1996), information access and distribution mechanisms can basically be divided into two models:

- "You go to the information source"
- "The information source comes to you"

In the "you-go-to-the-information-source"-model, the initiative and the responsibility for finding and accessing the information is located at the consumer end of the creator/consumer opposition. The creators of the information just wait for consumers to request or access the desired information. Typical examples of this model would be the World Wide Web, magazines, and bookstores. In "the-information-source-comes-to-you"-model information and entertainment are beamed to consumers. Consequently, consumers "do not have to try hard (with the exception of changing channels) to access the information – the information is delivered directly to the home (or is it the couch?)" (Kumar, 1996: 29). Typical examples would of course be cable TV, terrestrial broadcast or satellite broadcast.

In recent years, these information traffic patterns have frequently been described in terms of the buzzwords, 'push media' and 'pull media'.

Kelly et al. (1997) describe 'push media', typical examples of which are radio, television, and film, as follows: "Content is pushed to you ... Push media arrive automatically – on your desktop, in your email, via your pager ... The distinguishing characteristic of the new push media is that it finds you, rather than you finding it. That means the content knows where you are and what you are seeing" (1997: 14f, 23).

'Pull media', on the other hand, get their name from "the invitational pull you make when you click on the Web" (1997:14). In other words, pull media are media you (interactively) steer.

A similar, but slightly more complicated and sophisticated way of classifying interactive content and services, is the media typology originally developed by Bordewijk and Kaam (cf. Bordewijk & Kaam, 1986). They have designated this media typology as "a new classification of tele-information services" (1986: 16), *de facto* motivated by the present explosion of tele-information systems, to be understood here as the merger of digital telecommunication and computer technology. The distinctive mark of this typology is that it is defined independently of the technical design of the media, the form of presentation, and the content of information, and is instead based on social power relations and power positions,[14] which constitute different 'communication patterns' or 'information traffic patterns'. These patterns are described here in relation to who delivers the information and who controls the access to and use of the information, where the latter primarily refers to the choice of the content of information as well as the time that it is to be received.

One of the most widely used metaphors for computer networks as media has been the 'Information Superhighway'.[15] This is a metaphor that was already a cliché before the majority understood its implications, and a metaphor that is still heatedly debated and, among other things, has been heavily criticised for creating misconceptions. In this particular context, however, the metaphor is appropriate, since it relates directly to the mapping of information traffic on the Information Superhighway, which Bordewijk and Kaam refer to as the 'idealised information traffic patterns'. In the following, I will give a brief description of the different information traffic patterns, primarily based on Bordewijk and Kaam's presentation.

The typology takes its point of departure in two basic questions, partly concerning the central or decentral position of the sender and receiver, and partly concerning the ownership of the information and the control of the access to and use of the information. Here (C) is the information service provider, and (i) is the information service consumer.[16] The two questions can be stated as follows:

- Is the transmitted information owned by an information service providing centre (C) or an individual information service consumer (i)?
- Is the transmission and use of the information controlled by an information service providing centre (C) or an individual information service consumer (i)?

The answers to the two questions can be combined in a single matrix definition, thus giving four possible combinations of answers, representing what Bordewijk and Kaam describe as "four idealised information traffic patterns" (1986: 19): transmission, conversation, consultation, and registration (cf. Fig. 1)

	Information produced by a central provider	*Information produced by the consumer*
Distribution controlled by a central provider	TRANSMISSION	REGISTRATION
Distribution controlled by the consumer	CONSULTATION	CONVERSATION

Figure 1: Pattern matrix for the four 'idealised information traffic patterns'

Transmission. If the information service centre produces and is the owner of the information, as well as the sole controller of the choice of and time for distribution of the information to the information consumer, we have a case of *transmission*.[17] In this traffic pattern the flow of information will thus exclusively run in one direction, from the service centre (C) to the individual consumer (i) as illustrated in Fig. 2. If the information centre serves several consumers, which is of course often the case, we have the generalised pattern noted in Fig. 3, in which C is the service centre and i1, i2, i3, etc. are individual consumers. In other words, this is the kind of communication often referred to as one-way communication, one-to-many communication, mass communication or mass media. This corresponds to Kumar's 'the-information-source-comes-to-you'-model and to the concept of 'push media'.

Figure 2: Transmission, information flow from service centre (C) to individual consumers (i)

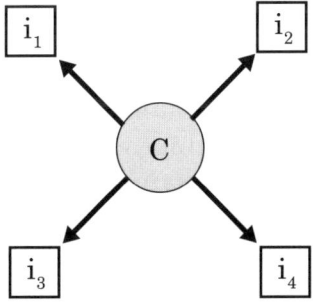

Figure 3: Transmission, generalised pattern, Information flow from service centre (C) to individual consumers (i1, i2, i3, etc.)

Characteristic features of transmitting media are that a large (potentially infinite) amount of information is available to the information centre; that all consumers in principle receive exactly the same information and often receive the information synchronously; and that, with respect to power, the media are strongly asymmetrical and centralistic, since the centre has maximum power over the information traffic by deciding content as well as programming, and the consumer has minimal power, being totally subject to the decisions of the centre in both respects. In actual practice, consumers will, more often than not, have the possibility of giving some kind of feedback, but because the model has been designed as an 'idealised' information traffic pattern, this aspect has been left out.

The prototypical examples of the transmission pattern are, of course, classical broadcast media such as TV and radio. If we refrain from the requirement for synchronous or simultaneous distribution and reception we could also include media such as films, books, newspapers, etc. The terms 'transmission' and 'broadcast' here offer a central characterisation of the activity and programs of these media.

It is a medium of this transmitting type that appears in *Fahrenheit 451*, and the critical point here is precisely that it is impossible to ask questions like "What do *you* think, Linda?" — it is impossible to participate in two-way communication or a dialogue — within this information pattern. It is only possible to 'simulate' such an interaction or interactivity.

Conversation. If the individual information service consumers produce and own the information, and if control of the means of distributing and handling the information are divided equally between those consumers (at least in this idealised case) the resulting situation is diametrically opposed to the one above, and we have a case of *conversation*. In this instance, the information flow runs in both directions, between the two individual consumers, and there is an equal exchange of information as illustrated in Fig. 4. In a more general model, the connection between the two information consumers ($i1$ and $i2$) will often be provided by an information service centre (C), but the centre represents a purely technical facility, neither intervening in the production of information or in the time of distribution, just as the centre often serves several consumers and handles numerous conversation connections, as noted in the generalised pattern of Fig. 5. This is the kind of communication often referred to as one-to-one communication or many-to-many communication, dialogue, conversation, etc.

*Figure 4: Conversation,
Information flow between individual consumers (i1, i2)*

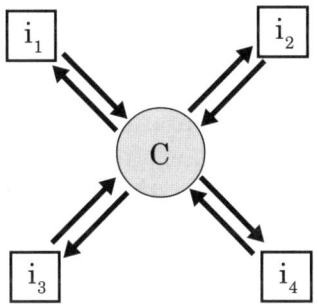

Figure 5: Conversation, generalised pattern

Characteristic features of the conversation pattern are therefore: that the information, as well as the time for exchange of information, are totally controlled by the consumers; that the distribution of power (at least in the idealised form) is completely symmetrical and decentralistic (contrary to the above mentioned transmission pattern); and that the traditional distinction between senders and receivers therefore tends to dissolve.

The prototypical example of the conversation pattern is, of course, the telephone, where the individual consumer decides whom to call, when to call, and what to talk about, whereas the telephone system plays a purely technical and mediating role in routing the telephone calls between the consumers. If we again refrain from requiring a synchronous mode and instantaneous interaction, other examples of conversation could be: telex, fax, e-mail, ordinary mail, etc.

It is only within media of this conversational type that it really makes sense to ask the question: "What do *you* think, Linda?" At least if one expects an answer to the question.

Until now, communication and media studies have primarily based their models and insights on the two above mentioned communication patterns: the transmission pattern in mass communication studies, and the conversation pattern in interpersonal communication studies, whereas the two following communication patterns have been markedly underexposed.

Consultation. If the information is produced and owned by a central information service centre (C), but the individual information service consumer (i) controls which information is to be delivered and when to deliver it, we have a case of *consultation.* In this instance, the information service centre only delivers information on request from the individual consumer (dotted line), and conversely the individual consumer only gets the information required, at the time required (thick line) as illustrated in Fig. 6. In this pattern too, the centre can normally be consulted by, and serve, several information consumers, resulting in the generalised pattern in Fig. 7.

The consultation pattern represents markedly different power relations in comparison with the two patterns considered above. Characteristic features of consultative media are that they have an asymmetric, but distributed division of power, where the power over the content is held by the centre, and the power over the distribution held by the consumer; that they — compared to the transmitting mode — require a higher degree of activity or interactivity on behalf of the consumer; but that they offer far more freedom and flexibility in the choice of information in return, making more individual and selective uses possible.

Exemplary representatives of the consultative pattern are found in various forms of on-demand services, online information resources, 'electronic memories' such as CD-ROMs, hard disk drives, and data bases, in various computer communication systems like World Wide Web, FTP, etc., and in various forms of printed media like reference works, dictionaries, and encyclopedias. It is even possible to argue that newspapers, magazines, periodicals and books belong in this category, to the extent that they are considered collections of information units which can be selected and read by the information consumer at a time that is convenient. On a more general level, you could also say that institutions like libraries, bookstores, etc. follow the consultation mode. This corresponds to Kumar's 'you-go-to-the-information-source'-model or the concept of 'pull media'.

Here the question "What do *you* think, Linda?" coming from the information centre really means "What are you looking for?" or "What do you choose?"

Figure 6: Consultation, information on request (request: dotted line)

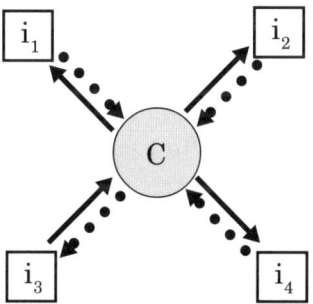

Figure 7: Consultation, generalised pattern (request: dotted line)

Registration. And finally, the opposite situation: when the information is produced by an individual information service consumer (i), but the use of the information is handled and controlled by an information service centre (C), we have a case of *registration*. Here the task of the centre is no longer to issue information, but to collect it. This information pattern has two variations. If the information is delivered by the individual on request from the centre we have an inversion of the information flow of the consultation pattern (Fig. 6 and Fig. 7) as illustrated by the generalised pattern in Fig. 8. If, however, the information is collected from the consumer without a request from the centre, we have an inversion of the information flow of the transmitting model (Fig. 2 and Fig. 3), where the centre no longer sends information to, but collects information from, the consumer as depicted by the generalised pattern in Fig. 9. The collected information can in turn be processed, computed, (re)arranged, etc. by the centre. This kind of pattern could perhaps be referred to as many-to-one communication.

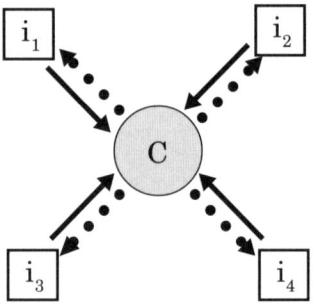

Figure 8: Registration, generalised pattern (on request: dotted line)

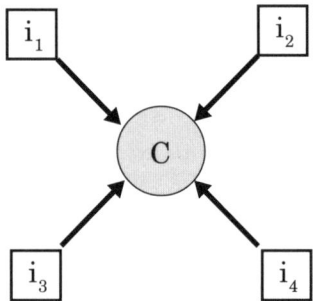

Figure 9: Registration, generalised pattern, without request

The registration pattern is thus also characterised by an asymmetric, but distributed division of power, only in reverse order from the transmission and the consultation patterns, since the information is produced and delivered by the consumers, whereas the use of the information, i.e. computation, interpretation and distribution (concealment, publication, etc.) is controlled by the central information service.

Examples of the registration pattern – in the reversed consultation version, i.e. 'on request' – would be (tele-)opinion polling, TV-viewers voting by letter or phone, shopping systems, various kinds of programmable software agents, customised services, etc., or – in the reversed transmission version, i.e. 'without request' – tele-alarm, video surveillance, logging of computer systems, electronic surveillance, security and alarm systems, etc., but also various kinds of adaptive media, intelligent interfaces, personalised services, etc. Other examples, on a more general level, could also be well known services such as news agencies, civil registration, tax authorities, and other public (accessible as well as non-accessible) registration systems, etc.

In this media pattern, too, you might very well be confronted with the question "What do *you* think, Linda?". But you will never know how your answer will be used.[18]

	Information produced by a central provider	*Information produced by the consumer*
Distribution controlled by a central provider	Broadcast TV and radio, films	Opinion polling, tele-alarm, video surveillance
Distribution controlled by the consumer	WWW, CD-ROMs, online information ressources	Telephone, fax, mail, e-mail

Figure 10: Matrix with examples of media and services as prototypical representatives of the various information traffic patterns

Fig. 10 indicates some examples of media and services within the matrix and its four information traffic patterns.

Another alternative way of classifying interactive content and services – somewhat similar to that mentioned above – is the media typology developed by Joan M. van Tassel (van Tassel, 1996). Van Tassel points out four types of content based on discrimination criteria such as: transient versus permanent and pre-packaged versus user-created.

- *Pre-packaged evergreen*: Pre-packaged content is text, graphics, audio, video, etc. that users may access. If the material is relatively permanent, it is called: 'evergreen', meaning it will be of common interest over some length of time.
- *Pre-packaged transient*: If pre-packaged material is replaced regularly, for example each week, it is called: pre-packaged transient.
- *User-created added data*: If the pre-packaged content is structured in a way so that the users can add to the material and thereby create a user-based database it is called: user-created added data.
- *User-created content*: If the content is created entirely by users, as for example in online 'chat rooms' or telephone conversations, it is called: user-created content.

These criteria and categories can be elaborated in a 3X2 matrix as shown in Fig. 11.

	Center produced	Center produced / user added data	User produced
Evergreen	Films & TV shows	User annotations to films, books etc.	User reviews of films and TV shows
Transient	News, weather forecasts	User discussions of current news	Chat rooms, telephone

Figure 11: Matrix based on van Tassel's typology

Interactive TV – Revisited

As is apparent from the above, the various information patterns and media types principally represent very different forms of communication and social power relations. There are now several points to be made from these media typologies in regard to interactive TV. The structure in the following is similar to Bordewijk and Kaam's matrix, but comments on all of the media typologies previously mentioned.

Transmission

The media of yesterday were based almost without exception on the transmission pattern, that is, in Kumar's terms, "the-information-source-comes-to-you"-model, or in Kelly et al.'s term 'push media'. Among the four information patterns enumerated in Bordewijk and Kaam's media matrix, this is the only one that does not have a return or back-channel that makes an information flow possible from the information user to the media system. Consequently, there is no possibility of – what van Tassel calls – user-created added data or user-created content.

As already mentioned, classic broadcast TV, is prototypic for the transmitting media pattern. As such it has strong synchronous ties, allowing the viewers to choose what they want (from the options offered) but not when to do so. Most television programming by far still works according to this synchronous transmission pattern and will probably continue to make up a considerable portion of interactive TV content.

Although most television today functions under the synchronous transmission pattern, recent developments in the available selection of TV channels alone have upset this idealised media pattern. As far as the viewer is concerned, there is in fact a decisive difference between a TV viewing situation where only one channel is available, or perhaps a very limited number of mostly identical channels, and the newly emerged so-called 'multi-channel situation', where a wide range of very different channels and programs can be picked up. In the last case, the extended number of options alone increases the possible choices available and tends to make the information pattern appear consultative. This is even more the case if the multi-channel system offers so-called 'theme channels' or 'genre channels', exclusively transmitting the same kind of information: news, sports, music videos, science documentaries, etc. since in principle the individual consumer actually controls when reception of the program in question takes place. In fact, just using a VCR to record a TV program in order to postpone its viewing, or fast forwarding past the boring commercials can be said to give the TV medium certain consultative qualities.

A currently available TV service based on transmission, which can be considered interactive TV in its embryo form, is teletext. The principle of teletext is that pages of text are broadcast in a hidden part of the television signal, and decoded by the television. Using the remote control, the viewer is able to choose which text he wants on the screen. In teletext services, TV transmission finds a specific application as a consultative medium. Here viewers have interactive and selective access to a large amount of information, which they do not necessarily receive or read synchronously, in the same specific order, or in its entirety.

These consultative features in the transmission pattern are even more obvious in TV services such as near-video-on-demand or multicasting, where the same program is broadcast on several channels at different times, so that the individual consumer only has to wait a short time from ordering a program to receiving it. In services of this type, you might say that TV as a transmitting medium is actually used consultatively. The same can be said about certain forms of interactive fiction or choose-your-own-story(-ending), where stories have built in options that require the viewer — either based on individual or majority decisions — to actively participate and make choices ("What do *you* choose, Linda?").

Consultation

While the media of yesterday – as mentioned – were based almost exclusively on the transmission pattern, current media developments including the arrival of 'new media' such as interactive television, the Internet, World Wide Web, networked multimedia, etc. have been more or less singularly characterised by a movement away from the transmission pattern toward the three other media patterns, especially the consultation pattern. The media of the future will thus most likely have much more to do with consultation, i.e. requests, content-on-demand, pull or 'you-go-to-the-information-source'-model.

With regard to services such as video-on-demand, where the selected programs are sent directly and immediately to the individual consumer the TV medium takes on purely consultative characteristics. The same is naturally true for similar services such as news-on-demand, sports-on-demand, music-on-demand, etc. as well as interactive advertisements or product information that, unlike traditional advertisements, are not sent to the consumer but which, on the contrary, the consumer himself interactively seeks and selects. Also 'electronic programming guides', understood as new computerised techniques or advanced software that use different menus and rapid scanning of current and future programs to ease navigation and to identify the programs one wants to see, can be said to contain consultative characteristics or to be a tool in the consultation mode.

From a more general point of view, Nicholas Negroponte argues in a discussion of the relationship between the current TV and the PC, that the main difference between the two media is not so much their functions, placement, or social aspects as their distribution. TVs as well as PCs are actually bit-processors, but there is an important difference in how these bits arrive: "The TV takes in bits radiated by cable, satellite, or terrestrial transmission. These bits are essentially thrown at the TV to catch-as-catch-can" (1995a). For TV it is a fact that "this process of pushing bits at people has been in real time only ... You don't download TV, you join an ongoing program" (1995a). Whereas conversely it applies that "the PC receives its bits because it (or you) asks for them explicitly (or implicitly). That's the difference" (1995a). Thus Negroponte's observation — stated in the terms presented here — is that TV is fundamentally a transmission medium or a 'push medium', whereas the PC is essentially a consultation medium or a 'pull medium'. His forecast for future developments is that the two media will converge in digitised TV, while retaining the PC's consultative form of distribution.

In his book, *Being Digital* (1995b), Negroponte mentions a form of distribution he calls "bit radiation", "bitcasting" or "datacasting" (1995b: 37ff.). During the 1980s Stewart Brand (1987) called it not broadcasting but "broad*catching*". Negroponte explains: "Digital life will include very little real-time broadcast ... With the possible exception of sports and elections, technology suggests that TV and radio of the future will be delivered asynchronously. This will happen either on demand or using 'broadcatching' ... Broadcatching is the radiation of a bit stream, most likely one with vast amounts of information pushed into the ether or down a fibre. At the receiving end, a computer catches the bits, examines them, and discards all but the few it thinks you want to consume later" (1995b: 168-9).

Whether bits are distributed on demand or as broadcatching, and whether they represent TV news, games, documentaries, etc., it will totally change the TV medium for: "once in the machine, there is no need to view them in the order they were sent. All of a sudden TV becomes a random access medium, more like a book or newspaper, browsable and changeable, no longer dependent on time or day, or the time required for delivery. / Once we ... begin to build it in its most general form, bit radiation, TV becomes a totally different medium" (Negroponte, 1995b: 49-50).[19]

George Gilder has a similar point in his book with the telling title, *Life after Television. The coming Transformation of Media and American Life*: "Computer networks respond to all the human characteristics that TV networks defy ... Rather than a system whereby a few 'stations' spray images at millions of dumb terminals in real time, computer networks put the customer in control, not settling passively for what is on the 'air' but actively seeking and even shaping the customer's first choices" (1994: 15-6).

Returning to Negroponte, he also describes the transformation of TV from a transmission to a consultation medium in terms of, as he says, "Where intelligence lives". He writes:

"Broadcast television is an example of a medium in which all the intelligence is at the point of origin. The transmitter determines everything and the receiver just takes what it gets. In fact, per cubic inch, your current TV set is perhaps the dumbest appliance in your home (and I'm not even talking about the programs). If you have a microwave oven, it likely has more microprocessors than your TV. Instead of thinking of the next evolutionary step of television as increased resolution, better colour, or more programs, think of it as a change in the distribution of intelligence — or, more precisely, the movement of some intelligence, from the transmitter to the receiver." (1995b: 19)

So, also with respect to technological *brain power*, the transformation of television involves the redistribution and the democratisation of power.

According to Negroponte, the nature of earlier 'mass media' will be totally changed and the whole concept of so-called 'mass communication' will be turned from a process where bits are thrown towards the audience, or variously defined groups of audience, into a process where, instead, people themselves are allowed to select them: "The economic models of media today are based almost exclusively on 'pushing' the information and entertainment out into the public. Tomorrow's will have as much or more to do with 'pulling', where you and I reach into the network and check out something the way we do in a library or video-rental store today. This can happen explicitly by asking or implicitly by an agent asking on your behalf" (1995b: 170).

In this connection, Robert L. Carberry has stated that TV will change from being uni-directional mass- or group-oriented to individually oriented and personal: "The resulting technologies will allow broadcasters to personalize broadcasts for a single individual ... Broadcasters will shift from 'narrowcasting' — broadcasting toward the wants of a group — to 'pointcasting' — broadcasting aimed at an individual".[20]

No matter whether it takes the form of video-on-demand or – what is variously termed – pointcasting, narrowcasting, bitcasting, digital radiation, or broadcatching, the interactive TV of the future is likely to have distinctive consultative features.

Registration

In his spiteful publication about TV, *Amusing Ourselves to Death* (1985), the culturally conservative American critic, Neil Postman, makes the caustic point that it is not the prophecy of George Orwell in *1984*, but the prophecy of Aldous Huxley in *Brave New World*, that appears to have come true:

"In America, Orwell's prophecies are of small relevance, but Huxley's are well under way toward being realized. For America is engaged in the world's most ambitious experiment to accommodate itself to the technological distractions made possible by the electric plug. This is an experiment that began slowly and modestly in the mid-nineteenth century and has now, in the latter half of the twentieth, reached a perverse maturity in America's consuming love-affair with television ... By ushering in the Age of Television, America has given the world the clearest available glimpse of the Huxleyan future." (1985: 156)

The significant difference between these two science fiction prophecies is that in Orwell's *1984* the TV media is represented as an intrinsically registering medium. Media watching us. However, it appears that economic, political and cultural developments have turned television into the exact opposite: a passive, transmission medium. Not the media watching all of us, but the medium watched by all of us. And it is in this respect that Postman found Huxley to be correct: "In the Huxleyan prophecy, Big Brother does not watch us, by his choice. We watch him, by ours" (1985: 155).

The development of the media during later years, however, seems to some extent to modify this unambiguous trend. In an article with the title "Caught. You used to watch television. Now it watches you" Phil Patton points out that shifts in the TV medium from a primarily transmitting medium have increasingly turned it into a registering medium due to the gradual but pervasive appearance of video surveillance cameras. From his American context Patton writes:

"For a long time now, America has seemed like a country where most people watch television most of the time. But only recently are we beginning to notice that it is also a country where television watches us. / We're all on security cameras ... At malls, hotels, airports, fast-food restaurants; in offices; on highways, in front of machines — we star in a TV system whose cast dwarfs that of broadcast and cable. In the world of security TV, the equation of home TV is reversed: the audience is small, the programming vast. No one can say for sure how many hours the average American is on TV ... We pay to watch ourselves" (1995).[21]

Also within the more traditional (mass) media system the TV medium has increasingly taken on registration characteristics. It takes place in the form of information services like polling, where the viewers are able to give their vote, mark their opinion, or state their point of view (e.g. new TV concepts such as Big Brother, etc.). Once registered, the media centre alone decides how to adapt, compute and distribute the information. It happens in the form of wagering understood as gambling services where it is possible to play the lottery, or place bets via the TV system — all more or less in real time. It can also take place in the form of a service such as pay-per-view (i.e. pay TV, where one only pays for the actual programs received), where the information centre collects information about the type and length of the TV viewing habits of the individual consumers. Information which the centre then likewise has at its exclusive disposal. Or explicitly in the form of automated ('smart') housing, where interactive TV systems are also coupled to surveillance functions, security alarms, etc. and thus maintain a connection with a security centre.

There are, in principle, two ways in which a media system can register the individual user's choice, behaviour, or preferences. These are called *personalisation* and *customisation,* respectively. The significant difference between the two concerns *the location of* the agency of the registration. *Personalisation* is driven by the media system, which tries to serve up individualised information to the user based on some model of that user's need. This form is also called adaptation or adaptive systems or interfaces, i.e. systems and interfaces that seem to intelligently adapt themselves to the user by noticing patterns of interaction or responding to user idiosyncrasies or desires according to expectations. *Customisation*, on the other hand, is driven by the user, i.e. is under direct user control: the user explicitly selects from certain options and thereby tailors the information. Thus, both personalisation and customisation obviously require the system to have some sort of information about the user. They are, in other words, related to the information traffic pattern Bordewijk and Kaam call registration.

To sum up, inside the (mass) media system and the entertainment industry, as well as the security and supervision area, developments are increasingly starting to (deny Postman and) agree with Orwell: That TV is (also) a medium of registration.

Conversation

Seventy-five years ago, Bertolt Brecht had a vision of the possible development of radio. He wrote:

> "... and finally — to find the positive aspect of the radio: I suggest that we convert it from a distribution device into a communication device. The radio would be the most impressive communication device in public life, a great system of channels or it would be, if it was able not just to receive, but also to send, which means not just to make the listener listen, but also to make him speak, and not only to isolate him, but to get in connection with him. Then the radio would have to give up its supplying position and organise the listener as a supplier."[22]

Thus what Brecht pointed out is that it is both possible and desirable to build up the radio not as a medium of transmission, but one of conversation. Today, however, it seems to be the TV medium, which is trying to implement this vision.

The connection between the conversational pattern and TV actually dates as far back as Brecht's vision, namely to the 1920s. Point-to-point, two-way communication (two-way-audio/one-way-video), i.e. a kind of video telephone, was actually one of the formats that was seriously considered and tried out when various TV technologies were first invented and tested.[23] In this aspect, too, economic, political and cultural forces quickly made TV the exact opposite: the archetype of the transmitting broadcast and mass media.[24]

Meanwhile, despite this characteristic, it is interesting to note that throughout its history, broadcast TV has attempted to develop communication forms and methods of addressing the audience that seek to contradict or compensate for the medium's transmission characteristic and one way communication. One of the most significant and wide spread of these methods of address is what could be called "simulated" or "mimed interaction" between the TV medium and the TV audience which seeks in various ways to give the primary illusion of a conversation media pattern. The 'simulated interaction' can take on a variety of forms: the studio host's direct appeal to the viewer; simulated 'eye contact' and imitated 'lively conversation' between *talking heads* and the viewer ("What do *you* think, Linda?"); the explicit inclusion of and 'play' with the viewer as a co-creating partner in the construction of the message of the media text; overhearing 'intimate' and 'private' conversations and interviews as a third silent partner; direct participation of representatives from the audience (in quizzes, vox pop, etc.); the inclusion of a studio audience that 'represents' and expands the TV audience and its reactions, etc. A method of address that naturally aims to 'speak to', involve and hold viewers, to create the illusion of a feeling of reciprocal obligatory social contact and communication — *in spite of* the transmission pattern's lack of dialogue and *in spite of* TV's reception situation and context of use which to an increasing degree has moved in the direction of the extensive, distractive and preoccupied.

Also in terms of conversational features, it seems that there is currently what could be called 'the return of the repressed' (in relation to the earliest history) as well as the realisation of what has, until now, been only 'simulated interaction' and dialogue with the viewer.

With the broadband, two-way (even 'switched', i.e. making it possible to call one TV terminal from another) networks available today, the conversational media pattern has become a realistic possibility within the framework of interactive TV systems. A traffic pattern of information used for service types such as e-mail, video telephone, network games, Internet connection via TV terminals, etc. Until now, this pattern has primarily been connected with the telephone.

Based on this background Christian S. Nissen, Director of Danish Broadcasting, states that: "The future digitisation of radio and TV will provide the technical conditions for Brecht's vision. In its utmost consequence it may provide a liberation and de-collectivisation of the radio and TV media" (1996: 4). Negroponte literally gives birth to this vision when he writes in the chapter "Cottage television": "On the Net each person can be an unlicensed TV station ... Every home movie won't be a prime-time experience (thank God). But we can now think of mass media as a great deal more than high production value, professional TV ... In the near future, individuals will be able to run electronic video services ... That's a television landscape of the future that is starting to look like the Internet, populated by small information producers" (1995b: 176). Once again, George Gilder makes a similar point when he writes, "Computer networks respond to all the human characteristics that TV networks defy. Computer nets afford peer-to-peer interactivity rather than top-down broadcasts. Rather than a few 'channels', computer networks offer as many potential connections as there are machines linked to the web" (1994: 15-6).

Finally, Alfred C. Sikes also predicts that interactive TV "will become a medium for social interaction", and also that: "All of the things that can be done gregariously will be done interactively".[25] So now we can genuinely speak of the "TV family" and "cousin" announcers. Negroponte has a similar point, when he, in connection with the above quote, argues that video services must necessarily be based on broadband cable systems — both to and from the home: "The channel needs to be two-way. An obvious example is teleconferencing, which will become a particularly valuable consumer medium for grandparents or, in divorced families, for the parent who does not have custody of the children" (1995b: 176). So who mentioned "Our family theatre" and who said, "Come in cousin"?

There is obviously a fair amount of naivete in these visions of everyone becoming their own TV producer and everyone starting their own TV station. The reality is naturally that it is relatively expensive to establish and run media servers, to keep them technologically updated, etc. just as it is expensive and requires a large team to produce content and maintain and update software — at least if the material is to have interest for anyone other than oneself. (It is already possible to note beginning tendencies of this type on the computer based and previously more anarchistic and grassroots-democratic Internet, which Negroponte uses as a frame of reference.) Likewise, there is (one of the key points already made by *Fahrenheit 451*) naturally a certain naivete in the idea of TV as a medium for the presentation of close and meaningful ('family' or) social contact. It is thus probable that it will become easier and quicker to carry out other functions connected to the other information patterns, while the conversation pattern will likely be the most expensive to establish and the most difficult to immediately profit from, in reasonable proportion to the investment.

This said, it must also be noted that in more humble versions — teletext-systems that enable viewer input, two-channel interaction, Internet connection via the TV set, e-mail, chat, network games, and perhaps even videophone — the TV's previously repressed or just 'simulated' conversational features will be revived.

'Multi-pattern Services' and 'Multi-pattern Networks'

As should be clear from the above, the typologies can be used for significant categorisation and meaningful description of various forms of ITV services, using the information pattern that the specific service is primarily based on, as illustrated in Fig. 12 (referring to Bordewijk & Kaam's matrix).

	Information produced by a central provider	*Information produced by the consumer*
Distribution controlled by a central provider	Broadcast TV, teletext, push, multi-channel TV near-video-on-demand be-your-on-editor	Polling, voting, pay-per-view, home shopping & banking, security systems
Distribution controlled by the consumer	True-video-on-demand, content-on-demand Web-on-TV, pull-media EPGs	Videophone, e-mail, chat, network games

Figure 12: Illustration of the four information traffic patterns in ITV

If you consider the actual and future trends of TV's development from the perspective of the matrix, they are best described as a relative movement from the top left position towards the other positions, i.e. from the traditional transmission information pattern toward the consultation, registration and conversation patterns. So, one way to conceptualise and describe interactive television is as the TV medium's transformation from a solely transmitting medium to a complex transmitting, consultation, registration and perhaps even conversation medium.

How pronounced this relative movement will become is still uncertain. Conflicting forces can be found in a number of characteristics, which have previously marked TV as a social and cultural phenomenon. Characteristics, which are partially connected with the facts: that TV consists not only of separate programs, but also the programming and the institution behind the program and the programming; that TV — at least in the Western European public service model — often makes up a national and regional community; and that TV is a simultaneous medium, i.e. built on synchronous reception, and a large part of TV's social function is precisely the experience of (large portions of the country) watching the same thing at the same time.[26] How strong these social and cultural forces are, to which extent they are able to retain the transmission pattern, or whether they will gradually be broken down is difficult to predict today. It does seem however, to be a relatively solid prediction that there will be at least a *relative* weakening of the transmission mode which will benefit one or several of the other modes.[27]

This also implies a general movement away from the strongly asymmetrical, centralistic power structure towards a larger symmetry in, or distribution of, the power. A shift in the social patterns of information traffic overall, that can moreover, generally be noticed within a large number of the new media which have arisen in connection with digitisation, telematics, computer media, etc. In connection with the discussion of Bordewijk and Kaam's matrix typology, Dennis McQuail writes: "The new media seem to offer the potential of a shift on the balance of power away from the sender and towards the receiver, making much more content of all kinds accessible to users and choosers without dependence on the mediating and controlling systems of mass communication" (1987: 40). Changes including: "abundance of supply of culture and information made available at low cost; more real choice and diversity; restored control to the receiver/user; decentralization; interactivity rather than one-way communication" (1987: 40). And he concludes: "This seems to indicate a general increase in individual freedom to gain information and a reduction in the dominance of centralized sources" (1987: 42).[28]

While this certainly can be said to be correct from a general perspective, both for the collective media landscape and for interactive TV, it cannot be said without noting considerable modifications and opposing movements. These modifications are, among other things, concerned with the dominance of the information centre in the growing registration patterns, that the centre continues to have power over content in the growing consultation pattern, and that the transmission pattern is still, and will continue to be, at work.

The above comments also make it obvious that in its current and future form, TV as a medium or service does not find itself exclusively in a single matrix position. On the contrary, it assumes the character of what Bordewijk and Kaam call 'multi-pattern-services', i.e. services where "several patterns occur ... simultaneously" (1986: 20).

Consequently, certain services are more adequately described as a combination of several information patterns, where for instance:

Pay-per-view (i.e. pay TV which functions on a 'taxi' principle so that one only pays for the programs that are actually received) can best be described as a combination of the transmission and registration patterns.

Near-video-on-demand (where the same program, typically a movie, is transmitted on different channels at different times, so that the individual viewer only has to wait briefly after having ordered the program before being able to see it on his home TV); *be-your-own-editor* (where the same event, e.g. a live transmission of a sports event, is transmitted on several parallel channels where each channel represents a certain camera angle on the event so that the viewer can 'zap' from channel to channel and edit his own coverage of the event), *interactive fiction,* etc. can all best be described as combinations of the transmission and consultation patterns.

Home shopping (i.e. electronic shopping centres where the consumer can browse through catalogues and exhibits to get information, compare, order and buy products and services and even pay using a smart card) as well as *home banking, ticketing,* etc. can best be described as a combination of the consultation and registration patterns.

And *game shows* (where the viewers can participate directly in TV quizzes and contests via interaction from their homes), etc. can best be described as combinations of the transmission and conversation patterns.

On a more general level, the new media also represent new combinations and the convergence of familiar patterns – including combinations of push and pull. A discernible trend is thus a new kind of hybrid media, so-called 'pull-push media' or 'networked push media', that allows you "to move seamlessly between media you steer (interactive) and media that steer you (passive)" (Kelly et al., 1997: 12). There are several reasons for this media development. One of them – according to Kelly et al. – is a more or less explicit demand from the users of the media: "What ... [people] want ... are more ways to zap. More ways to interrupt flow, more varieties ... of things done together with other people and things done alone. More states that flit between steering the media and being steered by it. More ability to tweak the dial, between twirling and being twirled, so that finally you can dance with the media. Networked media offer nothing more and nothing less than this: an expanding set of possible in-between states, combinations of push and pull and the means to slide between them" (1997: 19).

The promise of push-pull media is, in other words: "to marry the programmed experience of television with two key yearnings: navigating information and experience, and connecting to other people" (1997: 18). Using Bordewijk and Kaam's concepts, the promise of push-pull media is therefore a complex combination of transmission ('programmed experience of television'), consultation ('navigating information') and conversation ('connecting to other people'). A point, which is elaborated in the following, again from Kelly et al.: "With networked media you get TV's high production values along with the intense communal experience of watching something together – virtual communities. You also get the ability to address small self-organizing audiences that broadcast could never afford to find. And you get well-crafted stories seamlessly integrated into other media, such as on-line conversations. This heightened ability to extract meaning, experience, or community – rare with content pushed by broadcast – is almost the rule with content pushed on a network" (1997: 18).

One of the most significant consequences of these networked push media – compared to media known from the era of broadcasting – may be "the creation of a whole universe of small-scale (and not-so-small-scale) broadcast networks. Until now, broadcast had to be huge to be ubiquitous. Smaller ones were proprietary and fixed. Really small ones were called mailing lists or videoconferences. Networked media, on the other hand, can create broadcasting networks of any size and shape, especially the intermediate size between TV and, say, personal mailing lists. You can push-pull broadcast to llama keepers or home scholars, reconfiguring the shape of the network on the fly. Until now, the Net has been a place of pull-laden networks; now it will also be a Net of push-laden networks, a world of nichecasting – thousands of mini-networks, ranging from micro-TV stations to totally customized personal programming" (1997: 21).

These new mini-networked media that Kelly et al. predict, will fill the entire media continuum, taking us "one more step toward closing the gaps between existing media, toward one seamless media continuum, viewable in an infinite number of ingenious ways" (1997: 21f). So far, in the context of traditional media, push is better developed than pull. On the other hand, in the context of the Web, pull is better developed than push. But that is changing fast, and conceivably, the trend is towards a combination – or a re-balancing – of push and pull or, using Bordewijk and Kaam's concepts, towards a complex combination of transmission and consultation patterns.

TV will thus probably stop being a *purely* transmitting medium, but it will not simply stop being a transmission medium — it will *also* be a transmitting medium where this 'also' covers a complex combination of the other information patterns.

This is a characteristic that interactive TV shares with a number of other modern information services. The telephone, for example, which was originally a prototypical example of the idealised conversation media pattern, now offers specialised services with consultative traits (telephone based services such as 'information', 'time', news, sports news, weather reports, wagering, etc.), registration characteristics (registration of conversations for billing, telephone based polls, etc.), and even transmission characteristics ('parliamentary debate').

Even clearer within various computer based media, which from the start were supported by a combination of several of the four patterns:[29] computer based conferencing systems support e.g. a complex mixture of conversation functions (e-mail, input to topic groups), consultation functions (storage of debate input to theme conferences, address lists, etc.), and registration functions (logging and registration of input, information traffic, etc.). And advanced net systems such as World Wide Web have characteristics of consultation (visiting home pages, downloading text, pictures or sound files), conversation (built in e-mail facilities for one-to-one communication, web-'chat', etc.), registration (logging of data traffic, registration of visits to home pages and servers), and even transmission ('direct' network transmission of rock concerts, radio news, etc.).[30]

These examples primarily concern service and content, but where physical networks of distribution are concerned, a trend towards what Bordewijk and Kaam call "multi-functional, or perhaps better, multi-pattern networks" (1986: 21) can also be observed. Previously, individual information services typically had their own specific, technical distribution system, where the design was adapted to the type of service involved: terrestrial broadcast TV, terrestrial radio, cable TV, the telephone network, etc. Current trends indicate that networks which were originally designed for one particular form of communication or information service are now temporarily also being used for other information services. In the long run, various distribution systems for TV, teletext, radio, telephone, data, telefax, etc. may very well fuse together in the same networks. It will therefore become more and more difficult to characterise a certain information service based exclusively on the technical qualities of a medium. The reverse is also true. Purely technical qualities of a medium will not necessarily dictate a certain traffic pattern, but the two elements have a relative independence.[31]

Seen from these points of view — as 'multi-pattern services' and 'multi-pattern networks' — the matrix seems to deny itself to a certain extent. The very construction of the matrix and its application to current media phenomena demonstrates that the characteristic patterns and the sharp distinctions disintegrate in favour of more complex and hybrid information patterns and media forms. Despite the complexity of these multi-patterned and hybrid forms, the matrix is still an adequate framework and typology where new media and services can be significantly placed and classified (either in pure forms or at least as various combinations of information traffic patterns). It also offers a suitable description apparatus via which these media and services can be characterised and understood in a meaningful way.

Conclusion

As should now be apparent, interactive TV is many different things, and there are many notions as to how it can and should develop, i.e. compared to which levels of interactivity will be realised, which media patterns will be favoured, etc. For the user, of course, there will be a crucial distinction depending on which information pattern is dominant. An interactive TV system, which mainly follows the transmission pattern, would only make it possible to establish various forms of 'simulated' interactivity, two-channel interactions, datacasting, near-content-on-demand, etc. An interactive TV system following a registration pattern such as pay-per-view would, for example, make it possible to receive, consume and selectively pay for specific programs. An interactive system primarily based on the consultation pattern, in the form of video-on-demand, would allow the viewer/user to select, request and schedule specific programs of interest to that particular viewer. Finally, an interactive TV system that mainly follows the conversation pattern would give the individual consumer the possibility of acting as a sender as well as a receiver. This would make one-to-one, one-to-many and many-to-many forms of communication possible and would use the media in a flexible, open, productive and democratic way.

Specifically how the dream of interactive TV will be realised and how it will develop depends on complex co-operation among the economic, social, cultural and corporate interests surrounding the media in the years to come. Another important aspect involves the media politics, which will lead the sector while the media takes form, including the continued regulation of the relationship between commercial and public services. Last but not least, the media which emerges, will be dependent upon what the users want and what they are willing to pay for. Whether the media technology that gets the upper hand will look like the gloomy tele-vision from *Fahrenheit 451* with its passive viewers and simulated interactivity, or it will open up for receiver ruled, democratic information patterns and an active, productive relationship to a diverse and high quality assortment of information — this final decision will be up to ordinary consumers and the choices they make in the huge interactive system of the media marketplace.

"So, what do *you* think, Linda?"

Notes

1. *Fahrenheit 451* (1966). Directed by François Truffaut. Based on a novel by Ray Bradbury (1953).
2. Film dialogue from *Fahrenheit 451*.
3. "451 Fahrenheit, the temperature at which books ignite and burn...". Quoted from the colophon of Ray Bradbury's novel *Fahrenheit 451*.
4. The article will thus report my current research into the interactive modes of new media technologies and information services with special reference to interactive television and other consumer multimedia in the home. This work has been conducted as a sub-project of "The Aesthetics of Television", a research program sponsored by The Danish Research Council for the Humanities, 1993-1999 and as a sub-project of "Multimedia

in the Home", a research program, sponsored by Centre for IT Research, 1998-2001. An earlier and shorter version of this article was presented at the conference: Interactive Television 1996, "The Superhighway Through The Home?" (an international conference dedicated to personal and domestic media) in Edinburgh, Scotland, Sept. 3-5, 1996 under the title, *Mapping Interactive Television. A new media typology for information traffic patterns on the superhighway to the home*. Danish versions of the article can be found in the periodical *K&K* (*Kultur & Klasse/Kritik og Kulturanalyse*; Culture & Class/Criticism and Cultural analysis), no. 80, a theme issue on television in transition (*Fjernsyn i forvandling*) under the title: "Interaktivt TV, 'Coming soon to a screen near you'" and in a slightly longer version in: *Interaktivt TV*, working paper no. 12 from the research program "The Aesthetics of Television".

5. "The Superhighway through the home. Configuring and consolidating the vision. A world conference dedicated to interactive television", "First Call for Participation and Papers", Dec. 1995.
6. In contrast to the term 'multimedia', which indicates the integration of several media, cf. Jens F. Jensen (1995), in which this terminology was proposed.
7. The article is based on Jeffcoate and Matthews: *Interactive Television: The Market Opportunity,* Ovum Ltd. (1994), a report on the market for interactive TV. See also Dick Hackenberg (1995).
8. The three points are, among others, based on Jeffcoate (1995). See also IBMs home page "Interactive Television 101: Some basics" and Nolan, 1993.
9. Cf. for example Bill Gates (1995).
10. This service — and several of the services named below — can be found in both a pure, ITV based form, where orders and registration of consumption occur via two-way channels and, where the two-way systems have not yet been established, in a hybrid media form, as duo-media where ordering programs takes place over the telephone usually via a call to a voice response system from a touch tone telephone. The program is then transmitted via the (one-way) cable network.
11. Nicholas Negroponte, leader of MIT's Media Lab, expresses it like this: "In the future, advertising will be the converse of today — instead of advertisers soliciting response they will respond to solicitations by potential customers ... The reader will no longer stumble on the relevant information. It will percolate to the top of the information strata when the reader enters the

market for a car or a summer suit". Cited from T. Clarke (1995: 91).
12. A technological possibility that has naturally already caused utopian as well as dystopian speculation about 'direct TV democracy'. See f. ex. J. Alter (1995).
13. Cf. Jens F. Jensen (1995) for a more complete treatment of the competitive, cultural, political, and technological circumstances surrounding the development of multimedia and ITV.
14. The term 'power' as it is used in this context should not be taken too literally, but rather be understood as a sort of 'relative dominance' or 'right to dispose of'. For a discussion of power and technology in a related field of interactive entertainment technologies see also Gitte Jantzen & Jens F. Jensen (1993).
15. The extent of the metaphor's dissemination is reflected among other things by its many international variations: Der Infobahn (German), Autoroute de l'information (French), Autostrade dell'informazione (Italian), Autopistas de la informacion (Spanish), Autoestrada de informação (Portuguese), informationsmotorvejen (Danish). Cf. Ayer et al. (1995: 73).
16. The terms 'information service provider' or 'information service providing centre' and 'information service consumer' have been used here by Bordewijk and Kaam because they have the double advantage of including technical facilities, but leaving the direction of the information flow open, in contrast to concepts such as 'sender' and 'receiver'.
17. Bordewijk and Kaam use the term 'allocution', but for the sake of consistency in the terminology I have chosen the term 'transmission'.
18. For a full account of Bordewijk & Kaam's media typology and an elaboration of their matrix, cf. Jensen 1996a, 1996b, 1996c, 1996e, 1998c, 1999a, 1999c & 2000c.
19. Negroponte gives the following illustration: "Take the weather as an example. Instead of broadcasting the weatherman and his proverbial maps and charts, think of sending a computer model of the weather. These bits arrive in your computer-TV and then you, at the receiving end, implicitly or explicitly use local computing intelligence to transform them into a voice report, a printed map, or an animated cartoon with your favorite Disney character. The smart TV set will do this in whatever way you want, maybe even depending on your disposition and mood at the moment. In this example, the broadcaster does not even know what the bits will turn into: video, audio, or print. You decide that. The bits leave the station as bits to be used and transformed in a variety of different ways, personalized by a

variety of different computer programs, and archived or not as you see fit. / That scenario truly is one of bitcasting and datacasting and beyond the kind of regulatory control we have today, which assumes the transmitter knows that a signal is TV, radio, or data" (1995b: 55).
20. Cited from Eric Richard (1993).
21. And Patton continues by pointing out the following paradox: "Ironically, the people least on TV may be the TV stars. They don't buy their breakfast at Dunkin' Donuts. They avoid the cameras on malls and airports, of grocery stores and department stores (don't they all have personal buyers?). They travel in limousines, not buses. They enter buildings not through the lobbies with surveillance cams, but through back halls. The bigger the star, the less the surveillance. Even figuring their hours on broadcast TV, it's safe to say that Katie Couric and Barbara Walters, Dan and Connie and Ted, are on camera less than you are" (1995).
22. Cited from Christian S. Nissen (1996: 4).
23. Cf. John Carey (1994).
24. Cf. Derek William Nicoll (1995).
25. Cited from Richard (1993).
26. Cf. e.g. David Morley & Roger Silverstone (1990).
27. If only by virtue of the fact that the transmission mode is practically universal today.
28. Here, McQuail's viewpoint almost borders on technological determinism. However, it is modified considerably farther on when he writes: "... it would be unwise to depend on technology alone and even the new technology has its limitations and darker side. It will still be the case that what is available in central stores has to be decided centrally and diversity of control and management is not secured by technology, but by some form of politics. The range of what is actually available may come to depend on technology (including software) and it will probably not be so visible or open to direct observation, as with print media ... the chance of benefiting from the freedoms offered is increasingly dependent on possession of skills and equipment which are bound to be unevenly distributed ... The change in communication patterns and potential which is under way should not, for these reasons, be confused with a qualitative shift to 'better' social conditions of communication" (1987: 42). Similarly, media of registration can be said to cause an increase in the possibilities for central dominance through surveillance, registration and control.

29. For a more complete treatment of special computer media and computer networks in relation to information traffic patterns, see Jens F. Jensen (1996d): "Mapping the Web. A Media Typology for Information Traffic Patterns on the Internet Highway".
30. It is also worth noting that it is the transmission pattern that is the least represented within both computer media and telephone services.
31. Cf. Bordewijk & Kaam, p. 21. Naturally, this relative independence must not be overly emphasised. It is, for example, obvious that technical distribution systems, which are not able to carry two-way signals can not be used for conversation or consultation communication patterns. Similarly, two-way systems have only slight use in pure transmission. Bordewijk and Kaam also modify their view a little farther on when they point out a certain connection between technical features and communication patterns: "It should be realised, however, that the fact that the classification in traffic patterns does not depend on technological properties does not imply that technical developments and technical management may not exercise a certain influences on the relative balance of the four different patterns. The history of the art of printing proves that such influence can even be very marked" (1986: 21).

Bibliography

The Aesthetics of Television. Research Programme, sponsored by The Danish Research Council for the Humanities, 1993-1999, (1993). Aarhus.

Alter, J. (1995). "The Couch Potato Vote. Soon, you'll be able to vote from home — but should you?". In: *Newsweek, Technology '95,* February 27, 1995.

Andersen, Peter Bøgh, Berit Holmqvist & Jens F. Jensen (1993). *The Computer as Medium.* Cambridge: Cambridge University Press.

Anderson, Rich (1994). "Interactive Television: The Excitement Awaits". In: *High Technology Careers.*

Ayre, J., J. Callaghan & Signe Hoffos (1995). *The Multimedia Yearbook 1995.* Interactive Media Publications.

Bordewijk, Jan L., & Ben van Kaam (1986). "Towards a new classification of Tele-Information Services". In: *InterMedia,* vol. 14, no. 1.

Bradbury, Ray (1971). *Fahrenheit 451.* Copenhagen.

Brand, Stewart (1987). *The Media Lab.* Mass.: MIT.

Carey, John (1994). "The Interactive Television Puzzle". WWW document.
Cerami, Ethan (1998). *Delivering Push*. New York: McGraw-Hill.
Clarke, T. (1995). "Interactive Advertising". In: Ayer et al. (eds.) *The Multimedia Yearbook '95*.
Ernsberger, Richard Jr. (1994): "Game Wars". In: *Newsweek*, December 12, 1994
Fahrenheit 451 (1966). Directed by François Truffaut. Based on a novel by Ray Bradbury (1953).
Gates, Bill (1995). *The Road Ahead*. New York.
Gilder, George (1994). *Life after Television. The Coming Transformation of Media and American Life*. New York: W.W. Norton & Company.
Hackenberg, Dick (1995). "Interactive TV Gets Serious in 1995". WWW.
IBM (1995). "Interactive Television 101: Some basics". WWW document.
Interactive TV News (www.itvnews.co.uk)
Jantzen, Gitte & Jens F. Jensen (1993). "Powerplay – Power, Violence and Gender in Video Games". In: *AI & Society. The Journal of Human-Centred Systems and Machine Intelligence*.
Jeffcoate, Judith (1995). "Interactive TV". In: J. Ayre et. al. (eds.): *The Multimedia Yearbook '95*.
Jeffcoate, J., & Matthews (1994). *Interactive Television. The Market Opportunity*. Ovum Ltd.
Jensen, Jens F. (1993). "Computer Culture: The meaning of technology and the technology of meaning. A triadic essay on the semiotics of technology". In: Peter Bøgh Andersen, Berit Holmqvist & Jens F. Jensen: *The Computer as Medium*, Cambridge: Cambridge University Press.
Jensen, Jens F. (1995). *Multimedier og Teknologiudvikling. Rapport udarbejdet for Statsministeriets Medieudvalg, (Multimedia and technological development. A Report to the Media Commission under the Danish Department of State)*. Copenhagen.
Jensen, Jens F. (1996a). "Interaktivt TV – 'Coming soon at a screen near you'". In: *K&K* (Critique and cultural analysis), no. 80.
Jensen, Jens F. (1996b). *Interaktivt TV*. Working paper from the research project "The Aesthetics of Television", no. 12. Aarhus.
Jensen, Jens F. (1996c). *Mapping interactive television. A media typology for information traffic patterns on the superhighway to the home*, invited paper to the world conference for interactive television: "iTV-96, The Superhighway through the home?", Edinburgh University, 3-5 Sept. 1996.

Jensen, Jens F. (1996d). "Mapping the Web. A Media Typology for Information Traffic Patterns on the Internet Highway". In Herman Mauer (ed.): *WebNet 96 – World Conference of the Web Society Proceedings*, San Francisco.

Jensen, Jens F. (1996e). *Mapping Interactive Television*. Working paper from the research project "The Aesthetics of Television", no. 15. Aarhus.

Jensen, Jens F. (1998a). "Communication Research after the Mediasaurus? Digital Convergence, Digital Divergence?". In Ulla Carlsson (ed.): *Nordicom Review*, vol. 12, no. 1.

Jensen, Jens F. (1998b). "Interactivity. Tracking a New Concept in Media and Communication Studies". In Ulla Carlsson (ed.): *Nordicom Review*, vol. 12, no. 1.

Jensen, Jens F. (1998c). *Road Map of the Information Highway*. Working paper from the research project "The Aesthetics of Television", no. 25. Aarhus.

Jensen, Jens F. (1999a). "The concept of 'Interactivity' in 'Interactive Television' and 'Interactive Media'". In Jens F. Jensen & Cathy Toscan (eds.): *Interactive Television. TV of the Future or the Future of TV?*, Media and Cultural Studies 1, Aalborg: Aalborg University Press.

Jensen, Jens F. (1999b). "Trends in Interactive Content & Services over Multimedia Networks". In Borko Furth (ed.): *Proceedings of the IASTED International Conference on Internet, Multimedia Systems and Applications*. Nassau.

Jensen, Jens F. (1999c). "The Concept of 'Interactivity' in Digital Television". In Michael Rose et al.: *White Paper on Interactive TV*. Aarhus: Intermedia.

Jensen, Jens F. (1999d). "A short history of ITV trials and consumer studies". In Michael Rose et al.: *White Paper on Interactive TV*. Aarhus: Intermedia.

Jensen, Jens F. (2000a). "Interactivity – tracking a new concept". In Paul A. Mayer (ed.): *Communication, Computer Media and the Internet*. Oxford: Oxford University Press.

Jensen, Jens F. (2000b). "Trends in Interactive Content & Services on the Web". In Gordon Davies & Charles Owen: *Proceedings of the WebNet 2000 – World Conference on the WWW and Internet*. San Antonio, Texas.

Jensen, Jens F., & Cathy Toscan (eds.) (1999). *Interactive Television. TV of the Future or the Future of TV?* Media and Cultural Studies 1, Aalborg University Press.

Kelly et al. (1997). "PUSH! Kiss your browser goodbye: The radical future of media beyond the Web". In: *Wired*, no. 3

Kumar, Vinay (1996). *Mbone. Interactive Multimedia on the Internet*. Indianapolis: New Riders.

McQuail, Dennis (1987). *Mass Communication Theory. An introduction*. London.

Morley, D., & R. Silverstone (1990). "Domestic communication: Technologies and meanings". In: *Media, Culture and Society*, 12.

Negroponte, Nicholas (1995a). "Bit by bit TVs are becoming PCs. Or is it the other way round?" (http://www.wired.com/wired/archive/3.08/negroponte.html), also published in *Wired*, 3 vol., no. 8.

Negroponte, Nicholas (1995b). *Being Digital*. London.

Nicoll, Derek Williams (1995). "The Family History of Interactive Television", WWW document.

Nissen, Christian S. (1996). "TV aar 2000" ("TV year 2000"). In: *Weekendavisen*, January 26, 1996

Nolan, Chris (1993). "TV's Two-way street". In: *Cablevision*, Sept. 6, 1993.

Nolan, Chris (1995). "It's No Game". In: *Cablevision*, Feb., 20, 1995

Patton, Phil (1995). "Caught. You used to watch television. Now it watches you" (http://www.wired.com/wired/archive/3.01/caught.html), also published in: *Wired*, 1995, 3 vol., no.1.

Postman, Neil (1985). *Amusing Ourselves to Death*. London.

Richard, Eric (1993). "TV Ready for Massive Changes". In: *The Tech*, vol. 113, no. 42.

Rose, Michael, Claire Dorman, Henning Olesen, Berco Beute & Jens F. Jensen (1999): *White Paper on Interactive TV*. Aarhus: Intermedia.

"The Superhighway through the home" (1995). 'First Call for Participation and Papers' to the world conference dedicated to interactive television (http://www.ed.ac.uk/~rcss/iTV96/CONF13.HTM).

van Tassel, J. (1996). *Advanced Television Systems. Brave New TV*. Boston: Focal Press.